Diplomatic And Consular Reports. Annual Series, Issues 3075-3090

No. 3075.   Annual Series.

AUSTRIA-HUNGARY.

DIPLOMATIC AND CONSULAR REPORTS.

TRADE OF

BOHEMIA

FOR THE YEAR 1902.

FOREIGN OFFICE,

September, 1903.

DIPLOMATIC AND CONSULAR REPORTS.

AUSTRIA-HUNGARY.

REPORT FOR THE YEAR 1902

ON THE

TRADE OF BOHEMIA.

REFERENCE TO PREVIOUS REPORT, Annual Series No. 2857.

Presented to both Houses of Parliament by Command of His Majesty,
SEPTEMBER, 1903.

LONDON:
PRINTED FOR HIS MAJESTY'S STATIONERY OFFICE,
BY HARRISON AND SONS, ST. MARTIN'S LANE,
PRINTERS IN ORDINARY TO HIS MAJESTY.

And to be purchased, either directly or through any Bookseller, from
EYRE & SPOTTISWOODE, EAST HARDING STREET, FLEET STREET, E.C.,
and 32, ABINGDON STREET, WESTMINSTER, S.W.;
or OLIVER & BOYD, EDINBURGH;
or E. PONSONBY, 116, GRAFTON STREET, DUBLIN.

1903.

[Cd. 1766—9.]   *Price Twopence.*

CONTENTS.

No. 3075.   **Annual Series.**

Reference to previous Report, Annual Series No. 2857.

Report on the Trade of Bohemia for the Year 1902

By MR. CONSUL WENTWORTH FORBES.

(Prague, July 30, 1903; received at Foreign Office, August 3, 1903.)

The commercial arrangement with Hungary, which was brought *Depression in* to a satisfactory conclusion in the dying hours of the year 1902, *1902.* will be an important factor in restoring confidence, and will have a beneficial effect on the trade and industries of the Dual Monarchy. In many branches the depression that prevailed during 1901 was felt still more in 1902, particularly in the mining, machine and coal industries, and distress was prevalent throughout the land. In the metal industries alone it was estimated that about 30,000 workmen were without employment. In the great machine industry of the Empire, which has its chief seat in Prague and the surrounding neighbourhood, the distress was particularly felt during the winter months, and would have been greater had not the Government, corporations and private persons contributed fuel and food to the suffering thousands.

An epidemic of typhus broke out in Prague during the early *Public health.* summer of last year, owing to the unsatisfactory state of the water supply, and on analysing the water in both private and public wells, many were found to be unfit for use and had to be closed down. The pure water supply question has long been discussed by the authorities, and it is hoped that the great importance of a plentiful supply of good water being brought into the city will no longer be delayed.

This summer (1903) an Industrial Exhibition, on a large scale, *Exhibitions.* is being held at Aussig, an important commercial centre on the *At Aussig,* River Elbe, close to the Saxon frontier; it was opened by and is *1903.* under the patronage of the Archduke Ferdinand Carl, who is at present in residence at Prague, and it promises to be a great success.

The yearly Agricultural Exhibition at Prague was held at Whitsun- *Agricultural* tide, and the exhibits of agricultural machinery were very good, *Exhibition.*

(364)   A 2   *Prague, 1903.*

especially the heavy steam machinery and road rollers by British firms, who have branches established here. Two Bohemian firms also exhibited heavy steam rollers, which they are now manufacturing. The Government have placed some orders with them, but the price being nearly the same as the British-made machine, the competition so far has not done much harm to British firms, and prices are not reduced. The exhibits of light agricultural machinery, from the United States and Canada, attracted much attention, especially a light steam straw-binder in motion from the United States. This machine is particularly useful where threshing takes place on the field, and is very light and portable.

Next year (1904) an international exhibition of the spirit industry is to be held at Vienna from April 16 to the end of May, and is attracting the attention of the great spirit-producing nations of the Continent, especially of Germany and France. The German Emperor has expressed great interest in it, and his Government has voted 5,000l. in aid of the German section. The exhibition is to be divided into, first, raw materials ; second, the brewing industry, including malting, distilling and the manufacture of pressed yeast and starch ; third, uses to which the manufactured article can be applied ; fourth, spirit and its adaptability as a motive power for automobiles, &c.

An exhibition of Austrian industries, after the model of the " Paris in London " of last year, is to be held at Earl's Court next summer (1904), and the Austrian Government has already granted a subsidy.

The commerce of Austria-Hungary with the United Kingdom and its dependencies, both as to exports and imports, is of great importance, ranking second, Germany of course being first, I regret I am unable to give separate statistics for Bohemia as none are published, but commercially and industrially she is by far the most important of the many States which comprise this Empire. I also give data with reference to the trade of Austria-Hungary, particularly with the Indian Empire and the principal British colonies.

The value of the total imports and exports into Austria-Hungary was—

Year.				Value.	
				Imports.	Exports.
				£	£
1900	..	..	..	..	70,682,000	80,917,000
1901	..	..	..	..	68,860,000	78,561,000
1902	..	..	..	..	71,824,000	79,688,000

Margin notes:
oming hibitions. pirit hibition, ienna, 1904.

ustrian hibition in ndon, 1904.

iports and ports.

During the past five years the trade with the United ¦Kingdom, Trade with exclusive of India and the colonies, was— the United Kingdom.

Year.	Value.	
	Imports.	Exports.
	£	£
1898	5,773,471	6,198,751
1899	6,170,247	6,880,452
1900	6,205,901	8,385,412
1901	5,689,132	7,787,081
1902	5,946,790	7,190,608

The imports from Germany in 1902 amounted to 27,118,958*l*. Trade with and the exports to 38,459,556*l*., an increase on the year 1898 in Germany. imports of 3,638,593*l*. and in exports of 6,102,958*l*.

The imports from the United States in 1902 amounted to Trade with 5,658,576*l*. and the exports to 1,660,047*l*., an increase in the imports the United on 1898 of 63,680*l*. and in exports of 455,131*l*. States.

Both the imports from and the exports to the Indian Empire Trade with from the Dual Monarchy are considerable. The value of the India and imports for 1902 was 3,703,049*l*., and showed a falling-off on the Ceylon. previous year of 269,396*l*., and the value of the exports to India in the past year was 1,920,356*l*., a decrease on the year 1901 of 594,797*l*., of which 107,208*l*. was alone due to the fall in the export of sugar. The chief imports from and exports to India from the year 1897 to 1902, both years inclusive, are given in the following table :—

IMPORTS of Cocoa, Coffee and Tea from India and Ceylon. Imports.

Year.	Value.
	£
1897	342,250
1898	351,000
1899	315,500
1900	282,292
1901	263,583
1902	208,042

This gradual decrease is due to coffee, which fell from 317,417*l*. in 1897 to 157,041*l*. in 1902, but during this period there was an increase in tea to the value of 3,458*l*.

TOBACCO.

Year.				Quantity.	Value.
				Tons.	£
1897	..	..	..	..	139	13,417
1898	..	..	..	..	110	11,583
1899	..	..	..	..	44	9,500
1900	..	..	..	..	74	12,875
1901	..	..	..	..	111	20,625
1902	..	..	..	..	20	2,333

A very remarkable decrease, and as the Austrian Government is its own importer, it would be interesting to know the reason.

SPICES.

Year.				Quantity.	Value.
				Tons.	£
1897	..	..	..	..	2,729	104,417
1898	..	..	..	..	2,640	122,833
1899	..	..	..	..	2,824	143,167
1900	..	..	..	..	3,027	158,167
1901	..	..	..	..	3,024	172,708
1902	..	..	..	..	2,937	155,917

RICE.

Year.				Quantity.	Value.
				Tons.	£
1897	..	..	..	..	63,723	489,750
1898	..	..	..	..	58,166	469,888
1899	..	..	..	..	76,709	628,667
1900	..	..	..	..	65,615	523,958
1901	..	..	..	..	60,591	452,541
1902	..	..	..	..	62,055	427,250

OIL Seed, Linseed, Rape Seed, Palm Kernels, &c.

Year.				Quantity.	Value.
				Tons.	£
1897	..	..	..	..	7,769	74,250
1898	..	..	..	..	19,982	218,083
1899	..	..	..	..	23,141	285,250
1900	..	..	..	..	20,516	267,250
1901	..	..	..	..	35,628	430,250
1902	..	..	..	..	22,855	268,167

The great increase which marked the year 1901 was due to an

all round larger import, especially in rape seed, which was 8,596 tons, worth 84,167*l.*, whereas in 1902 it was only 5,172 tons, worth 45,000*l.*

Raw Hides and Skins.

Year.				Quantity.	Value.
				Tons.	£
1897	..	..	..	6,887	463,583
1898	..	..	..	5,938	419,833
1899	..	..	..	5,375	415,792
1900	..	..	..	7,949	630,917
1901	..	..	..	7,306	505,667
1902	..	..	..	6,606	522,709

Fat, Grease, &c.

Year.				Quantity.	Value.
				Tons.	£
1897	..	..	..	1,217	24,583
1898	..	..	..	1,550	35,917
1899	..	..	..	1,449	35,958
1900	..	..	..	2,014	41,708
1901	..	..	..	2,112	68,083
1902	..	..	..	3,587	91,208

The increase in 1902 was due to palm and coccanut oils.

Dyeing and Colouring Matter.

Year.				Quantity.	Value.
				Tons.	£
1897	..	..	..	5,612	242,750
1898	..	..	..	5,391	231,417
1899	..	..	..	3,668	216,958
1900	..	..	..	4,808	163,875
1901	..	..	..	4,495	180,541
1902	..	..	..	4,278	135,041

Showing a decreasing trade due to indigo, which fell from 532 tons, worth 208,333*l.*, in 1897, to 327 tons, worth 106,708*l.*, in 1902, whereas synthetic indigo imported from Germany rose during this period from 209 tons, worth 82,083*l.*, to 1,019 tons, worth 331,208*l.*

RAW COTTON.

Year.				Quantity.	Value.
				Tons.	£
1897	..	..	..	..	31,110	915,670
1898	..	..	..	..	27,145	755,583
1899	..	..	..	..	28,775	851,250
1900	..	..	..	..	14,356	569,458
1901	..	..	..	..	28,359 .	957,083
1902	..	..	..	..	27,872	939,541

JUTE.

Year.				Quantity.	Value.
				Tons.	£
1897	..	..	..	..	36,894	530,333
1898	..	..	..	..	45,805	572,591
1899	..	..	..	..	27,105	392,833
1900	..	..	..	..	33,727	534,000
1901	..	..	..	..	42,482	601,833
1902	..	..	..	..	49,196	635,417

TIN.

Year.				Quantity.	Value.
				Tons.	£
1897	..	..	..	..	894	57,000
1898	..	..	..	..	1,554	130,667
1899	..	..	..	..	1,136	137,291
1900	..	..	..	..	981	131,625
1901	..	..	..	..	1,065	129,583
1902	..	..	..	..	1,032	126,833

BONES and Bone Dust.

Year.				Quantity.	Value.
				Tons.	£
1897	..	..	..	..	459	1,667
1898	..	..	..	..	852	2,918
1899	..	..	..	..	1,432	4,833
1900	..	..	..	..	1,471	4,891
1901	..	..	..	..	427	1,417
1902	..	..	..	..	1,941	6,458

Exports to India.

The chief article of export to India is sugar.

SUGAR EXPORTS.

Year.				Quantity.	Value.
				Tons.	£
1897	..	..	..	..	41,605	434,583
1898	..	..	..	..	52,352	593,083
1899	..	..	..	..	46,899	580,167
1900	..	..	..	..	65,342	773,125
1901	..	..	..	..	133,752	1,432,792
1902	..	..	..	..	104,235	905,917

OTHER EXPORTS.

Year.			Value.			
			Cotton Goods.	Woollen Goods.	Paper.	Indiarubber Goods.
			£	£	£	£
1897	..	..	..	22,500	100,833	144,333	1,583
1898	..	..	..	51,500	141,583	163,591	7,167
1899	..	..	..	77,209	155,958	194,250	14,167
1900	..	..	..	103,667	159,958	184,917	23,208
1901	..	..	..	66,958	128,583	194,917	15,458
1902	..	..	..	41,875	132,542	181,625	18,333

The export of leather goods increased from 9,833*l.* in 1897 to 18,541*l.* in 1902, the most marked increase being in shoeware, which rose during this period from 175*l.* to 8,083*l.*

Woodware, furniture, &c., rose during the same period from 15,417*l.* to 28,208*l.*, due chiefly to the steadily increasing export of bentwood furniture, which rose from 4,333*l.* in 1897 to 13,958*l.* last year.

Glassware, chiefly exported from Bohemia, shows a rapidly increasing trade, which in 1897 was 64,167*l.* and rose to 126,917*l.* in 1902.

In beads, buttons, ornaments, &c., which are manufactured in the Gablonz district in Bohemia, and so called "Gablonz goods," the rise during this period was most marked, being from 8,000*l.* to 43,250*l.*, a jump in six years of 35,250*l.*

Jewellery, mother-of-pearl goods, &c., rose from 28,917*l.* in 1897 to 94,875*l.* in 1902, the increase being due to ornaments, &c., manufactured in non-precious metals.

In iron and ironware, during this period, the export rose from 55,250*l.* to 70,875*l.*, and in metal goods the export in 1902 was 208,958*l.*

TRADE WITH CANADA.

Year.				Value.	
				Imports.	Exports.
				£	£
1898	..	..	..	..	5,452	14,381
1899	..	..	..	..	3,845	10,726
1900	..	..	..	..	6,517	16,607
1901	..	..	..	..	14,227	6,926
1902	..	..	..	..	11,922	9,656

TRADE WITH AUSTRALIA.

Year.				Value.	
				Imports.	Exports.
				£	£
1898	..	..	..	..	224,531	24,167
1899	..	..	..	..	267,387	25,875
1900	..	..	..	..	156,388	26,750
1901	..	..	..	..	100,603	30,583
1902	..	..	..	..	159,084	40,083

TRADE with the British West Indies.

Year.				Value.	
				Imports.	Exports.
				£	£
1898	..	..	..	..	136,779	7,140
1899	..	..	..	..	104,868	5,915
1900	..	..	..	..	92,408	4,942
1901	..	..	..	..	96,970	3,887
1902	..	..	..	..	80,389	2,563

TRADE with the Cape.

Year.				Value.	
				Imports.	Exports.
				£	£
1898	..	..	..	..	18,454	14,056
1899	..	..	..	..	46,624	7,883
1900	..	..	..	..	6,676	165,404
1901	..	..	..	..	19,470	199,276
1902	..	..	..	..	22,007	105,150

TRADE with British Possessions in the Mediterranean.

Year.				Value.	
				Imports.	Exports.
				£	£
1898	..	..	..	..	7,280	464,276
1899	..	..	..	..	8,566	541,406
1900	..	..	..	..	10,480	557,778
1901	..	..	..	..	12,321	543,129
1902	..	..	..	..	9,231	538,789

During the past four years the brown coal fields of Bohemia Coal industry. produced :—

Production.

Year.							Quantity.
							Tons.
1899	..	..	..	..	..	..	17,900,000
1900	..	..	..	..	..	..	17,300,000
1901	..	..	..	..	..	..	18,300,000
1902	..	..	..	..	..	..	18,000,000

The export and consumption of Bohemian brown coal during Export and this period was :— consumption.

Year.					Quantity.	
					Export.	Consumed.
					Tons.	Tons.
1899	..	..	..	..	8,500,000	9,400,000
1900	..	..	..	..	7,700,000	9,600,000
1901	..	..	..	..	8,100,000	10,200,000
1902	..	..	..	..	7,400,000	10,600,000

The export in 1902, as compared with the year 1899, shows a falling-off of about 1,100,000 tons, whereas the home consumption increased during this period 1,200,000 tons. The decline in the export was due to the increased yield of the German coal fields and to the raising of freights on the railways in Bohemia in the autumn of 1900. The rise in home consumption was due not only to an increased demand by industrial undertakings, but also to the growth of the population in Bohemia, which, since 1899, has risen 8 per cent. The State Railways have recently contracted for a supply of 1,005,000 tons of Bohemian brown coal for next year (1904), being an increase on the present (1903) of 156,500 tons.

The export of brown coal from Bohemia to Saxony and Bavaria was :—

Year.				Quantity.	
				Saxony.	Bavaria.
				Tons.	Tons.
1899	..	..	..	3,650,000	1,820,000
1900	..	..	..	3,338,000	1,860,000
1901	..	..	..	3,450,000	1,900,000
1902	..	..	..	3,220,000	1,800,000

The price in 1902 declined by about 8d. to 10d. per ton, without any corresponding saving in the cost of production, and the result, compared with previous years, was unsatisfactory.

The increased export of coal by the River Elbe was unimportant, owing to low water in the autumn and the early closing of the river to navigation in consequence of ice.

The total export by river was, in round figures, 2,000,000 tons. The lowest freightage was in June, July and the middle of August, at the rate of 1·60s. per ton from Aussig to Magdeberg and the highest 3·96s. per ton in the middle of November.

The total import of coal into Austria-Hungary was :—

Year.				Quantity.	Value.
				Tons.	£
1900	..	..	..	6,935,795	4,680,097
1901	..	..	..	6,466,501	4,422,280
1902	..	..	..	6,346,618	4,215,000

The total export was :—

Year.				Quantity.	Value.
				Tons.	£
1900	..	..	..	8,982,217	3,969,215
1901	..	..	..	9,179,880	4,559,316
1902	..	..	..	8,819,736	3,706,750

The import of black coal, included in above figures, in 1902 was 5,766,380 tons and 547,406 tons of coke, the import from the United Kingdom was 287,669 tons, as compared with 176,539 tons in 1901.

The export of black coal, chiefly from the Bohemian pits, in 1902 was 691,680 tons and of coke 234,911 tons. For the first six months of this year, 1903, the output for both brown and black coal has improved in Bohemia. From the brown coal fields an increase of 10,000 tons and from the Pilsen black coal fields 1,180 tons on the first half of 1902.

The import of iron ore during the past six years was :—

Year.					Quantity.
					Tons.
1897..	..	..	..	..	..	134,778
1898..	..	..	..	..	..	178,507
1899..	..	..	..	..	..	212,412
1900..	..	..	..	..	..	233,156
1901..	..	..	..	..	..	218,476
1902..	..	..	..	..	..	197,525

During the latter year 104,827 tons were imported from Sweden, 30,472 tons from Germany and 46,869 tons from Greece.

The total production of the Austrian Iron Trust in pig iron, beams, sheet iron, rails, railway material, &c., was :—

Year.					Quantity.
					Tons.
1899..	..	..	..	..	..	478,540
1900..	..	..	..	..	..	431,254
1901..	..	..	..	..	..	430,228
1902..	..	..	..	..	..	480,000

The marked increase in 1902 on previous years was due to larger demands from Germany, owing to that country forcing her export trade. The prices, however, that ruled for the greater part of the year, were lower than in 1901. The home consumption was unfavourably influenced by the depression in the machine industry.

The State railways in Austria are commencing to relay with heavier rails the lines over which express trains run, the present 35·4 kilos. per metre is being gradually replaced by a 44·1 kilos. per metre rail. This means an outlay of about 834,000l., and as the North-West Railway is about to lay a second line of rails, the prospects for the iron industry are decidedly improving.

The import of iron and ironware was :—

Year.				Quantity.	
				Total Import.	From United Kingdom.
				Tons.	Tons.
1898	..	..	..	..	229,028	80,264
1899	..	..	..	..	161,953	66,714
1900	..	..	..	..	127,520	54,130
1901	..	..	..	..	126,591	48,490
1902	..	..	..	..	78,120	24,162

The import from Germany fell from 96,535 tons in 1898 to 44,657 tons in 1902. The total decrease in value of iron and iron-ware imported during this period was 519,229l., these figures show that the development of the home iron industry is gradually supplying the wants of the Empire.

Export of iron and ironware.

The export of iron and ironware was :—

Year.						Quantity.
						Tons.
1898 ..	..	..	..	..	..	61,758
1899 ..	..	..	..	..	..	108,757
1900 ..	..	..	..	..	..	158,788
1901 ..	..	..	..	..	..	101,655
1902 ..	..	..	..	..	..	118,246

The value in 1898 was 1,420,855l. and in 1902 1,712,330l. The export of the following was :—

	Quantity.				
	1898.	1899.	1900.	1901.	1902.
	Tons.	Tons.	Tons.	Tons.	Tons.
Iron and steel bars, rolled or malleable ..	18,348	36,377	43,318	20,243	33,179
Iron and steel plates ..	4,103	7,517	5,907	3,059	5,596
„ „ wire ..	23,231	1,826	7,769	1,662	6,509

To the United Kingdom.

The export to the United Kingdom fell from 2,348 tons in 1901 to 613 tons in 1902, of which, in the latter year, 244 tons were pig iron.

The machine industry.

The year 1902 was bad for the great engineering works in Bohemia, with the exception of the agricultural branch, and the internal depression that marked the year 1901 was last year still more keenly felt. The uncertainty as to the future with regard to the sugar industry, at home and abroad, was a principal factor in the depression, the sugar mills in Bohemia and throughout the Empire reduced all repairs to a minimum, and orders for new machinery were practically nil. The electrical works of Kolben and Co., in the vicinity of Prague, were the least effected, thanks to orders received from abroad, particularly from the United Kingdom and her dependencies. The value in exports of sugar machinery alone fell from 13,927l. in 1898 to 2,080l. in 1902.

Manufacturers of agricultural machinery, consequent on good harvests, have done well both in their home and foreign trade.

Fortunately, on the whole, the exports showed an improvement on the previous year, due to an increase in agricultural machinery, locomobiles and dynamos, &c.

In the locomotive industry the fluctuations in the export trade are shown in the following table :— Locomotive industry.

Year.				Locomotives Exported.	Value.
					£
1898	..	..	..	..	9	10,307
1899	..	..	..	..	1	209
1900	..	..	..	..	9	6,188
1901	..	..	..	..	13	7,562
1902	..	..	..	..	11	19,631

In 1902 the increase was due to Turkey importing to the value of 16,981l.

In locomobiles the number exported in 1898 was 47, worth 10,766l., which increased in 1902 to 183, worth 43,234l.

The total value of machinery exported was :— Machinery exports.

Year.						Value.
						£
1898	..	..	..	..	..	508,080
1899	..	..	..	..	..	615,420
1900	..	..	..	..	..	685,625
1901	..	..	..	..	..	457,540
1902	..	..	..	..	..	583,127

The export to the United Kingdom was 8,500l. in 1902, an increase on the previous year of 1,125l.

In agricultural machinery the export has been steadily increasing, and rose from 74,000l. in 1897 to 218,500l. in 1902. Russia is the best customer, and the value increased during this period from 24,417l. to 101,458l. last year. Agricultural machinery.

The effect of the Brussels Sugar Convention must diminish the area now under beet cultivation, and therefore that of cereals will be increased. Canada could extend her trade with Austria in light agricultural machinery ; the United States is increasing her competition in this direction.

A Prague firm has received a contract from Launceston, Tasmania, for four turbine dynamo groups of 450 horse-power each, in fact for the total installation ; the latter town is about to utilise the water-power of the River Esk for electric lighting purposes.

The value of dynamos exported in 1902 was 22,343l., an increase on the previous year of 4,961l.

The export of bicycles fell from 103,500l. in 1898 to only 36,917l. in 1902, and the import during this period from 60,000l. to 8,250l. Bicycle trade.

The works of Skoda, at Pilsen, Bohemia, are constructing 46 guns Government

order for
guns.

Imports from
the United
Kingdom.

Rolling-stock.

of varying calibre for the armaments of the new battleships A and B
now building for the Austro-Hungarian navy.

The import value of textile machinery and locomobiles from
the United Kingdom was :—

	Value.	
Year.	Textile Machinery.	Locomobiles.
	£	£
1897	302,417	38,917
1898	324,417	58,500
1899	239,501	61,583
1900	381,000	46,167
1901	305,708	36,000
1902	388,000	30,042

The import of sewing machines from the United Kingdom
was 68,891l., an increase on the previous year of 9,008l.

As several British engineering firms have written to me for
information with a view of establishing agencies at Prague, I would
suggest that an Englishman should be placed in charge of any such
agency, as, belonging to and siding with neither party, he would be
able to do business with both the rival nationalities that compose the
population of Bohemia. I can only add, I shall be very glad to give
anyone visiting this city for this purpose any help or further information which may be in my power.

The builders of railway and other rolling-stock had to discharge
about 4,000 workmen during the past year, and working hours were
reduced to an average of seven hours daily.

The total capacity per annum of the six carriage works in the
Austro-Hungarian Empire is 1,275 passenger carriages and 12,400
goods trucks, the most important is in Prague, and is able to turn
out 400 passenger carriages and 4,000 goods trucks in a year, or
nearly one-third of the total production.

During the past five years the Austrian works have delivered—

	Number.				
	1898.	1899.	1900.	1901.	1902.
Passenger carriages	729	374	479	414	358
Electric motor cars	180	290	505	343	198
Service cars	135	150	215	142	198
Goods trucks	5,316	5,224	5,645	5,163	3,372
Total	6,360	6,038	6,844	6,062	4,126

In April this year the orders to be placed by the State and private
railways from 1903–05 amount to 1,750,000l., this is in

addition to orders for this year already placed, and as the new lines of railway now being constructed are completed, under the scheme for the improvement of communication within the Austro-Hungarian Empire, the requirements and keeping up of railway plant will be continually increasing, consequently the outlook for this industry is decidedly encouraging. The export of rolling-stock in 1902 was 20,500*l*., a fall of 19,108*l*. on the previous year.

The import of raw cotton from the United Kingdom in 1902 was 1,403 tons, a reduction of 539 tons on 1901, but this was more than made up for by an increase of 1,280 tons in cotton yarn last year (1902). Raw cotton from the United Kingdom.

The import of cotton yarn and cotton goods from the United Kingdom was :— Cotton yarn and goods from the United Kingdom.

Year.	Cotton Yarn.		Cotton Goods.	
	Quantity.	Value.	Quantity.	Value.
	Tons.	£	Tons.	£
1897	6,089	665,000	301	141,500
1898	5,835	644,833	294	128,833
1899	5,321	726,083	305	114,000
1900	4,829	793,917	313	124,250
1901	4,726	695,917	299	115,042
1902	6,006	806,458	321	155,291

The import of wool from the United Kingdom rose from 1,930 tons in 1897 to 3,183 tons in 1902. Wool and woollen goods from the United Kingdom.

From the United Kingdom the import of woollen yarn and goods was :—

Year.	Yarn.		Goods.	
	Quantity.	Value.	Quantity.	Value.
	Tons.	£	Tons.	£
1897	2,754	635,333	674	357,333
1898	2,678	591,414	645	343,417
1899	3,283	751,041	698	406,542
1900	3,149	723,833	708	442,375
1901	3,022	652,583	696	414,042
1902	3,145	686,458	750	472,375

Flax, jute and hemp from the United Kingdom.

Flax, hemp and jute imports from the United Kingdom were :—

Year.			Flax, Hemp, Jute.		Jute Yarn.	
			Quantity.	Value.	Quantity.	Value.
			Tons.	£	Tons.	£
1897	..	..	1,400	21,833	977	21,167
1898	..	..	941	14,833	1,043	22,583
1899	..	..	735	14,875	660	16,375
1900	..	..	955	16,708	202	5,291
1901	..	..	1,061	16,625	237	6,125
1902	..	..	469	9,042	103	2,708

Linen and linen goods from the United Kingdom.

Linen yarn from the United Kingdom and linen goods were :—

Year.				Linen Yarn.		Value of Linen Goods.
				Quantity.	Value.	
				Tons.	£	£
1897	..	..	..	607	89,250	11,083
1898	..	..	..	569	90,167	9,500
1899	..	..	..	564	93,083	10,041
1900	..	..	..	523	93,458	10,167
1901	..	..	..	412	73,458	12,667
1902	..	..	..	487	77,750	9,958

Silk goods from the United Kingdom. Clothing, &c.

The value of silk goods imported from the United Kingdom in 1902 was 97,292l., an increase on the previous year of 17,375l.

The import from the United Kingdom of clothing, hats, hosiery, house and table linen, &c., was 55,750l. in 1902, a very slight increase on that of 1901.

The manufacture of articles of clothing, both for men and women, especially shirts, collars, hats, underclothing, ladies blouses, &c., is a large and growing industry in Bohemia and the export to the United Kingdom is steadily increasing.

At the exhibition now being held at Aussig shirt and collar makers may be seen at work, and labour-saving machinery of the latest type, worked by young girls of about 12 years of age; collars are cut out in blocks of 100, button holes made and buttons sewn on by these machines.

The export of articles of clothing and wearing apparel to the United Kingdom was :—

Year.						Value.
						£
1897 ..	..	..	..	..	..	38,000
1898 ..	..	..	..	..	..	42,750
1899 ..	..	..	..	..	..	46,583
1900 ..	..	..	..	..	..	52,208
1901 ..	..	..	..	..	..	100,583
1902 ..	..	..	..	..	..	117,208

During the year 1902 the spinning mills were fully occupied and the quantity produced increased, due to the replacement of old by new machinery of greater capacity and also to the increase in the number of spindles. During the past two years about 200,000 spindles have been added, and in the present year three new mills are being built, with a total capacity of 100,000 spindles. *Textile industry in Bohemia.*

Some new mills, working with Egyptian cotton, were adversely affected by the fluctuations in the market for raw material, which rose in one month 20 to 30 per cent. Cotton weavers have had a satisfactory year, there was an excellent demand, which also favourably influenced cotton printing and similar industries such as bleaching, dyeing and dressing. The close of 1902 left no heavy stocks on hand. This year, 1903, the high price of raw cotton has so far been most unfavourable, and spinning mills are considerably reducing their output.

In Austria there are about 3,054,000 spindles at work, of which 1,750,000 are in Bohemia, and there will probably be a temporary stoppage of about 1,000,000 spindles.

Reichenberg, in the north of Bohemia, is the seat of the cloth industry and of the manufacture of woollen goods. In the first part of the year 1902 the working was satisfactory, but this did not continue, owing to the fall in prices and the alteration in the fashion of ladies cloth, nevertheless weavers were fully occupied notwithstanding the increase of manufactories in recent years. *Cloth industry.*

The number of looms in Austria is about 120,000, of which about 70,000 are in Bohemia.

The export trade is steadily increasing and the industry is in a satisfactory state.

In the textile printing industry there are in Austria about 150 machines, of which more than half are in Bohemia. The hours of labour in the bleaching, printing and shirt making industries vary from 10 to 11½ hours per diem, there are some few printing works which run the whole 24 hours, but these are the exception, otherwise over-production and consequently a fall in price would result. *Labour conditions.*

The wages for regular hands in the cotton mills are from 2s. 6d. to 3s. 4d. per diem, occasional labour being paid proportionately less. Weavers are paid 2s. 6d. a day, but in the calico works in the east of Bohemia they only receive 1s. 8d. per diem. In the printing works skilled labour such as printers, engravers and others receive even as much as 8s. 4d. a day, the wage of the ordinary workman is 1s. 8d.

Exports.

The total value of the exports of the textile industry was :—

	Value.					
	1897.	1898.	1899.	1900.	1901.	1902.
	£	£	£	£	£	£
Cotton and cotton goods ...	1,772,417	1,987,000	2,248,666	2,431,625	2,181,200	2,174,570
Flax, hemp and jute goods ...	1,477,917	1,503,750	1,763,917	2,062,542	2,044,958	2,052,917
Wool and woollen goods ...	2,577,500	2,843,392	3,372,667	2,864,292	2,901,750	3,264,667
Clothing, &c.	1,754,583	1,834,000	2,063,750	1,992,000	2,046,958	2,211,542

By the foregoing it will be seen that the export trade is in a satisfactory state. Hungary being chiefly an agricultural country the textile industry is unimportant ; the chief centres of manufacture in Austria are in Bohemia, but for which I can give no separate statistics as none are published.

Glass, china and porcelain.

In Bohemia there are 43 china and porcelain manufactories employing over 7,000 people, and over 100 glass works employing more than 120,000 ; the most beautiful glass work, for which Bohemia is famous, is manufactured at Neuwelt. The value of glass and glassware exported in 1902 was 1,942,917l., but has decreased since 1900 by 254,291l.

The trade with the United Kingdom was 346,292l. in 1902, a falling-off on the previous year of 70,375l.

The export of china and porcelain rose from 684,000l. in 1897 to 812,375l. in 1902. The value exported to the United Kingdom in 1902 was 79,250l., a decrease on 1901 of 11,333l., but an increase on 1897 of 42,750l.

Chemicals.

The manufacture of chemicals is largely carried on throughout Bohemia, and the trade with the United Kingdom has increased from 1,504 tons, worth 49,333l., in 1897 to 4,076 tons, worth 130,000l., in 1902, the imports from the United Kingdom during this period also increased from 554 tons, worth 50,750l., to 823 tons, worth 59,967l.

Agriculture.

Of the ground under cultivation in Bohemia in 1902, 62·69 per cent. was under grain, 2·15 per cent. under pulse, root crops 19·34 per cent. and fodder herbage 12·92 per cent.

The result of the harvest was most satisfactory, and there was harvested in Austria :—

				Quantity.	
				1902.	1901.
				Tons.	Tons.
Wheat	..	..	..	1,250,000	1,200,000
Rye ..	..	..	..	2,090,000	1,900,000
Barley	..	..	..	1,610,000	1,460,000
Oats..	..	..	..	1,820,000	1,720,000
Maize	..	..	..	340,000	450,000

An all round increase in 1902 on the previous year, with the single exception of maize.

In Bohemia there was harvested in 1902 :—

				Quantity.	Increase as compared with 1901.
				Tons.	Tons.
Wheat	..	..	..	368,000	42,500
Rye ..	..	..	..	618,947	29,000
Barley	..	..	..	656,071	105,000
Oats..	..	..	..	573,042	83,000

Barley was the heaviest crop that has been harvested during the past five years and was only exceeded in wheat, rye and oats by that of 1899. A decrease in 1902 of 27·3 per cent. on the year previous in the area under beet cultivation in Bohemia resulted in an increased area of other crops being substituted.

ROOT Crops in Bohemia.

				Quantity.	
				1902.	1901.
				Tons.	Tons.
Potatoes	..	..	..	4,908,398	5,339,523
Sugar beet..	..	..	..	2,871,248	4,288,925
Clover	..	..	..	685,932	613,975
Rape	..	..	..	30,656	21,121

There was a slight increase, in Bohemia, in the area under hop cultivation in 1902 on the previous year, the production was 6,652 tons out of a total in the Austro-Hungarian Empire of 8,994 tons.

The export was :—

Year.				Quantity.	
				Total Export.	To United Kingdom.
				Tons.	Tons.
1897	..	..	..	3,707	114
1898	..	..	..	3,791	203
1899	..	..	..	5,040	178
1900	..	..	..	4,449	150
1901	..	..	..	10,159	468
1902	..	..	..	5,215	593

The greater portion went to Germany, which took 3,225 tons in 1902. Hop prospects for 1903 are at present anything but satisfactory in Bohemia.

Export of grain and flour. The export of grain and flour from Austria-Hungary is considerable and was :—

Year.				Quantity.		
				Grain.	Malt.	Flour.
				Tons.	Tons.	Tons.
1897	..	..	..	407,779	168,400	98,727
1898	..	..	..	348,610	164,551	77,153
1899	..	..	..	483,119	182,314	113,674
1900	..	..	..	344,797	185,369	105,973
1901	..	..	..	364,521	168,797	87,192
1902	..	..	..	488,102	173,228	99,284

Barley to the United Kingdom. The chief grain export to the United Kingdom is barley, which increased from 7,671 tons, worth 65,500l., in 1897, to 35,293 tons, worth 264,708l., in 1902.

Flour to the United Kingdom. Malt. The export of flour to the United Kingdom has increased from 1,385 tons in 1897 to 40,059 tons, worth 450,250l., last year.

Germany is the best customer of the Dual Monarchy; and in Bohemia, where malting for export is extensively carried on, her total production is taken by that country. The home consumption of malt has declined during the past year, owing to larger stocks being carried over from 1901 and to the diminished production of beer.

The prices for grain per met. centner. (220 lbs.) during the first Market prices
three months of 1903 on the Prague Corn Exchange were :— in Prague.

	January 1, 1903.		February 1, 1903.		March 1, 1903.	
	From—	To—	From—	To—	From—	To—
	s. d.	s. d.	s. d.	s. d.	s. d.	s. d.
Wheat ...	13 1	13 10	13 1	13 10	13 1	13 10
Rye ...	12 0	12 5	11 11	12 3	11s. 8d. to 12s. 1d.	11s. 6d. to 12s. 1d.
Oats ...	10 6	10 9	10 5	10 6	10s. 5d. 10s. 8d.	10s. 2d. 10s. 6d.
Barley ...	10 10	13 4	10 10	13 4	10s 10d.	13s. 4d.

The wet summer of 1902, combined with the distress that pre- Brewing.
vailed among the labouring classes, was detrimental to the brewing
industry, the production in Bohemia was :—

Year.						Quantity.
						Gallons.
1899–1900	..	..	..	..	..	203,023,964
1900–01	..	..	..	..	..	208,410,312
1901–02	..	..	..	..	..	201,471,094

In Austria the production last year was 431,809,774 gallons,
and the decrease on 1901 caused a loss to the revenue of 59,724l.,
the total amount derived from this source in 1902 was 3,110,235l.
The export trade is chiefly with Germany, which takes the light-
coloured Pilsen beers, and in return the heavy black beers of Bavaria
are extensively imported by Austria, and principally consumed by
the well-to-do classes.

The trade with the United Kingdom is unimportant, but at the
same time shows an increase, the export rising from 76 tons in 1897
to 227 tons in 1902. The import from the United Kingdom
last year was only 40 tons, worth 300l.

The total export of beer from Austria-Hungary was :—

Year.						Quantity.
						Tons.
1899	..	..	..	..	..	92,821
1900	..	..	..	..	..	91,640
1901	..	..	..	..	..	91,457

And in 1902, 95,664 tons, worth 566,750l., the bulk of which is
brewed at Pilsen, in Bohemia.

The import, which is chiefly from Bavaria, was 6,667 tons in
1902, a falling-off on the previous year of 348 tons.

The export price for rectified spirits fell from 17s. 6d. per hecto- Spirit
litre (22 gallons) at Trieste in 1901 to 9s. 7d. per hectolitre in 1902. industry.
At Hamburg the price fell from 17s. 6d. to 10s. 6d. per hectolitre.

The export in the 1901–02 campaign was 242,060 hectolitres, a reduction on the previous year of 15,404 hectolitres or 339,042 gallons; the decrease both in quantity and price was due to over-production, particularly in Germany. The export to the United Kingdom in 1902 was 80 tons, worth 23,167*l*., an increase of about 10 tons on the year previous.

Sugar industry.

The unusually large stocks carried over from the previous year, as well as a greater production, caused prices for sugar to fall to an unprecedented figure during the campaign of 1901–02, which would have been still more marked had not the beet sugar producing countries diminished the area under beet cultivation by about 10 per cent. When prices fell to 18*s.* per 220 lbs. in Bohemia in July, it was thought that the lowest point had been touched, but in September there was a still further decline at Aussig on the frontier to 13*s.* 4*d.* per met. centner. (220 lbs.), later prices recovered, and on December 26 the highest point was reached at 18*s.* 2*d.* per 220 lbs. from Aussig.

The Law authorising the contingent system passed by the Austrian Parliament, was brought forward by the Government with the avowed object of protecting smaller and less favourably situated mills and preventing them being swamped by the larger, in which case agriculturists would also suffer. The system proposed was, practically speaking, a Trust in favour of sugar producers, refiners and growers of beet. The Brussels Sugar Commission recently found that this law was not in keeping with the spirit of the Convention and it has been abandoned.

In consequence of the abandonment of the sugar bounty there is no doubt that assistance will be given to this industry by considerably reducing railway rates, not only to frontier stations and export ports, but also on the conveyance of raw sugar from the mills to the refineries, and on the carriage of beetroot, coal, &c.

'Rayon-irung."

The association of raw sugar manufacturers came to an arrangement whereby growers of beet were compelled to deliver their beet at fixed prices to the different sugar mills in their particular "rayon" or district; the unfairness of this system caused the farmers to petition the Government, and a law is about to be passed forbidding it.

In the 1901–02 campaign there were, in Bohemia, 128 mills using 4,000,000 tons of beet, which produced 658,285 tons of raw sugar out of a total production in Austria, Hungary and Bosnia of 1,291,127 tons.

The export from Bohemia was :—

	Quantity.	
	1900–01.	1901–02.
	Tons.	Tons.
Raw sugar	29,967	9,630
Refined sugar	307,334	389,611
Equivalent in raw sugar ..	371,450	442,531

The export from Austria-Hungary was :—

	Quantity.	
	1900–01.	1901–02.
	Tons.	Tons.
Raw sugar	87,792	33,985
Refined sugar	544,714	704,801
Equivalent in raw sugar ..	693,030	817,098

The bulk of the sugar exported from Bohemia goes to the United Kingdom.

The exports to the United Kingdom and to India from Austria-Hungary were :—

UNITED KINGDOM.

	Quantity.		
	1900.	1901.	1902.
	Tons.	Tons.	Tons.
Raw sugar	73,098	40,087	37,576
Refined sugar	252,030	279,464	240,646

INDIA.

	Quantity.		
	1900.	1901.	1902.
	Tons.	Tons.	Tons.
Raw sugar	1,515	1,085	1,723
Refined sugar	63,827	132,667	102,512

Having furnished information with regard to the Bohemian lace industry, in answer to applications made to this Consulate during the past year, the following brief description may be of interest :—

At Kleneč and Postřekov near Taus, at Drosan near Klattau, and at Sedlic near Blatuá, all in the Bohemian forest, not far from the Bavarian frontier, there is a widely spread lace industry. In nearly every house in these poor villages pillow-lace from thread, silk and twine is produced. The number of lace workers in this district is estimated at about 1,500. The lace is made chiefly during the long winter months, when little or no other work is to be had, and every member of the family is occupied in it, not only the females but also the males; in summer only old people and children from six years of age or those not fitted for heavier work are thus employed. In Drosan and Sedlic, where lace schools are founded, the girls who are learning and the women at their homes work the whole year through. The object of these schools is not only to teach the first rudiments, but also to guide in style and finish. The school buildings are light and airy, and in the winter are properly heated and frequented by an increasing number glad to benefit by being taught free of any cost. By the help of these schools this home industry has attained such perfection that it is able to compete with any lace made in Austria or outside the Empire; it is much sought after in Bohemia as well as in foreign lands, especially in France and the United States. The lace produced at Postřekov and Kleneč is collected, packed and forwarded by one Josef Kapic, dealer in Postřekov. At Drosan and Sedlic the lace made is sold by the curators of the schools; persons interested can address the Curatorium der Schule in Drosan, Böhmen and the Damengruppe der Národni Jednota Pošumavská in Sedlec bei Blatná, Böhmen, or the founders of the school at Prague, viz., der Damengruppe der Národni Jednota Pošumavská in Prag, Böhmen.

In the north of Bohemia, in several villages in the Erzgeberg and the Riesengeberg mountains, pillow-lace has been made by the peasantry since 1767, and in the year 1840 about 40,000 people were so occupied, but the introduction of machinery reduced the numbers considerably, and in 1870 only about 11,000, of whom 4,000 were children, were employed. In the year 1881 the Government opened a school at Gossengrün; schools already existed at Heinrichsgrüss and Hengstererben.

The Commercial Director of the Imperial Government in Vienna, Dr. Fritz Minkus, recently visited these districts and reported that the work produced was very beautiful and artistic in design. The increasing demand for this lace will be of great assistance in bettering the lot of these poor and industrious people. I am forwarding with this report a collection of samples* of hand-made lace, contained in three books, with prices marked in British currency

* Sent to Association of Chambers of Commerce.

against each sample, which I hope will be useful to those interested. I am indebted to the courtesy of the Prague Chamber of Commerce for these samples, which illustrate the various kinds of lace made by the peasantry in the Chamber's commercial district.

Basket work of all kinds is extensively carried on as a home industry in Bohemia, especially in those districts in the valleys of the Moldau and the Elbe, at Leitmeritz, Tetschen, Roudince, Meliuk, Könnigrätz, Saaz and Königsaal. *Basket and basketware.*

The manufactures are exclusively handwork, and special attention is bestowed upon willow culture by the Department for Agriculture, and there are several schools throughout the country for promoting this industry and especially for introducing elegant designs. These schools are supported partly by the State and partly by agricultural associations. Garden furniture is also manufactured in Prague, rushwork is chiefly made at Bakov and its environs, where also baskets, bathing shoes, caps, bags, &c., are made and largely exported. The Soudan and Egyptian armies are provided with caps manufactured at Bakov. I may here mention that a British manufacturer recently wrote to me for information regarding the basket industry, and stated that Bohemian basket goods were being imported in such quantities that it was very difficult for the home-made British article to compete on account of the cheapness of the Bohemian work.

The export of basket work to the United Kingdom was 50 tons in 1902, whereas in 1897 only 8 tons were sent.

To illustrate the condition of the labouring classes in Prague, I take the following from a report recently issued by the Government :— *Cost of living for a working man in Prague.*

A locksmith, married, without children, earned 2 kr. 60 h. (2s. 2d.) a day ; in a year 780 kr. (32l. 10s.).

His wife earned, by knitting stockings with a machine, 1 kr. 60 h. a week, or about 83 kr. a year, they therefore together earned 863 kr. a year (35l. 19s. 2d.). Their expenses were :—

	Expenses.				
	Currency.		Sterling.		
	Kr.	h.	£	s.	d.
Rent, one room	240	0	10	0	0
Food, including ¼ lb. of beef twice a week	416	0	17	6	8
Clothes, together	100	0	4	3	4
Shoes	32	0	1	6	8
Coal and wood	45	80	1	18	2
Subscriptions to clubs	16	0	0	13	4
Sundries	13	20	0	11	0
Total	863	0	35	19	2

LONDON :
Printed for His Majesty's Stationery Office,
By HARRISON AND SONS,
Printers in Ordinary to His Majesty.
(1400   9 | 03—H & S   364)

No. 3076.   Annual Series.

CUBA.

DIPLOMATIC AND CONSULAR REPORTS.

TRADE OF

C U B A

FOR THE YEAR 1902.

FOREIGN OFFICE,
September, 1903.

No. 3076 Annual Series.

DIPLOMATIC AND CONSULAR REPORTS.

CUBA.

REPORT FOR THE YEAR 1902

ON THE

TRADE AND COMMERCE OF THE ISLAND OF CUBA.

REFERENCE TO PREVIOUS REPORT, Annual Series No. 2909.

Presented to both Houses of Parliament by Command of His Majesty,

SEPTEMBER, 1903.

LONDON:
PRINTED FOR HIS MAJESTY'S STATIONERY OFFICE,
BY HARRISON AND SONS, ST. MARTIN'S LANE,
PRINTERS IN ORDINARY TO HIS MAJESTY.

And to be purchased, either directly or through any Bookseller, from
EYRE & SPOTTISWOODE, EAST HARDING STREET, FLEET STREET, E.C.,
and 32, ABINGDON STREET, WESTMINSTER, S.W.;
or OLIVER & BOYD, EDINBURGH;
or E. PONSONBY, 116, GRAFTON STREET, DUBLIN.

1903.

d. 1766—10.]   *Price Three Halfpence.*

CONTENTS.

———◆———

Note.—All values in this report have been reduced from United States currency at 5 dol. to the 1l. sterling.

Reference to previous Report, Annual Series No. 2909.

Report on the Trade and Commerce of the Island of Cuba for the
Year 1902, *by Mr. Lionel Carden, His Majesty's Minister at*
Havana.

(Havana, July 11, 1903; received at Foreign Office, July 30, 1903.)

The results of the year 1902, though not as good as might have Introductory
been expected in view of the large amount of sugar produced, remarks.
were by no means as bad as the pessimists had predicted would
be the case owing to the great fall in the price of that product.

On the other hand, it is very encouraging to note the steady
increase in the cultivation of fruit and vegetables for export
and in the development generally of the island's minor sources of
wealth, which up to comparatively recent times were quite neglected
in favour of the two staple products—sugar and tobacco.

From the following summary of the commercial movement in Commerce.
Cuba in the past two years, it will be seen that though the total
value of the exports fell off somewhat in 1902, the imports were far
more reduced:—

	1901.		1902.	
	Imports.	Exports.	Imports.	Exports.
	£	£	£	£
Merchandise	13,316,795	12,655,676	12,116,954	12,865,932
Coin and bullion	233,827	644,758	310,139	123,829
Total	13,550,622	13,300,434	12,427,093	12,989,761

I may mention that the decrease in the exports occurred only in
the movement of coin and bullion and not in merchandise, the
value of which was greater than in the previous year. The falling
off in the imports occurred chiefly in livestock and food products,
and is a rather encouraging feature, showing that Cuba is becoming
less dependent for her food supply on importations from abroad.

⌐ An exceptionally large stock of sugar remained unsold at the end of December, and as, besides this, the new crop promises to exceed that of 1902 by nearly 100,000 tons, a considerable increase may be looked for in the volume of Cuban trade during the current year.

Imports by
countries. In drawing up the accompanying table of imports by countries I have transferred to the United Kingdom and British Possessions the value of the sugar bags and rice which, although products of British India, figure in the Cuban customs returns as imported from Germany, owing to their having been shipped in transit from German ports :—

Country.	Value.	
	1901.	1902.
	£	£
United States	5,815,127	5,048,645
United Kingdom and British Possessions ..	2,267,346	2,076,657
Spain	1,899,771	1,908,332
France	588,856	609,145
Germany..	435,545	465,527
Other countries..	2,310,150	2,008,648
Total	13,316,795	12,116,954

A small increase took place in the imports from Spain, France and Germany, but a considerable falling off is observable in those from the United States, the United Kingdom and British Possessions, and from unspecified countries. The proportion of trade enjoyed by each has, however, been very little affected thereby.

In the case of British trade the falling off was mostly in rice and textile goods, while in that of the United States and other countries it occurred chiefly, as I have already mentioned, in livestock and food products.

Imports by
articles. Since the establishment of the Government of the Republic in May, 1902, a new system of classification has been adopted in the Customs, which makes it impossible for me to continue the analysis of the imports by groups of articles in quite the same form as I have given them in each of the past three years. Rather than omit the table entirely, I append the analysis of those groups in which exact comparison can be made with the year 1901, though it is to be regretted that iron and steel and machinery, in both of which British trade is largely interested, are not among them :—

Groups of Articles.	Value.	
	1901.	1902.
	£	£
Provisions and liquors	4,954,917	4,516,341
Textile goods	1,854,287	1,796,843
Livestock	1,863,616	1,277,150
Leather and manufactures of	412,075	558,655
Wood and manufactures of	480,831	457,505
Paper and manufactures of	232,138	257,639
All other articles	3,518,931	3,252,821
Total	13,316,795	12,116,954

In Annex 1 will be found a comparison of the importation of most of the principal articles for the past three years. I may mention that the large decrease in the number of cattle imported has considerably affected the British carrying trade, fewer cattle ships being now required than in former years. The falling off in this direction will be found under the head of British shipping.

In my report for 1901 I gave an account in some detail of the Products of trade in British Indian rice and sugar bags, which together represent British India. an important part of the total British import trade with Cuba.

To this there is little to add for 1902. The importation of rice fell off considerably, owing to the large stocks on hand at the beginning of the year. On the other hand, the larger production of sugar required a greater number of sugar bags, the increase in the imports of which represented a value of approximately 20,000*l.*

The total imports of British Indian produce into Cuba in 1902 were approximately as follows :—

Articles.	Value.
	£
Rice	610,000
Sugar bags	127,000
Total	737,000

The share of different countries in the export trade of Cuba Exports by shows no great change from the previous year, the United States countries. continuing to take rather over 75 per cent. of the total exports :—

Country.	Value.	
	1901.	1902.
	£	£
United States	9,614,714	9,899,657
United Kingdom and British Possessions ..	1,364,902	1,161,449
Spain	152,208	212,978
France	269,933	259,619
Germany..	848,043	793,558
Other countries..	405,876	538,671
Total	12,655,676	12,865,932

The increase in the United States trade occurs principally in ores and fruits, which are shipped exclusively to that country. The falling off in British trade occurs in cigars and cabinet woods.

Exports by articles. Although the quantities of the principal articles of export are given in Annex 1, which will be found at the end of this report, the variation in values, especially in the case of the products of sugar, has been so great this year that a continuation of the table I have given in former reports cannot but be of interest for purposes of comparison :—

Articles.	Value.	
	1901.	1902.
Sugar and its products—	£	£
Raw sugar	6,163,216	5,997,864
Refined sugar and candy	3,826	4,590
Molasses	243,866	130,056
Rum	41,308	40,195
Total	6,451,716	6,172,705
Tobacco and its products —		
Leaf and scrap	2,514,447	2,541,374
Cigars	2,496,355	2,474,982
Cigarettes	54,633	64,479
Total	5,065,435	5,080,835
Other articles—		
Mineral products, ores, &c. ..	187,607	428,515
Fruits	199,949	254,919
Cacao	78,735	110,490
Fibre	22,739	75,893
Honey and wax	91,947	136,270
Hides	45,496	74,896
Sponges	95,713	84,169
Woods	237,903	279,876
Miscellaneous	178,436	167,364
Total	1,138,525	1,612,392
Grand total	12,655,676	12,865,932

The prices of sugar which ruled during the past crop will be found under the head of sugar industry. It is sufficient to point out here that although over 200,000 more tons were exported in 1902 than in 1901 the gross value realised was roughly 150,000*l.* less, without taking into consideration the corresponding reduction in value of the molasses and other minor products.

Another noticeable feature is the remarkable increase in the shipment of iron and manganese ores and of fruits. The exports of pineapples alone increased from 50,000*l.* in 1901 to 90,000*l.* in 1902, and there seems to be scarcely any limit either to the quantity of these and other fruits for which a market can be found in the United States, or to the amount which can be produced in Cuba.

The prospect of the Reciprocity Convention recently concluded British trade. between Cuba and the United States being eventually sanctioned by the United States Congress has not failed to affect British trade. While it has not influenced the demand for those British goods which are of regular consumption in the Cuban market, it has nevertheless served in several cases which have come under my notice to deter Cuban merchants from accepting proposals to open up business relations with British manufacturers.

There can be no doubt that, with or without the Reciprocity Convention, British merchants will have to bestir themselves if they wish to retain the share they at present have of the Cuban trade. I cannot suggest any more effective way of attaining this end than by co-operating in the formation of trading companies combining a retail and wholesale business, such as I recommended in my report for the year 1901 and in many previous ones.

The enterprise of individuals may, it is true, in some cases win for them success even under very disadvantageous circumstances, but in my opinion combination alone is likely to prove effective in maintaining our commercial position in this part of the Continent of America, in view of the ever increasing keenness of competition.

The value of the Spanish silver dollar has varied during the past Currency and year in its relation to the Spanish gold dollar as follows :— exchange.

	Silver.	Equivalent to—
	Dollar.	Cents gold.
Highest	1	79
Lowest	1	74
Average	1	77½

The selling rates in Spanish gold dollars of bills on London at three days' sight during the same period were as follows :—

					Premium.	Equivalent of $1l$.
					Per cent.	Dol. c.
Highest ..	..	..	..		20$\frac{1}{2}\frac{3}{4}$	5 37
Lowest ..	..	..	..		18$\frac{7}{8}$	5 27$\frac{3}{4}$
Average ..	..	..	..		19$\frac{3}{4}$	5 31$\frac{1}{2}$

Sugar industry.

In spite of the continued phenomenally low price of sugar, its production in Cuba is steadily increasing year by year, showing that even under the existing unfavourable conditions cane-sugar can hold its own against beet.

When the abolition of the bounties comes into effect in September next, a fresh stimulus will be given to the industry, which it can hardly be doubted will result in a still larger production.

The highest price realised for sugar of 96° polarisation test during the past crop was 4$\frac{3}{16}$ reales per arroba of 25 lbs. Spanish (equivalent approximately to 8s. 9d. per cwt.), and was obtained at the commencement of the season. From this time on the quotations continued to fall, until in July they reached their lowest figure at 2$\frac{3}{4}$ reales (5s. 9d. per cwt.). The mean price for the whole crop is estimated at 3$\frac{3}{16}$ reales per arroba, or about 6s. 10$\frac{1}{2}$d. per cwt.

The following table shows the total production and exportation of all Cuban sugar in the past three years, as taken from the brokers' reports published monthly in Havana :—

Crop.			Produced.	Exported.
			Tons.	Tons.
1899-1900 ..	..	..	300,073	270,060
1900-1901 ..	..	..	635,856	560,700
1901-1902 ..	..	..	850,181	701,077
Estimated for				
1902-1903 ..	..	..	950,000	..

The difference between the amount produced and that exported represents the local consumption, which averages about 40,000 tons per annum, plus the stock in hand at the end of each year.

Owing to New York prices being below the corresponding European rates some shipments have been made to the United Kingdom during the current year (1903), and more would doubtless have been sent were it not for the system on which sugar is purchased there, which generally entails a delay of nearly three months before the final accounts of sale are rendered. The element of doubt thus introduced as to the ultimate result of each particular venture has had the effect, in view of the fluctuating nature of the market, of making most planters prefer to sell in New York, even on relatively disadvantageous terms, since a final settlement can always be obtained there a few days after delivery.

If the British market offered similar facilities, a not inconsiderable business might be done every year, with manifest benefit to our commerce, in buying sugar for shipment to the United Kingdom at moments when prices in New York happen to be unduly depressed.

The tobacco crop of 1902 proved rather short in quantity and of very inferior quality, so that good wrappers for the manufacture of cigars were in great demand and commanded high prices. *Tobacco industry.*

Opinions differ as to the success which has attended the experiment of affording artificial shelter to growing tobacco, a mention of which appeared in my report for the year 1901. The persons whom I have consulted on the subject seem, however, to agree on the following points :—

1. That tobacco grown under cover yields a far larger proportion of wrappers than that grown entirely in the open air.

2. That the colour of the leaf is lighter, and for this reason more acceptable, when made up into cigars, to the European, and especially the British market.

3. That the gain in the texture and colour of the leaf is to some extent offset by a loss in flavour.

4. That the awning serves to check the rapid evaporation of moisture from the soil and is therefore advantageous when the season is a dry one, but accentuates the bad effects of too much rain.

5. That it most effectually protects the plants from insects.

In view of the somewhat contradictory nature of these facts and of the undoubtedly heavy expense attending the first erection of the awnings, it is evident that the experience of several seasons is needed to determine conclusively whether or no the system can be considered to be a success from a commercial standpoint.

Thanks to the large amount of money invested in the most important industry of stock raising since the termination of the war, the number of cattle in the island has now nearly reached a point where the natural increase will suffice for the home supply of food, as well as of animals for draught purposes. It is therefore probable that the importation in 1903 will show a large falling off. *Stock raising.*

The total number of livestock inscribed in the local registry offices on December 31, 1902, was as follows :—

	Number.
Cattle	9,9,862
Horses..	167,933
Mules	30,950
Asses	1,838

In the course of 1902, 176,962 bullocks were killed for food in the different licensed slaughterhouses throughout the island, a slight increase over last year.

The results of the cattle industry in the four years from January, 1899, to December, 1902, may be briefly summed up as follows :—

	Head.	Head.
Killed for food in the 4 years (approximately)	700,000	
On hand on December 31, 1902..	999,862	
		1,699,862
Estimated on hand on January 1, 1899	192,343	
Imported in the 4 years ..	1,322,520	
		1,514,863
Difference representing natural increase ..	..	184,999

Cuban carrying trade. In Annex 3 will be found the number and tonnage of all vessels engaged in the foreign carrying trade entered at the different ports of Cuba in 1902, sub-divided into steamers and sailing vessels. I regret to be unable either to show the different flags or to make comparisons with previous years, owing to want of the necessary statistics.

Annex 2, however, shows the *value* of the merchandise carried under different flags in the import and export trade, specifying the countries from which imported and to which exported. From this it will be seen that only 17 per cent. of the merchandise introduced from the United Kingdom and British Possessions was brought in British bottoms, while the share of British vessels in the total import carrying trade was little more than 6 per cent. In the export trade the proportion of merchandise exported to the United Kingdom, carried in British bottoms, is still less, as the cigars which form the greater part of this trade are all sent in United States steamers to New York for transhipment to Liverpool.

In order to give some idea of the volume of the merchandise exported from Cuba in 1902, I may mention that the exports of sugar and its products, such as rum and molasses, represent over 860,000 tons ; of mineral products, principally iron ore, 737,000 tons ; of mahogany and other woods, 46,000 tons ; and of other articles 79,000 tons, without counting many smaller ones for which no weights were mentioned in the returns.

Almost all this tonnage went to the United States, as those products which found a market in Europe were mostly valuable freight such as cigars, &c., of comparatively little bulk.

The exportation of articles of a weighty nature, such as sugar, fruits and ores, is increasing rapidly, so that a corresponding demand for vessels to carry them may be confidently looked for.

British shipping in Cuba. In Annex 4 will be found a return of the British vessels entered at the ports of Havana, Matanzas, Cardenas, Guantanamo, Santiago and Cienfuegos. Besides these, the following British steamers called at the sub-port of Daiquiri, near Santiago, to load iron ore for the United States :—

Year.	Number of Vessels.
1900	55
1901	56
1902	61

British shipping has been considerably affected in the past two or three years by competition from Norwegian vessels, but somewhat greater activity has been observable in it of late, owing probably to the large sugar crop. In the past few months there has been a certain demand for vessels to take sugar cargoes to the United Kingdom.

The remarks in the following paragraph about British shipping at Havana are applicable equally to the other large ports of Cuba. British shipping at Havana.

The general features of the carrying trade in British bottoms to and from the port of Havana are practically the same as last year.

TABLE showing the Number and Tonnage of the British Vessels Entered and Cleared at the Port of Havana in 1902.

ENTERED.

Country.	With Cargo.		In Ballast.		Total.	
	Number of Vessels.	Tons.	Number of Vessels.	Tons.	Number of Vessels.	Tons.
United Kingdom and British Colonies ..	31	28,412	4	5,830	35	34,242
United States ..	77	82,058	19	32,244	96	114,302
Mexico, Central and South America ..	7	13,062	2	3,437	9	16,499
Cuban Ports ..	6	10,766	2	3,054	8	13,820
All other countries	8	17,488	..	..	8	17,488
Total ..	129	151,786	27	44,565	156	196,351
„ 1901 ..	143	181,890	20	33,579	163	215,469

CLEARED.

Country.	With Cargo.		In Ballast.		Total.	
	Number of Vessels.	Tons.	Number of Vessels.	Tons.	Number of Vessels.	Tons.
United Kingdom and British Colonies ..	..	..	2	954	2	954
United States ..	36	55,200	48	17,863	84	73,063
Mexico, Central and South America ..	6	12,267	7	8,939	13	21,206
Cuban Ports ..	23	47,343	28	44,410	51	91,753
All other countries	1	148	..	..	1	148
Total ..	66	114,958	85	72,166	151	187,124
„ 1901 ..	54	100,347	111	118,190	165	218,537

There was an increase in the number and tonnage of the steamers bringing cargoes from British ports to Cuba, whether direct or touching *en route* at one or two other ports such as Vigo, Antwerp, or Porto Rico, those entered in 1902 numbering 22 as against 17 in 1901. One steamer brought a cargo of coal from Cardiff, the remainder carrying general cargoes for Havana and other ports, principally Cuban. In the Canadian trade, 21 small sailing vessels entered with cargoes of potatoes and lumber as compared with 17 in 1901.

In the real indirect trade, 75 steamers and sailing vessels brought coal, lumber and general cargo from the United States as against 66 last year, but on the other hand, the vessels engaged in bringing cattle from Mexico and the Republics bordering on the Caribbean Sea fell off from 38 in 1901 to 7 in 1902, due to the decrease in the importations which I have mentioned in another part of this report.

In the outward trade there was a small increase in the number of British vessels which took full cargoes of sugar and molasses to ports of the United States.

The other clearances in cargo represented, as in former years, vessels which carried on part of the cargoes they brought in transit to a final port of discharge elsewhere, or which, having taken in some sugar here, proceeded to another Cuban port to finish loading.

Referring again to the possibility, to which I have called attention in several reports, of building up a profitable passenger trade between Cuba and Europe, I have to report the recent establishment by the Hamburg-America Steamship Company of a regular monthly line between Hamburg, Havana and Vera Cruz with first class passenger accommodation. It is to be regretted that British enterprise in this case has allowed itself to be forestalled by German, in a field which I am satisfied has great possibilities before it.

For the first time in the history of Cuba most complete and careful returns have been published, showing the births, deaths and marriages throughout the island for two consecutive years. The period embraced is from January, 1900, to December, 1901. The basis of population which has been adopted in these returns is that of the census of 1899, which showed a total of 1,572,797 inhabitants in the whole island. *Population and Lealth,*

The births registered in 1900 numbered 43,003, and in 1901 43,586, of which 47 per cent. were illegitimate.

The deaths registered numbered in 1900 28,779, and in 1901 27,754, representing respectively 18·29 and 17·64 per 1,000 inhabitants.

11,843 marriages were recorded in 1900, and 12,849 in 1901.

The principal causes of death were as follows :—

	Number.	
	1900.	1901.
Pulmonary tuberculosis ..	3,497	3,638
Heart and arterial diseases ..	3,100	8,511
Pernicious and paludic fevers ..	3,080	2,346
Pneumonia and bronchitis ..	2,547	1,829
Enteritis..	2,099	2,364

The deaths from yellow fever numbered 384 in 1900 and only 37 in 1901.

The healthiest province was that of Santiago, with a death-rate of only 11·95 per 1,000 inhabitants ; and the healthiest seaport town was Havana, with a death-rate of 19·34.

The increase of population arising from the excess of births over deaths amounted in 1900 to 14,224 and in 1901 to 15,832.

Annex 1.—RETURN of Principal Articles of Import and Export to and from the Island of Cuba.

A.—COMPARATIVE Table of the Principal Imports into Cuba.

Articles.		Imported in—			Increase or Decrease in 1902, compared with—		Remarks.
		1900.	1901.	1902.	1900.	1901.	
Agricultural implements ..	Value £	77,141	36,929	27,591	— 49,550	— 9,318	Two-thirds from the United States; remainder principally from the United Kingdom.
Bags (sugar) ..	Number	3,254,379	4,953,437	6,123,554	+ 2,869,175	+ 1,170,117	From British India. The great increase is due to the increased production of sugar.
Barrels ..	Value £	..	92,601	96,345	..	+ 3,744	From Spain and the United States, a little from the United Kingdom.
Beans and pease ..	Bushels	..	464,174	409,445	..	— 54,729	From Mexico, United States and Spain.
Beer (bottled) ..	Dozen	..	549,717	429,203	..	— 120,514	From United Kingdom and United States and a small amount from Germany. Falling off due to increased home production.
Boilers ..	Value £	..	29,495	11,603	..	— 17,892	Nearly all from the United States; very little from the United Kingdom.
Boots and shoes ..	Dozen pairs ..	210,571	183,737	186,032	— 24,539	+ 2,295	Two-thirds from Spain; remainder from the United States, whose trade is gaining ground.
Candles ..	Cwts. ...	..	22,045	20,252	..	— 1,793	Principally from Spain.
Cattle ..	Number	292,241	370,552	259,898	— 32,343	— 110,654	Three-quarters from Mexico and Central America; remainder from the United States.

Article	Unit				+/−		+/−		Remarks
Cement	Barrels	..	218,010	188,034	—	..		29,976	Principally from the United States; only a very small amount from the United Kingdom.
Cheese	Cwts.	35,216	29,076	27,856	—	7,360		1,220	Principally from the Netherlands; some from the United States and the United Kingdom.
China and earthenware	Value £	..	72,319	56,772		..		15,547	From the United States, United Kingdom, and Germany, and a little from France.
Coal	Tons	..	366,198	394,630	+	..		28,432	Almost entirely from the United States; a little from the United Kingdom.
Coffee	Cwts.	172,934	184,028	188,695	+	15,761	+	4,667	Principally from Porto Rico; some from Brazil.
Copper and manufactures of	Value £	95,668	40,898	55,748	—	39,920	+	14,850	All unmanufactured from the United Kingdom; manufactured principally from the United States.
Cotton— Piece goods	"	..	845,186	700,286		..		144,890	Two-thirds from the United Kingdom; remainder from Spain, United States, France, and Germany.
Knitted fabrics	"	..	125,701	118,811		..		6,890	Principally from Spain, France, and Germany.
Tulles and lace	"	..	66,042	75,317	+	..	+	9,275	Principally from the United States; some from France, Spain, and Germany.
Yarn and thread	"	..	43,891	52,784	+	..	+	8,893	Principally from the United Kingdom.
Cutlery (table and other)	"	..	16,991	16,953		..		38	Half from the United States; remainder from Germany, France, and the United Kingdom.
Eggs	"	147,033	87,186	40,282	—	106,751		46,904	From the United States.
Electrical machinery	"	16,000	16,886	8,082	—	7,918		8,804	Nearly all from the United States.
Fertilisers	Tons	7,294	7,356	6,155	—	1,139		1,201	Principally from Peru.
Fish (dried)	Cwts.	..	166,510	175,984	+	..	+	9,474	Cod and herring; from the United States, Canada, and Northern Europe.
Flour (wheat)	Barrels	556,170	602,202	595,360	+	39,190	—	6,842	From the United States.

COMPARATIVE Table of the Principal Imports into Cuba—continued.

Articles.			Imported in—			Increase or Decrease in 1902 compared with—			Remarks.
			1900.	1901.	1902.	1900.		1901.	
Furniture	Value £	..	..	56,133	47,435	+	..	− 8,698	Principally from the United States.
Glass and glassware	„	..	110,267	115,478	110,484	217	..	− 4,994	From the United States, Germany, Spain, France, and a little from the United Kingdom.
Hams	Cwts..	..	..	59,094	47,771	..	..	− 11,323	From the United States.
Hats and caps ..	Value £	..	..	66,522	68,906	..	..	+ 2,384	From Central America, France, United States, and in a smaller degree from the United Kingdom.
Horses and mules ..	Number	..	17,093	16,722	13,249	− 3,844		− 3,473	Two-thirds from Mexico and Central America; remainder from the United States.
Iron and steel— Pig, bar and sheet	Tons ..	..	..	7,592	7,617	+	..	+ 25	Half from the United Kingdom; remainder principally from the United States.
Structural ..	„ ..	..	..	6,291	2,131	..	..	− 4,160	Almost all from the United States.
Unspecified manufactures and castings ..	Value £	..	..	282,738	328,313	..	..	+ 45,575	Three-fifths from the United States; remainder from the United Kingdom and Germany.
Jerked beef	Cwts..	..	..	312,740	304,110	..	..	− 8,630	From the River Plate.
Jewellery	Value £	..	..	33,211	50,389	..	..	+ 17,178	Principally from Germany; some from France.
Lard	Cwts..	..	..	373,991	371,603	..	..	− 2,383	From the United States.

Article	Unit				+/−		+/−		Chief sources of supply
Linen manufactures	Value £	..	182,775	260,894		..	+	78,119	Four-fifths from the United Kingdom; remainder from Spain and a little from France.
Locomotives	"	..	30,487	21,999		..	−	8,488	All from the United States.
Lumber (pine)	Thousand feet	1,288,898	82,428	102,412		..	+	19,984	Principally from the United States; some from Canada.
Maize	Bushels	..	1,469,754	1,064,235	−	224,663	−	405,519	From the United States.
Milk (condensed)	Cwts	..	72,331	69,164		..	−	3,167	Principally from the United States; some from the United Kingdom.
Nails and spikes	"	..	60,730	47,462		..	−	13,268	Three-fourths from the United States; remainder from the United Kingdom and Germany.
Olive oil	Gallons	1,815,223	1,110,843	1,467,626	+	347,597	+	356,783	Principally from Spain; a little from France.
Onions	Bushels	..	243,613	247,588		..	−	1,080	Principally from Spain.
Paints and colours	Value £	..	44,410	46,283		..	+	1,873	From the United States and the United Kingdom; a little from France and Germany.
Paper, cardboard and manufactures of	"	167,193	188,189	252,258	+	85,065	+	64,069	From Spain, United States, France, and Germany.
Perfumery	"	..	40,009	42,767		..	+	2,758	Principally from France; some from the United States.
Petroleum (crude)	Gallons	..	4,175,900	5,085,988		..	+	860,038	All from the United States.
" (refined)	"	..	1,786,405	1,502,013		..	−	284,392	All from the United States.
Pianos and organs	Number	..	316	334		..	+	18	Principally from Germany; also from Spain, the United States, and France.
Pigs	"	28,894	10,772	1,988	−	26,906	−	8,784	Nearly all from the United States.
Pipes and fittings	Tons	..	2,291	900		..	−	1,391	Half from the United States; remainder almost all from the United Kingdom.
Pork (salt)	Cwts	..	117,986	77,879		..	−	40,607	From the United States.
Potatoes	Bushels	687,180	906,109	930,849	+	243,669	+	22,740	From the United States, the United Kingdom, Spain and Canada.
Pumps	Value £	41,349	15,083	9,741		..	−	5,342	Nearly all from the United States.
Railway cars	"	..	21,354	51,182	+	9,833	+	29,828	All from the United States.
Rice	Cwts	1,476,629	1,741,553	1,516,445	+	39,816	−	225,108	Nearly all from Rangoon and Patna; a little from Spain.

(362)

B

COMPARATIVE Table of the Principal Imports into Cuba—continued.

Articles.		Imported in—			Increase or Decrease in 1902 compared with—		Remarks.
		1900.	1901.	1902.	1900.	1901.	
Sewing machines ..	Value £ ..	26,429	17,027	20,533	− 5,896	+ 3,506	Nearly all from the United States; a very little from Germany and the United Kingdom.
Soap (common) ..	Cwts... ..	86,086	126,510	91,367	+ 37,270	− 35,143	Almost entirely from Spain.
Sugar machinery ..	Value £ ..	..	286,847	123,306	..	− 163,541	Two-thirds from the United States; remainder principally from the United Kingdom, and a little from France, Germany and Belgium.
Tinplate and manufactures ..	,, ..	29,748	25,887	21,652	− 8,096	− 4,235	All sheet tin from the United Kingdom; manufactures principally from the United States; remainder from the United Kingdom, Germany and Spain.
Tools of all kinds ..	,, ..	..	56,887	52,177	..	− 4,710	Half from the United States, remainder from the United Kingdom, Germany and France.
Typewriters ..	Number ..		641	670		+ 29	All from the United States.
Varnishes ..	Gallons ..	15,984	36,327	34,045	+ 18,061	− 2,282	Nearly all from the United States.
Wine in casks ..	..		7,170,726	6,999,672		− 171,054	Almost entirely from Spain.
,, bottles ..	Dozens ..		40,379	42,618		+ 2,239	From Spain and France.
Wire and wire cable ..	Tons ..		43,258	38,055		− 5,203	Almost all from the United States; a little from Germany.
Woollen manufactures ..	Value £ ..	163,598	122,127	134,949	− 28,649	+ 12,822	One half from the United Kingdom; remainder from France and Germany.

NOTE.—Owing to a re-classification in the returns of imports made in July, 1900, it has been impossible to furnish separate figures in the case of certain articles.

B.—COMPARATIVE Table of the Principal Exports from Cuba.

Articles.		Exported in—			Increase or Decrease in 1902 compared with—		Remarks.
		1900.	1901.	1902.	1900.	1901.	
Asphalt	Tons ..	734	2,544	5,939	+ 5,205	+ 3,395	All to the United States.
Bananas	Cwts...	* 215,880	* 392,165	449,220	+ 233,390	+ 57,055	All to the United States.
Cabinet woods (except mahogany)	1,000 cubic feet	† ..	20,036	24,375	..	+ 4,339	Half to the United States, rest principally to Germany.
Cacao	Lbs. ..	2,927,399	3,713,819	5,032,731	+ 2,095,332	+ 1,308,912	All to the United States.
Cocoanuts	Thousands	* 13,172	* 12,947	11,803	− 1,369	− 1,144	All to the United States.
Dye woods	Tons ..	† ..	* 3,012	3,832	..	+ 320	To Germany and unspecified European countries.
Hides	Cwts...	21,186	20,275	32,180	+ 10,994	+ 11,905	Two-thirds to Germany; rest to France and United States.
Honey	„ ..	38,346	42,807	75,920	+ 37,574	+ 33,113	Half to Germany, rest to United States, France and other countries.
Horns and bones	Tons ..	† ..	956	1,102	..	+ 146	Most to the United States, a little to Germany.
Iron ore	1,000 cubic feet	409,815	603,131	657,234	+ 247,419	+ 54,103	All to the United States.
Mahogany	„ ..	† ..	9,300	11,141	..	+ 1,841	Three-fourths to the United States; rest to the United Kingdom, Germany and France.
Manganese ore	Tons ..	† ..	25,653	89,522	..	+ 13,869	All to the United States.
Molasses	Gallons	5,906,040	12,627,950	13,824,149	+ 7,918,109	+ 1,196,189	All to the United States.
Pineapples	Cwts ..	† ..	* 175,180	323,940	..	+ 148,760	All to the United States.

* Only values were given in the Customs returns for these years. The quantities have been estimated according to the prices which ruled in 1902.

† Complete returns are not available for this year owing to re-classification.

COMPARATIVE Table of the Principal Exports from Cuba—continued.

Articles.			Exported in—			Increase or Decrease in 1902 compared with—		Remarks.
			1900.	1901.	1902.	1900.	1901.	
Rum	..	Gallons	867,063	1,043,508	1,308,634	+ 441,571	+ 265,126	Most to the United Kingdom, some to France and Germany.
Sponges	..	Lbs. ..	† ...	* 931,717	881,040	...	— 100,677	To France and the United States.
Sugar (raw)	..	Tons ..	286,996	589,281	795,278	+ 508,282	+ 205,997	All to the United States.
Tobacco— Cigars	..	Thousands	209,195	213,572	208,165	— 1,080	— 5,407	Nearly half to the United Kingdom, one quarter to the United States, remainder to Germany, France, Spain and other countries.
Cigarettes	..	Packets	*11,019,607	*9,755,964	11,507,549	+ 487,942	+ 1,751,585	Principally to Spanish American countries.
Leaf	..	Lbs. ..	30,585,303	29,864,881	34,321,335	+ 3,736,082	+ 4,456,454	Four-fifths to the United States, remainder to Germany, Spain and other countries.
Wax	..	Cwts...	8,281	9,142	11,980	+ 3,699	+ 2,838	Two-thirds to Germany, rest to United States, France, and other countries.

* Only values were given in the Customs returns for these years. The quantities have been estimated according to the prices which ruled in 1902.
† Complete returns are not available for this year owing to re-classification.

Annex 2.—RETURN showing the Share of Different Countries in the Carrying Trade of Cuba.

A.—VALUE of the Merchandise and Coin and Bullion Imported into Cuba, showing the Nationality of the Vessels in which they were carried and the Countries from which they were Imported in the Calendar Year 1902.

Nationality of Vessels.	From—						Total.
	United States.	United Kingdom and British Possessions.	Spain.	France.	Germany.	All other Countries.	
	£	£	£	£	£	£	£
Cuban..	562,072	14,568	1,152	3,244	2,356	170,363	753,755
American	3,195,736	362,139	38,253	149,144	46,779	678,471	4,470,522
British	254,082	369,288	24,296	33,151	25,001	133,037	838,795
French	310	40	9,893	210,613	13,728	12,491	247,075
German	2,151	280,198	12,772	81,932	194,665	78,187	649,905
Norwegian	835,084	25,138	722	1,096	18,048	565,431	1,445,519
Spanish	38,623	1,005,751	1,912,215	141,246	60,456	322,232	3,480,523
All other nationalities	322,671	19,535	21,859	23,991	104,494	48,449	540,999
Total	5,210,679	2,076,657	2,021,162	644,417	465,527	2,009,651	12,427,093

B.—VALUE of the Merchandise and Coin and Bullion exported from Cuba, showing the Nationality of the Vessels in which they were carried and the Countries to which they were exported in the Calendar Year 1902.

Nationality.	To—						
	United States.	United Kingdom and British Possessions.	Spain.	France.	Germany.	All other Countries.	Total.
	£	£	£	£	£	£	£
Cuban..	606,196	2,508		528	10,399	26,455	646,086
American	4,083,418	1,085,708		25,036	488,010	361,834	5,984,056
British	2,789,654	164			2,602	591	2,793,011
French		44,131	52,183	228,628	5,992	15,899	346,828
German	14,435	8,655	89	3,067	243,699	27,507	297,402
Norwegian	1,848,252	10,305		1,868	20,106	23,729	1,904,255
Spanish	380,566	4,633	284,087	451	12,770	78,278	710,735
All other nationalities	277,197	5,345			9,980	4,866	297,388
Total	9,899,718	1,161,449	336,259	259,618	793,568	539,159	12,989,761

Annex 3.—RETURN showing Foreign Carrying Trade of Cuba.

A.—VESSELS Entered in all Ports of Cuba during the Year 1902.

Ports.	Steam.		Sailing.		Total.	
	Number of Vessels.	Tons.	Number of Vessels.	Tons.	Number of Vessels.	Tons.
Baracoa..	56	47,884	40	5,593	96	53,477
Batabano	..	..	12	321	12	321
Caibarien	102	161,210	25	4,097	127	165,307
Cardenas	190	294,714	71	17,458	261	312,172
Cienfuegos	284	440,179	88	40,832	372	481,011
Gibara ..	207	187,948	19	2,154	226	190,102
Guantanamo	69	107,174	4	1,937	73	109,111
Havana..	1,129	1,918,321	232	84,368	1,361	2,002,689
Manzanillo	101	149,372	37	13,984	138	163,356
Matanzas	259	425,559	32	13,506	291	439,065
Nuevitas	120	149,979	31	7,858	151	157,837
Sagua ..	86	133,699	21	7,541	107	141,240
Santa Cruz	20	26,868	23	12,307	43	39,175
Santiago	480	787,159	64	25,656	544	812,815
Trinidad	12	13,484	6	1,468	18	14,952
Tunas ..	9	15,588	19	7,001	28	22,589
Total	3,124	4,859,138	724	246,081	3,848	5,105,219

B.—VESSELS Cleared from all the Ports of Cuba during 1902.

Ports.	Steam.		Sailing.		Total.	
	Number of Vessels.	Tons.	Number of Vessels.	Tons.	Number of Vessels.	Tons.
Baracoa ..	55	46,751	40	5,648	95	52,399
Batabano	..	..	9	256	9	256
Caibarien	102	161,207	23	3,004	125	164,211
Cardenas..	191	295,818	66	16,200	257	312,018
Cienfuegos	284	445,061	88	40,429	372	485,490
Gibara ..	208	189,224	19	2,254	227	191,478
Guantanamo	72	109,896	4	1,870	76	111,766
Havana	1,115	1,887,050	234	91,070	1,349	1,978,120
Manzanillo	100	147,227	36	13,911	136	161,138
Matanzas	259	427,543	33	14,221	292	441,764
Nuevitas	116	149,198	31	7,460	147	156,658
Sagua ..	84	132,414	20	7,321	104	139,735
Santa Cruz	20	26,868	22	11,394	42	38,262
Santiago	484	791,657	62	26,276	546	817,933
Trinidad	12	13,484	5	712	17	14,196
Tunas ..	9	15,588	20	7,345	29	22,933
Total	3,111	4,838,986	712	249,371	3,823	5,088,357

Annex 4.—RETURN of all British Shipping Entered at the following Ports of Cuba.

Ports.	Years.	Steam.		Sailing.		Total.	
		Number of Vessels.	Tons.	Number of Vessels.	Tons.	Number of Vessels.	Tons.
Havana	1900	164	235,293	64	15,990	228	251,283
	1901	132	207,890	31	7,579	163	215,469
	1902	102	182,550	54	13,801	156	196,351
Santiago	1900	62	96,394	44	3,040	106	99,434
	1901	66	112,639	18	2,154	84	114,793
	1902	76	129,386	11	2,537	87	131,923
Cardenas	1900	33	50,760	17	3,772	50	54,532
	1901	37	64,282	13	2,989	50	67,271
	1902	57	106,739	8	2,818	65	109,557
Cienfuegos	1900	35	79,105	18	4,176	53	83,281
	1901	49	137,177	25	5,701	74	142,878
	1902	37	70,508	34	8,012	71	78,520
Matanzas	1900	34	52,464	5	1,124	39	53,588
	1901	28	47,004	7	1,581	35	48,585
	1902	70	127,265	3	1,210	73	128,475
Guantanamo	1900	4	4,990	1	377	5	5,367
	1901	5	8,607	1	353	6	8,960
	1902	6	12,688	...	...	6	12,688

LONDON :

Printed for His Majesty's Stationery Office,

By HARRISON AND SONS,

Printers in Ordinary to His Majesty.

(1400   9 | 03—H & S   362)

No. 3078.   Annual Series.

NETHERLANDS.

DIPLOMATIC AND CONSULAR REPORTS.

TRADE OF

DUTCH GUIANA

FOR THE YEAR 1902.

FOREIGN OFFICE,
September, 1903.

No. 3077 Annual Series.

DIPLOMATIC AND CONSULAR REPORTS.

COSTA RICA.

REPORT FOR THE YEAR 1902

ON THE

TRADE AND COMMERCE OF COSTA RICA.

REFERENCE TO PREVIOUS REPORT, Annual Series No. 2776.

Presented to both Houses of Parliament by Command of His Majesty,
SEPTEMBER, 1903.

LONDON:
PRINTED FOR HIS MAJESTY'S STATIONERY OFFICE,
BY HARRISON AND SONS, ST. MARTIN'S LANE,
PRINTERS IN ORDINARY TO HIS MAJESTY.

And to be purchased, either directly or through any Bookseller, from
EYRE & SPOTTISWOODE, EAST HARDING STREET, FLEET STREET, E.C.,
and 32, ABINGDON STREET, WESTMINSTER, S.W.;
or OLIVER & BOYD, EDINBURGH;
or E. PONSONBY, 116, GRAFTON STREET, DUBLIN.

1903.

[Cd. 1766—11.]   *Price One Penny.*

CONTENTS.

—◆—

Report on the *Trade, Commerce and Agriculture of Dutch Guiana for the Year* 1902

By Mr. Consul Pigott.

(Paramaribo, July 7, 1903; received at Foreign Office, August 4, 1903.)

Owing to the prevalence of yellow fever in Paramaribo during the Shipping. first half of the year, 54 vessels discharged their cargoes in the river and left in ballast, only 22 vessels took cargo, most of these being small vessels plying between Paramaribo and Nickerie.

Appendix A gives a comparative statement of the British shipping, and Appendix B of the shipping, British and foreign, entered and cleared at the port of Paramaribo during the years 1899–1902.

The imports for the year were valued at 515,255*l.*, and the exports Total trade. at 343,058*l.*, as shown in the following table :—

Country.			Value.	
			Imports.	Exports.
			£	£
Netherlands	..	..	271,004	117,759
Dutch colonies	..	..	1,989	1,549
United Kingdom	..	..	64,488	5,624
British colonies	..	..	41,004	36,792
United States	..	..	96,595	173,897
France	..	..	2,227	7,433
French colonies	..	..	31,011*	..
Other countries	..	..	6,937	4
Total	..	..	515,255	343,058

* The imports from the French colonies include 243,955 grammes of raw gold, valued at 28,461*l.*

In Appendix C will be found a comparative statement of the total exports and imports from the United Kingdom and other countries during the years 1899–1902 ; while Appendix D shows the principal articles imported from the Netherlands, the United States and the United Kingdom during the same period.

As has been pointed out in former reports, this statement does not correctly show the origin of some of the articles, as a very large proportion of those shipped from the Netherlands, especially haberdashery, cottons, &c., are of British or German manufacture.

Appendix E gives the principal articles of export during the year and a comparative statement for the last four years.

The principal products sent to the United Kingdom were :—

Articles.					Quantity.	Value.
						£
Cocoa	..	..	..	Tons	44	2,535
Gold, raw	..	..	..	Grammes ..	1,046	119
Rum	..	..	..	Gallons ..	70,994	2,957

The following produce was shipped direct to the United States :—

Articles.					Quantity.	Value.
						£
Balata	..	..	..	Tons	7	1,053
Cocoa	..	..	..	,, ...	2,177	125,209
Gold, raw	..	..	..	Grammes ..	3,715	424
Coffee	..	..	..	Tons	165	4,829
Sugar	..	..	..	,, ...	4,666	42,379

In addition to these, sugar products, valued at 3,714*l.*, were sent to Demerara for transhipment, principally to the United States.

The amount of cane produced, and the yield, were on the whole satisfactory :—

Articles.					Quantity.	
					1902.	1901.
Vacuum pan	..	..	..	Kilos... ..	13,046,494	12,721,575
Rum	..	..	..	Litres ..	1,017,353	1,197,853

Cocoa is the most important industry of the colony, but the past year has been very unfavourable, the total crop being only 2,187 tons, against 3,004 tons in 1901.

There is very little doubt that this state of things might be much improved by higher and more scientific cultivation. Recognising this, the Government propose to establish an experimental station ; but much might be done on the part of the individual planters, by manuring, more thorough pruning, and when planting new areas or when supplying old fields, by using only plants raised from seed imported from other countries, *e.g.*, Trinidad or one of the other West Indian islands. The destruction of diseased pods and branches, by fire or otherwise, is almost entirely neglected, these are often left lying on the ground after gathering or pruning, and are, in all probability, the means of reproducing and spreading the disease " Kroloto," which has already done so much harm to the plantations and to the colony generally.

As stated in former reports, owing to the very low prices obtained, Coffee. the cultivation of Liberian coffee is being gradually dropped. The total crop for the year 1902 was 240 tons, against 304 tons in the previous year.

The total amount of rice produced was 373 tons, against 368 Rice. and 285 tons in 1901 and 1900. The imports during the year amounted to 4,407 tons. The area suitable for the cultivation of rice in the colony is practically unlimited.

The balata industry was more prosperous during the year Natural under review than it has been for several years past, the amount products. brought to town being 321 tons, against 237 tons in 1901 and Balata. 208 tons in 1900. This does not, however, represent the actual yield, as a very considerable amount was lost in transit from the bush to Paramaribo; most of this was, fortunately for the colony, insured. It is difficult to say how much was lost in this way, but within six months claims were made against a single insurance company for about 7,500*l.*, the value—insured—of some 90 tons lost in the rivers by the upsetting of the boats in which it was being transported; no lives were lost. It is understood that the insurance company in question has decided not to take any further risks of the sort.

In the last report it was stated that the gold industry continues Gold. in a very unsatisfactory condition; it is to be regretted that during the past year there has been no improvement, on the contrary, the amount produced has again fallen, but it is hoped that the current year may show some improvement.

A new Ordinance, dated January 22, 1903, revises the gold Ordinance of September 7, 1882; among other things it provides that holders of permits for searching for, or concessions for working, minerals in the colony, must be Netherlanders, inhabitants of the Netherlands, inhabitants of Surinam, or companies established in the Netherlands or in Surinam, *i.e.*, with the head office in those countries. The holder of a concession who is not himself resident in Surinam must always have a representative there.

The following are the amounts of gold obtained during the past five years, according to the official returns :—

Year.						Quantity.
						Grammes.
1898..	..	..	..	..	..	864,990
1899..	..	..	..	..	..	893,197
1900..	..	..	..	..	..	842,272
1901..	.	..	..	..	..	752,842
1902..	..	..	..	..	..	587,604

It is hoped that the long talked-of railway to the interior will be commenced during the current year, though so far no definite decision has been taken ; the home Government have now decided to do the work themselves.

Population. According to the official returns, the total population of the colony was, on December 31, 1901, 75,016 ; of these 746 were Europeans. The population of Paramaribo was, at the same date, 31,865. The above does not include the military, who number about 21 officers and 370 men.

Health. As was stated in the last report, an outbreak of yellow fever occurred at the end of 1901, and this continued until about the middle of June. Though the sickness was never epidemic, it interfered much with the trade of the colony. Since its disappearance the health of the colony has been, on the whole, satisfactory.

During the year there were 2,099 births and 1,959 deaths.

According to the official returns, rain fell on 229 days, the total fall being 118 inches.

Appendix A.—Return of British Shipping at the Port of Paramaribo Engaged in the Carrying Trade during the Years 1899–1902.

ENTERED.

From—	Year.	With Cargo.		In Ballast.		Total.	
		Number of Vessels.	Tonnage.	Number of Vessels.	Tonnage.	Number of Vessels.	Tonnage.
Demerara	1899	38	43,261	...	...	38	43,261
	1900	58	47,554	2	142	60	47,696
	1901	53	36,845	2	142	55	36,987
	1902	51	36,815	...	...	51	36,815
Other British West Indian and other colonies	1899	12	2,376	1	371	13	2,747
	1900	8	548	...	...	8	548
	1901	8	556	...	...	8	556
	1902	10	3,877	1	49	11	3,926
United States	1899	2	881	...	...	2	881
	1900	5	1,998	...	...	5	1,998
	1901	4	1,631	...	...	4	1,631
	1902	3	1,290	...	...	3	1,290
Other countries	1899	9	1,653	2	40	11	1,693
	1900	4	2,112	...	...	4	2,112
	1901	6	72	...	...	6	72

CLEARED.

To—	Year.	With Cargo.		In Ballast.		Total.	
		Number of Vessels.	Tonnage.	Number of Vessels.	Tonnage.	Number of Vessels.	Tonnage.
Demerara	1899	34	39,310	...	...	34	39,301
	1900	38	36,638	17	5,916	55	42,554
	1901	30	36,059	25	973	55	37,032
	1902	8	324	42	33,681	50	34,005
Other British West Indian colonies	1899	16	3,457	2	995	18	4,452
	1900	6	414	8	3,968	14	4,382
	1901	6	414	2	914	8	1,328
	1902	...	...	7	4,440	7	4,440
United States	1899	3	1,920	...	...	3	1,920
	1900	1	551	2	2,003	3	2,554
	1901	1	418	1	299	2	717
	1902	2	667	3	3,331	5	3,998
Other countries	1899	7	1,438	...	...	7	1,438
	1900	3	2,014	1	551	4	2,565
	1901	4	109	4	60	8	169
	1902	12	222	2	84	14	306

Appendix B.—RETURN of all Shipping Entered and Cleared at the Port of Paramaribo during the Years 1899–1902.

Nationality.	Year.	Entered.		Cleared.	
		Number of Vessels.	Tonnage.	Number of Vessels.	Tonnage.
British	1899	79	50,338	78	51,141
	1900	93	54,898	96	55,939
	1901	86	40,761	87	41,026
	1902	90	44,191	91	44,872
Netherlands..	1899	100	61,337	99	61,803
	1900	84	61,488	86	61,384
	1901	83	67,184	83	67,127
	1902	76	65,018	77	66,288
United States of America ..	1899	11	6,586	11	6,160
	1900	14	7,666	14	7,590
	1901	11	5,360	11	5,447
	1902	10	4,970	9	4,677
Denmark	1899	3	880	4	1,179
	1901	1	298	1	298
Norway and Sweden ...	1899	4	1,431	5	1,837
	1900	5	1,470	4	1,160
	1901	2	580	1	290
	1902	7	2,506	7	2,506
Portugal	1899	2	299	2	299
	1900	1	180	1	180
	1901	2	308	2	308
Venezuela	1899	5	381	5	381
	1900	8	677	8	677
	1901	2	144	2	144
Spain	1899	..	..	1	500
France	1899	27	14,350	27	14,350
	1900	25	13,652	25	13,652
	1901	28	14,711	28	14,711
	1902	30	13,864	30	13,864
Russia	1902	2	633	2	633
Total	1899	231	135,602	232	137,650
	1900	230	139,531	234	140,582
	1901	215	129,346	215	129,351
	1902	215	131,182	216	132,840

Appendix C.—RETURN of the Total Imports and Exports at the Port of Paramaribo during the Years 1899–1902.

Country.	Year.	Value.	
		Imports.	Exports.
		£	£
Netherlands	1899	266,906	147,588
	1900	249,375	162,358
	1901	282,238	140,250
	1902	271,004	117,759
Dutch colonies	1899	1,273	2,900
	1900	1,735	3,755
	1901	1,426	1,332
	1902	1,989	1,549
United Kingdom	1899	44,700	34,727
	1900	56,315	29,838
	1901	74,838	19,250
	1902	64,488	5,624
British colonies*	1899	46,739	5,980
	1900	45,589	12,494
	1901	48,771	26,341
	1902	41,004	36,792
United States	1899	110,828	267,556
	1900	118,270	252,073
	1901	118,879	256,382
	1902	96,595	173,897
France	1899	1,622	600
	1900	2,668	550
	1901	1,886	685
	1902	2,227	7,433
French colonies†	1899	31,249	1
	1900	33,124	116
	1901	54,555	75
	1902	31,011	..
Other countries	1899	6,851	422
	1900	6,706	554
	1901	7,222	2,815
	1902	6,937	4
Total	1899	510,176	459,782
	1900	513,882	461,738
	1901	589,815	447,180
	1902	515,255	343,058

* Includes goods transhipped at Demerara, imports from the United Kingdom and the United States of America, and exports of sugar products for the United States of America, &c.

† Including raw gold: 1899, 248,158 grammes; 1900, 266,444 grammes; 1901, 445,362 grammes; 1902, 243,955 grammes.

Appendix D.—COMPARATIVE Statement of the Principal Imports to Paramaribo during the Years 1899–1902.

Articles.	Year.	Total Value.	Whence Shipped.		
			Nether- lands.	United States of America.	United Kingdom and Colonies.
		£	£	£	£
Beer	1899	21,655	20,598	..	970
	1900	18,955	18,720	25	830
	1901	21,430	20,420	160	850
	1902	19,458	18,088	86	1,283
Biscuits	1899	5,409	20	5,209	178
	1900	3,913	1,523	1,616	646
	1901	2,631	12	2,497	121
	1902	2,755	12	2,695	48
Boots and shoes	1899	3,977	2,580	50	1,320
	1900	4,338	2,884	187	1,222
	1901	4,903	3,051	781	1,010
	1902	4,358	2,903	709	688
Butter and oleomargine..	1899	17,630	15,825	1,417	370
	1900	18,717	17,167	1,132	399
	1901	18,919	16,213	1,127	619
	1902	18,776	17,224	959	572
Cheese	1899	7,775	7,763	..	..
	1900	7,067	7,067	..	. ..
	1901	7,823	7,823	..	..
	1902	8,155	8,155	..	..
Clothing	1899	11,395	6,060	750	4,095
	1900	11,128	5,190	1,590	3,578
	1901	14,900	7,750	2,093	4,404
	1902	14,036	5,686	1,509	6,161
Cottons and woollens ..	1899	51,656	30,650	1,130	15,250
	1900	56,690	27,737	1,109	27,565
	1901	76,410	28,758	1,760	45,856
	1902	62,855	22,709	2,324	37,157
Coal	1899	2,017	..	148	1,845
	1900	3,055	..	956	2,095
	1901	2,096	..	..	2,096
	1902	2,349	66	..	2,283
Fish, dried and salted ..	1899	9,415	..	5,930	3,270
	1900	11,788	..	6,059	5,413
	1901	10,353	37	4,663	4,615
	1902	10,830	126	3,584	7,120
Flour and meal	1899	37,240	180	30,080	7,052
	1900	29,448	18	25,051	4,377
	1901	34,175	22	26,814	7,338
	1902	30,806	16	24,605	6,183
Grain and pulse	1899	12,160	3,270	2,280	6,600
	1900	11,309	3,885	1,950	5,447
	1901	12,423	4,266	2,244	5,910
	1902	12,650	4,572	2,029	6,045
Haberdashery	1899	9,170	6,325	1,085	1,400
	1900	10,168	6,090	796	1,456
	1901	12,423	4,266	2,244	5,910
	1902	10,415	7,266	1,553	1,184
Iron, wrought, &c. ..	1899	9,793	7,006	522	2,159
	1900	10,221	6,563	702	2,858
	1901	11,498	8,160	648	2,478
	1902	11,605	8,262	628	2,388
Lumber	1899	4,033	..	3,210	520
	1900	6,590	..	5,660	930
	1901	6,549	..	5,694	829
	1902	4,706	..	4,439	263

COMPARATIVE Statement of the Principal Imports to Paramaribo during the Years 1899–1902—continued.

Articles.	Year.	Total Value.	Whence Shipped.		
			Netherlands.	United States of America.	United Kingdom and Colonies.
		£	£	£	£
Machinery, &c.	1899	18,964	6,142	7,522	5,300
	1900	27,962	10,859	11,407	5,855
	1901	36,065	11,523	14,542	9,285
	1902	22,226	13,846	5,649	2,600
Meat, salted	1899	21,555	..	17,783	1,810
	1900	24,268	1,203	21,304	1,755
	1901	34,778	1,258	30,672	1,973
	1902	15,657	850	14,363	424
Oil, vegetable	1899	5,490	4,754	154	410
	1900	8,294	6,921	82	893
	1901	8,140	7,194	356	310
	1902	9,428	8,921	143	966
„ mineral	1899	6,740	..	6,625	102
	1900	8,347	..	8,237	110
	1901	6,485	..	6,399	85
	1902	7,234	..	7,082	154
Potatoes	1899	5,297	5,055	..	136
	1900	5,075	4,850	..	85
	1901	4,666	4,460	..	90
	1902	5,123	5,106	..	17
Provisions, tinned, &c. ..	1899	13,105	6,160	3,300	2,420
	1900	14,771	7,641	3,203	2,794
	1901	15,084	7,811	4,164	2,459
	1902	16,839	8,575	4,668	2,969
Rice	1899	45,425	43,320	45	2,020
	1900	30,062	27,453	..	2,608
	1901	35,747	34,350	..	1,393
	1902	38,569	38,099	..	461
Spirits	1899	7,804	7,100	88	290
	1900	10,277	9,373	69	517
	1901	11,434	10,717	118	234
	1902	13,093	12,851	17	502
Soap, unscented ..	1899	3,842	1,103	559	2,138
	1900	4,588	803	1,944	1,670
	1901	4,257	682	2,821	710
	1902	4,465	1,118	2,652	695
Tobacco and cigars ..	1899	8,105	6,570	1,403	125
	1900	9,533	7,292	1,926	305
	1901	10,350	7,752	2,329	209
	1902	10,419	8,165	2,090	144
Wines	1899	4,210	3,746	15	108
	1900	3,550	3,420	33	133
	1901	6,104	5,900	..	160
	1902	5,130	3,804	5	634

Appendix E.—RETURN of the Principal Exports from the Port of Paramaribo during the Years 1899–1902.

Articles.	Year.			Quantity.	Value.
					£
Balata	1899	Tons	..	118	13,836
	1900	,,	..	208	41,761
	1901	,,	..	237	49,456
	1902	,,	..	321	46,882
Cocoa	1899	,,	..	3,895	236,424
	1900	,,	..	2,927	182,950
	1901	,,	..	3,163	192,445
	1902	,,	..	2,355	135,423
Coffee, Liberian	1899	,,	..	268	7,618
	1900	,,	..	192	5,585
	1901	,,	..	159	4,680
	1902	,,	..	180	5,258
Gold, raw*	1899	Grammes	..	872,689	99,596
	1900	,,	..	873,095	99,679
	1901	,,	..	723,768	82,630
	1902	,,	..	583,423	66,607
Hides	1899	Tons	..	30	1,010
	1900	,,	..	31	1,065
	1901	,,	..	23	768
	1902	,,	..	15	527
Timber	1899	..		..	6,809
	1900	..		..	6,943
	1901	..		..	4,040
	1902	..		..	2,884
Rum	1899	Gallons	..	139,533	7,924
	1900	,,	..	221,388	15,087
	1901	,,	..	216,942	13,963
	1902	,,	..	168,150	7,003
Sugar, Muscovado ..	1899	Tons	..	180	1,502
	1900	,,	..	120	1,000
	1901	,,	..	179	1,500
,, vacuum-pan 1sts ..	1899	,,	..	6,179	77,244
	1900	,,	..	9,175	99,400
	1901	,,	..	9,198	91,983
	1902	,,	..	7,992	73,268
,, 2nds..	1899	,,	..	555	6,015
	1900	,,	..	846	7,055
	1901	,,	..	701	5,263
	1902	,,	..	754	5,032

* Including raw gold from French Guiana: 1899, 227,726 grammes; 1900, 239,726 grammes; 1901, 408,651 grammes; 1902, 223,346 grammes.

LONDON :
Printed for His Majesty's Stationery Office,
By HARRISON AND SONS,
Printers in Ordinary to His Majesty.
(1400   9 | 03—H & S   367)

PERU.

DIPLOMATIC AND CONSULAR REPORTS.

TRADE OF

PERU

FOR THE YEAR 1902.

FOREIGN OFFICE,
September, 1903.

No. 3079 Annual Series.

DIPLOMATIC AND CONSULAR REPORTS.

PERU.

REPORT FOR THE YEAR 1902

ON THE

TRADE OF PERU.

REFERENCE TO PREVIOUS REPORT, Annual Series No. 2807.

Presented to both Houses of Parliament by Command of His Majesty,
SEPTEMBER, 1903.

LONDON:
PRINTED FOR HIS MAJESTY'S STATIONERY OFFICE,
BY HARRISON AND SONS, ST. MARTIN'S LANE,
PRINTERS IN ORDINARY TO HIS MAJESTY.

And to be purchased, either directly or through any Bookseller, from
EYRE & SPOTTISWOODE, EAST HARDING STREET, FLEET STREET, E.C.,
and 32, ABINGDON STREET, WESTMINSTER, S.W.;
or OLIVER & BOYD, EDINBURGH;
or E. PONSONBY, 116, GRAFTON STREET, DUBLIN.

1903.

[Cd. 1766 – 13.]   *Price Twopence Halfpenny.*

CONTENTS.

Reference to previous Report, Annual Series No. 2807.

Report on the Trade of Peru for the Year 1902

By CONSUL-GENERAL ST. JOHN.

(Peru, June 12, 1903 ; received at Foreign Office, August 4, 1903.)

During the last few years efforts have been made to Preliminary
develop the agriculture as well as the mining and other industries remarks.
of Peru. These pursuits have been carried on with some
success and benefits of no small importance have already been
derived from this activity. It is true that during 1902 the economic
condition of Peru was depressed, owing to the fall in the prices
of sugar, copper and silver, which are some of the principal articles
exported from this country, but notwithstanding the unsatisfactory
condition of the value of the export trade, business was not unremunerative, owing to the stability of the exchange, whilst the
low level of freights favoured the exporter.

TABLE showing Total Trade of Peru during the Years 1898–1902.

	Value.				
	1898.	1899.	1900.	1901.	1902.
	£	£	£	£	£
Through Pacific ports and to Bolivia	3.077,469	3,072,591	...	4,298,378	3,454,733
From Department of Loreto	202,916*	288,940	...	412,000*	387,000*
Total	3,280,685	3.361,531	4,497.999	4.710,378	2,841,733

* Rubber only.

The statistics given only show the approximate value of the
trade of the country. In reproducing statistics given in previous
reports a few alterations have been made, in accordance with
official returns issued subsequently to the publication of the reports.

On examining the import tables appended to this report British trade.
it will be perceived that although British trade with Peru has not
shown a notable growth, it has increased to some extent during
the last quinquennial period. The imports of textile fabrics from
the United Kingdom have received a check, owing to the establishment of native manufactories which produce annually about

17,000,000 yards of grey domestics and drills and also a considerable quantity of cloth, blankets and knitted articles. However, but few articles of first necessity are produced in Peru cheaper than they could be imported ; therefore, there is still a large demand for foreign goods. Germany, the United States and Belgium are competing with the United Kingdom for most of the branches of the Peruvian trade. The manufacturers of those countries appear to send to this market many articles which are cheaper, of better appearance and more neatly packed than British goods of the same class.

Several large locomotives for one of the Transandine railways in British hands have recently been ordered from the United States. The alleged reason for placing the order in that country was that British engines are unsuitable for heavy grades. American engines of the type required are said to run more smoothly.

Possible openings for British trade.

By means of a national subscription about 70,000*l.* have been raised and deposited in the Lima banks with the object of acquiring a small war vessel. The money has been collected by a committee called the Patriotic Junta, which claims to have the exclusive control of the disposal of the money. It is understood, however, that the Junta will shortly have to consult with the Government as to the type of vessel which is to be built and also in order that application may be made to Congress for an appropriation, as the money collected, so far, is insufficient for the purpose which the subscribers have in view. British shipbuilders might communicate with the Minister of Marine and Señor Doctor Figueredo, the President of the Junta, upon the subject.

The reconstruction of the Government Palace at Lima is contemplated. The cost of the new building is estimated at 150,000*l.* Brick and iron are to be the principal materials used. Therefore, there may be sooner or later an opening for supplying a large quantity of iron. The presentation of plans has already been invited.

The Peruvian Government have in view the purchase of wire ropes or other aërial devices for crossing rivers or ravines in places in Cordillera, where bridges are likely to be destroyed.

British manufacturers of railway materials would do well to communicate occasionally with the London offices of the railway companies in Peru. The Lima, Callao and Chorrillos Railways are said to be in want of locomotives, and it may be pointed out that the Peruvian Corporation are the concessionnaires of nearly all the railways in the country.

In the near future there will be openings for the trade in electrical appliances of all kinds. There are already quite a number of installations for supplying electric light to towns and private houses. So far all orders for the plants have been placed with American, German and Italian firms. No tenders were invited. It would therefore be advisable for British manufacturers of electrical appliances to have active and reliable agents on the spot, so that no time may be lost as soon as an opening is heard of.

Pipes will be required for the drainage of Callao, but no tenders will be invited until the water-pipes recently ordered from the United Kingdom shall have been laid down and fresh funds obtained for the drainage of the town. There is little doubt but that this scheme will be carried out in due course.

Among the plans for the improvement of Lima, is a project for the acquisiton of refuse destructors. In a previous report this necessity was pointed out. The Municipality is now anxious to secure these furnaces, but for want of funds the purchase is being postponed. Callao, Arequipa, Cuzco, Piura, Trujillo, in fact almost all Peruvian towns, are worse off than Lima as regards sanitary arrangements of every kind.

On application to His Majesty's Consulate-General at Callao, *Sphere of usefulness of Consulate-General.* all available information concerning any branch of the Peruvian trade will be furnished without delay, and if so desired reliable firms will be recommended as agents.

Most of the small inland towns and several important mining *Communications.* and agricultural districts are still isolated. The only means of further developing the trade, as well as the agricultural and other industries, of Peru, will be to extend her internal communications. The Government are fully alive to the question and do what they can to open up the country by authorising the construction of railways or the surveys of new routes, and by giving small grants of money towards the making or improvement of roads and trails, but the process is slow.

The long-projected line between Oroya, the terminus of the Central Railway and Cerro de Pasco, 14,000 feet above sea level, is under construction and it is expected that it will be concluded before the end of 1903. Although constructed by an American company, a large quantity of materials have been imported from the United Kingdom. A short line connecting the Central Railway with the Morococha mining district was completed during 1902 by the Peruvian Corporation. This new line, which is 9 miles long, branches off at Ticlio, about 15,500 feet above sea level, rises some 135 feet higher and then descends to 14,900 feet.

A concession has been given for the construction of a railway from Chimbote to Recuay in the Department of Ancachs. Authorisation was also granted last year to lay down a line from the Department of Piura to the Marañon. The survey has been made and it is understood that the work would be feasible, but so far nothing further has been heard of this project.

A similar authorisation has been granted for the survey of a line from Chancay or Huacho to Cerro de Pasco, but the object of this line is very problematical, inasmuch as the necessary facilities for transportation will exist as soon as the line from Oroya to Cerro de Pasco shall have been completed. Permission has also been granted to make the survey of a line from Oroya to a navigable point on one of the affluents of the Amazon.

(309)

It is intended to build a carriage road between Ica and Ayacucho, and a survey has already been made by a Government engineer. The distance between those places is 186 miles. The culminating point which the road will cross is at Apacheta, about 15,500 feet above sea level. The town of Ayacucho is 8,940 feet high.

The Peruvian Corporation propose to take over the lines of the Lima and Callao and Chorrillos Railways for a long term of years, but the final arrangements have not yet been made.

Companies for the construction of electric tramways between Lima and some of the neighbouring sea-places were formed during 1902.

Telegraph lines. The telegraph line from the south to Talara has been extended as far as Zarumilla on the Ecuadorian frontier, thus connecting the Republics of Peru and Ecuador for the first time by an overland line. The Government have also constructed a line between Lima and Oroya. Other lines have been extended : the line to Casma has been extended as far as Huaraz, and the line to Pucara as far as Azangaro. A project to connect Huanuco by wire with Sullana, in the Department of Piura, viâ Huancabamba, is also under consideration.

Mining. A salient feature during the year has been the influx of American capital, which is being expended in the payment for hundreds of copper and silver mines, purchased at Cerro de Pasco by a syndicate, and in works which are being undertaken for the purpose of developing the copper mining industry on a large scale. These transactions should impart stimulus to the mining industry and contribute to the extension of the range of commercial activity. Further acquisitions of mining properties by foreign capitalists are contemplated in the Departments of Ancachs and Cuzco.

In 1902 there were 5,403 claims inscribed on the Register of Mines, as compared with 4,920 claims in 1901 and 5,178 claims in 1900. It is estimated that about two-thirds of the claims are worked. It is well nigh impossible to ascertain the real value of the ores exported from Peru, inasmuch as no pains are taken in order to insure accuracy in the declarations of value.

Sugar. The crisis experienced in the sugar industry in 1902 was of so acute a character that at one time it was thought that its effect would be disastrous, but towards the end of the year the price of that commodity improved. [At the beginning of 1902 sugar was quoted in Peru at 5s. 3d. per quintal of 100 lbs., the lowest point ever known, but during the month of December the price rose to about 8s. Producers are looking forward with great hopes to the operation of the Brussels Sugar Convention and urge the Government to adhere to it.

In July last a commission was appointed by the Government to report on the condition of the sugar industry and to suggest measures of relief. The commission recommended that scientific measures should be adopted and that improved machinery should be-substituted for all obsolete installations. This would no doubt be a step in the right direction and, if taken eventually, will be a matter of interest to British manufacturers of sugar machinery.

The limited amount of capital at the disposal of planters will prevent them from acting upon this suggestion for the present, but the necessity of cultivating the cane on scientific principles is recognised.

The scarcity of water in the coast valleys is the main obstacle to the development of the sugar industry. In the course of 1902 artesian wells were bored at Callao with great success, and similar experiments will now be made in some of the northern sugar districts.

Rain seldom falls within the coast belt of the Department of Cotton. Piura, the usual absolutely rainless periods being of six or seven years. However, the last rainless period was much longer, having lasted 11 years. At last rain fell in torrents in the month of February, 1902, and continued for several days. As is well known, the Peruvian cotton is of high quality. There exist in the Department of Piura and elsewhere on the coast of this Republic vast tracts of land where it could be grown, but the want of the necessary capital for production on a large scale prevents this. The planting of the Metafifi cotton has been tried of late and is giving very satisfactory results.

The cocaine industry is comparatively new. It was only in Cocaine. 1897 that it began to acquire some importance. There are now 21 small factories which manufacture this valuable product.

In accordance with the provisions of a law promulgated in Decem- Indiarubber. ber last, it is left to the discretion of the Government to extend the time for which concessions have already been granted, or which may hereafter be granted, to indiarubber companies. The exten- sion may be for any period not exceeding 40 years.

The sugar bags and metal pockets used in Peru come almost Products of entirely from India, viâ the United Kingdom. The total value India. of gunny bags imported in 1901 was 60,431l. The bags from the United Kingdom alone were valued at 53,162l., whilst bags of the value of 3,000l. were also imported during that year from Chili. Probably these bags also came originally from India. The balance was received from Italy, Germany, Belgium and the United States. The metal pockets are sent to the mining districts of Cerro de Pasco, Yauli, Casapalca, Huaylas, Caylloma, &c. The sugar bags are imported at the ports of Pimentel, Eten, Pacasmayo, Salaverry, Chimbote, Callao and Cerro Azul. Rice valued at 6,459l. was imported from India in 1900 and landed at Callao and Pisco. No other statistics are procurable at present.

The Peruvian tariff is about to be revised. Leaving aside the New tariff. general consideration of the present tariff, which places heavy duties on thousands of articles, it must be pointed out that the defective classification of the goods leads to frequent unavoid- able errors on the part of merchants, who are punished by the infliction of fines in the shape of double duties levied on the merchandise alleged to have been wrongly described.

Under the Insurance Law of 1895 the minimum amount of capital required to undertake insurance operations had been limited to 10,000*l.*, of which 30 per cent. only had to be invested in the country, but by a law promulgated at the end of 1901 it was made compulsory for every insurance company, and in the case of a foreign company represented in the country, for its branches or agencies to have a minimum capital of 200,000 soles, equivalent to 20,000*l.*, invested in Peru : 50 per cent. in real property and 50 per cent. in securities. A delay of six months was given for compliance with the provisions of this law. The effect of this measure has been to compel the agencies of several British and other foreign companies to liquidate their affairs. It should be pointed out that there were no grounds of complaint against any of these companies. There are four Peruvian insurance companies, three of which having a nominal capital of 200,000*l.* ; the other has a capital of 250,000*l.* These companies have only 10 per cent. of their capital paid up and a small reserve fund. They have, as a matter of course, availed themselves to the full of the opportunity and secured a considerable amount of business.

An exhibition of alcohol motors, lamps and other appliances was to be opened on January 1, 1903, but the arrangements were not completed by that date. Most of the exhibits came from France and Germany, only one having been received from the United Kingdom. It is believed that such machinery and appliances may meet with some success where alcohol can be obtained at a cheap rate. There is in this country a fairly large output of alcohol as a by-product of the sugar industry. The cost of the alcohol on the estates is about 10*d.* per gallon. At this price the alcohol might be utilised, but the cost of transport and dues are at present too heavy to allow of its wide use in places at any distance from the sugar mills. However, the Government propose to apply to Congress for the abolition or reduction of dues on alcohol intended to be used as fuel.

The cattle bred on the highlands of Peru, often at heights varying between 10,000 and 12,000 feet above sea level, are small, somewhat lean, and the young die in great numbers, about 50 per cent., owing to the severity of the climate and the want of care. Crossing has been tried to improve the breed, but without much success. The same may be said of the Peruvian sheep. It is small, with tall legs, and lean. It is bred for its wool, the flesh being of secondary importance. Meat is not only of indifferent quality but on the coast its price is high. Reference is made here to the pastoral industry of Peru simply with a view to draw attention to the possibility, at some future period, of bringing to the meat markets of the Pacific coast frozen or chilled carcases from Australia and Canada.

Foreign postage in Peru is high. The rate for the $\frac{1}{2}$ oz. is

20 c. if the letter is sent viâ Magellan Straits or San Francisco, or 22 c. if sent viâ Panama. The charge is thus about 5d. per ½ oz. The rate for letters forwarded to Brazil by the overland route, as well as for those sent to Bolivia, Colombia and Ecuador is only 10 c., or about 2½d. One may venture to predict that if the Peruvian Government would consent to the reduction of the high rates above referred to it would not be productive of injury to the revenue, as the bulk of foreign correspondence would soon increase, whilst the reduction of the charge would be to the benefit of trade.

Among the advantages of the metric system, one of the greatest is undoubtedly its importance for the purpose of facilitating commercial transactions between countries which have adopted it. Although in Peru several of the old Spanish weights and measures are still employed, the units used officially are the metre and kilogram. All who appreciate the manifold merits of the metric system look forward to its adoption by the United Kingdom as an additional means of promoting her foreign trade. *Weights and measures.*

All British steamship companies trading on this coast can now avail themselves of the option to pay the Peruvian Consular fees on coal cargoes sent to the Pacific for orders at the port where it is decided to send on the vessel to Peru, instead of at the port of loading. Formerly heavy fines were inflicted if the necessary documents relating to such cargoes were not procured at the port of origin. *Coal cargoes for orders.*

The quarantine restrictions on arrivals from the north during the latter part of 1902 were unusually severe and caused great inconvenience to trade and navigation owing to the want of lazarettos. However, it is satisfactory to report that a Decree has been issued whereby the construction of a quarantine station at Paita is ordered. It is to be hoped that the work will be taken in hand without delay, and that a similar establishment will be constructed at Callao. *Quarantine.*

As regards the correspondence brought by steamers put in quarantine, sometimes entire days are lost before t can be landed, for want of proper fumigating appliances.

The steamers of the Pacific Steam Navigation Company and of the Chilian Company were compelled last year to suspend their voyages between Panama and San Francisco owing to the hostility of the Panama Railroad Company, which refused to give through bills of lading for cargo shipped by those steamers north of Panama, thereby rendering the trade of the two steamship companies unprofitable. This action inflicted considerable injury on the Pacific Steam Navigation Company, which had built several fine steamers specially for that trade. The transit facilities appear to be monopolized by the Pacific Mail Company. The suspension of regular steam communication between this country and the United States is much to be regretted, as it was hoped that eventually the British passenger steamers trading on the west coast of South America would extend their voyages as far as British Co'ombia. *Transit difficulties across Isthmus of Panama.*

Want of dock
for large
vessels at
Callao.

As already remarked in the report for the previous year, the construction of a graving dock at Callao would be of importance. This matter gave rise to several projects and discussions during the last session of Congress. However, the Chambers separated without making any provision for the carrying out of the work. The cost of a graving dock is no doubt heavy, but for various reasons the Government might deem it advisable to guarantee the interest on the capital invested. However, if this cannot be done, they might give privileges or facilities to any company willing to bring out a floating dock capable of lifting 10,000 or 12,000 tons.

Rates of
freight.

The rates of freight from Peru to Europe were lower during 1902 than during the previous year. The rates by steamers varied between 1l. 8s. and 1l. 5s. for sugar, 1l. 10s. and 1l. 15s. for ores, and 4l. for cotton and wool. The rates for guano, by sailing vessels, fell from 1l. 10s. to 17s., owing to the large amount of tonnage on the coast and the cessation of nitrate charters in Chile. Towards the end of the year ships were brought up from the nitrate port to load sugar at 17s. and 18s. for Liverpool. The average freight on ores in 1902 was as stated above. However, it varied between 1l. 10s. and 2l. 12s. 6d., according to the declared value of the ores. During 1901 the rates of freight by steamers varied between 1l. 15s. and 1l. 8s. for sugar, 4l. 10s. and 4l. for cotton and wool, and 2l. 17s. 6d. and 1l. 17s. 6d. for ores. The rates by sailing vessels for guano were from 1l. 11s. 6d. to 1l. 17s. 6d.

TABLE showing Total Import Trade of Peru during the Years
1898–1902.

Country.	Value.				
	1898.	1899.	1900.	1901.	1902.
	£	£	£	£	£
United Kingdom ...	863,272	757,115	1,082,014	1,222,488	1,112,730
Belgium	60,035	59,191	72,382	128,131	138,169
Chile	136,840	152,565	91,329	64,944	179,267
China	52,663	53,441	76,857	74,884	89,494
France	155,396	172,895	162,681	274,215	196,169
Germany	340,185	345,151	354,283	456,075	516,967
Italy	66,160	76,653	98,155	128,116	147,425
Spain	15,590	14,663	14,269	21,604	26,233
United States ...	207,835	218,310	296,119	446,618	581,556
Other countries...	31,688	22,998	75,043	98,832	54,514
	1,929,679	1,873,481	2,317,132	2,716,907	3,052,531
Department of Loreto...	200,000*	249,523	...	145,500	250,928
Total	2,129,679	2,123,004	...	2,862,407	3,303,459

* Estimated value, as no data are available.

COMPARATIVE Table of Principal Exports from Peru during the Years 1900-02.

Articles.			Quantity.			Increase or Decrease in 1902 as compard with—		Character of Trade.
			1900.	1901.	1902.	1900.	1901.	
Borax	Tons		6,975	4,094	10,891	+ 3,916	+ 6,707	Exported chiefly to the United Kingdom
Coca	„		557	601	754	+ 197	+ 153	„ to Germany and the United States
Cocaine	Tons cwts		7-12	10-10	...	...	...	The bulk shipped to Germany
Coffee	Tons		1,432	890	1,565	+ 133	+ 685	Exported chiefly to Germany and Chili
Cotton	„		7,139	7,892	4,408	− 2,731	− 3,484	Principally to the United Kingdom and the United States
Cotton seed..	„		4,502	1,735	4,387	− 115	+ 2,652	The bulk exported to the United Kingdom
„ oil cakes	„		2,896	1,171	1,424	− 972	+ 253	„ „ United Kingdom
Guano	„		16,366	29,920	53,851	+ 37,485	+ 23,931	The whole exported on British account and bulk shipped to the United Kingdom
Hides and skins	„		2,252	2,218	2,413	+ 191	+ 225	Chiefly to France
Ores and metals	„		38,817	46,192	36,842	− 1,975	− 9,350	Principally to the United Kingdom
Rice	„		4,197	4,103	3,675	− 522	− 428	Exported to neighbouring republics
Rubber	„		...	1,726	1,782	...	+ 56	„ the United Kingdom and France
Spirits	Gallons..		284,031	149,157	213,636	− 70,395	+ 64,479	Principally to Bolivia and Chili
Sugar	Tons		110,564	112,942	115,427	+ 5,063	+ 2,685	Exported prncipally to the United Kingdom, Chili and the United States
Wool of all kinds ..	„		3,482	3,798	3,644	+ 162	− 154	The export is chiefly to the United Kingdom

TABLE showing Value of Imports into Peru through Pacific Ports and from Bolivia during the Years 1898-1902.

Country.	Year.	Cotton Goods.	Woollen Goods.	Linen Goods.	Silk Goods.	Apparel, Furniture and Empty Bags.	Articles of Food.	Wines and Liquors.	Drugs and Chemical Products.	Machinery, Coal, Tools, Hardware, Lumber, and Sundry Articles.	Total.
		£	£	£	£	£	£	£	£	£	£
United Kingdom ..	1898	286,623	87,075	13,685	10,147	58,024	17,703	6,261	41,514	342,240	863,272
	1899	274,945	90,845	14,434	7,402	60,564	25,997	4,004	38,922	240,502	757,115
	1900	252,456	87,617	13,518	9,873	74,945	11,836	7,456	30,327	593,986	1,082,014
	1901	320,007	136,432	15,108	10,351	77,446	26,058	8,168	40,383	389,562	1,023,488
	1902	318,670	92,796	12,417	15,700	67,336	33,380	10,423	28,075	533,942	1,112,739
Belgium	1898	5,341	2,907	952	271	2,328	1,008	1,110	716	44,472	60,035
	1899	5,113	8,552	897	230	3,595	1,899	945	2,381	40,679	59,191
	1900	6,726	2,764	1,389	1,488	4,161	3,197	1,344	2,817	48,496	72,382
	1901	9,607	7,894	1,207	1,247	4,510	3,457	2,203	3,057	94,919	128,131
	1902	13,591	9,353	2,016	1,680	7,621	2,951	6,607	5,261	89,086	138,169
Chile	1898	607	552	107	220	3,903	101,263	1,211	778	28,208	136,849
	1899	813	795	45	14	5,556	121,916	878	1,814	21,234	152,565
	1900	230	68	26	30	9,627	54,298	319	203	26,528	91,329
	1901	1,433	203	71	21	4,911	18,741	359	417	38,788	64,944
	1902	2,387	1,341	6,500	272	5,007	114,654	1,388	2,050	45,717	179,267
China.. ..	1898	27	7	..	3,805	1,054	37,588	538	1,171	8,480	52,663
	1899	27	..	..	1,625	1,399	39,377	646	1,663	8,697	53,441
	1900	106	4	9	6,429	2,069	41,495	632	9,071	11,046	70,857
	1901	34	..	..	9,142	3,059	44,391	936	2,667	14,651	74,884
	1902	183	89	32	3,824	1,787	62,477	1,032	2,276	17,794	89,494
France	1898	12,955	12,218	4,492	8,394	15,542	5,938	18,610	5,818	71,469	155,386
	1899	11,253	13,192	1,500	10,959	16,541	5,567	13,866	9,129	61,388	179,395
	1900	7,844	15,785	1,946	12,050	22,022	8,073	20,934	13,182	61,345	162,681
	1901	10,650	17,033	2,208	16,516	21,817	101,633*	19,157	12,052	73,140	274,215
	1902	15,829	23,257	1,621	24,916	25,604	6,920	17,270	11,742	69,010	196,169

Germany	1898	62,173	32,701	5,654	5,143	25,240	10,556	11,529	13,988	173,192	340,185
	1899	46,602	35,111	5,452	7,507	21,147	7,478	9,087	21,273	191,404	345,151
	1900	53,190	38,066	4,930	11,148	24,579	10,544	3,174	20,506	183,146	354,283
	1901	66,062	56,903	6,762	15,112	30,612	12,746	7,396	23,296	237,156	456,075
	1902	70,283	81,245	6,698	17,297	43,929	11,337	7,380	29,146	249,656	516,067
Italy	1898	20,506	1,822	741	878	9,498	12,574	6,715	3,963	9,484	66,166
	1899	24,549	1,606	850	729	14,353	12,896	3,398	4,308	13,966	76,653
	1900	30,962	2,452	1,123	1,736	20,490	15,983	6,864	3,997	14,540	98,155
	1901	43,133	3,380	1,207	2,157	25,927	20,560	5,733	5,174	20,895	128,116
	1902	50,294	5,578	729	1,973	22,872	18,389	13,024	6,224	28,395	147,423
Spain	1898	1,236	31	95	1	1,427	1,320	4,540	266	6,674	15,590
	1899	1,680	304	16	8	1,448	908	3,876	127	6,886	14,662
	1900	698	99	9	..	1,277	1,323	3,689	176	6,985	14,269
	1901	827	352	..	100	2,721	3,347	3,934	267	10,056	21,604
	1902	2,391	375	46	747	2,976	3,773	3,640	353	11,932	26,233
United States	1898	17,216	249	162	422	8,650	36,227	515	6,699	187,695	207,835
	1899	12,519	144	112	63	6,872	21,290	464	9,248	167,608	218,310
	1900	9,374	710	58	412	7,366	66,804	1,151	12,146	193,098	296,119
	1901	13,042	691	31	47	16,033	62,030	812	16,221	337,050	446,618
	1902	10,498	1,464	130	293	16,960	79,132	1,823	16,820	464,416	591,556
Other countries	1898	153	..	18	72	1,653	996	13	5,063	23,690	31,688
	1899	46	59	1	705	973	783	20	3,906	16,506	22,908
	1900	169	200	..	331	2,623	39,346	10	4,728	27,686	75,043
	1901	1,631	236	..	340	1,952	67,380	75	238	26,980	98,832
	1902	396	601	29	118	2,742	6,728	1,444	2,612	39,849	54,514

* So large and sudden an increase seems unlikely. However, the customs returns in the possession of the statistical department are said to show that amount.

RETURN of all Shipping Engaged in the Foreign Trade of Callao during the Years 1900-02.

ENTERED.

Nationality.	Year.	Steam				Sailing				Total			
		Number of Vessels		Tonnage		Number of Vessels		Tonnage		Number of Vessels		Tonnage	
		With Cargo.	In Ballast.	With Cargo.	In Ballast.	With Cargo.	In Ballast.	With Cargo.	In Ballast.	With Cargo.	In Ballast.	With Cargo.	In Ballast.
British	1900	181	..	307,938	..	33	..	36,571	..	214	..	346,539	..
	1901	197	..	346,190	..	35	..	47,293	..	232	..	393,483	..
	1902	192	1	343,808	1,511	23	..	31,235	..	215	1	375,013	1,511
Peruvian	1900	..	..	..	..	9	2	3,884	1,007	9	2	3,884	1,007
	1901	..	..	..	..	8	..	3,368	..	8	..	3,368	..
	1902	..	..	..	..	9	1	3,809	311	9	1	3,809	311
German	1900	42	..	93,872	..	7	..	7,682	..	49	..	101,554	..
	1901	51	..	123,567	..	6	..	7,190	..	57	..	130,757	..
	1902	52	..	123,428	..	6	..	8,376	..	58	..	131,804	..
Italian	1900	13	..	10,535	..	5	..	4,696	..	18	..	15,226	..
	1901	11	..	8,910	..	6	..	6,694	..	17	..	15,604	..
	1902	14	..	11,340	..	5	..	5,735	..	19	..	17,075	..
United States	1900	..	5	..	3,715	8	..	4,449	..	8	5	4,449	3,715
	1901	..	4	..	5,919	12	..	9,518	..	12	4	9,548	5,919
	1902	..	5	..	3,715	17	..	13,727	..	17	5	13,727	3,715
Chilian	1900	103	..	156,387	..	6	..	3,931	..	103	..	160,518	..
	1901	107	..	162,690	..	5	..	3,421	..	112	..	166,111	..
	1902	116	..	174,819	..	8	..	5,487	..	124	..	180,256	..

Norwegian	1900	2	..	3,217	..	3	..	2,661	..	.5	..	5,908	..
	1901	..	..	..	..	10	..	10,190	..	10	.1	10,190	..
	1902	1	..	2,260	..	3	1	2,935	1,022	4	..	5,201	1,022
Ecuadorian	1900	..	..	..	..	1	..	92	..	1	..	92	..
Danish	1901	..	..	..	..	.1	1	..	1,079	.1	.1	..	1,079
	1902	.1	..	..	..	..	..	964	..	1	..	964	..
Austro-Hungarian	1903	1	..	2,343	..	..	..	..	..	4	..	2,343	..
Belgian	1902	4	..	11,288	..	3	..	195	..	3	..	11,288	..
Colombian	1902	..	..	..	..	..	..	195	..	..	..	195	..
Total	1900	341	5	572,204	3,715	72	2	65,965	1,007	413	7	638,169	4,722
	1901	366	4	641,357	5,919	82	1	87,701	1,079	448	5	729,061	6,998
	1902	389	6	669,205	5,226	75	2	72,413	1,333	455	8	741,708	6,589

CLEARED.

Nationality	Year	Steam				Sailing				Total			
		Number of Vessels		Tonnage		Number of Vessels		Tonnage		Number of Vessels		Tonnage	
		With Cargo	In Ballast	With Cargo	In Ballast	With Cargo	In Ballast	With Cargo	In Ballast	With Cargo	In Ballast	With Cargo	In Ballast
British ..	1900	183	..	303,566	..	1	32	849	39,976	184	32	309,415	39,976
	1901	193	3	338,553	6,236	..	37	..	48,569	193	49	333,553	54,805
	1902	191	3	343,134	1,555	..	20	..	29,360	191	23	343,134	33,915
Peruvian ..	1900	..	..	..	..	4	8	312	4,301	4	8	312	4,301
	1901	..	..	..	..	6	6	504	2,670	6	6	504	2,670
	1902	..	..	..	..	4	5	1,457	3,002	4	5	1,457	3,002
German ..	1900	42	..	93,872	..	1	5	788	5,441	43	5	94,660	5,441
	1901	51	..	122,872	..	..	6	..	8,015	51	6	122,872	8,015
	1902	53	..	124,246	..	..	6	..	7,703	53	6	124,246	7,703
Italian ..	1900	13	..	10,530	..	2	3	1,349	3,347	15	3	11,878	3,347
	1901	11	..	8,910	..	2	2	1,598	2,543	13	2	10,508	2,543
	1902	13	..	10,533	..	1	6	1,625	6,663	11	6	12,155	6,663
United States ..	1900	..	4	..	2,972	1	3	86	1,917	1	7	86	4,889
	1901	..	5	..	6,662	..	16	..	11,993	..	21	..	18,655
	1902	..	5	..	3,715	..	15	..	11,849	..	20	..	15,564
Chilian ..	1900	103	..	155,391	..	1	3	760	2,224	104	3	156,151	2,224
	1901	106	..	160,586	..	..	4	..	2,817	106	4	160,586	2,817
	1902	115	..	178,409	..	..	8	..	5,299	115	8	178,409	5,299
Norwegian ..	1900	2	..	3,247	..	..	3	..	2,661	2	3	3,247	2,661
	1901	..	..	..	..	..	9	..	9,283	..	9	..	9,283
	1902	1	..	2,269	..	..	4	..	3,084	1	4	2,269	3,084
Danish ..	1901	..	..	..	..	..	1	..	1,079	..	1	..	1,079
Austro-Hungarian ..	1902	1	..	2,344	..	..	..	..	..	1	..	2,344	..
Belgian ..	1902	4	..	11,298	..	..	..	..	..	4	..	11,298	..
Colombian ..	1902	..	..	..	..	2	..	130	..	2	..	130	..
Total ..	1900	343	4	571,606	2,972	10	57	4,143	59,867	353	61	575,749	62,839
	1901	351	8	680,921	12,593	8	81	2,102	86,969	369	83	633,023	99,867
	1902	378	8	672,239	8,270	7	64	3,212	67,960	385	72	675,451	76,130

PERENÉ AND CHANCHAMAYO.

Mr. Vice-Consul Furlong reports as follows :—

Although there has been plenty of rain, and consequently good crops, there has been no marked improvement in trade during the year, the prices of most of the agricultural products having been so low as to be barely sufficient to meet ordinary working expenses. Planters have for this reason been worse off than in previous years, for although they had good crops, they have had great difficulty in obtaining money to harvest them, even though disposed to pay the usual ruinous rate of 3 to 5 per cent. per month interest. Preliminary remarks.

No data can yet be obtained relative to the quantity of coffee produced in the district, but it is roughly estimated at 40,000 bags of 100 lbs. each valued at 10 soles (1l.) net per bag. Germany receives nearly all coffee produced here. Few people care to export it to the United Kingdom. Coffee.

About 12,000 lbs. of tobacco have been produced in La Merced, San Luis and Oxapampa, one-half of which has been disposed of in Lima, the other half consumed locally. Including duties, the average price of tobacco has been 120 soles (12l.) per 100 lbs. Tobacco.

The output of rice for the year is estimated at 1,500 bags of 100 lbs. each, and valued at 10 soles (1l.) per bag. No rice is sent out of the district, the local demand being greater than the production. Rice.

About 60,000 lbs. of coca have been disposed of in Jauja, and about another 5,000 lbs. disposed of locally at an average price of 50 c. (1s.) per lb. Coca.

The production of rum has been about 400,000 gallons, value 1s. 9½d. per gallon. About 320,000 gallons have been consumed in Jauja alone, the balance being disposed of locally and in Cerro de Pasco. So many people are now going into this industry, and the production is increasing so rapidly, that it will soon exceed the demand. Common rum...

Of Peruvian bark, 15,000 lbs. of Cascarilla, picked in the forest, have been disposed of in La Merced at 4 soles (8s.) per quintal of 100 lbs. This bark is of inferior quality. Peruvian bark.

The importation business is entirely in the hands of Italians ; goods to the value of 100,000 soles (10,000l.), consisting principally of empty bags, sugar, flour, prints, wines, liquors and 1,200 head of cattle, have been imported during the year. Imports.

The road from Tarma to La Merced has been much improved and is at present in very good condition. From La Merced to San Luis de Shuaro the road is not well cared for, but owing to the nature of the ground it is always fairly passable. There has not been much care bestowed this year on the Pichis road. By the accounts of those who travel over it, this road is in a deplorable condition from La Pampa del Hambre to Puerto Bermudez. Communications.

A new suspension bridge is at present being built across the

River Paucartambo at Sogormo to replace the one destroyed
by the river two years ago. This bridge will once more put the
German colony at Oxapampa in communication with San Luis de
Shuaro and La Merced, and should be finished early in February,
1903. Nothing has yet been done towards the reconstruction
of the Capelo bridge, which was destroyed at the same time as that
of Sogormo.

Transport. Carriers have been quite plentiful, and no difficulty experienced
in getting out produce. Freights have been reduced by 3s. per
quintal between Perené and La Oroya.

Labour. There has been a good supply of labour all through the year,
part of which has been contributed by the Indian tribes of the
district.

CERRO DE PASCO.

Mr. Consular-Agent Stone reports as follows :—

Trade. The trade is almost entirely in the hands of natives, Italians
and Austrians, but an American company is opening up a mercantile store on a large and improved modern scale.

Silver and copper mines. Copper mines were formerly owned by Peruvians and some
foreigners. Most of them have been purchased by an American
syndicate at a cost of some millions of dollars. This syndicate
has now a large staff at work developing its property, and has sunk
five shafts to depths of from 150 to 300 feet. Pumping operations
have been commenced already at two of the shafts.

Gold mining. At about 9 miles from Cerro de Pasco is the site of a British
gold mining enterprise called the Chuquitambo Company, Limited,
which commenced working in October last with 40 stamps. The
output of gold is unknown.

Railway communication. To facilitate the transport of the ores to the coast, the syndicate
has in course of construction a railway from Oroya to Cerro de
Pasco, which is in an advanced state and will doubtless be
completed by the end of 1903.

The American syndicate has also under consideration the extension of the railway from Cerro de Pasco further into the interior,
for the development of the surrounding country, which is rich in
copper, silver and coal. This undertaking will absorb a large amount
of capital.

Rumiallana channel. The work of the Rumiallana tunnel is being carried out by a
Peruvian company. So far, 600 feet have been cleaned out, and
the tunnel driven to a distance of 1,466 feet.

Rates of wages. For native labour the average rate is about 3s. per day,
and for white labour about 8s. to 10s. per day.

Exports. The exports during the past year have been, roughly,
copper, 5,500 tons ; copper matte or regulus, 5,000 tons.

Pacasmayo.

Mr. Vice-Consul Jones reports as follows :—

In the absence of official statistics it is impossible to give Trade. reliable figures as to the volume of trade done through the port of Pacasmayo, but my opinion, based on personal observation, is, that there has not only been some shrinkage as regards quantities, but also a decided falling off in the value of the commodities dealt in.

This decrease in value is at once apparent when the lower prices which have ruled for the principal exports of the district, such as sugar and minerals, are considered; while rice, another important factor, though holding its own in price, has been produced in lesser quantity.

With a smaller export trade and, as a consequence, greater economies in the production of such exports, lower wages for unskilled labour and smaller field for the artisan class, the poor harvests the mountainous districts have yielded, and other causes, the power of spending has been reduced and the absorption of imports by the consuming classes curtailed, hence traders and importers comp'ain of the general stagnation of business.

The heavy duties on grey cotton cloths, matches, beer, liquors, Imports. &c., have a marked tendency to check business with the foreign countries producing these special articles, supplies being instead drawn from Lima, and in the case of liquors, cheap alcoholic adulterations superseding the genuine articles.

There is no noticeable change to report, nor has any new demand for specialities arisen. The trade does not show the balance it should in favour of British interests and, as mentioned in my last report, the principal business is not in British hands. British goods are not pushed and cheap German and Italian manufactures, specially made to suit the tastes and requirements of the country, compete with marked advantage in the district.

The production of sugar and alcohol, almost exclusively in the Exports. hands of British subjects, shows a slight increase in quantity, the former having been shipped principally to the United States, smaller quantities to Chile, while about 500 tons went in German steamers to Vancouver, British Columbia. Alcohol has only been sold locally and shipped to Bolivia, via Mollendo and Antofagasta. Rice has been in small supply, the result of an inferior crop last season, and only been shipped along the coast of South-West America.

Minerals and sulphides arrive from the mining districts; this business is in the hands of Germans.

The cattle trade has diminished of recent years.

Hides and goat-skins continue to be shipped to North American markets. In chemicals, barks, drug products and medicinal plants little trade, I am informed, has been done.

The principal valley crops being cane and paddy, both industries Agriculture.

suffered, the former from unprecedented low prices of sugar, developments having been curtailed on sugar-growing estates as a consequence, while last season's paddy suffered from drought in its early growth.

Climate.
The year has been cold, dry and unfavourable to agriculture.

Shipping.
Shipping has almost been restricted to the regular callings of the mail and coasting steamers from Valparaiso, with an occasional visit from an outside cargo boat with the object of discharging or receiving special cargo.

Communication.
Communication is limited to the Pacasmayo Railway system, a line which only extends as far as the towns of Chepen, Guadalupe and Tolon, all situated in the low lands.

Nothing has been done on the proposed Hualgayoc Railway, and the roads to the mountains and the interior have not been improved. Cajamarca is now in telegraphic communication with the coast and Lima, but the service is imperfect.

Money.
Capital is scarce in the district and good security for loans difficult to obtain.

Notwithstanding the introduction of a gold coinage, silver is still the common monetary medium in this district.

MOLLENDO.

Mr. Vice-Consul Robilliard reports as follows :—

General review.
Nothing of interest has occurred here during the year 1902, with the exception of excessive rains, that have caused several landslips on the railway between this port and Arequipa.

Exports.
The export tables annexed show in detail the nature of the trade.

Imports.
No detailed statistics can be obtained. The total value of imports during 1902 was 306,875l., as compared with 274,490l. in 1901.

Exchange.
The rate of exchange has ruled all through the year on the basis of 2s. to the sole.

British trade.
For staple articles the demand has kept up, but in novelties the Germans and Americans take the lead. British manufacturers do not appear to care to go out of the old groove to oblige intending purchasers.

Commercial travellers.
Not a dozen commercial travellers in all passed through this port during the year. Most of the commerce is carried on by direct communication with manufacturers and the sending of samples from this side showing the colours and styles of dress prints, &c., and also samples of the shape of tools most in demand for agricultural purposes, as these vary greatly in different districts.

Grey cottons.
The importation of grey cottons has fallen off greatly since the establishment of a factory in this Department, the produce of which competes favourably with European cloths. It uses native cotton, and gives a better class of article [at a less price. The amount of grey cottons made here now is sufficient for the demand for the interior and even for Bolivia.

Woollen baizes used to be, in former years, an article of large Woollen baizes.
consumption when the Indians clothed themselves chiefly in these
fabrics from Bradford. Of late years the imports have fallen off
to a tenth part, owing, doubtless, to the change in dress of the
Indians, who now make for themselves an inferior kind of baize
and buy the European article chiefly to take apart for the sake of
the colours, which are used for trimming, &c.

Beer is another article which has fallen off greatly, as the Beer.
breweries now established in this Department make enough and
of a fair quality to supply all the interior at, of course, a much
reduced rate. A little British stout and some German beers are
still introduced, but there is no comparison with former years.

During the war in South Africa the price of coal went up to 3l. a Coal.
ton, at which price it remains. Nearly all private houses are again
consuming firewood in their kitchens. A kind of brush grows
plentifully within a few leagues and costs less than coal as fuel.

The British Caylloma Silver Mining Company and the American Mining interests.
Inca Gold Mining Company continue to do well.

The alpaca fleece, which used to be shipped exclusively to Liver- Wool.
pool, now partly goes to New York; about 105 tons have
already been shipped to that port, but I feel convinced that the
bulk of it will always be sent to the British market.

Copper barilla is beginning to be shipped in large quantities Copper barilla.
again, about 500 tons monthly. This barilla comes from Corocoro
in Bolivia. There was a fear that those mines would shut down
if the price of copper fell below 48l. per ton. All the small mines
have stopped working, as it does not pay them now to do so.

Coca leaves are another of those articles which have looked for Coca leaves.
another market. It is now being exported chiefly to New York,
whilst in former years the bulk of it was sent to Hamburg.

A large amount of gold dust has been sent during the present Gold dust.
year to the mint in Lima; fully half the amount produced, which
is about 100,000l. The balance has nearly all gone to London.
A large quantity of ore has also been shipped to San Francisco.

RETURN of all Shipping Engaged in the Foreign Trade at Mollendo during the Years 1900–02.

ENTERED.

Nationality.	Year.	Steam – No. of Vessels With Cargo	Steam – No. of Vessels In Ballast	Steam – Tonnage With Cargo	Steam – Tonnage In Ballast	Sailing (with Cargo) – Number of Vessels	Sailing (with Cargo) – Tonnage	Total – No. of Vessels With Cargo	Total – No. of Vessels In Ballast	Total – Tonnage With Cargo	Total – Tonnage In Ballast
British	1900	177	1	319,877	80	8	10,189	185	1	330,066	80
	1901	189	..	336,870	..	13	18,534	202	..	355,413	..
	1902	198	2	382,844	2,023	9	14,054	207	2	396,898	2,023
Chilian	1900	104	1	158,068	38	..	..	104	1	158,068	38
	1901	102	1	157,949	37	..	..	102	1	157,949	37
	1902	114	1	175,856	37	..	..	114	1	175,856	37
German	1900	46	..	111,009	..	2	2,014	48	..	113,023	..
	1901	64	..	159,335	..	2	1,920	66	..	161,255	..
	1902	66	..	163,148	..	2	2,518	68	..	165,666	..
Italian	1900	2	..	1,620	..	..	..	2	..	1,620	..
	1901	1	..	810	..	1	798	2	..	1,608	..
	1902	2	..	1,620	..	..	..	2	..	1,620	..
Norwegian	1900	1	..	1,672	..	..	..	1	..	1,620	..
	1901	1	..	1,969	..	1	932	2	..	2,501	..
	1902	..	..	..	..	1	998	1	..	998	..
United States	1900	..	..	..	..	1	529	1	..	529	..
	1901	..	..	..	..	5	2,721	5	..	2,721	..
Total	1900	330	2	592,246	118	11	12,732	341	2	604,978	118
	1901	357	1	656,942	37	22	24,305	379	1	681,847	37
	1902	380	3	728,468	2,060	12	17,570	392	3	741,038	2,060

Nationality	Year	Steam				Sailing (in Ballast)		Total			
		Number of Vessels		Tonnage				Number of Vessels		Tonnage	
		With Cargo	In Ballast	With Cargo	In Ballast	Number of Vessels	Tonnage	With Cargo	In Ballast	With Cargo	In Ballast
British ..	1900	177	1	319,877	80	8	10,189	177	9	319,877	10,269
	1901	189	..	386,879	..	13	18,534	189	13	386,879	18,534
	1902	199	1	384,487	380	8	12,704	199	9	344,487	13,084
Chilian ..	1900	104	1	158,068	38	..	..	104	1	158,068	38
	1901	102	1	157,949	37	..	..	102	1	157,940	37
	1902	114	1	175,856	37	..	..	114	1	175,856	37
German ..	1900	46	..	111,009	..	2	2,014	46	2	111,009	2,014
	1901	64	..	159,335	..	2	1,020	64	2	159,335	1,920
	1902	66	..	163,148	..	2	2,518	66	2	163,148	2,518
Italian ..	1900	2	..	1,620	..	..	..	2	..	1,620	..
	1901	1	..	810	..	1	798	1	1	810	798
	1902	2	..	1,620	..	..	..	2	..	1,620	..
Norwegian ..	1900	1	..	1,672	..	1	932	1	1	1,672	932
	1901	1	..	1,969	..	1	998	1	1	1,969	998
	1902	..	..	..	..	1	529	..	1	..	529
United States ..	1900	..	..	..	..	1	..	..	1	..	..
	1901	..	..	..	..	5	2,721	..	5	..	2,721
Total ..	1900	330	2	592,246	118	11	12,732	330	13	592,216	12,850
	1901	357	1	656,942	37	22	24,905	357	23	656,942	24,912
	1902	381	2	725,111	417	11	16,220	381	13	725,111	16,637

RETURN of Bolivian Produce Exported through the Port of
Mollendo during the Year 1902.

Articles.			Quantity.		Value.
			Tons	cwts.	£
Sheep's wool ..	..	..	10	0	610
Bark ..	..	..	277	0	14,510
Copper barilla	..	..	3,483	0	141,000
Tin barilla ..	..	..	428	0	13,500
Dry ox-hides ..	..	..	35	0	1,452
Silver ores ..	..	..	44	0	909
Coca leaves ..	..	..	1	5	51
Rubber ..	..	..	293	10	119 250
Antimony ores	..	..	80	13	1,228
Coffee ..	..	..	2	10	104
Rhatany	..	..	1	5	127
Gold ..	..	..	..		2,380
Sundries	..	..	4	0	800
Total	..	..	..		295,951

RETURN of Peruvian Produce Exported through the Port of
Mollendo during the Year 1902.

Articles.			Quantity.		Value.
			Tons	cwts.	£
Alpaca wool ..	..	..	2,453	10	2 19,035
Sheep's wool ..	..	..	939	0	57,195
Vicuña wool ..	..	..	2	0	633
Borate of lime	..	..	4,828	0	34,300
Bark ..	..	..	8	10	453
Dry ox-hides ..	..	..	543	10	28,650
Silver ores ..	..	..	900	0	18,280
Copper ores ..	..	..	109	0	1,750
,, matte..	..	..	266	0	16,800
Coca leaves ..	..	..	697	0	28,300
Rubber ..	..	..	30	0	12,600
Coffee ..	..	..	17	0	8,437
Gold ores ..	..	..	22	10	56,500
Rhatany ..	..	..	16	0	1,640
Sheep-skins ..	..	..	43	0	480
Horns ..	..	..	10	0	145
Tartar ..	..	..	0	15	70
Cocaine	..	..	0	11	14,330
Maize ..	..	..	3	0	65
Hair ..	..	..	0	13	198
Gold ..	..	..	..		2,215
Silver bullion..	..	..	..		22,343
Bolivian coins..	..	..	..		16,590
Sundries	..	..	6	0	760
Total	..	..	..		571,769

SALAVERRY AND TRUJILLO.

Mr. Vice-Consul Reid reports as follows :—

Sugar is the principal article of export from Salaverry in which Sugar. British traders are interested, and nearly all of it goes to Chile, the United States or the United Kingdom. In the years 1897 and 1898 it was about equally divided between the countries named, but changes have since taken place whereby the quantity of sugar exported to the United Kingdom has been very much reduced, whilst that sent to the United States has been greatly increased.

The following table shows the quantity of sugar exported to Chile, the United States and the United Kingdom during 1900–02 :—

Year.				Quantity.		
				Chile.	United States.	United Kingdom.
				Tons.	Tons.	Tons.
1900 ..	..	..	..	10,484	26,032	2,487
1901 ..	..	..	.	17,564	20,360	2,741
1902 ..	..	..	..	14,522	20,670	6,569

The increased exportation of sugar to the United States during the last three years is due, in great measure, to the reduction in freights viâ Panama.

Although there are good mineral districts in the vicinity, the Ores. quantity of ores exported is very small. The railways do not extend in that direction and the roads are so bad that only high class ores can bear the cost of conveyance to the port.

In cotton goods the United Kingdom maintains the lead, Cotton goods. having supplied more than three-fourths of the quantity imported. Germany and Italy come next on the list, but very far behind. This market is now receiving a considerable amount of calicoes and other classes of cheap cotton goods from the mills in the vicinity of Lima, and apparently the use of these goods of native manufacture will go on increasing, as they are favoured by a duty of nearly 50 per cent. on the value of similar goods imported.

In woollen goods the imports from Germany have been of Woollen greater value than those from the United Kingdom, whilst a great goods. falling-off has taken place in the value of this class of goods imported from France, as shown hereunder :—

Year.				Value.		
				United Kingdom.	Germany.	France.
				£	£	£
1902 ..	..	..	..	1,309	1,730	366
1901 ..	..	..	..	1,521	736	911

The woollen mills in the country now supply a large proportion of the cheap class of goods, and it is generally admitted that the qualities made are improving. From Germany there comes a light class of goods which takes the market very well, as the appearance is quite satisfactory, and though it has not the durability in fibre or colour of first class goods, it seems to suit requirements. In this district, where there is virtually no rain and the climate is exceedingly mild, strong, well prepared unshrinkable goods are not indispensable, and it is often remarked that British-made goods have lasting qualities which purchasers here do not appreciate.

Food-stuffs. In food-stuffs the principal article is wheat imported from the United States and Chile. In canned provisions the United States and Germany are rapidly increasing the proportion they formerly supplied, whereas the value of the United Kingdom's contribution has fallen off from 1,734l. in 1901, to 294l. in 1902.

Sundries. The value of goods imported under the heading of sundries is more than half that of all the goods imported. They consist chiefly of goods introduced in large quantities which pay little or no duty, such as coal, rails, sleepers, timber, iron, steel, pumps, sugar mill and agricultural machinery, kerosene, nitrate of soda, electric installations, &c. There has been a falling-off in the imports of these goods from the United Kingdom and the United States, whilst those from Germany, Australia and Chile have increased very considerably. The increase of imports from Germany is mostly accounted for by the installation for lighting Trujillo by electricity.

New factory. A cigarette factory was opened in Trujillo during the year. The machinery seems well adapted to the purpose in view, for it receives the tobacco in leaves as imported, and with very little attention it turns out the cigarettes completely finished. This apparatus is the invention of a Spaniard, but was constructed in the United States.

Electric lighting. Notwithstanding the difficulties encountered in conveying the hydraulic and generating machinery to Poroto (the site of the power station), the installation of electric lighting in Trujillo has been carried out as was contracted for. On December 31 the inauguration of the public lighting took place, and has since been steadily maintained to the satisfaction of all concerned.

Telephones. The Trujillo Telephone Company having joined with that of Pacasmayo, now gives facilities for immediate communication with all the subscribers of both systems, which extend from Salaverry to the estates in the neighbourhood of Guadalupe. In connection with these companies another has been formed called the Compañia Telefonica Trasandina, and it has extended lines from Trujillo to Otuzco, Santiago de Huamachuco, Cajabamba and all the estates or mines of importance in these districts, employing in all 338 miles of wire. The subscribers to the Trasandina line number only 32, but to the Trujillo and Pacasmayo lines they are nearly 300.

The great reduction in the price of sugar which occurred about the beginning of this year had a most depressing effect upon the business of this district. Fears were entertained of a complete collapse in the staple industry. As the price of sugar has improved, so has confidence returned, and now business goes on as formerly, but with more caution. The sales of alcohol and rum have fallen off, and at present the stocks of these productions are unusually large, whilst the heavy tax on alcohol goes far to prevent its use for industrial purposes.

Value of produce.

TABLE showing Quantity and Value of Goods Exported from Salaverry during the Year 1902.

Country.	Sugar of all Kinds.		Rum and Alcohol.		Cocoa.		Cocaine.	
	Quantity.	Value.	Quantity.	Value.	Quantity.	Value.	Quantity.	Value.
	Tons cwts. qrs.	Soles.	Tons cwts. qrs.	Soles.	Tons cwts. qrs.	Soles.	Cwts. qrs. lbs.	Soles.
United Kingdom	6,569 14 1	433,137	..	..	..	..	5 1 14	24,400
Australia	506 1 3	40,000	..	..	..	..	..	..
Chile	14,522 10 0	972,301	249 2 3	43,464	..	..	..	..
Colombia	101 2 1	9,440	..	..	..	..	..	..
Ecuador	..	..	..	..	..	..	..	..
France..	..	..	..	..	..	..	0 1 14	..
Germany	..	..	..	..	3 10 0	1,610	6 3 20	25,625
United States.. ..	20,670 11 0	1,499,410	..	..	23 15 2	12,100	..	..
Total	42,369 19 1	2,954,288	249 2 3	43,464	27 5 2	13,710	12 2 20	50,095
Equiv. in sterling	..	£ s. 295,428 16	..	£ s. 4,346 8	..	£ 1,371	..	£ s. 5,002 10

TABLE showing Quantity and Value of Goods Exported from Salaverry during the Year 1902—continued.

Country.	Wool.		Coffee.		Hides.		Ores.		Silver and Sulphides.	
	Quantity.	Value.	Quantity.	Value.	Quantity.	Value.	Quantity.	Value.	Quantity.	Value.
	Tons cwts. qrs.	Soles.	Tons cwts. qrs.	Soles.	Tons cwts. qrs.	Soles.	Tons cwts. qrs.	Soles.	Tons cwts. qrs.	Soles.
United Kingdom	29 6 3	17,480	52 8 1	15,130	0 9 3	300	18 12 2	7,130	4 10 0	72,420
Australia	..	..	..	..	..	..	..	..	..	..
Chile	..	..	2 5 2	800	..	..	..	..	..	..
Colombia ..	..	..	..	..	..	..	..	..	..	..
Ecuador	..	..	..	..	..	..	..	..	..	..
France	2 14 0	1,000	5 11 0	1,800	1 0 3	350	..	..	..	..
Germany ..	..	..	3 5 0	2,289	..	..	103 0 3	24,290	2 4 1	35,250
United States ..	..	..	..	..	0 14 1	605	18 13 1	5,300	1 5 2	14,430
Total	32 0 3	18,480	63 9 3	20,019	2 4 3	1,255	140 6 2	36,720	7 19 3	122,100
Eq. in sterling	..	£ 1,848	..	£ s. 2,001 18	..	£ s. 125 10	..	£ 3,672	..	£ 12,210

TABLE showing Quantity and Value of Goods Exported from Salaverry during the Year 1902—continued.

Country.	Articles of Food.		Iron Goods.		Sundries.		Total Value.
	Quantity.	Value.	Quantity.	Value.	Quantity.	Value.	
	Tons cwts. qrs.	Soles.	Tons cwts.	Soles.	Tons cwts. qrs.	Soles.	Soles.
United Kingdom	..	..	..	1,000	1 12 2	8,860	579,857
Australia..	..	..	..	..	..	..	40,000
Chile	..	..	..	..	..	..	1,016,565
Colombia	..	..	..	..	1 4 0	210	9,650
Ecuador	1 1 3	55	..	..	4 8 2	370	425
France	..	..	..	..	7 8 2	250	3,050
Germany.. ..	..	..	..	..	0 11 2	2,100	91,511
United States ..	..	..	..	..	0 1 0	6	1,531,851
Total	1 1 3	55	4 6	1,000	15 6 0	11,796	3,272,912
Equiv. in sterling..	..	£ s. 5 10	..	£ 100	15 6 0	£ s. 1,179 12	£ s. 327,251 1

TABLE showing Value of Goods Imported at Salaverry during the Year 1902.

Country.	Value.									
	Cotton Goods.	Woollen Goods.	Linen Goods.	Silk Goods.	Apparel, Furniture, Empty Bags, &c.	Articles of Food.	Wines and Liquors.	Drugs and Chemical Products.	Sundries.	Total.
	£ s. d.	£ s. d.	£ s. d.	£ s. d.	£ s. d.	£ s. d.	£ s. d.	£ s. d.	£ s. d.	£ s. d.
United Kingdom ...	15,030 6 11	1,309 10 11	476 16 2	117 1 0	11,913 5 6	291 9 10	311 16 2	316 11 3	20,023 6 7	49,889 7 4
Australia	...	...	...	...	...	...	...	...	...	2,641 12 0
Belgium	110 10 0	62 8 0	...	...	...	...	42 7 0	66 17 1	2,806 9 8	3,088 11 9
Chile	...	...	...	...	683 2 0	1,601 9 8	...	...	4,922 10 0	7,207 1 8
China	...	...	...	...	...	277 8 0	...	...	117 11 2	394 19 2
Colombia	...	...	...	12 1	1 4 0	26 0 6	...	43 18 5	...	71 15 0
Cuba	...	...	...	...	...	...	...	...	31 9 2	31 9 2
Ecuador	...	...	...	...	...	...	...	...	46 0 0	46 0 0
France	497 10 11	366 15 0	3 18 4	296 5 0	674 12 6	165 4 6	400 4 11	841 1 7	1,664 1 4	4,389 14 1
Germany	2,134 18 11	1,730 1 9	235 6 1	330 16 4	1,459 5 1	837 1 0	42 0 0	1,291 17 11	22,772 15 2	30,531 2 3
Italy	1,173 16 0	...	30 17 9	...	311 15 2	206 8 0	187 14 10	103 15 6	215 9 0	2,262 16 11
San Salvador ...	...	...	...	...	...	...	...	·7	219 6 0	219 6 0
Spain	196 14 2	...	...	1 3 6	199 11 2	...	177 9 5	...	45 12 2	620 10 5
United States ...	412 2 8	...	...	...	483 19 9	2,317 17 0	84 16 11	698 1 3	15,487 1 3	19,483 19 10
Total ...	19,555 19 7	3,463 15 8	746 18 4	745 17 11	15,638 15 2	5,725 19 3	1,216 9 3	2,862 5 11	70,998 3 6	120,990 4 7

RETURN of all Shipping Engaged in the Foreign Trade of Salaverry during the Years 1900–02.

ENTERED.

Nationality	Year	Steam (with Cargo) Number of Vessels	Steam (with Cargo) Tonnage	Sailing Vessels With Cargo	Sailing Vessels In Ballast	Sailing Tonnage With Cargo	Sailing Tonnage In Ballast	Total Vessels With Cargo	Total Vessels In Ballast	Total Tonnage With Cargo	Total Tonnage In Ballast
British	1900	129	227,829	6	..	6,614	..	135	..	234,443	..
British	1901	125	227,730	4	2	3,464	1,549	129	2	231,194	1,549
British	1902	114	210,503	3	9	1,983	10,245	117	9	212,441	10,215
Chilian	1900	75	115,710	..	..	..	..	75	..	115,710	..
Chilian	1901	79	123,659	..	..	..	..	79	..	123,659	..
Chilian	1902	76	119,340	1	..	260	..	77	..	119,6'0	..
German	1900	17	33,595	..	..	..	..	17	..	33,595	..
German	1901	26	63,418	..	..	..	..	26	..	63,418	..
German	1902	20	42,456	4	..	2,591	..	24	..	45,077	..
Belgian	1902	1	2,982	..	..	..	..	1	..	2,982	..
United States	1900	..	..	2	..	1,334	..	2	..	1,334	..
Danish	1901	..	..	2	..	883	..	2	..	883	..
Norwegian	1901	..	..	1	..	1,079	..	1	..	1,079	..
Norwegian	1901	..	..	1	..	919	..	1	..	919	..
Total	1900	221	377,134	8	..	7,943	..	229	..	385,082	..
Total	1901	230	414,807	8	2	6,345	1,549	238	2	421,152	1,549
Total	1902	211	375,311	8	9	4,789	10,245	219	9	380,100	10,245

CLEARED.

Nationality	Year	Steam (with Cargo) Number of Vessels	Steam (with Cargo) Tonnage	Sailing No. of Vessels With Cargo	Sailing No. of Vessels In Ballast	Sailing Tonnage With Cargo	Sailing Tonnage In Ballast	Total No. of Vessels With Cargo	Total No. of Vessels In Ballast	Total Tonnage With Cargo	Total Tonnage In Ballast
British	1900	129	227,829	5	1	5,569	1,045	134	1	233,398	1,045
	1901	125	227,730	3	3	2,533	2,480	128	3	230,263	2,480
	1902	114	210,503	8	4	6,991	5,192	122	4	217,494	5,192
Chilian	1900	75	115,710	..	..	..	..	75	..	115,710	..
	1901	79	123,659	..	..	..	..	79	..	123,659	..
	1902	76	119,340	1	..	260	..	77	..	119,600	..
German	1900	17	33,595	..	..	..	..	17	..	33,595	..
	1901	26	63,418	..	..	..	..	26	..	63,418	..
	1902	20	42,486	4	..	2,591	..	24	..	45,077	..
Belgian	1902	1	2,982	..	..	..	..	1	..	2,982	..
United States	1900	..	..	2	..	1,834	..	2	..	1,334	..
Danish	1901	..	..	2	..	883	..	2	..	883	..
Norwegian	1901	..	..	1	..	1,079	..	1	..	1,079	..
		..	..	1	..	919	..	1	..	919	..
Total ...	1900	221	377,134	7	1	6,903	1,045	228	1	384,087	1,045
	1901	230	414,807	7	3	5,414	2,480	237	3	420,221	2,480
	1902	211	375,811	13	4	9,842	5,192	224	4	385,153	5,192

LONDON:
Printed for His Majesty's Stationery Office,
By HARRISON AND SONS,
Printers in Ordinary to His Majesty.
(1400   9 | 03—H & S   369)

No. 3080. Annual Series.

ITALY.

DIPLOMATIC AND CONSULAR REPORTS.

TRADE OF

SICILY

FOR THE YEAR 1902.

FOREIGN OFFICE,
September, 1903.

No. 3080 Annual Series.

DIPLOMATIC AND CONSULAR REPORTS.

ITALY.

REPORT FOR THE YEAR 1902

ON THE

TRADE AND COMMERCE OF SICILY.

REFERENCE TO PREVIOUS REPORT, Annual Series No. 2887.

Presented to both Houses of Parliament by Command of His Majesty,
SEPTEMBER, 1903.

LONDON:
PRINTED FOR HIS MAJESTY'S STATIONERY OFFICE,
BY HARRISON AND SONS, ST. MARTIN'S LANE,
PRINTERS IN ORDINARY TO HIS MAJESTY.

And to be purchased, either directly or through any Bookseller, from
EYRE & SPOTTISWOODE, East Harding Street, Fleet Street, E.C.,
and 32, Abingdon Street, Westminster, S.W.;
or OLIVER & BOYD, Edinburgh;
or E. PONSONBY, 116, Grafton Street, Dublin.

1903.

[Cd. 1766—14.]   *Price Twopence Halfpenny.*

CONTENTS.

———

Reference to previous Report, Annual Series No. 2887.

Report on the Trade and Commerce of Sicily for the Year 1902

By Mr. Consul Sidney J. A. Churchill.

(Palermo, July 31, 1903; received at Foreign Office, August 12, 1903.)

Palermo and Sicily generally are passing through a difficult period as regards trade and commerce. An abnormal frost in the United States gave the green fruit trade a fillip which caused some movement; but its prospects are not very bright, as the United States are gradually supplying their own wants. Agriculture is languishing owing to the depletion of the population by the continual flow of emigrants to the United States, to South America and Tunis. The wealthy houses of business for which Sicily was famous in the early part of the last century have disappeared, and instead of the commerce of the island being in the hands of a few important establishments, it is now divided up amongst a great number of individuals. *[margin: Commercial conditions of Sicily.]*

Formerly the Marsala wine trade was in the hands of a few old established firms, who turned out a sound wine famed all over the world. To-day it may be truthfully said that there are hundreds of individuals who are manufacturing a so-called Marsala wine, and in consequence this trade has reached a point where the making of Marsala wine is scarcely profitable. *[margin: Marsala wine.]*

The agricultural conditions in the interior of the Island of Sicily have been so little encouraging for the petty farmer and labourer that he has sought for better fortune across the sea; inquiries even being made for passages to South Africa and Australia. During 1902 no less than 11,000 emigrants were shipped from the port of Palermo direct for the United States. The numbers who went from the island by indirect means cannot be fixed with certainty, but they cannot be less than 30,000 during 1902, out of a population of some 3,000,000. *[margin: Emigration.]*

In the interior of the island the effects of the wholesale emigration have been such as to make it impossible to cultivate the lands without imported labour from the neighbouring province of Calabria. *[margin: Scarcity of population in the interior.]*

It was feared that the present extensive wine trade with Austria-Hungary was likely to suffer by new fiscal conditions to be imposed by that country on imports from Sicily, as also by the develop- *[margin: Wine trade.]*

ment of the restored vineyards in the Austro-Hungarian Empire after the ravages of the phylloxera pest. An agitation was accordingly started in order to persuade the Central Government at Rome to come to the aid of Sicily by legislation. In consequence,

Reduced railway rates for Sicilian products. reduced railway rates have been accorded to Sicilian products on Italian Continental railways on a progressive scale, increasing according to the distance travelled and without regard to the destination of the goods, whether for the home market or for export.

Shipping. The following table shows the shipping traffic of the port of Palermo during the last six years :—

Year.	Sailing.		Steam.		Total.	
	Number of Vessels.	Tons.	Number of Vessels.	Tons.	Number of Vessels.	Tons.
1897	1,793	113,912	1,962	1,719,150	3,755	1.833,062
1898	1,825	101,158	1,878	1,555,761	3,708	1,656,919
1899	1,937	117,584	1,817	1,518,626	3,754	1,636,210
1900	1,929	108,713	1,817	1,565,814	3,746	1,674,527
1901	1,790	97,466	1,938	1,752,865	3,728	1,850,331
1902	1,803	101,955	1,963	1,807,391	3,766	1,909,346

The freights carried to and from Palermo during the year 1902, as compared with the previous year, were as follows :—

Freights entered.

ENTERED.

Year.	Quantity.
	Tons.
1901	404,109
1902	389,810
Decrease, 1902	14,299

Freights cleared.

CLEARED.

Year.	Quantity.
	Tons.
1902	227,388
1901	210,431
Increase, 1902	16,957

The following table shows the number and tonnage of British British shipping.
vessels which called at the port of Palermo during 1902 and the
preceding five years :—

Year.				Number of Vessels.	Annual Tonnage.
1897	..	..	..	343	350,381
1898	..	..	..	321	399,744
1899	..	..	..	289	385,762
1900	..	..	..	262	351,319
1901	..	..	..	300	409,651
1902	..	..	..	293	427,750

Of these vessels during 1902 only one was a sailing craft with
a tonnage of 223 tons.

The British shipping during 1902 entered with 109,993 tons Freights by British shipping.
of freight and cleared with 82,185 tons of merchandise.

Following the practice begun last year, efforts have been again Coal trade of Sicily.
made to ascertain as accurately as possible the extent of the coal
trade of the Island of Sicily. Two tables are annexed to this
report, from which it will appear that, during 1902, the total import
of coals into Sicily from all sources reached 430,788 tons, of which
the United Kingdom supplied 420,526 tons; 278,332 tons from
Wales and the rest from North Britain. The foreign coal came
principally from the United States. It is understood that the United States coal.
trial of United States coal in Sicily has not been a financial success.

During 1902 the coal trade of Sicily made an advance on the Condition of coal trade in Sicily.
previous year to the extent of over 25,000 tons. Like all other
trades it suffers much from excessive competition. Apart from the
gas company, which has a long contract at prices favourable to
the vendor, the local selling price of coal has afforded little or no
margin to the importer.

The Palermo coal trade during 1902 employed 57 vessels, of Palermo coal trade.
which 37 were British, 9 Norwegian, 6 German, 2 Italian, 2 Greek
and 1 Danish. The total amount of coal imported into Palermo was
147,630 tons, of which 102,885 tons were carried in British bottoms.
Only 1,300 tons of this coal were not of British origin.

The coal trade of each of the principal ports of Sicily was as
follows during 1902 :—

IMPORTS of Coal during the Year 1902.

Port.					Quantity.
					Tons.
Palermo	..	..	..	..	..	147,630
Messina	..	..	..	..	..	105.942
Catania	..	..	..	..	..	90,810
Syracuse	..	..	..	..	..	8,806
Licata	..	..	..	..	..	23,928
Girgenti (Porto Empedocle)			..	..	22,802
Marsala	..	..	..	..	..	565
Trapani	..	..	..	..	..	25,158
Milazzo	..	..	..	..	..	5,647
Total	..	..	..	..	430,788

In June, 1902, their Majesties the King and Queen of Italy opened
an Agricultural Exhibition at Palermo. The native exhibits,
representative of nearly all Sicily, showed great industrial progress
and proved conclusively the great capacity of the native workmen.
Whilst there was little originality, the Sicilian proved that he
could turn out machinery and skilled work, under supervision, as
well as anybody else.

The Palermo shipbuilding yard during 1902 placed a 6,000 ton
freight steamer on the stocks to the order of the Navigazione
Generale Italiana. This is now almost ready for launching, with
machinery and masts complete.

The yard has an order from Messrs. Peirce Brothers, of Messina,
for a cargo steamer which is to be the biggest yet built in Italy,
for a tugboat for the Navigazione Generale, for a small cargo boat,
for Messrs. Corvaia, of Palermo, for a railway ferry boat to be used
in the Straits of Messina, and for some other small craft.

The Palermo shipbuilding yard, the full title of which is " Cantiere
Navale e Stabilimente Mecanici Siciliani, Palermo," is also the
owner of the dry dock now being constructed; the concession from
the Government for which has a duration of 70 years from the date
of the completion of the works. The construction is not to take
more than four years. The company receives the following sub-
ventions or grants in aid :—

	Amount.
	Lire.
From the Government	1,500,000
Municipality of Palermo	1,200,000
Cassa di Risparmio of Palermo (grant) ..	100,000
Palermo Provincial Council	200,000
Total	3,000,000

The land on which the works and the dock are built is granted by the Government rent free for the duration of the concession. The company is debarred from making over its rights in the working of the dock to any other parties except with the approval of the Minister of Public Works. The majority of the directors, the manager and the director-general must be Italian subjects.

The length of the dock is 172 metres 66 centims. (565 feet) by Dimensions of 8 metres 20 centims. deep (27 feet), width at top 25 metres 70 centims. the dock. (85 feet), at bottom 22 metres 40 centims. (73 feet 6 inches).

During the year 1902 the railway quay was widened and made Port accessible for ships to come alongside. By the completion of the improvements new quay for the Naples mail steamers f ther quay space has become available for merchant vessels.

The deepening of the channel in the harbour and the better protection of ships in bad weather whilst in the harbour are necessities not yet provided.

The following statement shows the condition of the sulphur Sulphur trade of Sicily during 1902 as compared with 1901 :—

		Quantity.	
		1901.	1902.
		Tons.	Tons.
Sulphur exported from Sicily	..	475,000	481,228
Stock in hand on December 31	..	242,438	329,836
Exported from Palermo	..	13,803	6,486

The asphalt exported during 1902 from Sicily amounted to Asphalt. 57,222 tons and went to the following countries :—

Country.				Quantity.
				Tons.
United Kingdom	..	..	..	10,660
Germany	..	..	..	26,150
United States	..	..	..	6,440
France	..	..	..	5,870
Netherlands	..	..	..	4,350
Austria-Hungary	..	..	..	1,750
Continental Italy	..	..	..	480
Egypt	..	..	..	400
Roumania	..	..	..	100
Miscellaneous	..	..	..	1,522

The coral beds of Sicily lie off the south-west coast and have Coral Trapani as the headquarters of the fishermen engaged in the industry, fisheries. mostly on behalf of Neapolitan capitalists from Torre dell'Annunziata and Torre del Greco. Formerly much coralwork was produced in Sicily ; but the industry has now completely died out. The harvest last season produced 265 tons of coral, 95 sailing vessels were engaged in the trade with crews of 908 men.

Liquorice
root and
juice.

Sicily produces wild liquorice to the extent of about 1,000 tons annually. This is not, however, sufficient for the requirements of the manufacturers of the juice, who are obliged to import root from Greece and Turkey. During 1902 it was estimated that about 4,000 tons were imported. It generally requires about 6 tons of root to make 1 ton of juice. The latter is principally employed in the tobacco trade, but for this the more bitter root from Asia Minor appears to have advantages over the Sicilian variety, which appears to affect the keeping quality of the tobacco.

Liquorice
exports.

Catania is the principal seat of the liquorice trade, and the output of juice there is estimated at between 300 and 500 tons annually, whilst Messina turns out from 100 to 150 tons per annum. Palermo, Caltagirone, Terranova, Termini and Trapani are all producers. The factory at Trapani is reported to be no longer working. During 1901 Palermo imported 115 tons of root, but in 1902 this diminished to 67 tons only. The exports of juice from Palermo during 1902 only reached 40 tons, half of which went to the United Kingdom.

Municipal
trading.

The first municipality in Sicily to attempt to trade on an important scale is Catania, where the municipality provides the citizens with bread. It is yet too soon to say whether the undertaking will be successful or not. The municipality of Palermo has also begun to grind corn and produce bread. The object in this latter case is to provide bread for the poorer class at the lowest rate possible, compatible with business.

Palermo has always had the reputation of being one of the most expensive places in Italy to live in. This is principally due to the fact that almost all the necessaries of life are imported. The municipality recently issued its standard of the prices of bread and meat, and, as the bakers and butchers protested that they could not supply at the standard rates, the municipality undertook the immediate production of bread and macaroni, the principal staples of food here. The result has been that the bakers and macaroni makers have since undersold the municipal products.

The burial of the dead in Palermo is also principally undertaken by the municipality. Formerly certain private cemeteries existed. They were the property of communities and corporations, but the municipality has imposed a tax of 4l. per burial in these cemeteries.

Hardware
trade.

The hardware trade of 1900, which had reached 242 tons during 1902, fell to 173 tons, or about 10 tons better than the imports of 1901. The Netherlands last year supplied about 69 tons, whilst the imports from the United Kingdom amounted to 49 tons.

Iron trade.

The pig iron imported during 1902 came entirely from the United Kingdom. The iron bars, T-iron, sections, &c., amounted to 825 tons, of which the Netherlands supplied 280 tons, Belgium 231 tons and the United Kingdom 140 tons; in iron plates the United Kingdom comes first with 196 tons to 53 tons from the German Empire and 33 tons from Belgium. In iron tubes the United States supplied 51 tons, to 22 tons from the United Kingdom. Of anchors, axles, &c., the United Kingdom supplied the major quantity. Railway wheels came mostly from Germany. Of partly manufactured ironware, out of 309 tons, 113 tons came from Germany and 73 tons from the United Kingdom. Galvanised iron sheets came entirely from the United Kingdom. In the supply of tools, Germany takes first place owing to her cheaper prices, the United Kingdom comes second.

The main source of supply of the Palermo market for brass, copper and bronze is the United Kingdom. Brassware, copper and bronze.

Zinc is principally imported from Belgium and Germany. Zinc.

Out of 408 tons of machinery the United Kingdom supplied 314 tons, most of which consisted of sewing machines. Machinery.

The population of Palermo on December 31, 1902, was estimated to be as follows :— Population.

	Number.
In the city	257,354
Suburbs	55,981
Garrison	3,159
Total	316,494

The daily average births during 1902, excluding stillborn children, was 22·51. Births.

The average daily mortality of Palermo during 1902, excluding stillborn births, was 19·22. Mortality.

The exchange at Palermo during 1902 varied but a few centimes, and scarcely reached higher than 25 lire 30 c. or lower than 25 lire 8 c. per 1*l*. This exchange was to the advantage of trade with the United Kingdom. Exchange.

For the first time in Sicily a night service of trains has been organised between Palermo, Messina and Catania. There is also now a service with Messina, allowing that town to be visited from Palermo in time for return in the same day. Train service.

The railway extension from Corleone to San Carlo, has been completed. Extension of railways.

In view of the difficulty experienced by foreigners in establishing their identity to the satisfaction of the post and telegraph authorities it is necessary to repeat the information given last year as to the possibility of obtaining certificates of identity from the post office on being presented by two known local residents. The identity ticket of the Cyclists Touring Club, with portrait, is often accepted as sufficient. Telegraph money orders.

A society has been formed in Palermo for the protection of foreigners and travellers and for the encouragement of travelling in Sicily. Foreigners in trouble or who have complaints to make have but to address themselves to this association at the Town Hall of Palermo. This society is affiliated with a similar institution on the continent of Italy. Travellers' Protection Society.

Strict regulations governing the employment of automobiles on public roads and thoroughfares in the province of Palermo have been issued. All cars must be registered, and exhibit a number and the name of the place of registry. Automobile on public ways.

RETURN of all Shipping at the Port of Palermo during the Year 1902.

Nationality.	Steam						Sailing					
	Entered.			Cleared.			Entered.			Cleared.		
	Number of Vessels.	Tonnage.	Freight.	Number of Vessels.	Tonnage.	Freight.	Number of Vessels.	Tonnage.	Freight.	Number of Vessels.	Tonnage.	Freight.
Italian	1,289	984,276	101,417	1,235	983,228	60,981	1,795	100,502	113,115	1,769	97,042	22,366
British	292	427,527	109,688	279	417,907	82,185	1	223	305	1	223	..
German	112	158,982	16,644	111	149,838	28,500	..	..	..	..	..	..
Austro-Hungarian	132	152,897	6,749	132	152,397	19,253	..	..	..	..	..	..
French	52	48,503	3,658	48	44,381	3,023	..	..	..	..	..	..
Greek	16	16,945	15,019	20	20,318	2,031	5	962	1,062	5	962	..
Dutch	38	23,874	865	32	23,324	3,309	..	..	..	..	..	..
Norwegian	14	18,579	19,452	14	18,579	1,887	..	..	..	..	..	..
Spanish	6	8,895	680	6	8,895	1,676	..	..	..	..	..	..
Danish	9	7,628	1,900	9	7,623	1,280	..	..	..	..	..	..
Russian	5	5,949	240	5	5,949	1,147	..	..	..	..	..	..
Swedish	2	1,850	..	2	1,350	300	..	..	..	..	..	..
Ottoman	..	..	..	..	..	..	2	288	116	1	172	..
Uruguayan	1	1,191	..	1	1,191	..	..	..	..	..	..	..

RETURN of Coal Imported into the Island of Sicily during the Year 1902.

Port.	Flag.		Quantity.			
			Welsh.	North Country.	Foreign.	Total.
			Tons.	Tons.	Tons.	Tons.
Palermo	British	..	79,530	23,085	..	102,615
	Foreign	..	20,657	23,058	1,300	45,015
Total		..	100,187	46,143	1,300	147,630
Messina	British	..	29,039	4,680	..	33,719
	Foreign	..	46,432	18,566	7,225	72,223
Total		..	75,471	23,246	7,225	105,942
Catania	British	..	23,079	15,894	..	38,973
	Foreign	..	39,569	10,763	1,000	51,337
Total		..	62,648	26,662	1,000	90,310
Syracuse	British	..	7,619	..	..	7,619
	Foreign	..	740	447	..	1,187
Total		..	8,359	447	..	8,806
Licata	British	..	4,091	6,333	..	10,424
	Foreign	..	4,179	8,275	1,050	13,504
Total		..	8,270	14,608	1,050	23,928
Porto Empedocle ..	British	..	4,703	11,908	..	16,611
	Foreign	..	4,144	2,047	..	6,191
Total		..	8,847	13,955	..	22,802
Marsala	Foreign	..	..	565	..	565
Trapani	British	..	4,120	..	415	4,535
	Foreign	..	5,055	15,568	..	20,623
Total		..	9,175	15,568	415	25,158
Milazzo	British	..	4,244	..	..	4,244
	Foreign	..	1,131	..	272	1,403
Total		..	5,375	..	272	5,647
Grand total ..		..	..	..	..	430,788

TABLE showing Quantity of Coal Imported into Sicily during the
Years 1901–02.

			Quantity.	
			1901.	1902.
			Tons.	Tons.
Welsh coal	..	..	243,579	278,332
North Country coal	..	..	68,006	141,194
Other coal	..	..	8,122	11,262
Carried in—				
British ships ..	..	..	216,655	218,740
Foreign ships..	..	..	188,774	212,048
Grand total—				
British coal	..	..	405,429	419,526
Foreign coal ..		..	8,122*	11,262*

* Principally from the United States of America.

RETURN of Principal Articles of Import into Palermo during the
Year 1902 compared with the Years 1900–01.

Articles.				Quantity.		
				1900.	1901.	1902.
Mineral waters	..	..	Tons	38	31	38
Wines, in casks	..	..	Gallons	3,740	43,076	97,047
„ in bottle	..	..	„	1,760	2,410	1,917
Spirits	..	..	„	2,420	2,817	1,572.
Oil, olive	..	..	Tons	365	17	..
„ mineral	..	..	„	245	295	384
Petroleum	..	..	Gallons	670,780	624,602	548,300
Coffee	..	..	Tons	284	318	347
Sugar	..	..	„	17	13	40
Cocoa	..	..	„	13	8	20
Pepper	..	..	„	85	80	88
Tobacco	..	..	„	1,548	3,859	430
Caustic soda	..	..	„	319	380	440
Oxides	..	..	„	..	35	58
Carbonates	..	..	„	290	385	504
Chlorides	..	..	„	227	241	184
Nitrates	..	..	„	155	110	140
Sulphates	..	..	„	929	1,194	839
Paraffin, solid	..	..	„	113	166	215
Liquorice root	..	..	„	85	114	67
Resins	..	..	„	33	125	117
Herbs	..	..	„	955	3,446	3,545
Colours	..	..	„	..	30	28
Horsehair	..	..	„	546	365	422
Timber	..	..	„	19,820	21,506	24,737
Cardboard	..	..	„	..	230	242
Hides	..	..	„	207	163	131
Metallic dross	..	..	„	180	119	..
Iron, scrap	..	..	„	326	149	..
„ pig	..	..	„	1,540	757	193
Stearic acid	..	..	„	104	108	832.
Fertilisers	..	..	„	62	114	266
Oleic acids	..	..	„	214	169	39
Steel and iron, in bars	..	„	832	516	825	
„ „ plates	..	„	1,080	383	308	
„ „ tubes	..	„	131	136	95	
„ „ manufac-						
tured	..	..	„	1,640	454	309
Steel and iron rails	..	„	905	2,457	40	
„ „ galvanised		„	88	329	404	
Copper and brass	..	„	59	29	43	
Zinc	..	..	„	130	109	184
Guns	..	..	Number	1,172	728	1,078
Revolvers	..	..	„	1,845	658	2,367
Machinery	..	..	Tons	1,223	318	408
Cement	..	..	„	1,287	1,297	1,475
Fire-bricks	..	..	„	296	387	233
Coal	..	..	„	84,659	97,754	85,327
Glassware	..	..	„	171	119	132
„ bottles	..	..	„	66	65	65
Grain, corn, wheat	..	„	36,170	30,160	30,290	
„ other kinds	..	„	5,330	4,228	4,617	
Feculæ	..	..	„	..	169	188
Starch	..	..	„	41	27	31
Fish, dried	..	..	„	285	375	378

RETURN of Principal Articles of Import into Palermo during the
Year 1902 compared with the Years 1900–01—continued.

Articles.		Quantity.		
		1900.	1901.	1902.
Seeds, oleaginous.. ..	Tons ..	..	108	178
„ non-oleaginous ..	„ ..	..	232	252
Cheese	„ ..	67	148	58
Lard	„ ..	277	214	126
Eggs	„ ..	..	29	97
Hardware..	„ ..	242	164	173

RETURN of Principal Articles of Export from Palermo during the
Year 1902 compared with the Years 1901–1900.

Articles.		Quantity.		
		1902.	1901.	1900.
Wines	Gallons ..	865,338	533,800	1,078,473
Olive oil	Tons ..	2,470	2,174	745
Essences and volatile oils	„ ..	52	72	58
Mustard seed	„ ..	115	94	30
Tomato paste	„ ..	1,454	949	418
Tartar	„ ..	1,842	1,538	..
Citrate of lime	„ ..	627	446	540
Liquorice root	„ ..	..	3	..
Manna	„ ..	91	86	109
Dried orange peel ..	„ ..	101	69	..
Lemon juice	„ ..	896	498	757
Liquorice juice	„ ..	39	34	38
Shumac	„ ..	24,503	22,206	..
Cork	„ ..	607	276	342
Hides	„ ..	124	134	99
Sulphur	„ ..	6,486	13,803	13,616
Grain, other than cereals..	„ ..	378	2,520	1,185
Macaroni	„ ..	526	805	421
Oranges, lemons	„ ..	102,875	61,729	46,600
Fresh vegetables ..	„ ..	67	185	104
Fish, sardines, anchovies..	„ ..	66	23	..
Cheese	„ ..	183	1,422	..
Fertilisers..	„ ..	353	145	..

RETURN of British Shipping engaged in the Indirect Carrying Trade of Foreign Countries and British Possessions at the Port of Palermo during the Year 1902.

ENTERED (WITH CARGO).

Countries whence Entered.	Number of Vessels.	Tons.
United Kingdom	63	89,900
Italy	215	286,899
France and French possessions..	1	1,994
Austria-Hungary	2	3,330
United States	4	5,689
Greece	5	7,837
Turkey	1	1,037
Total	291	396,686

CLEARED (WITH CARGO).

Countries to which Cleared.	Number of Vessels.	Tons.
United Kingdom	45	55,252
Italy	90	119,808
France and French possessions..	6	7,571
Austria-Hungary	3	4,581
United States	68	111,568
Greece	3	3,924
Turkey	21	30,140
Russia	2	4,594
Belgium	2	2,472
Spain	51	70,670
Total	291	410,580

MESSINA.

Mr. Acting Vice-Consul G. Vadalà reports as follows :—

In 1902 there was an increase in the import of coal into Messina Coal. of 6,027 tons compared with 1901, caused by the increased consumption of the railway and tramways running through Messina and Barcelona to the north of the town and Messina and Giampilieri to the south ; and also to gas lighting, which is becoming more and more general every year, and even electric lighting which has been introduced on the square of the municipality and in a few buildings. The amount imported from Norfolk, United States, was 7,225 tons in 1902, against 7,312 tons in 1901.

All other articles of importation show a decline in quantity as compared with the previous year, especially iron and steel, pig iron and maize.

The coal imported into Messina was carried by 50 steamships. Of these 15 were British vessels, 11 Austro-Hungarian, 7 Norwegian, 7 German, 2 Spanish, 2 Greek, 2 Italian, 3 Danish and 1 was Russian.

The following table shows the various places whence the coal came to Messina and the flag under which it was carried during the year 1902 :—

| Flag. | From— | | | | | | | Total Quantity per Flag. |
	Cardiff.	New-port.	Blyth.	New-castle.	Sunder-land.	Barry.	Norfolk, U.S.	
	Tons.	Tons.	Tons.	Tons.	Tons.	Tons.	Tons.	Tons.
British	12,358	14,645	...	4,680	...	2,036	...	33,719
Austro-Hungarian ...	20,814	3,138	...	...	...	...	...	23,952
Norwegian	4,048	...	5,694	...	4,948	...	...	14,690
German	3,656	4,407	3,417	...	...	...	...	11,480
Spanish	...	...	...	...	...	...	7,225	7,225
Greek	...	3,481	1,945	...	...	...	...	5,426
Italian	2,504	2,254	...	...	...	...	...	4,758
Danish	...	...	1,032	1,630	...	...	...	2,662
Russian	2,630	...	...	...	...	...	...	2,630
Total ...	45,410	27,925	12,088	6,310	4,948	2,036	7,225	105,942

The average price at Messina for coal during the year 1902 was 1l. per ton for Welsh coal and 19s. per ton for North Country coal.

Sulphates.

The following chemical products were exclusively imported from the United Kingdom in 1902 :—

| | Quantity. |
	Tons.
Sulphate of—	
Ammonia..	231
Copper ..	137
Sodium ..	126

Exportation.

Exportation shows an augmentation on the principal articles, viz., wine, olive oil, essences, wine lees, citrate of lime, raw silk, pumice stone, walnuts and filberts, and pickled orange and lemon peels.

Exports to the United Kingdom.

The principal exports to the United Kingdom comprised—

Articles.		Quantity.
Citric acid .	Tons ..	16
Citrate of lime	,, ..	1,146
Raw silk ..	Lbs. ..	26,400
Wine lees ..	Tons ..	2,150
Wine ..	Gallons	4,420
Oranges and lemons	Tons ..	7,378
Pickled orange and lemon peel ..	,, ..	8,127
Citrons in brine ..	,, ..	953

The population of the commune of Messina on December 31, 1902, was 157,886 persons, whilst at the census taken on February 10, 1901, it amounted to 152,878.

The trade in brined lemon and orange peels and lemon and orange skins plays an important part in the commerce of Messina. The method of pickling these peels is very simple. The lemons and oranges are brought down from the gardens to Messina, they are then cut in halves and put in pipes and filled up with sea water ; they are allowed to remain in the sea water for four or five days until the fruit ferments, they are then taken out and the sea water thrown away, the fruit is weighed into other pipes (350 kilos. or about 770 lbs. being put into each cask) and about 85 lbs. of Trapani salt is added, the pipes are then filled up with fresh sea water, and, after being re-coopered, the process is completed and the pipes are ready for shipment. In regard to lemon and orange skins the process is almost identical, with the exception that the pulp is taken out by means of a spoon, and the skins are packed into half pipes containing about 4 cwts. of skins net, and the quantity of salt added is about 40 lbs.

It is estimated that about 3,000 tons of pickled orange and lemon peels and orange and lemon skins are exported annually from the port of Messina. During the year 1902 3,796 tons were shipped to the United Kingdom, Austria-Hungary, United States of America, Germany, Australia, &c. The greater part of this fruit (3,427 tons) was shipped to the United Kingdom.

In the year 1902 the price for pipes of pickled lemon peels of about 770 lbs. weight varied from 16s. to 18s., and that of bitter orange peels was from 1l. to 1l. 1s. 6d., both f.o.b. Messina.

The best citrons for this purpose come from Pizzo, Paola, Cetraro, Cipollina and Diamante to the north of Sicily under the denomination of "Diamante citrons," and from Villa S. Giovanni, Catona and Gallico "Calabrian citrons." Citrons are sliced in half with their pulp. The dimensions of the pipes are as follows :—Length, 4 ft. 3 ins. ; diameter, 3 ft. 4 ins. Half pipes : length, 2 ft. 6 ins. ; diameter, 2 ft. 4 ins. About 44 gallons of salt water and 88 lbs. of salt are added to each 770 lbs. weight of peels. The half pipe contains from 440 to 485 lbs. of peels and 44 lbs. of salt. Diamante citrons weighing above 1 lb. (Sicilian) each cost 5l. 12s. per 770 lbs., those weighing above 2 lbs. (Sicilian) each, cost 6l. 7s. per 770 lbs. Calabrian citrons weighing 1 lb. (Sicilian) each cost 4l. 2s. per 770 lbs., whilst those weighing above 2 lbs. (Sicilian) each cost 4l. 12s. per 770 lbs. One Sicilian lb. is equivalent to 11¼ ozs.

The cotton mill at Messina employs about 300 persons, of whom 100 are women. Printed and white tissues, of an excellent quality, are manufactured, and are sold throughout the Kingdom of Italy. The cotton yarn used is imported from Venice and Naples. It is estimated that about 420 tons are manufactured every year.

A considerable trade in live quails takes place from this port to the United Kingdom. The birds are caught in the neigh- bourhood of Messina, chiefly at Faro, Massa San Giorgio to the north ; and at Galati, Giampilier, Santa Teresa and Santo Stefano to the south of the town. They are kept from three to four days in Messina in cages before being shipped, and are fed on hemp seed and ground corn and are watered freely every day. It is estimated that from 90,000 to 100,000 are caught annually by means of running nooses and traps. The price of the quails in Messina is from 45 c. to 50 c. per head. The birds are shipped in cages from Messina to Genoa, whence they are sent by rail viâ Chiasso to the United Kingdom. In October a few quails arrive in Messina from Egypt and Tripoli for transhipment to the United Kingdom.

RETURN of Principal Articles of Export from Messina during the Year 1902 compared with the Year 1901.

Articles.		Quantity.	
		1901.	1902.
Wine	Gallons ..	30,967	97,868
Olive oil..	Tons	1,360	1,906
Essences and volatile oils ..	,, ...	302	425
Tartaric acid	,, ...	1½	26
Citric acid	,, ...	79	27
Wine lees	,, ...	4,700	6,003
Citrate of lime	,, ...	870	2,260
Manna	,, ...	8½	4
Lemon juice, concentrated ..	,, ...	1,741	2,290
Liquorice juice..	,, ...	210	200
Hair, raw	,, ...	14¾	76
Silk —			
Raw	Lbs.	70,151	113,421
Waste..	,, ...	31,222	34,631
Hides—			
Raw	Tons	4½	15
Dry	,, ...	120	111
Pumice stone	,, ...	4,654	7,652
Sulphur	,, ...	20	¼
Chestnuts	,, ...	86	108
Bitter orange and lemon peel, in brine	,, ...	1,982	3,796
Oranges and lemons, in boxes..	,, ...	53,155	53,815
Citron, halved, in brine ..	,, ...	1,264	1,477
Pistachio	,, ...	34	21
Almonds—			
Shelled	,, ...	1,187	1,479
In the shell	,, ...	5	9
Walnuts and filberts	,, ...	2,437	3,532
Linseed..	,, ...	1	¼

RETURN of Principal Articles of Import into Messina during the Year 1902 compared with the Year 1901.

Articles.	Quantity.	
	1901.	1902.
	Tons.	Tons.
Linseed oil	22	19
Mineral oils (various)	164	99
Petroleum	1,267	1,018
Coffee	178	195
Sugar	8	129
Pepper and allspice	22	36
Caustic potash and soda	415	429
Carbonate of soda	37	43
Sulphate of—		
Ammonia	102	231
Copper	135	137
Soda	17	126
Argol and wine lees	43	38
Gum and resins	48	35
Esparto grass	170	294
Tissues—		
Cotton	17	18
Woollen	17	15
Cocoons	83	130
Timber—		
Common	½	1
Squared	20,400	22,750
Woods, cabinet	1	5
Hides—		
Raw	63	258
Dry	400	452
Pig iron	521	426
,, wrought	16	57
Iron and steel	2,700	1,017
Sheet iron	10	11
Copper, brass, and bronze manufactured articles	290	266
Cement and hydraulic lime	74	98
Fire bricks, tiles, &c.	9	17
Coal	99,915	105,942
Earthenware	4	6
Wheat	9,170	33,510
Maize	11,810	9,597
Seeds, non-oleaginous	65	69
Palm and cocoanut oil	30	144
Stockfish and codfish	1,770	2,987
Herrings	252	270
Fish, salted	2½	3
Cheese	58	19
Lard	166	78
Manure	79	35

RETURN of all Shipping at the Port of Messina during the Year 1902.

ENTERED.

Nationality.	Sailing.		Steam.		Total.	
	Number of Vessels.	Tons.	Number of Vessels.	Tons.	Number of Vessels.	Tons.
Italian	1,415	57,968	1,199	1,119,626	2,614	1,177,594
British	2	243	217	283,328	219	283,571
Austro-Hungarian	..	..	339	370,440	339	870,440
German	..	..	120	139,435	120	139,435
Greek	27	4,776	34	37,077	61	41,853
Norwegian ..	..	..	26	24,433	26	24,433
Dutch	..	..	31	21,718	31	21,718
Danish	..	..	25	17,113	25	17,113
Spanish	..	..	10	13,183	10	13,183
Russian	..	..	6	5,137	6	5,137
French	..	..	3	3,743	3	2,743
Swedish	..	..	5	3,373	5	3,373
Turkish .. , ..	16	2,692	1	76	17	2,768
Total ..	1,460	65,679	2,016	2,038,632	3,476	2,104,311

CLEARED.

Nationality.	Sailing.		Steam.		Total.	
	Number of Vessels.	Tons.	Number of Vessels.	Tons.	Number of Vessels.	Tons.
Italian	1,337	50,459	1,194	1,115,115	2,531	1,165,574
British	1	149	217	283,328	2,8	283,477
Austro-Hungarian	..	..	337	367,533	337	367,533
German	..	..	119	138,101	119	138,101
Greek	24	4,005	34	37,077	58	41,082
Norwegian ..	..	..	25	23,390	25	23,390
Dutch	..	..	31	21,718	31	21,718
Danish	..	..	25	17,113	25	17,113
Spanish	..	..	10	13,133	10	13,133
Russian	..	..	6	5,137	6	5,137
French	..	..	3	3,743	3	3,743
Swedish	..	..	5	3,373	5	3,373
Turkish	14	2,480	1	76	15	2,556
Total ..	1,376	57,093	2,007	2,028,837	3,383	2,085,930

RETURN of British Shipping engaged in the Indirect Carrying
Trade of Foreign Countries and British Possessions at the
Port of Messina during the Year 1902.

ENTERED.

Countries whence Entered.	With Cargo.		In Ballast.		Total.	
	Number of Vessels.	Tons.	Number of Vessels.	Tons.	Number of Vessels.	Tons.
Italy	133	166,896	14	22,112	147	189,008
Austria-Hungary	8	14,806	..	..	8	14,806
Greece	7	10,857	..	..	7	10,857
Roumania	3	5,990	..	..	3	5,990
Russia	3	4,849	..	..	3	4,849
Spain	..	..	2	3,800	2	3,800
Turkey	2	3,095	..	..	2	3,095
Egypt	1	1,885	..	..	1	1,885
France	..	..	1	1,795	1	1,795
Malta	..	..	1	1,721	1	1,721
Tunis	1	1,617	..	..	1	1,617
Newfoundland	2	243	..	..	2	243
Total	160	210,238	18	28,928	178	239,166

CLEARED.

Countries to which Cleared.	With Cargo.		In Ballast.		Total.	
	Number of Vessels.	Tons.	Number of Vessels.	Tons.	Number of Vessels.	Tons.
Italy	49	70,011	3	1,390	52	71,401
United States	26	36,558	..	..	26	36,558
Russia	1	1,714	7	11,543	8	13,257
Roumania	..	..	7	9,200	7	9,200
Canada	5	8,409	..	..	5	8,409
Spain	2	3,843	2	2,907	4	6,250
Turkey	..	..	4	5,700	4	5,700
Netherlands	2	3,974	..	..	2	3,974
Austria-Hungary	4	3,757	..	..	4	3,757
France	1	1,204	1	1,079	2	2,283
Belgium	1	2,208	..	..	1	2,208
Denmark	1	1,868	..	..	1	1,868
Germany	1	994	..	..	1	994
Total	93	134,040	24	31,819	117	165,859

CATANIA.

Mr. Vice-Consul Elford reports as follows :—

Sulphur.

The average price for best thirds brimstone during 1902 was 3l. 17s. 1d. per ton f.o.b. Catania.

Population.

The municipal returns show the population to be 153,743 in 1902.

Industries.
Petroleum.

The Società Francese dei Petroli, of Paris, are still actively conducting at Nicosia their researches for petroleum, and have one tube-well down 500 metres and another 100 metres, without so far finding any petroleum, although they have had an abundance of gas, and hope that their operations will be successful.

Spirit.

A distilling firm at Misterbianco, near Catania, is now erecting plant for the distillation of spirit from Indian corn ; this is quite a new industry in Sicily, and there are only four other similar establishments in Italy.

Cotton
spinning.

The owners of the cotton spinning mill, mentioned in my 1899 report, are about to double their plant by erecting another 200 horse-power gas engine and 5,000 spindles.

Agriculture.
Wheat.
Rice.
Wine.

There was a fair wheat crop of about 658,530 quarters.

The production of rice was about 118,300 bushels.

The production of wine in this province was very abundant, about 39,618,000 gallons.

Oil.

The quantity of oil produced was 8,253,750 gallons.

Harbour improvements.

The Government, recognising the growing importance of this port, have voted 140,000l. for the consolidation of the breakwater and the making of new quays. The present quays of the outer harbour have been properly paved and are now lighted by 12 arc lights, so that discharging can be conducted at night when necessary.

Municipality
bread.

The Town Council, decided in October last to municipalise the making and selling of bread, and, on October 17, the city was supplied with municipal bread, the daily production of which is 60 tons, principally machine-made. The public are supplied at about ½d. per lb. less than the average price paid during the previous five years. The municipality have established 15 depôts in the city ; some of the bakers have become municipal employés. their pay is about 6s. per day, and there are also many small retailers who retail the bread on 3 per cent. commission. The journeymen bakers under the municipality have improved pay and shorter hours. The municipality expect to realise an annual profit of 2,000l. Several cities have sent committees to study the working of the system, which gives great satisfaction to the public.

RETURN of Principal Articles of Import at Catania during the Years 1902-1901.

Articles.	1902.		1901.	
	Quantity.	Value.	Quantity.	Value.
	Tons.	£	Tons.	£
Petroleum	2,882	28,248	2,706	13,580
Colonials	179	7,949	182	8,649
Chemicals	4,853	95,314	2,332	15,267
Colour and dyes ..	1,141	2,844	4,265	35,936
Linen goods and yarns	97	2,619	74	5,012
Cotton „ „	451	23,666	452	40,468
Woollen „ „	59	23,270	43	22,188
Silk goods and „	0·378	600	1	2,700
Timber and furniture ..	26,595	100,251	22,262	51,592
Hides and skins ..	630	60,955	663	64 740
Iron and metals ..	1,787	15,241	2,864	48,666
Machinery	119	871	222	7,218
Glassware	1,871	83,561	224	927
Coals	90,310	102,533	76,263	93,210
Cereals and vegetable produce	53,720	446,391	28,625	301,380
Animals and their produce	502	17,798	679	26,804
Other articles	380	8,007	279	9,001
Total	..	1,020,118	..	747,338

RETURN of Principal Articles of Export from Catania during the Years 1902-1901.

Articles.		1902.		1901.	
		Quantity.	Value.	Quantity.	Value.
			£		£
Wine...	Gallons				
Cognac	„				
Marsala	„	1,518.218	65,905	1,375,761	41,744
Vermouth	„				
Beer	„				
Oil	„	325,028	60,940	137,359	25,735
Spirits	„	302	44	250	37
Colonials, drugs and tobacco ...	Tons ...	1,827	59,896	280	4,687
Wool...	„ ...	32	1,282	39	1,898
Argols, manna, liquorice root and lemon juice...	„ ...	1,825	83,505	1,085	39,636
Hemp, flax and jute	„ ...	14	692	58	2,980
Staves, casks and cork-wood ...	„ ...	183	17,839	35	1,567
Kid, skins and gloves	„ ...	162	28,242	58	3,755
Lava stone	„ ...	21,298	14,724	10,261	5,809
Asphalt and mastic	„ ...	6,441	10,345	456	9,600
Cereals	„ ...	4,118	69,653	1,586	13,668
Green and dry fruit	„ ...	5,879	118,608	10,158	366,952
Oranges and lemons	„ ...	93,655	536,603	75,216	333,984
Cheese, salt fish, &c.	„ ...	457	25,727	142	3,895
Sulphur	„ ...	107,040	546,754	160,672	597,451
Other articles	„ ...	296	16,333	10,560	54,200
Total	...	...	1,656.092	...	1,511,698

TABLE showing Total Value of all Articles Exported from and Imported into Catania to and from Foreign Countries during the Years 1902–1901.

Country.	Exports.		Imports.	
	1902.	1901.	1902.	1901.
	£	£	£	£
United Kingdom ..	240,222	185,269	137,902	176,284
France	69,047	164,314	28,142	13 800
Germany	186,733	151,724	36,884	21,000
United States	93,859	145,427	33,881	9,875
Austria-Hungary ..	366,925	364,294	224,704	138,459
Netherlands	208,138	96,659	42,260	15,780
Russia	83,224	78,270	224,770	288,670
Turkey	44,567	83,981	27,280	23,997
Greece	153,667	101,872	175,246	8,510
Other countries ..	209,910	139,888	89,050	55,963
Total	1,656,092	1,511,698	1,020,118	747,338

RETURN of all Shipping at the Port of Catania during the Year 1902.

ENTERED.

Nationality.	Sailing.		Steam.		Total.	
	Number of Vessels.	Tons.	Number of Vessels.	Tons.	Number of Vessels.	Tons.
British	..	..	139	179,517	139	179,517
Italian	1,954	78,507	984	807,714	2,938	881,221
German	..	..	112	123,437	112	123,437
Greek	64	11,823	26	32,718	90	44,541
Other nationalities	12	2,674	272	225,842	284	228,516
Total ..	2,030	88,004	1,533	1,369,228	3,563	1,457,232
,, 1901..	2,013	82,673	1,403	1,237,009	3,416	1,319,682

CLEARED.

Nationality.	Sailing.		Steam.		Total.	
	Number of Vessels.	Tons.	Number of Vessels.	Tons.	Number of Vessels.	Tons.
British	..	..	138	178,404	138	178,404
Italian	1,941	72,218	986	809,951	2,927	882,169
German	..	..	111	122,715	111	122,715
Greek	60	10,230	27	33,719	87	43,949
Other nationalities	12	2,592	272	224,658	284	227,250
Total ..	2,013	85,040	1,534	1,369,447	3,547	1,454,487
,, 1901..	2,014	81,944	1,398	1,231,867	3,412	1,313,811

RETURN of British Shipping engaged in the Indirect Carrying Trade of Foreign Countries and British Possessions at the Port of Catania during the Year 1902.

ENTERED.

Countries whence Entered.	With Cargo.		In Ballast.		Total.	
	Number of Vessels.	Tons.	Number of Vessels.	Tons.	Number of Vessels.	Tons.
United Kingdom and British Colonies ..	104	136,212	3	2,691	107	138,903
Italy	19	22,976	1	2,003	20	24,979
Austria-Hungary	10	14,618	1	1,588	11	16,206
Turkey	1	1,884	..	..	1	1,884
America	1	1,158	..	..	1	1,158
Africa	..	..	1	1,694	1	1,694
Total ..	135	176,848	6	7,976	141	184,824

CLEARED.

Countries to which Cleared.	With Cargo.		In Ballast.		Total.	
	Number of Vessels.	Tons.	Number of Vessels.	Tons.	Number of Vessels.	Tons.
United Kingdom and British Colonies ..	4	5,142	1	2,003	5	7,145
Italy	86	111,345	2	2,996	88	114,341
Austria-Hungary	26	35,328	..	..	26	35,328
Turkey	..	..	9	11,686	9	11,686
America	1	1,557	..	..	1	1,557
Africa	..	..	1	1,073	1	1,073
Russia	4	5,476	2	2,222	6	7,698
Denmark ..	1	1,226	..	..	1	1,226
Greece	1	1,229	1	1,134	2	2,363
Spain	..	..	1	1,192	1	1,192
Total ..	123	161,303	17	22,306	140	183,609

SYRACUSE.

Mr. Vice-Consul Lobb reports as follows :—

The value of imports for the year 1902 was 177,048*l.* and of the Trade and exports 263,560*l.*, as against 123,375*l.* and 199,290*l.* respectively commerce. for the year 1901.

Coals.

The quantity of coal imported from the United Kingdom during the year 1902 was 7,619 tons, as against 5,560 tons for the year 1901.

Oranges and lemons.

The total number of cases of lemons and oranges exported during the year 1902 was 69,863 for the United Kingdom and 119,833 for Austria-Hungary.

Pickled orange and lemon peel.

The total number of casks of pickled orange and lemon peel exported during the year 1902 was 12,472, of which 11,592 went to the United Kingdom and 880 to New York.

Carobs.

The yield of carobs in the province of Syracuse for the year 1902 was estimated to be about 45,000 tons. The chief markets are at Syracuse, Avola, Pozzallo and Mazzarelli.

Olive oil.

The olive crop for the year 1902 was somewhat better than that of 1901. The quantity is calculated to be 990,000 gallons and of excellent quality. The increase in quantity is attributed to the fact that the olive trees in most districts in the province of Syracuse were less infected with the olive fly (*Mosca olearia*) than in previous years.

Wine.

The quantity of wine produced in the province of Syracuse during the year 1902 was 12,381,600 gallons, as against 14,700,000 gallons for the year 1901. This diminution was caused by the peronospera, which attacked the vines in early spring and also by the scarcity of rain from the month of May up to the time of vintage.

Tunny fish.

The tunny fishery, which begins about May 1 and ends about September 15, gave the following results :—

Name of Fisheries.			Quantity.	Value.
			Tons.	£
Santa Panagia ..	..	..	301	4,816
Marina di Avola..	..	..	124	1,884
Marzamemi	..	..	266	4,256
Capo Passero (large and small)			278	3,336
Total ..	..	..	969	14,292

Olive husks.

The demand for husks of olive exceeded the supply. The quantity exported from the port of Syracuse was 6,203 tons, the price varying from 1l. 4s. to 1l. 8s. per ton f.o.b.

Tomato paste.

The quantity of tomato paste exported from Syracuse during the year 1902 was 488 tons. There is a new factory established at Melilli, a town 12 miles from Syracuse, for preparing and preserving in tins concentrated tomato sauce, whole tomatoes, peperoni (capsicums) and melanzane (egg plant). The quantity exported during the year 1902 was : tomato sauce, 120,000 tins of 1 lb. each ; peperoni (capsicums), 10,000 tins of 1 lb. each ; and 2,000 tins of melanzane (egg plant ; about one-third of the above quantities was exported to Glasgow.

Rock asphalt.

The exportation of asphalt was less than in the preceding year, the quantity shipped was :—

Rock Asphalt Shipped from Syracuse.

					Destination.							Total.
	London.	France.	Austria-Hungary.	Hamburg.	New York.	Italy.	Netherlands.	Russia.	Turkey.	Roumania.	Alexandria, Egypt.	
	Tons.	Tons.	Tons.	Tons.	Tons.	Tons.	Tons.	Tons.	Tons.	Tons.	Tons.	Tons.
Sicula Company..	860	8,820	1,150	2,500	8,140	10	4,050	12	10	100	..	15,152
H. and A. B. Aveline ..	500	..	..	300	..	..	..	..	..	..	..	800
French Company ..	3,902	2,500	300	100	..	470	300	..	..	..	260	7,832
Total	5,262	5,820	1,450	2,900	8,140	480	4,350	12	10	100	260	28,784

The above figures include 8,486 blocks of compressed bitumen, equal to 235 tons, and 20,194 sacks of pulverised asphalt rock equal to 1,014 tons, shipped by the Sicula Company to various destinations.

Rock Asphalt shipped from Mazzarelli.

	Destination.				Total.
	London.	Germany.	New York.	Austria-Hungary.	
	Tons.	Tons.	Tons.	Tons.	Tons.
The United Limmer ..	5,486	6,350	3,251	300	15,387
H. and A. B. Aveline..	..	5,050	..	..	5,050
French Company ..	..	5,050	90	..	5,140
Total	5,486	16,450	3,341	300	25,577

Grain.

The total quantity of grain produced in the province of Syracuse during the year 1902 was 61,000 tons.

Salt.

The quantity of salt exported from the salines of Augusta during the year 1902 was as follows :—

Salt shipped from Augusta.

Destination.					Quantity.
					Tons.
Italy	..	..	..		5,919
United Kingdom ..	..	..	..		690
Bulgaria	..	..	..		1,450
Germany	..	..	..		200
Malta	..	..	..		88
Roumania	..	..	..		600
Sweden and Norway	..	..	..		1,625
European Turkey ..	..	..	..		51
United States ..	..	..	..		7,605
Total ..	..	..			18,228

The salt sent to Italy was bought by the Italian Government.

Essential oil of lemon and orange.

The quantity of essential oil of orange and lemons produced at Syracuse and Avola and sent by railway to Messina, from where it is exported, was 20,000 lbs.

Water.

The supply of drinking water being insufficient for the requirements of the town, the municipality of Syracuse have been making active researches for water, and have found abundant supplies in the mountains of Canicattini-Bagni, a distance of 20 miles. The cost of bringing this water into the city, plant for distribution, &c., is estimated at 48,000l.

The public works completed during the year 1902 were : First, Public works.
a new market, its cost being 3,200*l*. It is constructed on the
most modern system, furnished with a good supply of fresh water,
good cellarage and electric light. Secondly, the interior of the
" Camera di Commercio " (Chamber of Commerce), the exterior
having been built about five years ago. It is a fine edifice,
situated in Via Duca degli Abruzzi and partly in Piazza Mazzini,
overlooking the port of Syracuse. One section of the buildingis
allotted to a school of commerce.

RETURN of Articles of Export from Syracuse during the Year
1902.

Articles.		To the United Kingdom and Colonies.		To other Countries.		Total.	
		Quantity.	Value.	Quantity.	Value.	Quantity.	Value.
			£		£		£
Wine	Gallons...	2,190	72	151,644	4,961	153,834	5,033
Olive oil	Tons ...	254	10,160	1,107	44,280	1,361	54,440
Lemons and oranges ...	,, ...	5,589	15,649	7,190	20,132	12,779	35,781
Lemon and orange peel, in brine	,, ...	5,796	7,419	440	563	6,236	7,982
Carobs	,, ...	725	2,320	1,227	3,926	1,952	6,246
Tomato paste	,, ...	59	2,124	429	15,444	488	17,568
Olives, in brine	,, ...	43	723	6	101	49	824
Olive husks	,, ...	...	...	6,203	7,445	6,203	7,445
Firewood	,, ...	2,695	1,617	33	19	2,728	1,636
Wheat	,, ...	...	...	2,269	21,419	2,269	21,419
Linseed	,, ...	...	...	533	17,056	533	17,056
Barley	,, ...	...	...	353	1,836	353	1,836
Oats	,, ...	...	...	164	1,512	164	1,512
Cereals	,, ...	...	...	436	4,360	436	4,360
Cheese	,, ...	59	2,360	76	3,040	135	5,400
Tunny—							
In oil	,, ...	2	108	143	7,722	145	7,830
In salt	,, ...	4	160	18	720	22	880
Asphalt, rock	,, ...	5,262	5,262	18,522	18,522	23,784	23,784
Almonds—							
Shelled	,, ...	1	72	338	24,336	339	24,408
In the shell	,, ...	...	...	4	57	4	57
Citrate of lime	,, ...	49	1,799	...	...	49	1,799
Concentrated lemon juice	,, ...	...	...	28	829	28	829
Vegetable fibre	,, ...	...	...	66	79	66	79
Lupins	,, ...	...	...	592	2,131	592	2,131
Rough wax	,, ...	...	...	27	3,510	27	3,510
Macaroni...	,, ...	...	...	11	176	11	176
Fresh—							
Fish	,, ...	73	2,920	...	...	73	2,920
Fruit	,, ...	242	1,936	...	...	242	1,936
Potatoes	,, ...	205	820	278	1,112	483	1,932
Sundries	,, ...	...	...	263	2,751	263	2,751
Total	...	...	55,521	...	208,039	...	263,560

RETURN of Articles of Import to Syracuse during the Year
1902.

Articles.				From the United Kingdom and Colonies.		From other Countries.		Total.	
				Quantity.	Value.	Quantity.	Value.	Quantity.	Value.
					£		£		£
Wine	...	...	Gallons	...	...	130,857	5,948	130,857	5,948
Marsala	...	...	,,	...	...	4,581	225	4,581	225
Vermouth	...	...	,,	...	...	989	48	989	48
Cognac	...	...	,,	...	...	60	22	60	22
Beer	...	...	,,	38	6	23	4	61	10
Spirits	...	...	,,	...	...	1,302	219	1,302	219
Coals	...	...	Tons	8,541	10,932	265	336	8,806	11,268
Coke	...	...	,,	811	1,297	963	1,540	1,774	2,837
Petroleum	...	...	Gallons	152	11	224,146	28,528	224,298	28,539
Olive oil	...	...	Tons	5	204	15	635	20	839
Charcoal	...	...	,,	...	...	404	1,616	404	1,616
Flour	...	...	,,	...	...	3,341	40,092	3,341	40,092
Wheat	...	...	,,	...	...	2,649	25,906	2,649	25,906
Indian corn	...	...	,,	...	...	92	662	92	662
Coffee	...	...	,,	1	150	22	3,300	23	3,450
Sugar	...	...	,,	2	120	233	13,980	235	14,100
Rice	...	...	,,	...	...	409	9,816	409	9,816
Macaroni	...	...	,,	...	...	92	1,472	92	1,472
Potatoes	...	...	,,	...	...	233	932	233	932
Timber	...	...	,,	12	29	4,455	10,692	4,467	10,721
Iron	...	...	,,	...	...	69	632	69	632
Tissue—									
Cotton	...	...	,,	...	...	36	5,760	36	5,760
Woollen	...	...	,,	...	...	18	5,832	18	5,832
Cotton and woollen	...	,,	...	...	4	928	4	928	
Hides and skins	...	...	,,	...	...	17	3,128	17	3,128
Sundries	...	...	,,	...	...	758	2,946	758	2,946
Total	...	...		...	12,749	...	164,299	...	177,048

TABLE showing Total Value of all Articles Exported from and
Imported to Syracuse to and from Countries during the
Year 1902.

Countries.					Value.	
					Exports.	Imports.
					£	£
United Kingdom and colonies				..	55,521	12,749
Italy	..	..	..	..	140,903	126,355
France	..	..	..	..	28,194	95
Germany	..	..	..	..	2,900	..
United States	..	..	..	..	3,703	6,987
Austria-Hungary		..	..	..	27,591	9,933
Netherlands	..	..	..	..	4,350	..
Russia	..	..	..	..	12	16,582
Greece	..	..	..	..	..	72
Tripoli	..	..	..	..	26	..
Turkey	..	..	..	..	260	165
Roumania	..	..	..	..	100	2,235
Brazil	..	..	..	..	..	1,875
Total	..	..			263,560	177,048

RETURN of all Shipping at the Port of Syracuse during the Year 1902.

ENTERED.

Nationality.	With Cargo.		In Ballast.		Total.		Value of Cargoes.
	Number of Vessels.	Tons.	Number of Vessels.	Tons.	Number of Vessels.	Tons.	
							£
British	2	2,521	39	48,029	41	50,550	7,618
Italian	541	153,362	165	73,171	706	226,533	167,870
Austro-Hungarian	1	238	327	187,017	328	187,255	1,440
German	...	...	12	13,397	12	13,397	...
Greek	1	144	...	...	1	144	120
French	...	...	1	1,445	1	1,445	...
Norwegian	...	...	2	1,944	2	1,941	...
Spanish	...	...	1	1,032	1	1,032	...
Total	545	156,265	547	326,035	1,092	482,300	177,048

CLEARED.

Nationality.	With Cargo.		In Ballast.		Total.		Value of Cargoes.
	Number of Vessels.	Tons.	Number of Vessels.	Tons.	Number of Vessels.	Tons.	
							£
British	39	48,029	2	2,521	41	50,550	29,479
Italian	529	166,563	146	53,009	675	219,572	194,962
Austro-Hungarian	327	187,017	1	238	328	187,255	27,223
German	12	13,397	...	...	12	13,397	8,427
Greek	...	...	1	144	1	144	...
French	1	1,445	...	...	1	1,445	2,500
Norwegian	2	1,944	...	...	2	1,944	1,367
Spanish	1	1,032	...	...	1	1,032	602
Total	911	419,427	150	55,912	1,061	475,339	263,560

RETURN of British Shipping engaged in the Indirect Carrying Trade of Foreign Countries and British Possessions at the Port of Syracuse during the Year 1902.

ENTERED.

Country.	With Cargoes.		In Ballast.		Total.	
	Number of Vessels.	Tons.	Number of Vessels.	Tons.	Number of Vessels.	Tons.
Italy	..	..	36	46,153	36	46,153
United Kingdom	2	2,521	..	..	2	2,521
Malta	..	..	3	1,876	3	1,876
Total ..	2	2,521	39	48,029	41	50,550

CLEARED.

Country.	With Cargoes.		In Ballast.		Total.	
	Number of Vessels.	Tons.	Number of Vessels.	Tons.	Number of Vessels.	Tons.
Italy	39	48,029	1	1,177	40	49,206
Russia	..	..	1	1,344	1	1,344
Total ..	39	48,029	2	2,521	41	50,550

MARSALA.

Mr. Vice-Consul Gray reports as follows :—

The return, as regards aggregate value of exports, is rather less than last year, but the return of imports shows a considerable increase.

The shipments of "Marsalas" are practically the same as last year, but the falling-off in shipments of common young wine (vino grezzo) continues.

During the first half of the year large quantities of poor wine, resulting from the abundant vintage of 1901, were used for distillation; but as this year's vintage was so short, there will be very little wine available for distilling.

There is still a falling-off in the return of vessels trading here, due to the diminished shipments of common young wine.

For the first time for a number of years, a cargo of salt has been shipped from here instead of from Trapani, but the vessel had to load outside the harbour. If money was spent in making the harbour deeper, a considerably larger trade would be carried on here.

Large quantities of wine lees are produced, but the amount cannot be calculated correctly, as they are sent by rail or sea to Messina and Trapani, whence they are exported, and consequently they do not figure in the statistics of this custom-house.

No further work has been done this year towards lengthening the new mole on the west side of the harbour.

The production of Marsala may be calculated in general at about half or a third less than last year, but the quality is considerably better and more alcoholic than that of last year's wines. Owing to the small production, prices are naturally higher than those of the previous vintage. Phylloxera continues its destructive course, so that, except in the case of the weather being specially favourable for the vines, the production must continue to decrease until the American vines, which are now being planted, begin to bear. There are numbers of small landowners here whose vines have been destroyed by phylloxera, and as they are unable to meet the expense of planting American vines, they have to resort to sowing cereals.

Annex A.—RETURN of all Shipping at the Port of Marsala
during the Year 1902.

ENTERED.

Nationality.	Sailing.		Steam.		Total.	
	Number of Vessels.	Tons.	Number of Vessels.	Tons.	Number of Vessels.	Tons.
British	11	779	16	20,211	27	20,990
German	..	..	3	3,160	3	3,160
Swedish and Nor-						
wegian.. ..	..	..	2	1,672	2	1,672
Danish	..	..	4	3,305	4	3,305
Dutch	..	..	1	747	1	747
Spanish	..	..	1	1,711	1	1,711
Greek	1	94	..	..	1	94
Tunisian	1	25	..	..	1	25
Italian	379	18,869	298	165,152	677	184,021
Total ..	392	19,767	325	195,958	717	215,725
,, 1901 ..	538	28,588	287	186,902	825	215,490

CLEARED.

Nationality.	Sailing.		Steam.		Total.	
	Number of Vessels.	Tons.	Number of Vessels.	Tons.	Number of Vessels.	Tons.
British	10	708	16	20,211	26	20,919
German	..	..	3	3,160	3	3,160
Swedish and Nor-						
wegian.. ..	..	..	2	1,672	2	1,672
Danish	..	..	4	3,305	4	3,305
Dutch	..	..	1	747	1	747
Spanish	..	..	1	1,711	1	1,711
Greek	1	94	..	..	1	94
Tunisian	1	25	..	..	1	25
Italian	379	18,604	298	165,152	677	183,756
Total ..	391	19,431	325	195,958	716	215,389
,, 1901 ..	537	28,360	287	186,902	824	215,262

Annex B.—RETURN of Principal Articles of Export from Marsala during the Years 1902-1901.

Articles.			1902.		1901.	
			Quantity.	Value.	Quantity.	Value.
				£		£
Wine (Marsala) ..	Pipes	..	21,205	318,075	21,184	317,760
,, (grezzo) ..	,,	..	15,501	52,703	27,823	83,469
Dried fruit	Cwts.	..	26	26	218	242
/ Cheese .. {	Tons	..	372	18,005	..	..
	Cwts.	..	..	..	375	1,125
Olive oil	,,	..	76	155	42	103
Salted fish	,,	..	48	55	28	32
Stone for building purposes	Tons	..	3,017	200	2,631	143
Salt	,,	..	690	1,380	..	..
Other articles ..	..		..	2,145		119
Total	..		..	392,744	..	402,993

RETURN of Principal Articles of Import into Marsala during the Years 1902-1901.

Articles.			1902.		1901.	
			Quantity.	Value.	Quantity.	Value.
				£		£
Wine (Mistel) ..	Gallons ..		66,998	4,120	..	..
Coffee and sugar {	Tons	..	40	2,778	..	..
	Cwts.	..	..	..	218	1,088
Pepper	,,	..	6	19	10	27
Cattle	Head	..	723	8,676	290	3,480
Coal..	Tons	..	4,753	4,951	1,359	2,174
Staves .. {	,,	..	8,404	26,894	..	..
	Thousand		..	..	866	8,947
Iron..	Tons	..	1,064	9,830	145	1,450
Sulphate of copper .	,,	..	..	..	15	420
Petroleum	,,	..	452	9,040	491	9,820
Hardware .. {	,,	..	21	430	..	..
	Cwts.	..	..	..	80	80
Cloth .. {	Tons	..	48	3,840	..	..
	Cwts.	..	..	..	6	24
Spirit	Pipes	..	1,025	10,250	799	7,990
Chemical manure ..	Tons	..	.	..	3	35
Wood for building purposes	,,	..	330	3,964	..	..
Cereals	,,	..	78	891	..	..
Other articles ..	..		..	1,020	..	621
Total	..		..	86,703	..	36,156

Annex C.—TABLE showing Total Value of all Articles Exported
from and Imported to Marsala to and from Foreign Countries
during the Years 1902–1901.

Country.	Exports.		Imports.	
	1902.	1901.	1902.	1901.
	£	£	£	£
United Kingdom and colonies ..	4٩,600	71,267	1,585	2,881
America	2,919	10,980	17,053	16,795
France	3,705	3,856	6	
Germany, Russia and Baltic	15,550	19,80٩	1,173	4,540
Italy	285,191	273,582	46,668	..
Tunis and other foreign counties	86,779	23,505	٤0,228	11,940
Total	392,744	402,993	86,703	36,156

TRAPANI.

Mr. Vice-Consul Marino reports as follows :—

The yield of marine salt from the Trapani Salines in 1902 Salt.
amounted to about 220,000 tons, which is a little higher than
the annual average. The salt has been sold at 5s. 6d. per ton.

According to the official custom-house statistics, 304,300 gallons Wine trade.
of wine were exported from Trapani in 1902 to the Continent
of Italy and abroad, against 130,220 gallons in 1901. The large
difference is due to the fact that this year some foreign speculators
purchased big lots of grapes while unripe on the vine, and at
the proper season they made the wine according to a special
method of their own. This is not the first time that such a specu-
lation has been made ; but in former years the wine so produced
has been shipped in other ports of the province, while this year
all the wine came to Trapani, where it was loaded on board several
steamships in order to spare unnecessary expenses.

The phylloxera continues to occasion immense damage all over Phylloxera.
this province.

The Italian Legislature has lately voted 24,000l. with which to Public works.
commence the works for a new breakwater to protect the port of
Trapani from the south-west and west.

During the year the erection of a lighthouse upon the Porcelli Lights.
Rocks has been proceeded with, and the building is nearly
completed.

The mercantile marine of Trapani has been considerably Mercantile
increased of recent years, and additional vessels are now being built. Marine.

In my report for 1901 I mentioned the labour disturbances, and Labour
now I am pleased to state that these have ceased. Certain con- disturbances.
cessions have been made to the working classes, but, owing to the
hardness of their lot, emigration to Tunis and other countries
continues.

RETURN of British and Foreign Shipping at the Port of Trapani during the Year 1902

ENTERED.

Nationality.	With Cargoes.		In Ballast.		Total.		Value of Cargoes.
	Number of Vessels.	Tons.	Number of Vessels.	Tons.	Number of Vessels.	Tons.	£
British	4	2,803	19	9,349	23	12,152	4,619
Italian	16	15,815	25	21,135	41	36,950	105,325
Norwegian	9	8,641	27	30,954	36	39,595	13,218
Greek	6	7,691	1	346	7	8,037	47,066
Russian	3	3,380	2	449	5	3,829	22,616
Swedish	..	..	1	3,806	1	3,806	..
Danish	2	1,831	1	102	3	1,933	2,728
German	1	923	..	..	1	923	923
Dutch	..	..	1	1,952	1	1,952	..
Spanish	..	..	2	645	2	645	..
Austro-Hungarian	1	368	2	1,095	3	1,463	200
Total	42	41,452	81	69,333	123	110,785	196,695

CLEARED.

| Nationality. | With Cargoes. | | In Ballast. | | Total. | | Value of Cargoes. |
	Number of Vessels.	Tons.	Number of Vessels.	Tons.	Number of Vessels.	Tons.	
							£
British ...	19	10,481	4	1,671	23	12,152	3,682
Italian ...	26	21,637	15	15,313	41	36,950	9,088
Norwegian ...	35	38,926	1	669	36	39,595	21,799
Greek ...	1	346	6	7,691	7	8,037	160
Russian ...	3	945	2	2,884	5	3,829	280
Swedish ...	1	3,306	..	..	1	3,306	925
Danish ...	3	1,933	..	..	3	1,933	1,200
German ...	..	..	1	923	1	923	..
Dutch ...	1	1,952	..	..	1	1,952	1,125
Spanish ...	1	491	1	154	2	645	222
Austro-Hungarian ...	2	1,095	1	368	3	1,463	495
Total	92	81,112	31	29,673	123	110,785	38,966

Annex B.—RETURN of Principal Articles of Export from Trapani during the Years 1902–1901.

Articles.			1902.		1901.	
			Quantity.	Value.	Quantity.	Value.
			•	£		£
Marine salt..	..	Tons ..	140.942	40,520	97,944	27,342
Wine	..	Gallons ..	304,300	45,645	130,220	19,533
Wood	..	Tons ..	61	134	91	200
Empty casks	..	Number..	4,967	1,118	3,374	759
Stone for building..		Tons ..	1,147	1,778	3,670	5,690
Alimentary paste	..	,, ..	89	1,424	62	992
Salt fish	..	,, ..	290	52,925	346	63,145
Cheese	..	,, ..	69	5,244	29	2,204
Esparto rope	..	,, ..	21	609	56	1,624
Beans of all kinds..		,, ..	131	1,048	345	2,760
Other articles	..	,, ..	..	..	1,622	3,580
Total ..	..	..	..	150,445	..	127,829

RETURN of Principal Articles of Import to Trapani during the Years 1902–1901.

Articles.			1902.		1901.	
			Quantity.	Value.	Quantity.	Value.
				£		£
Coals	..	Tons ..	25,158	25,158	19,393	23,270
Wheat	..	,, ..	17,609	140,872	17,431	139,448
Olive oil	..	,, ..	18	540	3	90
Mineral oil..	..	,, ..	270	7,560	301	8,428
Iron..	..	,, ..	19	266	..	..
Cotton goods	..	Lbs. ..	436	48	343	38
Woollen goods	..	,, ..	826	155	2,255	427
Esparto grass	..	Tons ..	31	434	14	196
Cattle	..	Number..	119	1,547	200	2,600
Horses, mules and donkeys ..	..	,, .	1,215	6,075	767	3,835
Salt fish	..	Tons ..	296	932	195	620
Sponges	..	Lbs. ..	6,992	1,748	2,222	555
Coffee	..	Tons ..	16	1,936	18	2,178
Seeds	..	,, ..	..	..	31	620
Staves, deals, planks, &c.	..	,, ..	3,346	45,170	2,997	40,846
Empty casks	..	Number..	77	14	383	67
Chloride of potash..		Tons ..	35	175	..	..
Sulphate of ammonia		,, ..	68	408	...	..
Other articles	..	,, ..	2,520	3,750	3,750	5,320
Total	..	..	..	236,788	...	228,538

Annex C.—TABLE showing Total Value of all Articles Exported
from and Imported into Trapani to and from Foreign Countries
during the Years 1902–1901

Country.	Exports.		Imports.	
	1902.	1901.	1902.	1901.
	£	£	£	£
United Kingdom	12,335	11,452	27,158	25,185
Turkey	24,000	42,200	41,230	42,920
Tunis	29,808	19,298	11,290	8,387
United States of America	17,989	7,300	48,580	48,032
Austria-Hungary	21,140	7,127	3,170	1,792
Norway and Sweden ..	31,799	24,226	..	..
Russia	2,280	2,023	101,372	96,724
Spain	1,270	850	..	..
Egypt	..	5,690	..	..
Germany	6,424	..	..	..
Other countries	3,400	7,663	3,988	5,498
Total	150,445	127,829	236,788	228,538

RETURN of British Shipping engaged in the Indirect Carrying Trade of Foreign Countries and British Possessions at the Port of Licata during the Year 1902.

ENTERED.

Countries whence Entered.	With Cargoes.		In Ballast.		Total.	
	Number of Vessels.	Tons.	Number of Vessels.	Tons.	Number of Vessels.	Tons.
United Kingdom	6	6,029	..	..	6	6,029
Italy	..	..	9	12,837	9	12,837
Turkey	..	..	1	1,694	1	1,694
Total ..	6	6,029	10	14,531	16	20,560

CLEARED.

Countries to which Cleared.	With Cargoes.		In Ballast.		Total.	
	Number of Vessels.	Tons.	Number of Vessels.	Tons.	Number of Vessels.	Tons.
United Kingdom	2	3,116	..	..	2	3,116
United States of America ..	5	8,137	..	..	5	8,137
Sweden	3	3,415	..	..	3	3,415
Italy	..	..	2	1,930	2	1,930
Russia	1	927	1	871	2	1,798
Spain	..	..	1	1,035	1	1,035
Turkey	..	..	1	1,129	1	1,129
Total ..	11	15,595	5	4,965	16	20,560

RETURN of British Shipping engaged in the Indirect Carrying Trade of Foreign Countries and British Possessions at the Port of Girgenti during the Year 1902.

ENTERED.

Countries whence Entered.	With Cargoes.		In Ballast.		Total.	
	Number of Vessels.	Tons.	Number of Vessels.	Tons.	Number of Vessels.	Tons.
United Kingdom	7	8,441	..	..	7	8,441
Italy	..	..	23	32,489	23	32,489
Austria-Hungary	..	..	8	10,837	8	10,837
Egypt	..	..	2	3,606	2	3,606
Greece	..	..	1	1,075	1	1,075
Total ..	7	8,441	34	48,007	41	56,448

CLEARED.

Countries to which Cleared.	With Cargoes.		In Ballast.		Total.	
	Number of Vessels.	Tons.	Number of Vessels.	Tons.	Number of Vessels.	Tons.
United Kingdom	9	11,511	1	814	10	12,325
United States of America ..	22	33,450	..	..	22	33,450
Sweden	1	1,174	..	..	1	1,174
Germany.. ..	1	1,058	..	..	1	1,058
Turkey	..	..	4	4,930	4	4,930
Greece	..	..	1	1,086	1	1,086
Italy	..	..	1	1,252	1	1,252
Russia	..	..	1	1,173	1	1,173
Total ..	33	47,193	8	9,255	41	56,448

LONDON :
Printed for His Majesty's Stationery Office,
By HARRISON AND SONS,
Printers in Ordinary to His Majesty.
(1400   9 | 03 — H & S   374)

No. 3081.   Annual Series.

CHINA.

DIPLOMATIC AND CONSULAR REPORTS.

TRADE OF

W U H U

FOR THE YEAR 1902.

FOREIGN OFFICE,
September, 1903.

No. 3081 Annual Series.

DIPLOMATIC AND CONSULAR REPORTS.

CHINA.

REPORT FOR THE YEAR 1902

ON THE

TRADE OF WUHU.

REFERENCE TO PREVIOUS REPORT, Annual Series No. 2802.

Presented to both Houses of Parliament by Command of His Majesty,
SEPTEMBER, 1903.

LONDON:
PRINTED FOR HIS MAJESTY'S STATIONERY OFFICE,
BY HARRISON AND SONS, ST. MARTIN'S LANE,
PRINTERS IN ORDINARY TO HIS MAJESTY.

And to be purchased, either directly or through any Bookseller, from
EYRE & SPOTTISWOODE, East Harding Street, Fleet Street, E.C.,
and 32, Abingdon Street, Westminster, S.W.;
or OLIVER & BOYD, Edinburgh;
or E. PONSONBY, 116, Grafton Street, Dublin.

1903.

[Cd. 1766—15].   *Price One Halfpenny.*

CONTENTS.

———◆———

Reference to previous Report, Annual Series No. 2802.

Report on the Trade of Wuhu for the Year 1902

By Mr. Consular-Assistant V. L. Savage.

(Wuhu, June 29, 1903 ; received at Foreign Office, August 10, 1903.)

The total value of the foreign trade of Wuhu during the year Total value of 1902 was 2,490,966*l.*, as compared with 1,977,007*l.* in 1901, an the trade. improvement of 513,959*l.* The depreciation of silver having brought down the average value of the Haikuan tael to 2*s.* 7½*d.*, as compared with 2*s.* 11*d.*, the rate at which the values of 1901 were computed ; an addition of 14 per cent. should be made to the above increase for purposes of correct comparison.

The total value of the trade in Haikuan taels was second only Low rate of to that of 1899, and was over 1,000,000 taels in excess of exchange to that of 1900. The following table, which shows the highest figures be taken into reached hitherto, may serve to indicate to what extent allowance account. must be made, under existing circumstances, for the variations of exchange in comparing the trade of any one year with that of other years :—

Year.	At per Haikuan Tael—	Value of Total Trade.	
		Currency.	Sterling.
	s. d.	Haikuan taels.	£
1899	3 1¼	20,305,440	3,045,816
1900	2 11¼	18,181,986	2,814,235
1901	2 11	13,327,718	1,977,007
1902	2 7⅙	19,161,280	2,490,966

The imports for 1902 show a decline all round, when their value is converted into sterling, as compared with 1901.

The higher total is, therefore, entirely due to a large increase in Rice, a good exports, the result of an excellent rice crop. For several months crop. in the autumn Wuhu was the principal granary for Southern China, where the rice crop was a failure in many districts. The supplies of rice usually conveyed to Swatow and Canton by steamer from Annam and Siam had also apparently fallen below the average.

The total export of rice from Wuhu amounted to some 259,281 tons, representing a value of 1,178,537l., or approximately 75 per cent. of the total export trade.

Large as this amount is, it falls considerably short of the total export of rice in 1899 and 1900, although the crop was, to all appearances, a full one. The action of the Chinese authorities in imposing an extra likin of 1 mace per picul on rice for export on the ground that, in view of the comparative failure of the crop in the Lüchou Fu district from drought, precautions had to be taken to prevent rice leaving the port in too great a quantity and too rapidly for safety, was, no doubt, the reason why the export of rice did not reach a total amount comparable with that of previous good rice years.

Shipping.

As will be seen by the table given in Annex I appended to this report, 2,086 vessels cleared from the port during the year 1902 with a total tonnage of 2,302,445, as compared with 2,020 vessels with a tonnage of 2,104,763 in 1901. Of this tonnage 50 per cent. was British, 19 per cent. German, 17 per cent. Chinese, 13 per cent. Japanese and 1 per cent. Norwegian and Danish. These figures correspond closely to those of last year, except that the tonnage of Japanese shipping has increased by 4 per cent. at the expense of British and German shipping.

In value of cargo, however, the figures tell a different tale, British shipping leading far ahead, as the following table shows :—

Nationality.				Value of Cargo.	
				1901.	1902.
				Per cent.	Per cent.
British ..	..	..	..	64	72
German ..	..	..	..	14	10
Chinese ..	..	..	..	17	7
Japanese..	..	..	..	5	4
Norwegian	..	..	..	..	7
Total	..	..		100	100

There is also, therefore, a noticeable increase in the Norwegian shipping, the number of ships in 1902 being 15, as against 2 in 1901.

Imports.
Opium.

Of the imports, Indian opium has declined in value by nearly 70,000l., notwithstanding the failure of the opium crop in Ssuch'uan. This considerable decrease suggests that the import of foreign opium varies a good deal *pari passu* with the exchange rate of silver ; for the usual effect of a good rice crop is to increase the demand for the foreign drug.

Native opium.

On the other hand, native opium, of which only four chests passed through the hands of the Imperial Maritime Customs last year, shows an improvement, 46 cwts., valued at 15,929l., having been imported in 1902.

Cottons.

Cottons have maintained themselves notwithstanding the fall

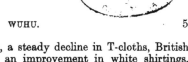

in silver. There is, however, a steady decline in T-cloths, British sheetings and chintzes, and an improvement in white shirtings, dyed and figured brocades, drills and lastings. Particularly noteworthy is the manner in which American sheetings are rapidly superseding the British article, which is said to be of lower quality. Within the last three years the import of British sheetings has declined from 89,710 to 54,629 pieces, while Americans have risen from 2,000 to 20,625 pieces.

Indian yarn has further improved, while Japanese has declined. The British yarn has become a negligible quantity altogether. Yarn.

Woollen piece-goods have decreased slightly all round. Woollens.

The importation of kerosene oil has fallen off a good deal this Kerosene oil. year as compared with 1901 and previous years. The total amount imported was 2,389,390 gallons against 3,105,720 gallons last year. Sumatra oil has improved by 171,000 gallons, while Russian fell from 1,065,500 to 646,790 gallons. American oil, however, still retains its hold of the market with 1,307,100 gallons, or 55 per cent. of the total oil imported.

The next item which calls for special notice is sugar, the total Sugar. of 188,370 cwts. being the highest on record. White refined sugar Foreign. especially seems to have found favour in the neighbouring markets, the import this year having risen by about 33 per cent. as compared with 1901. Sales of sugar have improved considerably of late, thanks to a system of Chinese agencies which have been established at various places in the interior in connection with a British firm, for the special purpose of selling foreign sugar wholesale. Some opposition was made at first by likin officials, but it has been, so far, successfully overcome in most cases.

The decline in the import of native sugar continues, the total Native. amount imported in 1902 being 75,224 cwts., as against 107,213 cwts. in 1901.

With regard to other native imports, the most noteworthy are native cloth and nankeens, which have increased by some 8,000l. On the other hand, native cotton yarn shows a falling-off Native yarn. of over 8,000 cwts. valued at some 15,079l.

Chief among the exports this year, after rice, the staple article, Exports. is wheat, the total export of which, 389,760 cwts., is more than Wheat. double that of any other year except 1900, when it was 203,306 cwts. This considerable increase is traceable, of course, to the favourable climatic conditions which resulted in a full rice crop ; but it was also due to the small demand for groundnuts from Wuhu, which has induced the farmers to sow wheat and rape in larger quantities as a substitute for the groundnut. Thus 194,620 cwts. of rape seed Rape seed. were exported during the year, a total which falls short of last year's exportation of this article by over 86,200 cwts., but which is, nevertheless, nearly treble the largest amount previously exported. On the other hand, the export of sesamum seed shows a considerable falling-off, as also that of beans, of which only Beans. 30,580 cwts. were exported. This is the lowest total on record, with the exception of that of 1897.

Of the remaining exports flour, from the Wuhu rice and flour Flour. mill, has improved, so also has tobacco leaf, while feathers, medicines, coal, hemp, paper, tea and prepared tobacco are normal.

The export of albumen shows a further decline. There is only one factory still working which is a foreign one. The prohibition of the import of foreign salt and boracic mixture is still enforced, and makes the cost of production of albumen unduly high, but the chief cause of the decline this year was the comparative scarcity and consequent high price of eggs.

On the whole the trade of Wuhu is flourishing, although the port itself is somewhat severely handicapped by local conditions. The scarcity of godowns and their unsuitable position, the necessity for the use of cargo boats, of which the number is at times insufficient, the danger to steamers from huge and unwieldy rafts floating down the river, and the delays in loading and unloading ships occasioned by the accumulation of native boats which seek the shelter of the creek in windy weather and block the passage of the cargo boats ; all these adverse circumstances are so many obstacles in the way of the progress of the port and the development of its trade. The anxiety of the larger foreign firms to secure a footing on the foreshore upon the site long ago set apart for a foreign settlement, is growing ; and it is to be hoped that the opposition of the officials and others to the establishment of this much needed settlement and to the legitimate use by foreigners of their treaty right to buy land within the port limits may ultimately be overcome.

In conclusion I have to acknowledge the courtesy of the Commissioner of Customs for the use of statistics compiled in his office prior to their publication.

Annex I.—RETURN of all Shipping at the Port of Wuhu during the Year 1902.

ENTERED.

Nationality.	Steam.		Sailing.		Total.		Total Value of Cargo.
	Number of Vessels.	Tons.	Number of Vessels.	Tons.	Number of Vessels.	Tons.	
							£
British	967	1,147,712	1	827	968	1,148,539	589,583
Chinese	255	370,408	256	24,748	511	395,156	231,193
German	392	448,701	...	...	392	448,701	101,647
Japanese	204	297,103	1	1,145	205	298,248	139,319
Norwegian	15	13,177	...	...	15	13,177	1,337
Danish	1	1,158	...	...	1	1,158	...
Total	1,834	2,278,259	258	26,720	2,092	2,304,979	1,063,079
,, 1901	1,732	2,068,753	270	30,087	2,002	2,098,841	1,155,362

CLEARED.

Nationality.	Steam.		Sailing.		Total.		Total Value of Cargo.
	Number of Vessels.	Tons.	Number of Vessels.	Tons.	Number of Vessels.	Tons.	
							£
British	968	1,148,272	1	347	969	1,148,619	1,032,769
Chinese	254	369,087	250	24,221	504	393,648	95,222
German	392	448,701	...		392	448,701	140,578
Japanese	204	297,103	1	319	205	297,422	55,192
Norwegian	15	13,177	...	...	15	13,177	95,572
Danish	1	1,158	...	...	1	1,158	8,599
Total	1,834	2,277,498	252	24,947	2,086	2,302,725	1,427,932
,, 1901 ...	1,737	2,074,901	283	29,862	2,020	2,104,763	821,645

Annex II.—RETURN of Principal Articles of Export from Wuhu during the Years 1902–1901.

Articles.			1902.		1901.	
			Quantity.	Value.	Quantity.	Value.
				£		£
Beans	Cwts.	...	30,580	6,863	88,014	18,538
Coal	Tons	...	1,143	941	1,626	1,527
Egg albumen, preserved...	Cwts.	...	83	251	102	346
,, yolk, preserved	,,	...	561	277	712	394
Feathers	,,	...	24,723	27,067	28,121	29,844
Groundnuts	,,	...	22,938	6,415	57,576	16,496
Hemp	,,	...	6,546	4,652	7,170	6,026
Paper	,,	...	3,290	11,295	3,120	8,742
Rice	Tons	...	259,281	1,178,537	138,358	545,723
Seed, rape	Cwts.	...	194,635	45,291	280,907	59,619
,, sesamum	,,	...	9,431	3,436	13,542	4,911
Silk, raw, white	Lbs.	...	47,066	12,746	184,933	48,347
Tea	,,	...	108,933	2,567	87,867	2,281
Wheat	,,	...	387,760	72,429	166,644	30,259
Sundries, unenumerated...	...	...	...	55,165	...	42,968
Total	...	...	...	1,427,932	...	816,021

Annex III.—RETURN of Principal Articles of Import into Wuhu during the Years 1902–1901.

Articles.			1902.		1901.	
			Quantity.	Value	Quantity.	Value.
				£		£
FOREIGN GOODS.						
Opium, Malwa	Lbs.	...	176,395	137,350	263,733	205,007
,, Patna	,,	...	266	236	320	260
Total opium ...	,,	...	176,661	137,586	264,053	205,267
Cotton goods—						
Shirtings, grey, plain ...	Pieces	...	106,399	64,172	119,860	61,594
,, white ...	,,	...	59,800	32,797	51,885	27,688
T-cloths	,,	...	7,250	2,331	11,714	3,506
Drills	,,	...	20,550	12,626	17,920	11,689
Sheetings... ...	,,	...	75,254	36,565	64,117	33,136
Chintzes, &c. ... }	,,	...	14,430 {	317	1,550	518
Cotton prints ...				4,268	16,222	6,164
Turkey-reds	,,	...	9,785	3,241	10,200	3,800
Cotton lastings and Italians ...	,,	...	34,096	22,917	28,064	23,518
Yarn, British	Cwts.	...	46	119	18	49
,, Indian	,,	...	43,769	110,484	38,961	102,474
,, Japanese	,,	...	10,900	27,512	12,649	29,422
Other cotton goods ...	...	...	...	8,761	...	12,982
Total cottons	...	...	...	316,110	...	316,540

RETURN of Principal Articles of Import into Wuhu during the
Years 1902–1901—continued.

Articles.			1902.		1901.	
			Quantity.	Value.	Quantity.	Value.
				£		£
FOREIGN GOODS—continued.						
Woollen goods—						
Camlets, British... ...	..	Pieces ...	1,190	1,916	1,250	2,237
Long ells...	...	,, ...	5,655	4,075	6,655	5,489
Italian cloth	...	,, ...	1,273	1,070	1,050	1,467
Other woollen goods ...	...	...	...	13,747	...	11,667
Total woollens ...	...	...	...	20,808	...	20,860
Miscellaneous piece-goods	...	...	...	801	...	461
Metals	...	...	...	19,474	...	18,514
Sundries—						
Bags, gunny and hemp } ,, straw and mat ...	...	Pieces ...	4,889,171	51,415	3,140,730	18,085
Matches	...	Gross ...	367,510	12,990	369,580	15,428
Oil, kerosene, American	..	Gallons ...	1,307,100	28,716	1,685,720	47,886
,, Russian	...	,, ...	646,790	12,253	1,065,500	25,328
,, Sumatra	...	,, ...	425,500	5,735	254,500	4,926
Sandalwood	...	Cwts. ...	18,354	19,159	14,452	17,185
Sugar	...	,, ...	188,360	110,092	135,430	91,289
Umbrellas	...	Pieces ...	54,537	6,349	63,864	8,057
Sundries, unenumerated	...	...	...	63,065	...	70,695
Total sundries ...	...	...	...	309,774	...	298,879
Re-exported foreign goods	...	...	...	2,725	...	...
Total foreign goods	...	...	...	806,278	...	860,521
NATIVE GOODS.						
Bags, gunny and hemp, old	...	Pieces ...	...	4,964	271,596	1,992
Cloth, native and nankeens	...	Cwts. ...	9,712	48,202	8,506	45,786
Coal	...	Tons ...	5,801	4,922	5,425	5,429
Cotton yarn, Chinese ...	...	Cwts. ...	6,757	16,255	13,649	31,334
Fans, paper... ...	...	Pieces ...	1,655,110	2,475	349,466	3,330
Grass-cloth...	...	Cwts. ...	1,271	5,582	1,806	11,684
Gypsum	...	,, ...	45,818	4,194	64,144	6,633
Lung-ngans (dried fruit)...	...	,, ...	4,125	5,626	1,630	2,901
Medicines	...	...	...	4,803	...	4,038
Oil, bean, tea, sesamum ...	...	Cwts. ...	5,242	6,430	5,582	5,164
,, wood	...	,, ...	18,238	15,930	15,900	16,338
Opium (Yünnan)	...	,, ...	46	15,929	5	224
Paper	...	,, ...	2,340	6,567	...	5,290
Samshu (spirits) ...	...	,, ...	3,525	2,562	2,545	1,539
Seeds, melon	...	,, ...	6,664	4,695	7,437	6,064
Silk goods	...	,, ...	215	10,948	...	11,816
Sugar	...	,, ...	75,224	58,698	107,213	80,203
Tobacco	...	,, ...	8,275	7,268	7,751	9,470
Wood poles	...	Pieces ...	26,752	9,082	17,264	6,427
Sundries, unenumerated...	...	...	...	20,443	...	27,420
Total native goods	...	...	...	255,575	...	283,073
,, imports ...	...	...	...	1,061,853	...	1,143,594

LONDON :
Printed for His Majesty's Stationery Office,
By HARRISON AND SONS,
Printers in Ordinary to His Majesty.
(1400 9 | 03—H & S 373)

No. 3082.   Annual Series.

AUSTRIA-HUNGARY.

DIPLOMATIC AND CONSULAR REPORTS.

TRADE OF

F I U M E

FOR THE YEAR 1902.

FOREIGN OFFICE,
September, 1903.

No. 3082 Annual Series.

DIPLOMATIC AND CONSULAR REPORTS.

AUSTRIA-HUNGARY.

REPORT FOR THE YEAR 1902

ON THE

TRADE AND COMMERCE OF FIUME.

REFERENCE TO PREVIOUS REPORT, Annual Series No. 2895.

Presented to both Houses of Parliament by Command of His Majesty,
SEPTEMBER, 1903.

LONDON:
PRINTED FOR HIS MAJESTY'S STATIONERY OFFICE,
BY HARRISON AND SONS, ST. MARTIN'S LANE,
PRINTERS IN ORDINARY TO HIS MAJESTY.

And to be purchased, either directly or through any Bookseller, from
EYRE & SPOTTISWOODE, EAST HARDING STREET, FLEET STREET, E.C.,
and 32, ABINGDON STREET, WESTMINSTER, S.W.;
or OLIVER & BOYD, EDINBURGH;
or E. PONSONBY, 116, GRAFTON STREET, DUBLIN.

1903.

[Cd. 1766—16.]   *Price One Penny.*

CONTENTS.

———◆———

————

NOTE.—For purposes of this report the word "average" implies the average of the last five years, unless otherwise stated.

Reference to previous Report, Annual Series No. 2895.

Report on the Trade and Commerce of Fiume for the Year 1902

By Mr. Consul Faber.

(Fiume, July 31, 1903 ; received at Foreign Office, August 7, 1903.)

Trade was influenced by and is still suffering under the intense *Preliminary.* political tension and the uncertainty due to the suspense in the conclusion of the financial and customs accord (Ausgleich) between Austria and Hungary and the treaties of commerce with foreign countries. If the political tension is not brought to an early conclusion an acute commercial crisis can hardly be avoided in the near future.

Exports amount to 750,000 tons (decrease 37,000 tons) in *General trade.* weight and 6,460,000*l.* (decrease 432,000*l.*) in value ; and imports to 355,000 tons (decrease 45,000 tons) in weight and 3,678,000*l.* (decrease 227,000*l.*) in value.

The shipment of remounts to South Africa amounted to 36,258 *Remounts.* (increase 19,232), and account for 755,000*l.* of the above exports in 1902 and 370,000*l.* in 1901, so that the actual value of exports would appear to be (deducting the remounts) 6,522,000*l.* in 1901 and 5,705,000*l.* in 1902, a decrease of 817,000*l.*, or 12½ per cent. for the year.

Exports to the United Kingdom and British colonies have risen *Exports to* from 2,073,000*l.* in 1901 to 2,375,000*l.* in 1902, and deducting the *British* value of remounts as above, the amounts are 1,703,000*l.* in 1901 and *Empire.* 1,620,000*l.* in 1902.

Imports from the United Kingdom and British colonies have *Imports from* risen from 1,140,000*l.* in 1901 to 1,427,000*l.* in 1902, an increase of *British* 25 per cent. *Empire.*

In this amount nine steamers built in the United Kingdom for Austro-Hungarian steamship companies figure for 485,000*l.*, as against three steamers in 1901 valued at 127,000*l.*, which would account for more than the whole increase in the value of imports.

The percentage of British trade is 37½ per cent. (increase 7½ per *Percentage of* cent. of the total trade), and 47 per cent. (increase 10 per cent.) *British trade.* of the foreign trade (excluding the national coasting trade, which is one-fifth of the total sea-borne trade).

The percentage of foreign countries in the foreign trade is as *Percentage of* follows : Italy, 16 ; France, 12 ; Turkey, 5 ; and sundries, 20. *foreign trade.*

Shipping has increased as follows, viz. : Entries in 1902, *Shipping.*

1,964,000 tons, an increase of 205,000 tons, of which 85,000 tons were British ; 139,000 tons Austro-Hungarian ; and 36,000 tons local ; other flags show a decrease of 55,000 tons.

Values of cargoes under the British flag.

As regards the values of cargoes under the British flag, we find—

					Value.
					£
Entered	..	..	..	..	700,000
Cleared	..	..	..	..	1,485,000
	Total	..	..	..	2,185,000
	„ 1901	..	..	..	1,818,000
	Average ..	..	..	..	1,857,000

of which was—

DIRECT TRADE.

				Value.	
Year.				Entered.	Cleared.
				£	
1902	..	..	..	507,000	1,350,000
1901	..	..	..	522,000	860,000
	Average	..	..	610,000	812,000

CARRYING TRADE.

				Value.	
Year.				Entered.	Cleared.
				£	£
1902	..	..	..	193,000	135,000
1901	..	..	..	196,000	240,000
	Average	..	..	170,000	270,000

SHIPPING Trade with India under the British Flag.

Year.						Value Entered.
						£
1902 ..	..	..	..	..	..	303,000
1901 ..	..	..	..	..	..	303,000
	Average ..	..	..			330,000

SHIPPING Trade with India under the Austro-Hungarian Flag.

Year.				Value.	
				Entered.	Cleared.
				£	£
1902	..	..	..	380,000	384,000
1901	..	..	..	370,000	760,000
Average	..	..		330,000	520,000

The exports to India, and the greater bulk of the imports, with a tendency to increase, are carried entirely under the Austro-Hungarian flag, owing to shipping bounties and the refund of Suez Canal dues.

The percentage of British tonnage is 18 per cent. (increase 3 per cent.) and of values of cargoes under the British flag, $21\frac{1}{2}$ per cent. (increase $4\frac{1}{2}$ per cent.), but this increase is due to the remount business which is temporary.

The British trade was disposed as follows :— British trade.

	Value.	
	Imports.	Exports.
	£	£
Under the British flag	512,000	1,359,000
„ Austro-Hungarian flag	557,000	1,025,000
Nine steamers bought in the United Kingdom	358,000	..
Total	1,427,000	2,375,000

These figures comprise—

TRADE with India and Burmah.

Year.				Value.	
				Imports.	Exports.
				£	£
1902	..	..	..	685,000	385,000
1901	..	..	..	723,000	760,000
Average	..	..		700,000	520,000

TRADE with the United Kingdom and British Colonies.

Year.					Value.	
					Imports.	Exports.
					£	£
1902	..	..	..	..	742,000	1,990,000
1901	..	..	..	..	414,000	1,313,000
Average		..		..	410,000	1,270,000

Imports from the United Kingdom.

The imports from the United Kingdom comprise : coal, 55,000 tons (increase 12,000 tons), ships (9), 485,000£. (increase 358,000£.), iron and steel goods, 2,100 tons ; tobacco, 400 tons ; cocoanut and palm oils, 650 tons ; cotton goods and yarn, 500 tons ; machinery, 320 tons ; chemicals, 400 tons ; copper ; vitriol ; various metals ; lubricating oils, &c. Total, 62,000 tons and nine ships.

Imports from India.

Imports from India were : rice, 52,000 tons ; jute, 11,000 tons ; cotton, 2,000 tons ; indigo , pepper ; cocoanut oil ; superphosphates. Total, 67,000 tons.

Exports to the United Kingdom.

The exports to the United Kingdom comprise : flour, 41,000 tons (increase 3 per cent.) ; sugar, 34,000 tons (increase 29 per cent.) ; oak extract, 16,000 tons (increase 3 per cent.) ; barley, 21,000 tons (increase 8 per cent.) ; lumber, 20,000 tons (increase 5 per cent.) ; mineral waters, 500 tons ; hemp, 250 tons ; starch, 1,700 tons ; chemicals, 1,000 tons ; magnesite and magnesite bricks, 730 tons ; prunes, 450 tons ; paper ; cellulose ; bentwood furniture, &c. ; Total, 141,000 tons.

Exports to India.

Exports to India were : sugar, 43,000 tons (decrease, 21 per cent. ; hardware ; lumber ; flour ; glassware ; paper ; &c. Total, 46,000 tons.

Exports to South Africa.

Exports to South Africa were : remounts, 36,258 ; hay and straw, 5,500 tons ; oats, 1,800 tons ; bran, 2,600 tons ; railway trucks, 1,300 tons ; sugar ; pine boards ; cement hardware ; wooden furniture ; wine ; beer ; brandy ; flour ; glue ; leather ; soap ; salt ; brushware ; sieves ; &c. Total, 12,000 tons and 36,258 remounts.

Exports to Gibraltar, Malta and Cyprus.

Exports to Gibraltar consist of native grown tobacco, 660 tons ; and to Malta, pine boards, 850 tons ; besides staves, 1,100 tons ; sugar ; leather ; wooden furniture ; beans ; rice ; flour ; firewood ; hardware ; bran ; starch ; matches ; brushware ; sieves. Total, 3,500 tons.

Exports to Aden.

Exports to Aden were : sugar, 900 tons ; flour ; pine boards ; paper glassware ; brushware ; bentwood furniture. Total, 1,040 tons.

Exports to Hong-Kong.

Exports to Hong-Kong were : sugar, 1,800 tons ; spirits ; and mineral waters. Total, 1,830 tons.

Sugar.

Exports of sugar to India have ceased owing to Indian duties on bounty-fed sugar. Cheap freights have enabled shipments viâ British ports, and the Adria Steamship Company closed a charter for 150,000 tons at 9s. per ton to British ports of the United Kingdom and shipments have been sublet much below this figure.

Imports of Italian wine have fallen to 32,000 tons (317,000l.), Wine. from 93,000 tons in 1898 (average 62,000 tons). The question of the preferential duty in favour of Italian wines is the great difficulty which stands in the way of the renewal of the commercial treaty with Italy. A compromise will no doubt be effected, limiting the imports to what is required for raising the alcoholic grade of cheap Hungarian wines (coupage). Dalmatian and Istrian wines were imported to the extent of 23,000 tons (214,000l.), which is the average.

Lumber shows a notable decrease of 55,000 tons (excluding Lumber. staves). This is owing chiefly to the circumstance that the Dalmatian ports (Sebenico and Spalato) are attracting supplies from Bosnia and Slavonia, now the railways are being extended.

Oak staves have been a sluggish market. Over production Oak staves. is the chief cause, and markets are surfeited with stocks. It is contemplated to limit the production, but in order to bring trade to a healthy condition, it would be necessary to stop shipments for a whole season at least. Shipments reached 30,000,000 (decrease 12,000,000), the average being 37,000,000 ; of these France alone absorbed 29,000,000 (decrease 11,000,000), the average being 35,000,000.

The Adria Steamship Company has increased its fleet by eight Austro-steamers of 14,620 tons ; the Ungaro-Croats by four steamers of Hungarian 661 tons for coasting traffic ; and private firms for " free naviga-navigation. tion " (non-subsidised) by three steamers of 7,211 tons. The aggregate of steam shipping consists of 91 steamers of 84,923 tons, of which 15 steamers of 30,851 tons are not subsidised.

Emigration from Croatia and Hungary is increasing by leaps Emigration. and bounds. The number of emigrants registered at Fiume is officially given at 7,500 in 1902 and 4,250 up to June, 1903, but these numbers are far exceeded. At present they proceed viâ Genoa, Hamburg and Bremen. An Act has been passed to bring the flow of emigration under Government control. For this purpose it is proposed to organise national lines of steamers with Fiume as port of call, but at present the inducement does not seem to warrant the expense, as the subsidy would no doubt have to be very large.

An extension of the harbour is decided upon. The outer break- Harbour water is to be lengthened, another inner mole and quay frontage works. constructed which will form another basin with moorage for six large steamers. These works are to be concluded in five years at a cost of 420,000l.

The Austrian Lloyd has started a monthly service to Durban Line of and intermediate ports with new steamers of 4,000 tons. They steamers to make 14 to 16 knots and have good accommodation for passengers. east coast of Africa.

Annex A.—RETURN of all Shipping at the Port of Fiume during the Years 1901–02.

ENTERED.

Flag	Sailing						Steam						Total						Value of Cargo in 1,000l.		
	Number of Vessels			Tonnage in 1,000 Tons.			Number of Vessels			Tonnage in 1,000 Tons.			Number of Vessels.			Tonnage in 1,000 Tons.					
	1901.	1902.	Average, Five Years.	1901.	1902.	Average Five Years.	1901.	1902.	Average, Five Years.	1901.	1902.	Average, Five Years.	1901.	1902.	Average, Five Years.	1901.	1902.	Average, Five Years.	1901.	1902.	Average, Five Years.
British ...	1	...	1	0·9	...	0·8	155	176	156	296	352	260	156	176	157	267	352	261	718	700	777
Austro-Hungarian ...	1,186	1,133	1,231	38	34	40	4,217	4,749	4,278	1,020	1,164	977	5,403	5,882	5,509	1,058	1,198	1,017	2,300	2,461	2,218
Austro-Hungarian (local) ...	...	...	...	...	...	...	4,091	4,514	4,194	220	256	218	4,091	4,514	4,194	220	256	218			
Italian ...	739	715	750	46	32	40	216	208	232	104	81	106	935	923	982	150	113	146	496	417	565
German ...	...	...	...	...	...	...	24	22	...	26	25	...	24	22	...	25	25	...	390	100	190
Other flags ...	33	22	31	11	7	9	22	11	39	26	12	41	55	33	70	38	19	50			
Total ...	1,959	1,870	2,013	96	73	90	8,725	9,680	8,899	1,662	1,890	1,602	10,684	11,550	10,912	1,758	1,963	1,692	3,904	3,678	3,750

CLEARED.

Flag	Sailing						Steam						Total						Value of Cargo in 1,000l.		
	Number of Vessels.			Tonnage in 1,000 Tons.			Number of Vessels.			Tonnage in 1,000 Tons.			Number of Vessels.			Tonnage in 1,000 Tons.					
	1901.	1902.	Average, Five Years.	1901.	1902.	Average, Five Years.	1901.	1902.	Average, Five Years.	1901.	1902.	Average, Five Years.	1901.	1902.	Average, Five Years.	1901.	1902.	Average, Five Years.	1901.	1902.	Average, Five Years.
British	...	...	1	...	...	0·6	157	175	156	266	354	259	157	175	156	266	354	260	1,100	1,485	1,080
Austro-Hungarian	1,178	1,125	1,226	37	33	40	4,206	4,741	4,270	1,016	1,155	971	5,384	5,866	5,496	1,053	1,188	1,011	5,010	4,357	4,278
Austro-Hungarian (local)	...	...	...	...	...	...	4,091	4,514	4,195	220	256	218	4,091	4,514	4,195	220	256	218			
Italian	746	712	745	44	31	40	221	207	232	103	81	105	967	919	977	147	112	145	501	485	478
German	...	...	...	...	...	...	25	22	...	26	26	...	25	22	...	26	25	...	281	133	210
Other flags	38	27	34	12	9	10	22	12	39	26	12	41	60	39	73	38	21	51			
Total	1,962	1,864	2,006	93	73	91	8,722	9,671	8,891	1,657	1,883	1,594	10,684	11,535	10,897	1,730	1,956	1,685	6,892	6,460	6,046

Annex C.—TABLE showing Total Value of Imports and Exports at the Port of Fiume during the Years 1901–02.

Country.	Value of Exports in 1,000l.			Value of Imports in 1,000l.		
	1901.	1902.	Average, Five Years.	1901.	1902.	Average, Five Years.
United Kingdom ...	2,073	2,375	1,691	1,140	1,427	1,113
Austria-Hungary ...	1,235	1,373	1,166	792	665	716
Italy	815	681	695	720	642	836
France ...	977	818	960	74	139	97
United States ...	222	194	226	180	206	180
Turkey	230	161	198	330	225	326
Brazil	98	93	100	122	14	62
Russia	65	5	20	24	7	60
Netherlands ...	210	237	242	18	6	28
Belgium	145	133	162	13	35	10
Spain	91	68	86	...	4	2
Egypt	355	65	176	60	58	44
Greece	40	55	33	15	14	17
Japan	162	100	158	40	60	34
Roumania	15	11	6	109	30	72
Chili ...	...	...	...	72	32	43
Portugal	75	29	48	...	...	...
Tunis	14	10	28	...	...	...
Germany	43	30	70	69	37	33
Philippines... ...	...	...	...	102	34	48
Other countries ...	27	22	32	25	43	29
Total	6,892	6,460	6,047	3,905	3,678	3,750

Annex B.—RETURN of Principal Articles of Import to the Port of Fiume during the Years 1901–02.

Articles.	Quantity in 1,000 Metric Tons.			
	1901.	1902.	Average, Five Years.	From the United Kingdom and British Colonies in 1902.
Coal	79	75	67	United Kingdom, 55
Rice	57	60	60	Burmah, 52
Wine	64	57	85	
Fruit	12	13	13	
Jute	14	11	15	India, 11
Salt	8	8	8	
Sulphur	6	8	4·5	
Phosphates..	12	8	8	
Resin	7	7	5·6	
Valonea	6	6	5	
Maize	20	6	16	
Nitrates	9	3	5·6	
Naphtha .. ,. ..	3	3	7·6	
Tobacco	5	3	4	United Kingdom, 0·4
Cotton, raw	2	3	2·6	India, 2
,, goods and yarn ...	0·6	0·7	0·6	United Kingdom, 0·5
Copper	1	2	1·5	
Pig iron	10	3	7·6	United Kingdom, 1·3
Iron ore	2	2	2·2	
Bitumen	2·3	1·3	2·7	
Coffee	2·8	1·1	2	
Lubricating oil	4	1	2·5	United Kingdom, 0·2
Palm oil	1·2	1·2	1	United Kingdom, 0·6
Cocoanut oil	0·9	1	0·9	United Kingdom, 0·6
Cotton oil	0·9	0·7	0·7	United Kingdom, 0·7
Chemicals	1·5	1·1	1·5	United Kingdom, 0·4
Machinery	0·6	0·9	0·7	United Kingdom, 0·3
Hemp	0·4	0·7	0·8	
Pepper	0·4	0·3	0·3	India, 0·3

RETURN of Principal Articles of Export from the Port of Fiume during the Years 1901–02.

Articles.	Quantity in 1,000 Metric Tons.			
	1901.	1902.	Average, Five Years.	To the United Kingdom and British Colonies in 1902.
Sugar	127	123	109	United Kingdom, 34; India, 43; Colonies, 0·5
Oak—				
Staves	100	72	84	
Square	25	15	22	
Extract	19	23	18	United Kingdom, 16
Lumber	213	183	208	United Kingdom, 20; India, 1·2; Colonies, 1
Horses (number) ..	17,147	36,403	22,000	South Africa, 36,258
Flour	109	113	101	United Kingdom, 41; India, 0·7
Wheat..	28	16	13	
Barley..	25	37	25	United Kingdom, 21
Maize	28	39	28	
Oats	4	5	6	South Africa, 1·8
Beans	24	25	24	United Kingdom, 0·8
Hardware	13	4	6	United Kingdom, 0·07; India, 1·3
Tobacco	5	3·4	3·6	Gibraltar, 0·6
Hemp seed	2·3	0·9	1·6	
Petroleum	2·2	2·5	2·2	
Bentwood furniture ..	1·1	3·2	0·8	Gibraltar, 0·2
Leather	0·5	0·5	0·5	
Wooden goods ..	0·5	0·5	0·5	
Mineral water ..	5	3·4	3·3	United Kingdom, 0·5
Rice, shelled	5	6	4	
Paper, cellulose ..	3	3·3	3	United Kingdom, 0·09
Pig iron	0·7	0·9	2	
Spirits..	2	1·3	2	
Dried prunes	1·3	2·1	3	United Kingdom, 0·45
Potatoes	2·2	2·7	2·5	
Iron ore	1	1	1	
Magnesite	6	10	8	United Kingdom, 0·73
Cotton goods	0·6	0·8	0·6	
Hemp	0·7	0·4	0·5	United Kingdom, 0·25
Soap	0·4	0·5	0·4	
Starch..	2	3·5	2	United Kingdom, 1·7
Machinery	0·3	0·8	0·7	
Chemicals	3	2	3	United Kingdom, 1
Glue	1	1	0·8	United Kingdom, 0·5
Bran	3·4	6	4	South Africa, 2·6
Hides	1·2	4	3	United Kingdom, 0·15
Millstones	0·7	1	0·8	

LONDON:
Printed for His Majesty's Stationery Office,
By HARRISON AND SONS,
Printers in Ordinary to His Majesty.
(1400   9 | 03—H & S   372)

No. 3083. Annual Series.

NETHERLANDS.

DIPLOMATIC AND CONSULAR REPORTS.

FINANCES OF THE

NETHERLANDS

FOR THE YEARS 1902–03.

FOREIGN OFFICE,
September, 1903.

No. 3083 Annual Series.

DIPLOMATIC AND CONSULAR REPORTS.

NETHERLANDS.

REPORT FOR THE YEARS 1902-03

ON THE

FINANCES OF THE NETHERLANDS.

REFERENCE TO PREVIOUS REPORT, Annual Series No. 2882.

Presented to both Houses of Parliament by Command of His Majesty,
SEPTEMBER, 1903.

LONDON:
PRINTED FOR HIS MAJESTY'S STATIONERY OFFICE,
BY HARRISON AND SONS, ST. MARTIN'S LANE,
PRINTERS IN ORDINARY TO HIS MAJESTY.

And to be purchased, either directly or through any Bookseller, from
EYRE & SPOTTISWOODE, EAST HARDING STREET, FLEET STREET, E.C.
and 32, ABINGDON STREET, WESTMINSTER, S.W.;
or OLIVER & BOYD, EDINBURGH;
or E. PONSONBY, 116, GRAFTON STREET, DUBLIN.

1903.

[Cd. 1766—17.]   *Price Three Halfpence.*

CONTENTS.

———◆——

Reference to previous Report, Annual Series No. 2882.

Report on the Finances of the Netherlands for the Years 1902–03
*by Mr. A. F. G. Leveson-Gower, Secretary of His Majesty's
Legation at the Hague.*

(Hague, July 31, 1903 ; received at Foreign Office, August 5, 1903.)

This report is based on the statement made by the Netherlands
Minister of Finance when presenting the budget for the year 1903
to the Second Chamber of the States General.

The results for the year 1900 (which are now closed) indicate a **Results, 1900.**
surplus of 1,229,897 fl. (102,491*l.*), or nearly 700,000 fl. (58,334*l.*)
over and above the estimated surplus for that year, as stated in
September, 1901.

The revenues for the year 1900 exceeded the original estimates
by no less than 10,308,204 fl. (859,017*l.*), and were 7,576,248 fl.
(631,354*l.*) in excess of those of the year 1899.   Against this increase
in the revenues, increased outlays caused an extra expenditure to
the extent of 7,555,643 fl. (629,637*l.*) above the original estimates.

The actual results are as follows :—

	Amount.	
	Currency.	Sterling.
	Florins.	£
Revenue	155,391,389	12,949,282
Expenditure	154,161,492	12,846,791
Surplus	1,229,897	102,491

The results, so far as they are known for the year 1901, are as follows :—

	Amount.	
	Currency.	Sterling.
	Florins.	£
Revenue	153,049,321	12,754,110
Expenditure	152,904,749	12,742,063
Surplus	144,572	12,047

The expenditure in 1901 was 2,489,665 fl. (207,472*l.*) below, and the revenue 4,757,419 fl. (396,452*l.*) in excess of the original estimates.

The most productive sources of revenue have been : sugar, registration dues, distilled liquors, post and telegraph service, the Netherlands Bank, slaughtered cattle, property tax, imports, stamp duties, income tax, mortgage dues, and the beer and vinegar tax. But there has been a considerable falling-off in the returns from death duties and a slight decrease in the returns from the pilotage service.

Compared with the year 1900 there is an apparent decrease in the returns to the amount of 2,342,068 fl. (195,172*l.*) which is entirely attributable to a decrease in the death duties which in 1900 were abnormally productive. This decrease was not made good by a corresponding increase of returns from other sources, which only amounted to 2,182,802 fl. (181,900*l.*), while the decrease in the death duties amounted to 4,524,870 fl. (377,072*l.*).

The summary of results for the last 10 years shows a total deficit during that time of 6,946,821 fl. (578,901*l.*), as shown in detail in the following statement :—

Year.	Surplus.		Deficit.	
	Currency.	Sterling.	Currency.	Sterling.
	Florins.	£	Florins.	£
1892	1,074,248	164,521	..	..
1893	..	..	8,118,106	676,509
1894	1,645,603	137,134	..	..
1895	..	..	839,105	69,925
1896	1,323,580	110,298	..	..
1897	..	..	2,542,390	211,866
1898	..	..	2,974,480	247,873
1899	1,209,360	100,780	..	..
1900	1,229,897	102,491	..	..
1901	144,571*	12,048	..	..
Total	7,527,260	627,272	14,474,081	1,206,173

* Estimate.

It should be borne in mind, however, that this includes the expenditure on public works, which was as follows :—

Description.			Amount.	
			Currency.	Sterling.
			Florins.	£
Rotterdam Waterway	..	..	2,738,065	228,172
Mouth of the Maas	..	..	10,125,174	843,764
Merwede Canal ..	..	..	1,071,684	89,307
Railways	..	..	19,317,754	1,609,813
Total	..	..	33,252,677	2,771,056

It includes also an expenditure of (net) 21,516,800 fl. (1,793,066*l.*) in the reduction of the National Debt.

Little of a definite kind can as yet be said with regard to the results of the year 1902. The estimates of expenditure, which were first stated at 167,333,726 fl. (13,944,477*l.*), were subsequently augmented by supplementary grants, raising the total estimate of expenditure to the sum of 168,365,420 fl. (14,030,452*l.*). Results, 1902.

The revenue for the first eight months of 1902 exceeded that of the corresponding period of the preceding year by 3,460,000 fl. (288,333*l.*), while the returns for the whole year (*see* annexed Table XVII) indicate an increase on the ordinary resources of more than 6,000,000 fl. (500,000*l.*).

The estimates, as originally stated, were 154,002,245 fl. (12,833,520*l.*), so that the results, as far as they have been made public, may roughly be taken as follows :—

Description.	Amount.	
	Currency.	Sterling.
	Florins.	£
Expenditure (including public works and reduction of debt)	168,365,420	14,030,452
Revenue, roughly (or 6,000,000 fl. above estimate)	160,000,000	13,333,333
Deficit..	8,365,420	697,119

NETHERLANDS.

The estimates for the year 1903 are as follows :—

				Amount.	
				Currency.	Sterling.
				Florins.	£
Expenditure	..	..	..	164,574,170	13,714,514
Revenue ..	..	..	..	156,504,260	13,042,022
	Deficit	..	..	8,069,910	672,492

This budget at first sight may appear more satisfactory than that of the year 1902, the deficit being represented at a considerably lower figure ; but it must be borne in mind that the so-called extraordinary expenditure this year will call for a much smaller outlay, while the ordinary expenditure, on the contrary, is estimated at 4,777,994 fl. (398,166*l.*) in excess of that of last year, while further allowance is made for only 2,502,015 fl. (208,501*l.*) increase in the revenue.

Only two departments show a diminished estimate, the Naval Department and the Department of Waterstaat, Commerce and Industry, while all the other departments anticipate an increase in their expenditure.

The increased expenditures are to be ascribed to : The costs in connection with the diplomatic mission to China ; building expenses in connection with courts of justice and penal institutions ; the Education Act, the Public Health Act, the Housing Act and the Workmen's Accidents Insurance Act; the Militia Law ; the increased expenditure in connection with the postal and telegraph service and increased expenditure in connection with the colony of Curacao.

Increased receipts are looked for, especially from the postal service, the sugar industry and the registration dues, and, moreover, higher returns may be expected from the property and income taxes, the excise on slaughtered cattle and imports. On the other hand, the returns from distilled liquors, death duties and pilotage service are estimated at a somewhat lower figure.

On more careful examination it may be allowed that the following so-called extraordinary expenditure might be deducted from the deficit :—

Description.	Amount.	
	Currency.	Sterling.
	Florins.	£
Railways	1,838,465	153,205
Mouth of the Maas	840,000	28,333
State management of mines	561,500	46,792
State insurance bank	300,000	25,000
Total	3,039,965	253,330

'. These sums, together with the usual margin allowed in making up the estimates—about 2,000,000 fl. (166,667*l.*) reduces the deficit to about 3,000,000 fl. (250,000*l.*). The Minister of Finance in making his statement gave expression to the warning that, in view of the uncertain outlays in connection with the Workmen's Accidents Insurance Act and other prospective measures, the expectation of reduced expenditure was not great.

The deficit is occasioned principally by the measures adopted in the course of the year 1901, as follows (exclusive of the expenditures mentioned in the preceding table) :—

Description.	Amount.	
	Currency.	Sterling.
	Florins.	£
Workmen's Accidents Insurance Act	235,000	19,583
The Educational Act of 1901	2,000,000	166,667
Public Health Act.	120,100	10,008
Housing Act	4,500	375
Militia Act of 1901	1,815,300	151,275
Horse Breeding Act	100,680	8,390
Total	4,275,580	356,298

and, moreover, the re-adjustment of the army pensions and the expenditure on the Java, China and Japan Steamship Line will call for outlays of 84,000 fl. (7,000*l.*) and 62,500 fl. (5,208*l.*) respectively.

To meet these calls on the Treasury, which, as will be observed, are of a more or less permanent nature, it is proposed that the excise on distilled liquors shall be increased from 63 fl. (5*l.* 5*s.*) per hectolitre (22 gallons) to 70 fl. (5*l.* 16*s.* 8*d.*), and that a re-adjustment of the property tax law shall be effected.

With regard to the condition of the Treasury it was stated that, although during the year 1902 recourse had been had to the issue of Treasury bills to meet current expenses, it was fully expected that these would be entirely redeemed before the close of that year.

A subsequent memorandum issued by the Minister of Finance is to the following effect :—

By the different budget bills, the estimates of expenditure came to a total of 162,932,414 fl. 94 c. Later estimates have augmented this sum by 913,100 fl., consequently a total sum has been estimated amounting to 163,845,514 fl. 94 c., as a supplement to this is the sum of 4,223,970 fl. 24 c., applied for in bills already before the House, or shortly to be proposed (this includes an increase in the Navy estimates of 2,302,283 fl. 99 c.). The total estimated expenditure therefore amounts to 168,069,485 fl. 18 c. The receipts are estimated at 156,504,260 fl.; consequently a deficit of 11,565,225 fl. 18 c. is to be calculated on. From this must be deducted the amounts which come under the head of extraordinary expenses, such as the sum of 3,039,965 fl. already mentioned, the taking over of the claims of officials and private persons upon the Chinese Government amounting to 359,700 fl., and the loan in Surinam for the Lawa Railway amounting to 1,650,000 fl. These extraordinary expenses amount altogether to 5,049,665 fl., there remains, therefore, a deficit of 6,515,560 fl. 18 c. A somewhat large proportion of this sum, probably some millions, will not be included in the expenses.

On the other hand, however, new supplementary estimates to a considerable amount are inevitable, including one in connection with the strikes. From the nature of the case it is impossible to state accurately how much will be saved, or to how much the new increase in expenditure will amount.

On the whole, excepting the receipts from sugar, from which an increase of about 800,000 fl. may be reckoned, the Minister of Finance did not consider the situation more favourable than when the estimates were originally presented, when the deficit on the ordinary expenses was reckoned by him at between 3,000,000 and 4,000,000 fl. He therefore is of opinion that all resources require strengthening by good financial management.

Annex I.—TABLE showing the Estimates of Expenditure for the Year 1903 as Introduced by the Netherlands Minister of Finance.

Number.	Description.		Amount.	
			Currency.	Sterling.
			Florins.	£
I	Queen's Civil List		800,000	66,667
II	State Councils and Cabinet		689,402	57,450
III	Department of Foreign Affairs ..		1,136,148	94,679
IV	„ Justice		6,356,369	529,697
V	Home Department		18,636,103	1,553,009
VI	Department of Marine		16,512,820	1,376,068
VIIA	National Debt		34,733,843	2,894,488
VIIB	Finance Department		25,734,131	2,144,511
VIII	War Department		25,202,456	2,100,204
IX	Department of Waterstaat		33,104,918	2,758,743
X	„ Colonies		1,617,979	134,832
XI	Unforeseen expenditure		50,000	4,167

Annex II.—TABLE showing Revised Estimates of Expenditure for the Year 1903 as Finally Passed by the States-General.

Number.	Description.		Amount.	
			Currency.	Sterling.
			Florins.	£
I	Queen's Civil List		800,000	66,667
II	State Councils and Cabinet		689,402	57,450
III	Department of Foreign Affairs ..		1,136,148	94,679
IV	„ Justice		6,384,494	532,041
V	Home Department		18,831,365	1,569,280
VI	Department of Marine		14,349,740	1,195,812
VIIA	National Debt		33,743,833	2,811,986
VIIB	Finance Department		25,944,731	1,162,061
VIII	War Department		25,257,736	2,104,811
IX	Department of Waterstaat		33,087,607	2,757,301
X	„ Colonies		1,667,349	138,946
XI	Unforeseen expenditure		50,000	4,167

Annex III—Table showing the Revenue during the Years
1891–1901 inclusive.

CURRENCY.

Year.			Amount.			
			Ordinary Receipts.	Sale of Crown Lands.	Other Receipts.	Total.
			Florins.	Florins.	Florins.	Florins.
1891	..	..	129,450,298	150,000	563,175	130,163,473
1892	..	..	131,115,706	150,000	420,000	131,685,706
1893	..	..	126,537,164	150,000	140,000	126,827,164
1894	..	..	131,517,521	150,000	1,235,552	132,903,073
1895	..	..	132,257,968	200,000	..	132,457,968
1896	..	..	134,233,424	..	180,000	134,413,424
1897	..	..	135,508,388	260,000	200,000	135,968,388
1898	..	..	138,669,363	250,000	8,308,717	147,228,080
1899	..	..	146,480,122	500,000	835,019	147,815,141
1900	..	..	154,574,593	600,000	216,796	155,391,389
1901	..	..	152,466,167	300,000	283,154	153,049,321

STERLING.

Year.			Amount.			
			Ordinary Receipts.	Sale of Crown Lands.	Other Receipts.	Total.
			£	£	£	£
1891	..	..	10,787,525	12,500	46,981	10,846,956
1892	..	..	10,926,309	12,500	35,000	10,973,809
1893	..	..	10,544,764	12,500	11,667	10,568,930
1894	..	..	10,959,793	12,500	102,963	11,075,256
1895	..	..	11,021,497	16,667	..	11,038,164
1896	..	..	11,186,119	..	15,000	11,201,119
1897	..	..	11,292,365	21,667	16,667	11,380,699
1898	..	..	11,555,780	20,833	692,393	12,269,007
1899	..	..	12,206,677	41,667	69,583	12,317,928
1900	..	..	12,881,216	50,000	18,066	12,949,282
1901	..	..	12,705,514	25,000	23,596	12,754,110

Annex IV.—TABLE of Expenditure during the Years 1891-1901 inclusive.

CURRENCY.

Year.	Amount.					
	General Service.	Interest.	Redemption of Debt.	State Railway.	Other Expenses.	Total.
	Florins.	Florins.	Florins.	Florins.	Florins.	Florins.
1891 ..	86,268,385	31,239,302	2,872,545	1,350,000	8,433,240	130,163,473
1892 ..	89,036,077	31,519,317	24,923,048	276,950	6,033,317	151,788,710
1893 ..	91,057,689	31,462,359	5,185,458	2,025,000	5,214,763	134,945,270
1894 ..	90,895,492	31,383,939	3,032,728	1,504,358	4,440,951	131,257,471
1895 ..	92,069,641	31,499,888	3,275,372	748,368	5,703,803	133,297,074
1896 ..	93,529,240	30,628,060	1,507,556	899,137	6,525,849	133,089,844
1897 ..	99,287,728	30,363,846	2,708,473	1,129,499	5,021,230	138,510,778
1898 ..	102,995,262	30,819,413	2,638,043	10,735,304	3,014,537	150,202,560
1899 ..	106,042,298	31,678,869	6,295,365	3,750,216	1,921,876	149,688,625
1900 ..	110,700,781	31,553,248	3,255,881	4,591,748	4,059,834	154,161,492
1901 ..	114,765,663	30,860,362	3,120,924	1,760,026	2,397,774	152,904,749

STERLING.

Year.	Amount.					
	General Service.	Interest.	Redemption of Debt.	State Railway.	Other Expenses.	Total.
	£	£	£	£	£	£
1891 ..	7,189,032	2,603,275	239,378	112,500	702,770	10,846,956
1892 ..	7,419,673	2,626,609	2,076,920	23,079	502,776	12,649,059
1893 ..	7,588,141	2,621,863	432,121	168,750	434,564	11,245,439
1894 ..	7,574,624	2,615,328	252,727	125,363	370,079	10,938,123
1895 ..	7,672,470	2,624,991	272,948	62,364	475,317	11,108,090
1896 ..	7,794,103	2,552,338	125,629	74,928	543,821	11,090,820
1897 ..	8,273,977	2,530,320	225,706	94,125	418,436	11,542,565
1898 ..	8,582,939	2,568,284	219,837	894,608	251,211	12,516,880
1899 ..	8,836,858	2,639,906	524,614	312,518	160,156	12,474,052
1900 ..	9,225,065	2,629,437	271,323	382,646	338,319	12,846,791
1901 ..	9,563,805	2,571,697	260,077	146,669	199,814	12,742,062

Annex V.—TABLE showing how the "other Expenditure" comprised in the Fifth Column of the preceding Table is made up.

Description.	1891.		1892.		1893.		1894.		1895.		1896.	
	Currency.	Sterling	Currency.	Sterling	Currency.	Sterling	Currency.	Sterling	Currency.	Sterling	Currency.	Sterling.
	Florins.	£	Florins.	£	Florins.	£	Florins.	£	Florins.	£	Florins.	£
Expenditure on prevention of cattle disease	55,183	4,599	210,620	17,518	127,939	10,662	255,901	21,383	98,266	8,189	438,419	36,535
Extraordinary expenditure in the War Department	3,434,792	286,233	2,643,296	220,275	2,889,129	240,761	2,556,415	213,034	4,135,345	344,612	4,384,121	365,343
Extraordinary expenditure in the Marine Department	71,472	5,956	30,354	2,529	92,534	7,711	39,623	3,302	237,511	19,793	252,841	21,070
Revision of the taxable revenue on house property	..	..	..	..	..	..	..	..	..	..	..	..
Improvements to river at Rotterdam	1,457,811	121,484	989,970	82,414	457,245	40,601	413,270	36,939	584,101	48,675	162,654	13,555
Expenditure on Merwede Canal	1,994,713	166,226	803,098	66,925	268,585	22,382	..	..	..	..	..	..
Works at the mouth of the Maas	1,419,267	118,272	1,357,076	113,089	1,349,329	112,444	1,145,651	95,471	649,577	54,048	1,287,812	107,318
Total	8,433,240	702,770	6,033,317	502,776	5,214,763	434,564	4,440,950	370,079	5,703,803	475,317	6,525,849	543,821

TABLE showing how the "other Expenditure" comprised in the Fifth Column of the preceding Table is made up—continued.

Description.	1897.		1898.		1899.		1900.		1901.	
	Currency.	Sterling.	Currency.	Sterling.	Currency.	Sterling.	Currency.	Sterling.	Currency.	Sterling.
	Florins.	£	Florins.	£	Florins.	£	Florins.	£	Florins.	£
Expenditure on prevention of cattle disease	243,644	20,304	57,594	4,799	60,770	5,064	52,222	4,352	75,590	6,299
Extraordinary expenditure in the War Department	3,392,754	282,730	1,933,414	161,118	1,097,188	91,432	2,987,493	248,957	1,305,920	108,827
Extraordinary expenditure in the Marine Department	..	..	..	..	17,991	1,499	23,696	1,975	19,918	1,660
Revision of the taxable revenue on house property	13,654	1,138	35,115	2,926	167,290	13,941	407,462	33,955	115,000	9,583
Improvements to river at Rotterdam ..	71,825	5,985	..	..	..	..	..	..	..	..
Expenditure on Merwede Canal ..	..	..	..	..	..	..	588,959	49,080	881,345	73,445
Works at the mouth of the Maas ..	1,299,352	108,279	988,423	82,368	578,636	48,220	..	..	..	..
Total..	5,021,230	418,486	3,014,537	251,211	1,921,876	160,156	4,059,834	338,319	2,397,774	199,814

Annex VI.—Chapter II.   STATE Councils and Queen's Cabinet.

Year.				Amount.	
				Currency.	Sterling.
				Florins.	£
1891	..	..	..	..	628,590	52,882
1892	..	..	..	..	654,768	54,564
1893	..	..	..	..	639,887	53,324
1894	..	..	..	..	602,637	50,219
1895	..	..	..	..	646,522	53,877
1896	..	..	..	..	648,322	54,027
1897	..	..	..	..	646,942	53,912
1898	..	..	..	..	675,144	56,262
1899	..	..	..	..	649,504	54,125
1900	..	..	..	..	650,837	54,236
1901	..	..	..	..	661,726	55,144

Annex VII.—Chapter III.   DEPARTMENT of Foreign Affairs.

Year.				Amount.	
				Currency.	Sterling.
				Florins.	£
1891	..	..	..	..	714,935	59,578
1892	..	..	..	..	742,895	61,908
1893	..	..	..	..	725,890	60,491
1894	..	..	..	..	758,044	63,170
1895	..	..	..	..	788,541	65,712
1896	..	..	..	..	812,429	67,702
1897	..	..	..	..	802,153	66,846
1898	..	..	..	..	836,218	69,685
1899	..	..	..	..	886,468	73,872
1900	..	..	..	..	854,692	71,224
1901	..	..	..	..	854,153	71,179

Annex VIII.—Chapter IV.   DEPARTMENT of Justice.

Year.				Amount.	
				Currency.	Sterling.
				Florins.	£
1891	..	..	..	..	5,176,008	431,334
1892	..	..	..	..	5,301,851	441,821
1893	..	..	..	..	5,308,016	442,335
1894	..	..	..	..	5,150,465	429,205
1895	..	..	..	..	5,235,934	436,328
1896	..	..	..	..	5,216,476	434,706
1897	..	..	..	..	5,317,080	443,090
1898	..	..	..	..	5,610,882	467,573
1899	..	..	..	..	6,111,133	509,261
1900	..	..	..	..	6,092,326	507,694
1901	..	..	..	..	6,287,188	523,932

Annex IX.—Chapter V. Home Department.

Year.				Amount.	
				Currency.	Sterling.
				Florins.	£
1891	..	..	..	..	11,280,203	940,017
1892	..	..	..	..	12,431,392	1,035,949
1893	..	..	..	..	12,315,006	1,026,250
1894	..	..	..	..	12,676,544	1,056,379
1895	..	..	..	..	12,824,677	1,068,723
1896	..	..	..	..	13,627,254	1,135,604
1897	..	..	..	..	14,046,883	1,170,574
1898	..	..	..	..	14,273,788	1,189,482
1899	..	..	..	.	14,725,914	1,227,159
1900	..	..	..	.	15,425,008	1,285,417
1901	..	..	..	..	16,107,087	1,342,257

Annex X.—Chapter VI. Department of Marine.

Year.				Amount.	
				Currency.	Sterling.
				Florins.	£
1891	..	..	..	..	13,829,690	1,152,474
1892	..	..	..	..	13,942,213	1,161,851
1893	..	..	..	..	15,180,634	1,265,053
1894	..	..	..	..	14,782,999	1,231,916
1895	..	..	..	..	15,365,425	1,280,452
1896	..	..	..	..	15,774,978	1,314,581
1897	..	..	..	..	15,378,065	1,281,505
1898	..	..	..	..	15,257,474	1,271,456
1899	..	..	..	..	15,913,486	1,326,124
1900	..	..	..	..	16,948,200	1,412,350
1901	..	.	..	..	16,778,445	1,398,204

Annex XI.—Chapter VIIA. National Debt.

Year.				Amount.	
				Currency.	Sterling.
				Florins.	£
1891	..	..	..	..	34,111,848	2,842,654
1892	..	..	..	..	56,442,366	4,703,530
1893	..	..	..	..	36,647,817	3,053,985
1894	..	..	..	..	34,416,668	2,868,055
1895	..	..	..	..	34,775,261	2,897,938
1896	..	..	..	..	32,135,616	2,677,968
1897	..	..	..	..	33,072,320	2,756,027
1898	..	..	..	..	33,457,456	2,788,121
1899	..	..	..	..	37,974,234	3,164,519
1900	..	..	..	..	34,809,129	2,900,761
1901	..	..	..	..	33,981,285	2,881,774

Annex XII.—Chapter VIIB. FINANCE Department.

Year.			Amount.	
			Currency.	Sterling.
			Florins.	£
1891	..	..	18,814,838	1,567,903
1892	..	..	18,825,505	1,568,792
1893	..	..	18,890,364	1,574,197
1894	..	..	19,024,156	1,585,346
1895	..	..	19,059,655	1,588,305
1896	..	..	19,300,163	1,608,347
1897	..	..	21,045,533	1,753,794
1898	..	..	24,168,017	2,014,001
1899	..	..	24,739,163	2,061,597
1900	..	..	25,069,539	2,089,128
1901	..	..	25,059,517	2,088,293

Annex XIII.—Chapter VIII. DEPARTMENT of War.

Year.			Amount.	
			Currency.	Sterling.
			Florins.	£
1891	..	..	22,180,173	1,848,348
1892	..	..	21,763,932	1,813,661
1893	..	..	21,882,673	1,823,556
1894	..	..	21,664,069	1,805,339
1895	..	..	23,085,956	1,923,829
1896	..	..	23,168,008	1,930,667
1897	..	..	24,494,454	2,041,204
1898	..	..	22,013,942	1,834,495
1899	..	..	21,606,659	1,800,555
1900	..	..	23,718,775	1,976,565
1901	..	..	22,942,064	1,911,839

Annex XIV.—Chapter IX. DEPARTMENT of Waterstaat.

Year.			Amount.	
			Currency.	Sterling.
			Florins.	£
1891	..	..	21,365,933	1,780,494
1892	..	..	19,631,267	1,635,939
1893	..	..	21,181,933	1,765,161
1894	..	..	19,980,927	1,665,077
1895	..	..	19,310,731	1,609,228
1896	..	..	20,249,222	1,687,435
1897	..	..	21,603,889	1,800,324
1898	..	..	31,330,710	2,610,892
1899	..	..	25,043,758	2,086,980
1900	..	..	28,291,223	2,357,602
1901	..	..	27,941,390	2,328,449

Annex XV.—Chapter X. DEPARTMENT of Colonies.

Year.				Amount.	
				Currency.	Sterling.
				Florins.	£
1891	..	..	..	1,211,421	100,952
1892	..	..	..	1,121,821	93,485
1893	..	..	..	1,363,240	113,603
1894	..	..	..	1,372,106	114,342
1895	..	..	..	1,368,898	114,075
1896	..	..	..	1,333,688	111,142
1897	..	..	..	1,281,664	106,805
1898	..	..	..	1,563,221	130,268
1899	..	..	..	1,209,100	100,758
1900	..	..	..	1,462,551	121,879
1901	..	..	..	1,465,787	122,149

Annex XVI.—COMPARATIVE Table showing the Estimates of Revenue for the Years 1903–1902.

CURRENCY.

Sources of Revenue.	Amount.			
	1903.	1902.	Increase.	Decrease.
	Florins.	Florins.	Florins.	Florins.
Direct taxes—				
Land tax	13,104,000	13,016,000	88,000	..
Assessed taxes..	9,150,000	9,022,000	128,000	..
Tax on professional and trade incomes	6,554,000	6,300,000	254,000	..
Property tax	7,665,000	7,464,000	201,000	..
Excise—				
Sugar	16,100,000	14,900,000	1,200,000	..
Wine	1,800,000	1,800,000	..	..
Spirits	26,400,000	26,700,000	..	300,000
Salt	1,580,000	1,520,000	60,000	..
Beer and vinegar	1,450,000	1,400,000	50,000	..
Slaughtered cattle	3,900,000	3,700,000	200,000	..
Indirect taxes—				
Stamp duty	3,540,000	3,530,000	10,000	..
Registration duty	5,600,000	5,200,000	400,000	..
Mortgage duty..	570,000	510,000	60,000	..
Succession duty or death duty	8,670,000	8,950,000	..	280,000
Percentages	3,864,600	3,971,000	..	106,400
Import duties—				
Customs	9,900,000	9,600,000	300,000	..
Stamped forms..	18,600	18,000	600	..
Tax on gold and silver wares..	330,850	320,900	9,950	..
Crown lands—				
Ordinary domain	1,500,000	1,500,000	..	..
War Department domain	62,000	60,000	2,000	..
Highways	28,000	30,000	..	2,000
Canals, ferries and harbours..	90,000	86,000	4,000	..
Postal service	11,760,000	11,122,000	638,000	..
Telegraph service	2,350,000	2,487,000	..	137,000
State lottery	657,000	651,000	6,000	..
Shooting and fishing licenses	138,000	135,000	3,000	..
Pilotage service	2,000,000	2,350,000	..	350,000
Mining	19,665	26,220	..	6,555
State railways	4,188,150	4,188,150	..	..
Miscellaneous receipts	7,832,695	7,811,975	20,720	..
Netherlands - Indies contribution—				
On account of interest and redemption of 3½ per cent. loan	3,856,700	3,865,000	..	8,300
Sums accruing from sale of domain..	300,000	360,000	..	..
Netherlands Bank contribution..	1,350,000	1,300,000	50,000	..
Receipts in virtue of Law of May 9, 1890	175,000	168,000	7,000	..
Total..	156,504,260	154,002,245	3,692,270	1,190,255
Net increase..	..	..	2,502,015	

COMPARATIVE Table showing the Estimates of Revenue for the
Years 1903–1902—continued.

STERLING.

Sources of Revenue.	Amount.			
	1903.	1902.	Increase.	Decrease.
	£	£	£	£
Direct taxes—				
Land tax	1,092,000	1,084,667	7,333	..
Assessed taxes	762,500	751,833	10,667	..
Tax on professional and trade				
incomes	546,167	525,000	21,167	..
Property tax	638,750	622,000	16,750	..
Excise—				
Sugar	1,341,667	1,241,667	100,000	..
Wine	150,000	150,000	..	..
Spirits	2,200,000	2,225,000	..	25,000
Salt	131,667	126,667	5,000	..
Beer and vinegar	120,833	116,667	4,167	..
Slaughtered cattle	325,000	308,333	16,667	..
Indirect taxes—				
Stamp duty	295,000	294,167	833	..
Registration duty	466,667	433,333	33,333	..
Mortgage duty..	47,500	42,500	5,000	..
Succession duty or death duty	722,500	745,833	..	23,333
Percentages	322,050	330,917	..	8,867
Import duties—				
Customs	825,000	800,000	25,000	..
Stamped forms..	1,550	1,500	50	..
Tax on gold and silver wares..	27,571	26,742	829	..
Crown lands—				
Ordinary domain	125,000	125,000	..	..
War Department domain ..	5,167	5,000	167	..
Highways	2,333	2,500	..	167
Canals, ferries and harbours ..	7,500	7,167	333	..
Postal service	980,000	926,833	53,167	..
Telegraph service	195,833	207,250	..	11,417
State lottery	54,750	54,250	500	..
Shooting and fishing licenses ..	11,500	11,250	250	..
Pilotage service	166,667	195,833	..	29,167
Mining	1,639	2,185	..	546
State railways	349,012	349,012	..	..
Miscellaneous receipts	652,724	650,998	1,727	..
Netherlands - Indies contribu-				
tion—				
On account of interest and				
redemption of 3½ per cent.				
loan	321,392	322,083	..	692
Sums accruing from sale of				
domain	25,000	25,000	..	..
Netherlands Bank contribution..	112,500	108,333	4,167	..
Receipts in virtue of Law of				
May 9, 1890	14,583	14,000	583	..
Total..	13,042,022	12,833,520	307,689	99,188
Net increase.. ..	..	..	208,501	

Annex XVII.—COMPARATIVE Table showing the Estimates and Results of Revenue for the Year 1902, so far as they were known to December 31, 1902; and Results for the Year 1901.

CURRENCY.

Sources of Revenue.	Amount.		
	Estimates, 1902.	Results, 1902.	Results, 1901.
	Florins.	Florins.	Florins.
Direct taxes—			
Land taxes	13,016,000	13,046,418	12,836,524
Assessed taxes	9,022,000	9,213,908	8,847,016
Tax on professional and trade			
incomes	6,300,000	6,657,189	7,188,831
Property tax	7,464,000	7,649,080	7,547,515
Excise			
Sugar	14,900,000	16,705,335	15,543,024
Wine	1,800,000	1,794,298	1,802,958
Spirits	26,700,000	26,676,657	26,807,939
Salt	1,520,000	1,567,063	1,571,300
Beer and vinegar	1,400,000	1,428,356	1,458,764
Slaughtered cattle	3,700,000	4,105,289	3,890,401
Indirect taxes—			
Stamp duty	4,100,000	4,512,991	4,242,195
Registration duty	5,200,000	6,013,736	5,834,717
Mortgage duty	510,000	631,875	592,406
Succession duty or death duty ..	12,351,000	15,037,734	11,443,964
Import duties—			
Customs	9,600,000	10,112,088	9,899,297
Stamped forms	18,000	19,301	18,738
Tax on gold and silver ware ..	320,900	348,340	338,093
Crown lands—			
Ordinary Crown land ..	1,676,000	1,666,345	1,706,753
War Department domain ..			
Postal service	11,122,000	11,491,979	10,750,769
Telegraph service	2,487,000	2,396,400	2,320,646
State lotteries	651,000	657,476	656,157
Shooting and fishing licenses	135,000	141,813	139,085
Pilotage service	2,350,000	2,160,911	2,122,240
Mining	26,220	19,759	26,158
Total	136,369,120	144,049,347	137,585,580

COMPARATIVE Table showing the Estimates and Results of Revenue for the Year 1902, so far as they were known to December 31, 1902 ; and Results for the Year 1901—continued.

STERLING.

Sources of Revenue.	Amount.		
	Estimates, 1902.	Results, 1902.	Results, 1901.
	£	£	£
Direct taxes—			
Land tax	1,084,667	1,087,201	1,069,710
Assessed taxes	751,833	767,825	737,251
Tax on professional and trade incomes	525,000	554,767	599,069
Property tax..	622,000	637,423	628,960
Excise—			
Sugar..	1,241,667	1,392,111	1,295,252
Wine..	150,000	149,525	150,246
Spirits	2,225,000	2,223,055	2,233,995
Salt	126,667	130,588	130,942
Beer and vinegar	116,667	118,613	121,564
Slaughtered cattle	308,333	342,107	324,200
Indirect taxes—			
Stamp duty ..	341,667	376,082	353,516
Registration duty	433,333	501,144	486,226
Mortgage duty	42,500	52,656	49,375
Succession duty or death duty	1,029,250	1,253,144	953,664
Import duties—			
Customs	800,000	842,674	824,941
Stamped forms	1,500	1,608	1,561
Tax on gold and silver ware	26,741	29,028	28,174
Crown lands—			
Ordinary Crown land	} 139,667	} 138,862	} 142,229
War Department domain			
Postal service ..	926,833	957,665	895,897
Telegraph service	207,250	199,700	193,387
State lotteries ..	54,250	54,789	54,680
Shooting and fishing licenses..	11,250	11,817	11,590
Pilotage service..	195,833	180,076	176,853
Mining ..	2,185	1,646	2,180
Total	11,364,093	12,003,940	11,465,455

Annex XVIII.—TRANSLATION of the Chapter in the Budget, which deals with the National Debt, after Revision in the States-General.

Article.	Description.	Amount.	
		Currency.	Sterling.
		Florins.	£
I.	Interest on a capital of 623,891,500 fl. (51,990,958l.), inscribed debt, at 2½ per cent., falling due June 30 and December 31, 1903	15,597,287	1,299,774
II.	Interest on an inscribed interest bearing debt of bonds issued in virtue of the law of December 30, 1895, of that of June 9, 1898, and of that of June 29, 1899, at 3 per cent., on a capital of 512,981,200 fl. (42,748,433l.), falling due March 1 and September 1, 1903, in addition to a provision of one-eighth per cent. of the nominal amount of the coupons paid abroad with regard to the said bonds ..	15,391,436	1,282,619
III.	Interest and expenditure in the preparation and issue of Treasury bills and promissory notes, also the interest and cost of pledging Treasury bills the issue of which is permitted by law, as also the interest on the money, which according to the law of August 7, 1888, revised bank octroi, has been advanced by the Netherlands Bank	300,000	25,000
IV.	Interest on the caution money paid by tax-payers at 2½ per cent., falling due June 30 and December 31, 1903	6,000	500
V.	Interest at 3 per cent. on capital sums, together amounting to 3,976 fl. (331l.), raised for the maintenance and improvement of high roads in what was formerly known as the Valkenburg, in the province of Limburg, by virtue of agreements entered into with the communes interested, now charged to the State, falling due in 1903	119	10
VI.	Interests, fixed charges and disbursements falling due in 1902 on account of State domains, for so far as they are not met by the domain authorities, and on highways and canals ..	38,000	3,167
VII.	Interest on voluntary and judicial assignments	20,000	1,667
		31,352,843	2,612,737
	PART II.		
	Redemption of the National Debt.		
VIII.	Redemption and discharge of interest bearing National Debt, including the discharge of certain payments belonging to the administration of domain, fixed burdens and payments	3,381,000	281,750
	Total	34,733,843	2,894,487

LONDON :
Printed for His Majesty's Stationery Office,
By HARRISON AND SONS,
Printers in Ordinary to His Majesty.
(1400   9 | 03—H & S   371)

No. 3084.   Annual Series.

<u>JAPAN</u>.

DIPLOMATIC AND CONSULAR REPORTS.

TRADE OF

NAGASAKI

FOR THE YEAR 1902.

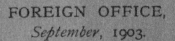

FOREIGN OFFICE,
September, 1903.

No. 3084 Annual Series.

DIPLOMATIC AND CONSULAR REPORTS.

JAPAN.

REPORT FOR THE YEAR 1902

ON THE

TRADE OF NAGASAKI.

REFERENCE TO PREVIOUS REPORT, Annual Series No. 2899.

Presented to both Houses of Parliament by Command of His Majesty,
SEPTEMBER, 1903.

LONDON:
PRINTED FOR HIS MAJESTY'S STATIONERY OFFICE,
BY HARRISON AND SONS, ST. MARTIN'S LANE,
PRINTERS IN ORDINARY TO HIS MAJESTY.

And to be purchased, either directly or through any Bookseller, from
EYRE & SPOTTISWOODE, EAST HARDING STREET, FLEET STREET, E.C.,
and 32, ABINGDON STREET, WESTMINSTER, S.W.;
or OLIVER & BOYD, EDINBURGH;
or E. PONSONBY, 116, GRAFTON STREET, DUBLIN.

1903.

[Cd. 1766—18.]   *Price Twopence.*

CONTENTS.

———◆———

Reference to previous Report, Annual Series No. 2899.

Report on the Trade of Nagasaki for the Year 1902

By Mr. Acting-Consul John B. Rentiers.

(Tokio, July 15, 1903 ; received at Foreign Office, August 25, 1903.)

The value of the foreign trade of the port of Nagasaki during the year 1902 amounted to 1,408,752*l.*, consisting of imports 952,012*l.* and exports 456,740*l.* *Value of foreign trade in 1902.*

These figures show a decline from those of the preceding year in imports of 453,916*l.* in exports of 38,952*l.*, and in the total trade of 492,868*l.* *Decline as compared with 1901.*

The total values of the trade of the port during the past five years were :— *Trade during five years 1898-1902.*

Year.				Value.		
				Imports.	Exports.	Total.
				£	£	£
1898	..	..	..	2,010,903	672,451	2,683,354
1899	..	..	..	1,137,975	633,710	1,771,685
1900	..	..	..	1,540,916	693,911	2,234,827
1901	..	..	..	1,405,928	495,692	1,901,620
1902	..	..	..	952,012	456,740	1,408,752
Total (five years)			..	7,047,734	2,952,504	10,000,238
Average (five years)			..	1,409,547	590,501	2,000,048

While, therefore, the value of the total trade of 1902 shows a decrease of 492,868*l.* on that of the preceding year, the decrease as compared with the average total trade for the past five years is still more marked, amounting to 591,296*l.* ; the imports for 1902 falling below the average for this period by 457,535*l.* and the exports by 133,761*l.*

The value of the total trade in 1902 was indeed lower than that in any previous year since 1895, when it amounted to 1,140,639*l.* The value of imports also was lower than in any previous year since 1895 when it amounted to 680,852*l.*, and of exports since 1894 when it amounted to 374,406*l.*

Trade at ports
other than
Nagasaki in
1902.
Compared
with that of
previous year.
The value of the foreign trade at two other ports, Karatsu and
Kuchinotsu, included within the Consular district of Nagasaki,
amounted in 1902 to 651,101*l*., consisting of imports 63,036*l*. and
exports 588,065*l*. These figures show a general increase, as compared
with those of the preceding year. of 94,076*l*. in the total trade,
of 15,859*l*. in imports and of 78,217*l*. in exports.

Value of trade
of southern
district of
Japan.
Adding these figures to those already given of the trade of
Nagasaki, the whole trade of the southern Consular district of
Japan during the year 1902 as compared with 1901 is shown to
have been :—

					Value.	
					1902.	1901.
					£	£
Imports	..	..	..	..	1,015,048	1,453,105
Exports	..	..	..	..	1,044,805	1,005,540
		Total	..	..	2,059,853	2,458,645

Comparing these figures with those given at the commencement
of this report of the values of the trade of the port of Nagasaki, it
will be seen that the decline in the total trade of the three ports
above mentioned is not so great as in that of this port alone ; for
the amount of the total trade of the three ports during 1902 falls
short of that during the preceding year by only 398,792*l*. and that
of imports by 438,057*l*., while the exports of 1902 exceed those of
1901 by 39,265*l*.

On comparing the table given above with that given in last
year's report, it will be noticed that the figures here given for the
trade of 1901 are smaller than those given last year. This is due
to the fact that during the year 1901 the Prefecture of Fukuoka,
in which lies the port of Hakata, was added to the Consular district
of Shimonoseki, and the trade of that port can consequently no
longer be included in a report on the trade of Nagasaki. For the
sake of comparison with this year's trade, the value of the trade of
Hakata has therefore been omitted from the figures here given for
1901, which represent the trade of Nagasaki, Karatsu and
Kuchinotsu.

Distribution
of trade of
Nagasaki
among foreign
countries.
Decrease in
imports.
The distribution of the trade of the port of Nagasaki is shown
in Annex III. It will be seen that the decline in the value of
imports is general, and that, if we exclude the almost microscopic
import trade of Italy, the only countries from which the imports
to Japan have increased are China and British India. In the
case of the latter country the import consists almost entirely of rice
and raw cotton, and, although it amounts to half as much as it
did in 1900, the recovery is very small when compared with the
import of 1899, of which it is little more than one-tenth. The

increase is accounted for by the increased import of Indian rice, although the decline in the import of cotton has continued.

The decline in the imports from the United Kingdom from those of the previous year amounts to 224,674*l*., or nearly one-half, while Hong-Kong suffers in still greater proportion, the imports from that colony having decreased by 150,737*l*., and being little more than one-seventh of those of the previous year. This decrease is entirely accounted for by the fall in the import of sugar from Hong-Kong. The small import trade from Canada also fell to nearly one-twentieth of that of 1901. The total imports from the British Empire show a decrease of 375,097*l*. from those of the preceding year. *Imports from the United Kingdom and colonies.*

In the export trade there has also been a falling-off, though a slight one. Exports to the United Kingdom and to British India have slightly increased. The only noticeable increase, however, is that of exports to Russia, which have advanced 10,000*l*., an advance of five-sevenths on the preceding year. *Decrease in exports. Exceptions.*

Reviewing the most prominent imports in detail, the following results will be found :— *Imports reviewed in detail.*

A decrease in the quantity of coal imported to the extent of 32,027 tons and 82,489*l*. in value. The whole import was from the United Kingdom and the United States, and consisted of Welsh coal to the value of 31,500*l*., and Pocohontas 5,299*l*. The first experimental cargo of this coal was imported here from Philadelphia early in 1900, when the price of Welsh coal was the highest yet seen, and sold to the United States and German navies. Since then it has been regularly imported for the United States Navy. Its price at that time was 3*l*. per ton, while Cardiff fetched nearly 4*l*. 10*s*. per ton. During 1902 the lowest price here for Cardiff was 2*l*. 2*s*. per ton ; at the close of the year it had risen to 2*l*. 8*s*. per ton. The general price of Pocohontas was 2*l*. 2*s*. per ton, prices in both cases being duty paid and f.o.b. *Coal.*

A slight increase in the quantity but decrease in the value of raw cotton imported, which was divided as follows :— *Raw cotton.*

From—				Quantity.	Value.
				Lbs.	£
China	..	..	..	2,589,067	43,100
British India	..	..	..	243,333	3,800
United States	..	..	..	73,200	1,700
	Total	..	..	2,905,600	48,600

The fall in the value of cotton imported has been persistent, as the following table will show, the loss falling most heavily on British India. This has continued, while the import for the United States shows a slight recovery :— *Continuous decrease.*

From—	Value.			
	1899.	1900.	1901.	1902.
	£	£	£	£
China	45,382	48,904	47,567	43,100
British India	102,118	8,980	5,860	3,800
United States	28,461	42,168	40	1,700
Total	175,961	100,052	53,467	48,600

Drugs. The import of drugs and chemicals was insignificant, the largest item being for caustic soda 2,897l., the whole of which came from the United Kingdom.

Paints. A large decrease in the import of dyes and paints. Of these the only noticeable item is paint in oil, the entire import of which, to the value of 2,609l., came from the United Kingdom.

Flour. A decrease of 3,941l. in the import of flour, which was imported to the value of 10,833l. from the United States.

Instruments and tools. A decrease of over 3,209l. in the import of instruments and tools, most of which were of British manufacture.

Glass. An increase of 1,579l. in the value of the import of glass manufactures. Of the whole import the value of window glass amounted to 9,213l., of which 8,958l. came from Belgium, the rest from Germany ; while plate glass to the value of 257l. came from Belgium and only 97l. from the United Kingdom. Cheap glassware has for some years been made in Nagasaki, and its quality is steadily improving.

Machinery. A decrease of 14,197l. in the import of machinery. Of the total value of 44,543l. imported, 35,708l. was of British manufacture, 6,935l. American, and 1,840l. French, the small balance coming from Russia and Norway. The British included lifting machinery to the value of 4,307l. ; drilling machinery, 3,137l. ; lathes, 4,534l. ; other machine tools, 4,618l. ; electric machinery and motors, 4,140l. The largest items in the American imports are for lathes, sawing and other machine tools, 3,108l. ; electric machinery and motors, 1,326l. ; and drilling machinery, 909l. The largest in the German import is 1,134l. for fire engines.

Manure. An increase of 10,758l. in the import of bone and bone dust for manure. This came, to the value of 31,570l., from China, 4,083l. from Corea, the small balance from Russia.

Salted meat. A decrease of 2,824l. in the import of salted meat. This came, to the value of 5,926l., from Corea, 3,628l. from Russian Asia, the rest from America.

Metals. The total value of the import of metals in 1902 was 178,769l., showing a falling-off, as compared with 1901, of 8,741l.

A slight increase is noticeable in the import of manufactured iron, of pipes and tubes and of steel ; the other items show a decrease.

Metals principally British. Of the total import of metals of the value of 178,769l., the value of that coming from the United Kingdom was 146,450l., the principal items contributing towards it being :—

Articles.	Value.		Value of import from the United Kingdom.
	Total Import.	British Import.	
	£	£	
Manufactured iron—			
Pig	9,368	8,589	
Bar and rod	19,410	10,397	
Plate and sheet	44,315	40,977	
Galvanised sheet	2,229	2,156	
Other manufactured iron ..	16,880	15,008	
Iron manufactures—			
Pipes and tubes	15,125	14,749	
Rails	549	433	
Nails	4,296	954	
Screws and bolts	5,671	5,546	
Anchors and chain cables ..	5,688	5,573	
Steel and steel manufactures—			
Steel	4,790	4,468	
„ wire rope	5,435	4,423	
Other steel manufactures ..	6,295	6,256	
Brass, tubes, &c.	2,741	2,527	
Copper „	8,085	7,748	

The entire quantity of pig iron came from the United Kingdom, with the exception of 769l. worth from the Hanyang foundry near Hankow. Bar and rod were imported from Belgium to the value of 7,473l., and 1,540l. from Germany. Plate and sheet, 1,714l. from Belgium, 1,255l. from France, 369l. from Germany and United States. Of the total import (92,202l.) of manufactured iron, 77,127l. came from the United Kingdom. Steel wire rope, 606l. from Germany and 406l. from Belgium. Nails, 1,574l. from the United States, 1,398l. from Germany and 370l. from Belgium. *From other countries.*

IMPORT of Metals during the Year 1902.

Country of Origin.				Value.
				£
United Kingdom				146,450
United States				11,837
Belgium				10,921
Germany				5,242
France				1,976
Other countries				2,343
Total				178,769

The import of kerosene oil in 1902 shows a decrease from that of 1901 of 1,346,545 gallons in quantity and 43,502l. in value. The American oil is imported in cans containing 10 gallons. Russian *Kerosene.*

oil is imported almost entirely in bulk in tank steamers, a very
small quantity only arriving in cases. The import of Russian oil
is in British, while that of American oil is in American hands :—

				Quantity.	Value.
				Gallons.	£
American oil	..	..	..	7,583,950	166,980
Russian tank oil	..	..	..	2,833,877	44,277
Russian case oil	..	..	..	6,870	157
Total	..	..	..	10,424,697	211,414

Oil cake.   An advance of 11,502*l.* in the value of the import of oil cake,
the greater part of which comes from China.

Provisions.   A decrease of 6,634*l.* in the value of the import of provisions,
under which heading are included all comestibles other than flour
and salted meat, the principal ones being fresh eggs, condensed
milk and butter, to the respective values of 6,697*l.*, 2,300*l.*, 1,764*l.*,
the first being slightly in excess of last year's value, the two last
below it. Eggs come chiefly from China, a comparatively small
quantity from Corea.

Rice.   An increase of 14,697*l.* in the value of rice imported. The
largest amount of this came from the French Indo-Chinese possessions
and was valued at 44,030*l.* ; the import from China comes next at
7,966*l.* ; Siam, 7,680*l.* ; British India, 6,940*l.* ; and finally Corea,
998*l.* It may be noted that the value of rice imported in 1901
from British India was only 563*l.*

Steam boilers.   Steam boilers were imported to the value of 6,782*l.*, all of which,
with the exception of 8*l.* from France, came from the United
Kingdom.

Sugar.   The trade in sugar is of great importance to British interests,
forming, as it has done for many years, about 95 per cent. of the
total value of the imports to Japan from Hong-Kong. The import
into Nagasaki in 1902 amounted to 78,177 cwts., valued at 44,599*l.*
These figures show a decrease from the import of 1901 of 254,878
cwts. and of 183,103*l.* in value.

Classification of import of 1902.   The import into Nagasaki in 1902 was classified in the customs
return as follows :—

Brown sugar.—This includes not only raw and brown sugar
strictly so called, but also all qualities of partially refined sugar
up to and including refined sugar of No. 14 Dutch Standard in
colour. Class I—(*a*) up to No. 7, inclusive, Dutch Standard of
colour, 26,386 cwts., of the value of 10,526*l.* ; (*b*) up to No. 14,
inclusive, Dutch Standard, 13,234 cwts., of the value of 6,492*l.*
Class II—(*a*) up to No. 20, inclusive, Dutch Standard, 3,636 cwts.,
of the value of 2,450*l.* ; (*b*) above No. 20, Dutch Standard, 34,921
cwts., of the value of 27,581*l.*

Increased import in 1901.   The increase in the import during 1901 was attributable, as

remarked in last year's report, to the attempt to evade payment Increased taxation.
of the consumption tax which came into operation on October 1,
1901. This tax is collected, as regards imported refined sugars,
before they are removed from the customs. It is true that the
regulations allow of their being stored in bond ; but the charges
for storage in the bonded warehouses are too heavy to make this
course practicable, and these warehouses, too, are unwilling to store
large quantities.

The great decline noticeable in the amount of sugar imported
during 1902 is due in part to this anticipatory import of 1901,
in part also to the increasingly keen competition of the native Competition of Japanese refineries.
refineries in Japan and Corea, which will, there is little doubt,
gradually supply more and more of the refined sugar required in Japan.

Of Class I, 7,191l. came from China, 7,276l. from the Distribution of import.
Philippines, 1,230l. from Hong-Kong, and small quantities from
the Dutch, British and French colonies. Of Class II, the import
from Hong-Kong amounted to 20,700l., and the balance, under 7,000l.,
from Germany. The total value of sugar imported into Nagasaki
from Hong-Kong in 1901 was 171,298l.

The fall in the import of textiles too, during 1902, was great, Textiles.
showing a decrease from that of the preceding year of 13,870l., or
more than the entire value of the import of 1902.

The value of cotton textiles imported from the United Kingdom
was only 965l., of which the largest item was cotton satins 176l.,
while the United States figures with only 208l. for duck and Russia
824l. for cotton prints. In woollen textiles the decrease from last
year was 2,942l. ; the British import amounted to 2,732l., of which
1,533l. was for woollen and worsted cloths. The small balance
was divided among Germany, Russia, France and Holland.

Of silk, nearly the whole import came from China, the value
of silk goods coming from that country being 1,747l.

The value of timber imported in 1902 was 8,912l. less than in Timber.
1901. Of the 10,624l. worth imported in 1902, 9,002l. was teak,
all of which comes from Siam, while lumber, boards and planks
from the United States and British North America amounted
respectively to only 743l. and 653l.

Of the 8,911l. set down as the value of four steam vessels imported, Steam vessels.
the only import in the ordinary sense of the word was a steam launch
built at Hong-Kong, of the value of 930l. 4,083l. is the value given
of the steamship "Tauais," which was bought from the Messageries
Maritimes Company by the Osaka Merchant Steamship Company ;
3,318l. is the value of the German steamship "Samoa," bought by
a Japanese subject, and now being refitted at the Kawasaki dock
at Kobe, while 530l. was the value of the wreck "Yoshino Maru,"
a British steamship, sold, but not yet transferred, to Japanese,
which was broken up.

The imports at the port of Kuchinotsu amounted in 1902 to Import trade of subsidiary ports.
61,981l., of which 39,426l. was raw cotton, 17,791l. oil cake, and
2,234l. rice. The imports at Karatsu amounted only to 1,056l.

The principal exports from Nagasaki during the year were, in Principal exports.

the order of their value, products of fisheries, coal, tea, provisions. Of the total value of the export of dried fish, &c., viz., 108,501*l.*, no less than 71,822*l.* was dried cuttlefish, of which 68,937*l.* worth went to Hong-Kong; 6,058*l.* worth of mushrooms also went to Hong-Kong, the rest to China.

Brick tea.

Of the export of tea, 20,081*l.* was brick tea, which all went to Russia, while practically all the other tea exported, viz., 8,531*l.*, went to China. The advance of this export of brick tea has been very rapid, for in 1899 it amounted to only 191*l.*, in 1900 to 1,808*l.*, in 1901 to 10,288*l.*, and in 1902 to 20,081*l.*

Raw silk.

A practically new export from Nagasaki is that of raw silk, which appeared in the customs returns for the first time in 1899, when it amounted to 1,021*l.* In the following year it disappeared, reappearing in 1901 with a total of 3,047*l.*, and rose still further last year to 9,253*l.*, the whole of which went to Russia.

The whole of the export of Awabi shells went to the United Kingdom.

Of the raw cotton exported, 4,923*l.* worth went to Corea, 2,660*l.* to Russian Asia, the rest to China, which country also took the whole of the export of cotton yarn, amounting in 1902 to little over 2,000*l.*, less than one-seventh of the export of the previous year.

The decline in the export of rice, mentioned in the last report, has continued in 1902.

The export of Portland cement continued during 1902, but fell to about one-sixth of its value in 1901. Nearly the whole of this went to China.

Of other manufactures, lacquered ware, paper, porcelain and textiles all show a decreased export, while clothing alone shows an increase of 2,794*l.*, the principal items under this heading being European clothes to the value of 3,344*l.*, boots and shoes 1,254*l.*, and cotton underclothing 1,173*l.*, all made in Japan.

Exports from subsidiary ports.

Although the export trade from the two subsidiary ports is chiefly in coal, cotton yarn was exported last year from the port of Kuchinotsu of the value of 87,833*l.*, and from Karatsu of the value of 1,288*l.*

Coal from Nagasaki.

In the export of coal from Nagasaki there was a decrease as compared with the previous year of 16,340 tons and 12,431*l.* in value. This is to be ascribed chiefly to the transfer of the export from Nagasaki to Moji and to the ports of Kuchinotsu and Karatsu. The coal coming from the Takaslima mines at this port is considered the best of all Japanese coal, and that from the Miike mines, near Kuchinotsu, ranks next to it, being an excellent coal both for steaming and for gas. But at Moji coal in large quantities for cargoes can be obtained at cheaper rates than in Nagasaki. and the former port also lies in the direct route from Yokohama and Kobe to Shanghai, Hong-Kong and Singapore, and large ships, after discharging their outward cargo at these Japanese ports, very frequently call at Moji, taking thence a full cargo of coal for the three ports mentioned, where there is a good demand for Japanese coal, and whence they can readily obtain freight for Europe.

The Miike mines are situated at Omuta, 35 miles from the port **Miike coal** of Kuchinotsu, at which ships often call after discharging cargo at **mines.** Nagasaki, and there fill up with coal for China or Singapore. The water there is, however, so shallow that the shore is approachable only by small junks, and even these can only be lightly loaded, and they are then towed to Kuchinotsu, which they reach in five hours. There are at times periods of low tides when even these are unable to approach for a week at a time. To obviate the inconvenience arising from this state of things, the Mitsui Company, to whom the mines belong, have decided to construct a dock and wharves at this spot. Work was commenced in June of last year, and is to be completed in five years at a cost of 3,500,000 yen, or a little over 357,000*l*.

The dock will be approached by a passage 2,000 yards long and 820 yards wide, protected on each side by a breakwater. At the entrance to this channel the sea is 30 feet deep and the depth of water in the channel itself will be 15 feet at neap tides. A double lock with three gates will give entrance into the dock, where quays will be built of sufficient size to allow three or four vessels of from 7,000 to 8,000 tons to lie alongside. Rails will be laid along the quay, and the coal trucks will be brought alongside the ships. Adjoining the dock a large reservoir will be built, by means of which, together with the lock gates, a constant depth of water will be maintained in the dock. The dock itself can be readily enlarged if necessary, and an almost unlimited number of wharves can be constructed by reclamation to right or left of the breakwaters forming the approach. The work is reported to have progressed more quickly than was expected, and the broken stone for the dam for the left breakwater has already been laid down. The present output of these mines averages 1,000,000 tons a year, which quantity, it is expected, will be very greatly increased after the completion of this dock, the working of the mines having hitherto been hampered by the lack of facilities for shipping the coal.

While, therefore, the export of coal from Nagasaki during the **Coal from** last five years shows a continuous fall, that from Kuchinotsu, **Kuchinotsu** though it was lower in 1901 than in the previous year, has, with that **and Karatsu.** exception, continually risen, and although the export from Karatsu was lower last year than in 1901, still the aggregate exports from the three ports of this district was nearly 100,000 tons greater than the aggregate of 1901 :—

Year.		Quantity.				Total Value.
		Nagasaki.	Kuchinotsu.	Karatsu.	Total.	
		Tons.	Tons.	Tons.	Tons.	£
1898 ..	..	413,715	370,732	80,547	864,994	705,993
1899 ..	..	343,001	432,885	71,211	847,097	673,674
1900 ..	..	374,771	562,990	129,537	1,077,298	722,346
1901 ..	..	187,823	487,353	184,296	859,472	537,480
1902 ..	..	171,483	619,014	165,803	956,300	590,507

From Moji.   Although Moji is no longer included in the Nagasaki Consular
district, having been included in that of Shimonoseki in 1901, the
following table, showing the continuous increase in the export of
coal from that port, will explain the corresponding decrease in that
from Nagasaki :—

Year.						Quantity.
						Tons.
1898	..	..	..	..	..	788,027
1899	..	..	..	..	..	832,226
1900	..	..	..	..	..	949,638
1901	..	..	..	..	..	1,929,910
1902	..	..	..	..	..	1,833,165

From these figures it will be seen that the great fall of 186,000
tons in the export from Nagasaki in 1901 was contemporaneous
with a far greater rise of 980,000 tons in that from Moji.   Thus, while
the export trade in coal has practically been transferred to other
ports, to Moji chiefly, but also to Kuchinotsu and Karatsu, there
is every prospect that the trade of Nagasaki in bunker coal will
continue steady.   The splendid and safe anchorage of Nagasaki,
vastly superior to that of Moji, which the swift current running
through the Shimonoseki Straits renders somewhat unsafe, the facilities it affords for transhipment to all ports of North China and
Russian Asia, and the remarkable rapidity with which the vessels
can be coaled, in both of which the smooth and still water in this
harbour is of great importance—all these circumstances combine to
render it probable that Nagasaki will still remain the coaling port in
this southern island for mail steamers and other large vessels.

Takashima   The output in the year 1902 of the mines of the Mitsui Bishi
mines.   Company on Takashima and Hashima, islands lying close to this
harbour, was 186,929 tons, valued at 157,464*l*.   The average prices
for the year were : for lump, 9 yen 275 sen (18*s.* 11*d.*) ; for mixed
lump and small 8 yen 12 sen (16*s.* 7*d.*) ; and for small coal,
7 yen 31 sen (14*s.* 11*d.*), showing a considerable advance on the
prices for the previous year, which were respectively 8 yen 41 sen
(17*s.* 2*d.*), 7 yen 42 sen (15*s.* 2*d.*) and 6 yen 99 sen (14*s.* 3*d.*), and
when the greater output of 198,579 tons was valued at 154,064*l*.

Owing to the poor quality of coal obtained from the mine on
Yokoshima, the workings there were abandoned in January, 1902.
At about the same time a new shaft was commenced on the opposite
side of Takashima to that on which were the existing workings.
This will be in full working order by the beginning of next year,
and an output of over 1,000 tons a day is expected from it ; but it
is probable that the output from the present workings will decrease.
There are five seams of coal, the uppermost is one of 8 feet thick-
ness, and thence in order downwards come seams of 12, 5,

18 and 3 feet. This last is not being worked. The 18 feet seam is that chiefly worked, both at Takashima and at Hashima, another island lying about 2½ miles distant, where it is worked at a depth of 1,500 feet. This is lower than the level of the same seam at Takashima. It is expected that many faults will be found in the seam; but, if the displacement in these be not excessive, it is intended to drive a tunnel through the seam from the one island to the other. Should this be found impracticable, the seam must continue to be worked from either end, or another shaft be sunk from one of several islets near.

It is estimated that the coal at present known to exist immediately around the Islands Takashima and Hashima affords a supply at the pesent rate of working for at least 30 years.

The Mitsui Bishi Company owns coal mines also at Ochi, near Karatsu, and at Namadzuta and Shinuyu, near Moji. It has a contract for the supply of coal from these two last-named mines to the Peninsular and Oriental Company at Shanghai and Hong-Kong. The entry of this company on the coal mining industry dates from 1881, when it purchased the Takashima mine from the late Count Goto. The company's other mines have been opened since then.

Of the three principal factors in the prosperity of Nagasaki, viz., (1) the trade with China, and especially with North China; (2) the coal mining industry; and (3) the shipbuilding industry, mention has been made at some length of one, the coal industry. The third, the shipbuilding industry, is of great importance, not Shipbuilding, alone to this port and country, but also to British shipowners, to docks, &c. whom it must be a matter of interest to know the facilities offered for the repairs of their ships at this distant port of the Far East.

A somewhat full account of the works and of alterations and additions to them up to last summer was given in last year's report. Some important alterations have, however, been made since then. By an extension, and also by a re-arrangement of the shipbuilding yard, it now contains eight berths, on which as many ships, ranging from 170 to 700 feet in length, can be built at the same time, and at a little extra expense in cutting away the hill at the back of the yard two ships of 1,000 feet each could be built alongside of each other. The building capacity of this yard has been increased, and it is now able to turn out vessels of an aggregate gross tonnage of 20,000 tons in the year.

The shipbuilding yard possesses an extensive pneumatic plant for riveting, caulking, clipping and cutting plates, &c. A much larger plant has, however, been ordered, and when that is set up it is intended to remove the present plant to the machine shop.

The plans for the dock mentioned last year as being in course of construction have been enlarged; the intention now is to give it a length of 714 feet on the keel blocks, with a breadth at the entrance at the top of 96 feet 7 inches and at the bottom of 88 feet 7 inches. Depth of water at ordinary spring tides, 34 feet 6 inches. It is further the intention not to build up the dock head, and the length of the dock can be readily extended by further cutting away of the hill side into which the head of the dock is cut.

Forty machines of the newest pattern were installed in the machine shop last year. These included a planing machine to plane 21 feet horizontally and 18 feet vertically ; a 54-inch centre crank shaft lathe ; a 30-inch centre-gap lathe ; two 24-inch centre shaft lathes, having a common centre line to turn a shaft up to 67 feet in length ; one 5½-inch spindle double universal horizontal drilling, boring, tapping, studding and milling machine to move 10 feet vertically and 15 feet horizontally ; a cylinder boring machine, to bore cylinders up to 100 inches diameter. About 40 more new small machines have been acquired up to date. In the boiler shop electric shell drilling machines, screwing machines and a plate roller for rolling plates up to 2 inches thick by 11 feet 9 inches wide have been set up, and a duplicate of the 40-ton overhead electric travelling crane set up last year has been ordered.

The foundry shop as previously enlarged being insufficient, a further extension of 102 by 50 feet has been made to be used for brass founding only ; the part hitherto used for that purpose being added to the iron foundry.

The heaviest casting made at these works was one of 22 tons, and it is improbable that it will be repeated, the practice being to reduce the size of individual castings by making them in sections, which greatly increases the facility of handling the new casting, to which the weight of the mould adds enormously, and also reduces the risk of loss in case of misadventure ; 50 tons of castings can be easily turned out in a day.

Steel castings are not made here, and such as are required, as, for instance, stern frames for steamers, are obtained from the United Kingdom. Small steel castings can, however, be made at Osaka.

Steam power in all parts of the works is rapidly being superseded by electricity and compressed air. The reason for this is the scarcity of water on that side of the harbour, which necessitates water being brought to the works by boat at an annual cost of 2,000l.

The electric power house is furnished with condensing apparatus for recovering the water employed by the steam engines in driving the dynamos.

Among the vessels completed last year at this yard is a salvage steamer of 712 tons, with a speed of 12 knots, fitted with all the necessary pumps and gear of the most powerful description. With this and with its large staff of experienced workmen and drivers the company is prepared at short notice to undertake salvage operations. When not engaged in salvage operations this steamer is employed as a passenger boat, making trips on fixed days to places on the neighbouring coasts and outlying islands. On the last day of December, 1902, there were 5,245 workmen employed in the works. During 1902 four steamers were completed, of an aggregate gross tonnage of 8,361 tons. The details of these are as follows :—

No.	Description.	Length.	Breadth.	Depth.	Tons.	I.H.P.
		Feet.	Ft. in.	Ft. in.		
1	Single-screw steel salvage steamer ...	186	29 0	16 2	712	690
2	,, ,, iron-ore carriers ...	320	42 0	25 0	2,774	2,779
3	,, ,, ,,	320	42 0	25 0	2,795	2,366
4	,, composite steam yacht	90	17 8	9 6	80	220

Mention has already been made of the first vessel on this list. The second and third are employed under contract in conveying iron ore from the Chinese mines at Taishan, in the neighbourhood of Hankow, to the Government steel works at Yawata, near Wakamatsu. On the return journeys they take cargoes of coal from Moji to the Hanyang Iron Works. The fourth is a yacht built for the use of the Prince Imperial of Japan.

The work in hand at the close of 1902 was as follows :—

No.	Description.	Length.	Breadth.	Depth.	Tons.	I.H.P.
		Feet.	Ft. in.	Ft. in.		
1	Twin-screw steel cargo and passenger steamer	445	49 2	33 6	6,443	5,448
2	Single-screw steel cargo and passenger steamer	256	36 0	16 4	1,933	1,565
3	Single-screw steel cargo steamer ...	279	39 6	23 3	2,000	1,200
4	Twin-screw steel passenger steamer	420	50 0	30 6	5,400	6,500
5	Single-screw steel cargo and passenger steamer	256	36 0	16 4	1,933	1,565
6	Twin-screw steel ferry boat	115	20 0	10 3	223	320
7	,, ,, ,, ...					
8	Single-screw steel cargo steamer ...	385	48 6	29 9	5,000	3,200
9	Twin-screw steel cargo and passenger steamer	445	52 0	33 6	7,000	5,900
10	Small cargo and passenger steamer	112	...	...	...	...
11	Steam launch	60	...	...	...	...
12	,, ...	50	...	...	...	...

Of these vessels No. 1 was delivered to the Japan Mail Steamship Company in March, and is now running on its American line to Seattle. No. 2 was delivered to the same company early in the year, and is running on its North China line. No. 3 was launched early last month, and by the end of June will go to Osaka to take Government material to the Pescadores. No. 4 will be launched in September, and is intended for the Japan Mail Steamship Company's Australian line. No. 5, to be launched in July, is for the same company's North China line. No. 6 is already running in the Inland Sea in connection with the Sanyo Railway, for which service No. 7 is also intended. No. 8, of which the keel plate has already been laid, is for the Japan Mail Steamship Company's Bombay line. Of the last four, which have not been commenced, No. 9 is for the same company's American line ; No. 10 is for the Merchant Steamship Company of Osaka ; and the last two are launches for the use of the Dock Company itself. The engines of the earlier of these large steamers, which the company commenced to build in 1897, were imported from the United Kingdom. Three years ago, however, they engaged the services of a British engineer, under whose supervision the engines also are now built in the company's workshops. The excellent quality of the work turned

out by the shipbuilding yard of this company has obtained for it
a high reputation, and compares favourably with that of many
British yards. Great care is exercised in its supervision, and the
over-lapping of rivet holes in the hull plates, giving what are
technically termed " blind " or " half blind " holes. is unknown ;
all the rivet holes being " true."

The docking business of the company in 1902 shows a great
falling-off both in number and tonnage, from that of the previous
year :—

	1902.		1901.	
	Number of Vessels.	Tons.	Number of Vessels.	Tons.
Japanese—				
Vessels of war ..	9	3,942	23	6,666
Merchant vessels ..	27	38,014	51	85,306
Foreign—				
Vessels of war ..	7	9,561	21	·53.498
Merchant vessels ..	48	118,146	54	147,673

Transhipment
cargo.

During 1902 17,974 tons of goods, valued at 719,592l., were
transhipped at Nagasaki, showing an increase in value of 20,469l.
over those transhipped in the preceding year. Of this amount,
50,161l. was the value of goods brought to Nagasaki from Siberia,.
Corea and North China for transmission to South China, Europe and
America, while the value of exports from Europe and America to
Port Arthur and Vladivostock transhipped at Nagasaki amounted
to 384,762l., and those to Corea 274,113l.

Shipping.
aggregate
tonnage.

The aggregate tonnage of the merchant shipping under all
flags entered in Nagasaki, and the ports of Kuchinotsu and Karatsu,.
included in this Consular district in 1902, shows a slight advance
on that of the previous year. The most marked changes are a
great increase in Japanese and decrease in French shipping. Entries
at the port of Hakata were included in the total of entri s in the
Nagasaki Consular dist:ict. This port, which lies in the Prefecture
of Fukuoka, being now comprised in the district of Shimonoseki
Consulate, the entries at Hakata have, for the sake of comparison,
been deducted from the totals for 1901.

Japanese
shipping at
Nagasaki.

At Nagasaki 504 Japanese vessels of 616,507 tons entered in
1902, as against 415 vessels of 585,373 tons in 1901, and 456 vessels
of 552,551 tons in 1900.

At
Kuchinotsu.

At Kuchinotsu the increase is still more marked, 138 vessels
of 193,197 tons having entered in 1902, against 107 vessels of
156,908 tons in 1901, and 98 vessels of 147,143 tons in 1900,

Aggregate of
the three
ports.

while the aggregate of the three ports in 1902 was 642 vessels of
809,704 tons, against 698 vessels of 797,203 tons in 1901, and
629 vessels of 738,183 tons in 1900. In none of these figures are

included the numbers or tonnage of the small coasting steamers which ply in large numbers between Nagasaki and small towns on the neighbouring coasts not opened to foreign trade.

The majority of the steamers entered belong to the two great shipping companies of Japan, the Nippon Yusen Kaisha (Japan Mail Steamship Company) and the Osaka Shosen Kaisha (Merchant Shipping Company of Osaka). The former company has five lines calling at Nagasaki, viz., a weekly service to Shanghai, a monthly service to Australia, and others to North China direct, to North China viâ Corean ports, to Vladivostock and to Formosa. The steamers of this company's European, American, Indian and direct Formosan lines do not call at this port.

The Osaka Company has fortnightly services from Nagasaki to Corean ports, and also to Formosan ports.

A third company, the Toyo Kisen Kaisha (Oriental Steamship Company) owns three large steamships running between Hong-Kong and San Francisco in conjunction with the vessels of the Pacific Mail and the Occidental and Oriental Steamship Companies.

The British shipping entered at Nagasaki shows a decrease in 1902 of 32 vessels and 41,960 tons as compared with the previous year. The aggregate of British shipping in the three ports of the district was, in 1902, 250 vessels of 652,144 tons, of which 4 were sailing ships, showing a decrease of 14 vessels but an increase in tonnage of 7,904 tons on the previous year, when, of the 264 vessels entered, 13 were sailing ships. *British shipping at Nagasaki.*

The extension between China and Japan of the Peninsular and Oriental Company's Mail Steamship service from Europe, which used to be carried on by two steamers, was abandoned in the autumn of 1900, and there seems to be no immediate prospect of its renewal The "Intermediate" or cargo and passenger steamers of this company have also almost ceased to call at Nagasaki, for of these vessels only 3, of a tonnage of 8,050 tons, entered the port. In 1901 the number was 4, and in 1900 it was 18 vessels, with a tonnage of 55,202 tons. In view of the tonnage dues charged in Japanese ports and the small amount of cargo consigned to Nagasaki, it is found to be more economical for a ship bringing cargo from Europe to tranship it at Shanghai. This view is supported by the fact that the steamers of the European line of the Japan Mail Steamship Company do not call at Nagasaki; but, running direct from Hong-Kong to Kobe, they tranship their Nagasaki cargo at the latter port into steamers of their Shanghai, Australian or Formosan lines which call here.

The decrease of British shipping at Nagasaki is counterbalanced by an increase at Kuchinotsu, the port for the Miike coal mines, where the increase in 1902 was 24 vessels, all of which were steamships, and 62,660 tons. Now of those ships which enter at Kuchinotsu many have not called at Nagasaki; but, having brought out a cargo of Welsh coal for the use of the Japanese Navy and discharged it at the Admiralty port of Sasebo, they proceed to

Kuchinotsu, and there take in a return cargo of Japanese coal for Hong-Kong or Singapore.

Classification of British shipping at Nagasaki.

Of the British shipping which entered Nagasaki during 1902, the numbers and tonnage of vessels belonging to the principal well-known lines were as follows :—

Lines by Red Sea route.

The Ocean Steamship Company.—30 steamers of 82,806 tons, as compared with 30 steamers of 113,114 tons in 1901.

" Ben " Line.—16 steamers of 29,370 tons, as compared with 18 steamers of 32,622 tons in 1901.

China Mutual Steamship Company.—15 steamers of 51,060 tons, as compared with 17 steamers of 52,795 tons in 1901.

" Shire " Line.—8 steamers of 19,701 tons, as compared with 7 steamers of 15,946 tons in 1901.

" Glen " Line.—6 steamers of 15,907 tons, as compared with 9 steamers of 27,683 tons in 1901.

All the above are cargo steamers only from the United Kingdom viâ the Suez Canal, and calling at Nagasaki on the outward voyage only.

Trans-Pacific.

Of the Trans-Pacific lines, 50 steamers of the Canadian Pacific Railway Company of 142,487 tons, and 29 steamers of 80,774 tons of the White Star Line, under charter to the Occidental and Oriental Steamship Company, called at this port in 1901, as compared with 34 steamers of 100,117 tons belonging to the former and 30 steamers of 85,820 tons belonging to the latter lines in 1901.

Of ocean-going steamers of the tramp class, or which, while belonging to the well-known lines do not call regularly at Nagasaki, there were 29 entr'es of an aggregate tonnage of 59,768 tons, as compared with 40 entries with a tonnage of 99,356 tons in 1901.

French shipping.

French steam shipping continues to be represented solely by the mail steamers of the Compagnie des Messageries Maritimes. There was last year a decrease of 32 vessels with a tonnage of 42,521 tons, the entries being 46 vessels and tonnage 101,905 tons, as compared with 78 entries with a tonnage of 144,426 tons in 1901. This falling-off was not in steamers only, as only one sailing ship entered in 1902 as against six in 1901. This ship brought Cardiff coal, as did all those in 1901.

In the returns for 1903 the entries of French shipping will be practically nil, the steamers of the French Mail Company having ceased to call at Nagasaki since February 15 of the present year.

German shipping.

German shipping at the port of Nagasaki shows a decrease of 16 vessels with a tonnage of 22,733 tons, 80 vessels with a tonnage of 290,372 tons having entered in 1902, as compared with 96 vessels with a tonnage of 313,105 tons in 1901. Of the entries in 1902 53 vessels with a tonnage of 254,061 tons belonged to the German mail steamers, in which service there were employed four steamers of a net registered tonnage of over 6,500 tons, two of 3,900 tons, and five of a little over 3,000 tons each.

A report has been current for some time that it is intended to withdraw the large passenger steamers of over 6,500 tons net tonnage of the Norddeutscher Lloyd and Hamburg-American lines, which have been running here since the autumn of 1899, and to replace them by steamers of the size of those alone previously employed, viz., of a net tonnage of little over 3,000 tons.

Russian shipping again shows an advance, and has maintained the position which it acquired in 1901, of second, numerically, though not in tonnage, to that under the Japanese flag. Russian shipping.

The following figures, which include steamers only, show its advance since 1897 :—

Year.	Number of Vessels.	Tons.
1897	75	144,005
1899	157	268,459
1901	228	378,109
1902	249	385,609

The fine steamers of the Russian Volunteer Fleet call here regularly on both the outward and homeward voyages between Odessa and Vladivostock, and the 13 vessels engaged in this service made the round trip 20 times during the year 1902, making a total, including one call by a ship which was sold on her return home, of 41 entries with a tonnage of 184,374 tons. Of these vessels, nine have a net tonnage of over 4,700 tons, one of them having a net tonnage of 5,787 tons, and one 6,188 tons. A still larger one was built last year, but has not yet come out.

The Chinese Eastern Railway Company's fleet consists of 19 vessels, which called here 163 times in 1902. The company maintains regular direct communication between Nagasaki and Dalny and Shanghai and Dalny ; it has also regular steamers running between Shanghai and Vladivostock viâ Nagasaki and Corean ports, between Shanghai and Dalny viâ Corea and Port Arthur, and between Chefoo and Port Arthur. Inconvenience is caused, however, to shippers here, by its ceasing to run steamers direct from Nagasaki to Port Arthur, for which place a large quantity of cargo was transhipped at Nagasaki last year, much of it being taken on from Dalny to its destination in sea-going lighters, which afford insufficient protection to the cargo. The company has also services between Vladivostock and ports in Northern Siberia.

Two ships of the Russian Steam Navigation and Trading Company of Odessa made each one voyage out to Vladivostock and home during 1902, calling here twice each. In the previous year six steamers of this company called here, and they are expected to call more frequently during the present year.

Three vessels of the Northern Steamship Company of St. Petersburg, a Danish company under the Russian flag, called here twice each ; more are expected to call this year.

One steamer of the Archangel Mourmoa Steamship Company called here twice, but will not come again.

United States shipping. United States shipping shows an increased tonnage but a decrease of one in the number of entries. The customs table includes only steamships strictly engaged in commerce, and these all belonged to the Pacific Mail Steamship Company, whose vessels run between San Francisco and Hong-Kong viâ Japanese ports. In addition to these, however, 38 steamers of the aggregate tonnage of 117,150 tons, all under the United States flag, and employed as United States Army transports, entered Nagasaki during the year, principally on their homeward journey from Manila to San Francisco.

Public works, waterworks extension. The extension of the municipal waterworks, of which details were given in the report for 1899, was commenced in 1900, and was to have been completed by the end of March, 1903, owing, however, to the epidemic of cholera which occurred here last year, and to the consequent difficulty of obtaining the requisite amount of labour, the period for its completion has been extended to March, 1904.

The old reservoir had a capacity of 12,000,000 cubic feet ; two new reservoirs have now been constructed, the one near to the old one with a content of 14,000,000 cubic feet, and the other in a valley at some distance from the former with a content of 39,000,000 cubic feet, giving a total content of 65,000,000 cubic feet. The capacities of these reservoirs is given as 74,880,000, 87,360,000 and 243,360,000 gallons respectively, though, when quite full, they will all contain somewhat more ; the full capacity of No. 2 being estimated at 90,000,000 gallons. This gives a total of 405,240,000 gallons, which, at the present rate of distribution of 1,390,000 gallons, means a supply for 291 days. The former reservoir was constructed to supply a population of 60,000, when the actual population of Nagasaki was 44,921 ; the present two additional reservoirs are estimated to be sufficient for a further 122,000, or the whole three reservoirs to suffice for a total population of 182,000. The entire population of Nagasaki on December 31, 1902, was, however, 150,479 persons.

The extension as actually carried out differs somewhat from the proposals made in 1899. In addition to the two new reservoirs, there have been constructed six new filter beds, measuring 130 feet in length by 100 feet in breadth. The three old ones only measure 120 by 80 feet. These measurements are less than those originally proposed. Further, instead of the two service reservoirs, each 100 feet square, as proposed, two of 80 feet square have been built, and a third, of the same size, is now under construction, giving thus a larger quantity for immediate use than was proposed. This extension, the cost of which was estimated at 1,527,000 yen (about 155,800*l*.) has been carried out at an actual expenditure of 1,462,300 yen, or 6,600*l*. less than the sum estimated. It is furthur proposed to carry the supply pipes down the western side of the harbour, and thus to include the Mitsubishi Company's dockyard in the area of water supply.

Harbour works. In 1900 it was estimated (vide report for 1899) that the dredging and reclamation works, which would, it was hoped, be completed

in less than three years, would be sufficiently advanced to enable
the railway terminus to be brought down to the water's edge.
The terminus still remains where it was at that time, viz., 2½ miles from
the foreign quarter of the city. The new site proposed was certainly
much nearer to the main part of the city than the original site; but
it was still inconveniently distant, and the object of moving it, viz.,
of bringing sea and land communication into actual contact, was
not achieved thereby, as it was accessible on the level by only one
narrow street, for by other and nearer routes from a great portion
of the city a steep ridge had to be crossed rendering them impracticable for heavy traffic. However, the Minister for Home Affairs has
now ordered that the site be prepared in front of Deshima, the
historical Dutch settlement, where a very large area has already
been reclaimed. A further area of 741 tsubo (2,964 square yards)
is now to be reclaimed for this purpose.

The dredging and reclamation works in this harbour, which
were commenced in October, 1897, were to have been completed by
September, 1903. About one-third of the work still remains to be
done, the amount of dredging required having proved to be greater
than was estimated through the silting up again of places previously
dredged. Within the present year, too, a very large part of the
stone facing of the reclaimed land has had to be taken down and
rebuilt. At the commencement of the work the dredging was
undertaken by a company formed for this purpose, and was to be
completed in three years. The company, being unable to carry out
its undertaking, dredging operations were commenced by the
municipality and carried on simultaneously with those of the company. Further delay was met with last year, when, owing to the
prevalence of cholera at this port, a sufficient supply of labour to
carry on the work properly was not obtainable. The period for
completion of the work has now been extended by one year, bringing
it to September, 1904, by which time it is hoped that the whole
undertaking may be finished.

Work has also been started on the opposite (the west) side of
the head of the harbour, with the object of forming a coal station
there. This, however, is to be completed only by the autumn
of 1905.

ı The Japanese population of Nagasaki on December 31, 1902, Population.
numbered 148,880 persons, 80,892 being males and 67,988 females,
living in 20,483 houses. This shows an increase as compared with
that of the previous year of only 6,069 persons, or less than half the
increase of the preceding year. The foreign population of the port
shows a decrease, principally amongst American and French citizens.

The following table shows the actual figures of the foreign
population :—

FOREIGN Population of Nagasaki on December 31, 1902.

Nationality.	1902.			Total, 1901.
	Males.	Females.	Total.	
British	67	58	125	138
Russian..	56	57	113	132
American (U.S.) ..	53	46	99	160
German..	28	19	47	45
French	27	16	43	90
Austro-Hungarian .	18	9	27	33
Portuguese	9	4	13	..
Swedish and Norwegian	6	6	12	21
Danish	8	3	11	..
Italian	6	4	10	..
Roumanian	5	5	10	22
Turkish..	4	4	8	22
Dutch	2	2	4	..
Greek	1	1	2	..
Other Europeans ..	..	..	..	55
Unknown	4	5	9	..
Total	294	239	533	718
Chinese..	970	94	1,064	1,288
Corean	..	2	2	20
Grand total ..	1,264	335	1,599	2,026

Annex I.—RETURN of Import Trade of Nagasaki during the Years 1902–1901.

Articles.			1902.		1901.		Average, 1897–1901.	
			Quantity.	Value.	Quantity.	Value.	Quantity.	Value.
				£		£		£
Beans, peas, pulse	..	Tons	..	14,203	..	11,483	..	18,999
Coal	..	Lbs.	21,482	36,799	53,509	119,288	49,801	83,866
Cotton, raw	..		2,905,600	48,600	2,862,827	58,460	10,220,898	152,861
Dyes and paints	..			7,551		14,364		12,304
Flour	..	Cwts.	27,082	10,833	30,602	14,774	25,366	11,158
Glass and manufactures of	..		..	9,674	..	8,095	..	4,991
Instruments, tools and implements	..			3,791		7,000		11,262
Machinery	..			44,543		58,740		87,764
Manure, bone	..	Lbs.	23,778,852	36,508	16,086,965	25,750	15,177,818	20,843
Meat, salted	..	,,	3,233,998	9,932	3,494,548	12,756		12,264
Metals—								
Iron, manufactured	..	Tons	13,042	92,202	12,571	92,152	12,371	83,502
,, manufactures	..			29,262		30,393		34,288
Pipes and tubes	..	Tons	1,259	15,125	1,108	14,417	..	16,172
Rails and fittings thereof	..	,,	..	..	136	1,373	3,985	22,200
Steel and steel manufactures	..			16,520		15,719		10,973
Brass and manufactures of	..			2,741		5,320		⎫
Copper	..			8,085		11,035	..	⎬ 38,061
Lead	,,			..		5,459		⎭
Miscellaneous	..			14,884		11,642		
Oil, kerosene	..	Gallons	10,424,697	211,414	11,771,242	254,916	8,606,469	152,467
,, cake	..	Lbs.	59,081,867	86,831	47,767,333	75,329	49,669,718	76,441
Provisions	..			18,738		25,872		18,176
Rice	..	Tons	9,973	67,614	7,501	52,917	9,832	74,862
Steam boilers	..		..	6,782	..	7,406		11,575

RETURN of Import Trade of Nagasaki during the Years 1902-1901—continued.

Articles.		1902.		1901.		Average, 1897–1901.	
		Quantity.	Value.	Quantity.	Value.	Quantity.	Value.
			£		£		£
Submarine telegraph cables	..	..	..	..	15,119	..	..
Sugar—							
Brown	Cwts.	39,620	17,018	104,975	51,943	91,937	43,622
White	,,	38,557	27,581	228,080	175,759	278,503	200,114
Textiles—							
Cotton manufactures	..	..	2,585	..	8,953	..	5,402
Silk ,,	..	..	1,867	..	6,282	..	12,501
Woollen ,,	..	..	3,369	..	6,311	..	4,980
Miscellaneous	..	..	3,731	..	3,876	..	4,480
Timber	..	..	10,624	..	19,596	..	12,603
Vessels, steam	Number	4	8,911	5	81,803	3	131,678
Wine, beer and spirits	..	..	8,933	..	12,862	..	11,894
Sundries	..	..	74,074	..	92,198	..	..
Total foreign produce	..	..	950,675	..	1,403,603	..	1,381,753
Re-imports	..	..	1,337	..	2,116	..	..
Grand total	..	..	952,012	..	1,405,719	..	1,381,753

Annex II.—RETURN of Export Trade of Nagasaki during the Years 1902–1901.

Articles.		1902. Quantity.	1902. Value.	1901. Quantity.	1901. Value.	Average, 1897–1901. Quantity.	Average, 1897–1901. Value.
			£		£		£
Cement, Portland	Lbs.	2,148,207	2,007	11,405,036	11,842	342,432	6,841
Coal	Tons	171,483	102,096	187,823	114,527	565,386	280,906
Cotton, raw	Lbs.	406,300	9,229	406,403	10,084	918,023	12,174
„ yarn	„	82,263	2,102	586,067	15,910		22,007
Fish—							
Cuttle	„	4,714,355	71,822	4,849,997	80,990	3,845,848	67,741
Bêche-de-mer	„	225,556	6,888	241,158	7,202	302,363	8,536
Miscellaneous, dried	„	...	29,841	...	24,586	...	22,422
Grains and provisions		...	22,931	...	25,266	...	36,745
Lacquered ware		...	7,845	...	8,923	...	5,046
Mushrooms	Lbs.	286,619	14,730	213,717	9,534	211,612	8,978
Paper and paper manufactures		...	14,156	...	17,230	...	12,846
Porcelain and earthenware		...	5,588	...	5,700	...	5,973
Rice	Tons	1,277	12,868	1,525	15,448	2,424	22,549
Shells, Awabi	„	98	4,437	135	5,077	135	5,918
Silk, raw	Lbs.	13,987	9,263	...	...	...	...
Tea	„	2,546,573	28,970	1,808,841	17,169	896,301	6,931
Textiles—							
Cotton	„	...	1,884	...	1,913	...	10,464
Silk	„	...	3,324	...	7,347		
Clothing	„	...	10,425	...	7,631		
Miscellaneous	„	...	687	...	583		
Sundries	„	...	71,705	...	73,862	...	...
Total, Japanese produce		...	432,688	...	460,364	...	486,076
Re-exports		...	24,092	...	34,828	...	60,897
Grand total		...	456,780	...	495,692	...	546,973

Annex III.—RETURN showing Total Value of all Articles Exported from and Imported into Nagasaki to and from Foreign Countries during the Years 1902–1901.

Country.	Exports.		Imports.	
	1902.	1901.	1902.	1901.
	£	£	£	£
British Empire—				
United Kingdom ..	6,486	5,896	267,633	492,307
Hong-Kong ..	106,409	115,265	23,643	174,380
British India ..	14,846	13,215	11,848	8,090
Canada	21	85	127	2,366
Australia ..	515	140	497	1,702
Total British trade	127,777	134,601	303,748	678,845
China	215,923	238,042	216,272	202,373
United States ..	1,054	364	219,317	244,221
Corea	26,329	40,700	24,427	37,793
Russia	24,845	14,610	6,467	7,465
Russian Asia ..	51,071	59,544	51,583	55,980
France	495	22	9,263	. 17,246
Italy	1,654	5,800	445	308
Germany	583	1,412	20,216	21,095
Other countries ..	7,009	597 .	100,274	140,652
Total	328,963	361,091	648,264	727,083
Grand total ..	456,740	405,692	952,012	1,405,928

Annex IV.—RETURN of all Shipping Entered in the Consular District of Nagasaki during the Year 1902.

ENTERED NAGASAKI.

Nationality.	Sailing.		Steam.		Total.	
	Number of Vessels.	Tons.	Number of Vessels.	Tons.	Number of Vessels.	Tons.
Japanese.. ..	55	2,143	449	614,364	504	616,507
British	4	4,190	173	481,873	177	486,063
Russian	..	..	249	385,609	249	385,609
German	5	10,301	75	280,071	80	290,372
French	1	1,417	45	100,488	46	101,905
American (U.S.)	1	2,302	28	92,955	29	95,257
Norwegian ..	..	.	32	28,306	32	28,306
Other nationalities	7	4,154	11	12,232	18	16,386
Total	73	24,507	1,062	1,995,898	1,135	2,020,405
„ 1901 ..	116	33,233	1,094	2,050,201	1,210	2,083,434

ENTERED KUCHINOTSU.

Nationality.	Sailing.		Steam.		Total.	
	Number of Vessels.	Tons.	Number of Vessels.	Tons.	Number of Vessels.	Tons.
Japanese.. ..	6	321	132	192,876	138	193,197
British	..	..	65	153,748	65	153,748
German	1	1,894	11	25,033	12	26,927
Norwegian ..	..	..	10	10,716	10	10,716
Other nationalities	..	..	8	14,203	8	14,203
Total	7	2,215	226	396,576	233	398,791
„ 1901 ..	4	55	169	293,721	173	293,776

TOTAL for the Three Ports within the Consular District of Nagasaki.

Nationality.	Sailing.		Steam.		Total.	
	Number of Vessels.	Tons.	Number of Vessels.	Tons.	Number of Vessels.	Tons.
Japanese.. ..	61	2,464	581	807,240	642	809,704
British	4	4,190	238	635,621	242	639,811
Russian	..	..	249	385,609	249	385,609
German	6	12,195	86	305,104	92	317,299
French	1	1,417	45	100,488	46	101,905
American (U.S.)	1	2,302	28	92,955	29	95,257
Norwegian ..	..	..	42	39,022	42	39,022
Other nationalities	7	4,154	19	26,435	26	30,589
Total entries— Nagasaki and Kuchinotsu	80	26,722	1,288	2,392,474	1,368	2,419,196
Karatsu* ..	35	2,898	74	80,586	100	83,484
Grand total ..	115	29,620	1,362	2,473,060	1,468	2,502,680
„ 1901	145	35,153	1,340	2,435,682	1,485	2,470,835

* Of these, 2 sailing vessels of 90 tons were Corean, the rest Japanese; 35 steam vessels of 37,886 tons, Japanese; 8 of 12,333 tons, British; 19 of 15,819 tons, Norwegian; 12 of 15,048 tons, other nationalities.

LONDON:
Printed for His Majesty's Stationery Office,
By HARRISON AND SONS,
Printers in Ordinary to His Majesty.
(1400   9 | 03—H & S   379)

GERMANY.

DIPLOMATIC AND CONSULAR REPORTS.

TRADE OF

GERMANY

FOR THE FIRST HALF OF THE YEAR 1903

FOREIGN OFFICE.

September, 1903.

No. 3085 Annual Series.

DIPLOMATIC AND CONSULAR REPORTS.

GERMANY.

REPORT FOR THE FIRST HALF OF 1903

ON

GERMAN TRADE AND INDUSTRY.

REFERENCE TO PREVIOUS REPORT, Annual Series No. 2959.

Presented to both Houses of Parliament by Command of His Majesty,
SEPTEMBER, 1903.

LONDON:
PRINTED FOR HIS MAJESTY'S STATIONERY OFFICE,
BY HARRISON AND SONS, ST. MARTIN'S LANE,
PRINTERS IN ORDINARY TO HIS MAJESTY.

And to be purchased, either directly or through any Bookseller, from
EYRE & SPOTTISWOODE, EAST HARDING STREET, FLEET STREET, E.C.,
and 32, ABINGDON STREET, WESTMINSTER, S.W.;
or OLIVER & BOYD, EDINBURGH;
or E. PONSONBY, 116, GRAFTON STREET, DUBLIN.

1903.

[Cd. 1766—19.] *Price Twopence.*

CONTENTS.

———◆———

———·———

NOTE.—Conversions have been made at the rate of 20 marks to the 1*l.* and 1,000 kilos. to the ton.

Report on the Trade and Industry of Germany for the First Half of 1903

By Mr. Consul-General Schwabach.

(Berlin, August 12, 1903; received at Foreign Office, August 15, 1903.)

The noteworthy improvement in several branches of German commerce and industry which it was possible to record in the latter half of the preceding year, has been maintained more generally and in a higher degree during the first six months of 1903.' In fact, the economic situation of Germany may be said to be better than at any time during the last two years. The dearth of employment is much less apparent, and a number of industries, more especially the textile industries, the building trade, and several branches of the iron and steel industries—which have been fairly busy—were able to put on new hands; whereas in coal mining and in the electrical industry there has been hardly any increase in the number of workmen, although the coal mines at least have considerably increased their output. *(margin: General remarks.)*

Although business is, on the whole, much more active than during the last two years, prices have only improved in a much smaller degree. Conspicuous among those industries which suffer from low prices are the electrical, the Portland cement, and several branches of the iron and steel trades, notably the machine building and the mechanical tool industries.

Harvest prospects being favourable in the greater part of the German Empire, the consuming power of the agricultural part of the population may be expected to improve still further. Unfortunately, very severe inundations during the month of July have done great damage in the Prussian provinces of Silesia and Posen, and in some parts of West Prussia and Brandenburg, but with the exception of the districts affected by the floods the condition of the crops continues to be satisfactory.

The volume of the freight traffic on German railways increased very considerably during the first half of the year, and the receipts of that department compare with those in the corresponding period of the preceding year, as follows :— *(margin: Railway traffic.)*

Month.					Increase.
					Per cent.
January	..	..	..	..	..	8·48
February	..	..	..	..	..	8·33
March	..	..	..	..	..	9·47
April	..	..	..	..	..	2·33
May	..	..	..	..	..	6·89
June	..	..	..	..	..	4·40

The receipts from the passenger traffic were, with one exception, likewise better than last year, viz. :—

Month.					Increase or Decrease.
					Per cent.
January	..	..	..	..	..	+ 1·88
February	..	..	..	..	..	+ 5·19
March	..	..	..	..	..	− 2·11
April	..	..	..	..	..	+ 11·0
May	..	..	..	..	..	+ 2·59
June	..	..	..	..	..	+ 9·81

The total receipts from goods and passenger traffic increased in—

Month.					Increase.
					Per cent.
January	..	..	..	..	..	6·25
February	..	..	..	..	..	6·93
March	..	..	..	..	..	5·97
April	..	..	..	..	..	4·69
May	..	..	..	..	..	4·95
June	..	..	..	..	..	5·83

The figures represent the absolute increase, the mileage increase would be somewhat less owing to the extension of the railway system.

The foreign trade of the German Empire was much larger than last year, both for imports and exports.

Total imports.

The imports of merchandise reached 21,720,000 tons, valued at 153,400,000l., against 19,660,000 tons of the value of 141,960,000l. in 1902 and 20,770,000 tons amounting to 137,600,000l. in 1901 (January to June). This shows an increase of 2,060,000 and 950,000 tons, and 11,440,000l. and 15,800,000l. respectively. The principal advances have taken place in the following commodities :—

Articles.	Increase, compared with January to June, 1902.	
	Quantity in 1,000 Tons.	Value in 1,000l.
Earths and ores	764	1,150
Coal..	309	200
Corn	289	1,800
Wood and wooden wares.. ..	397	920
Waste	135	550
Mineral oils	42	200
Cotton and cotton goods	36	2,850
Stone and stone wares	50	50

The imports of jute, rice and salt have fallen off considerably.

Exports for the first six months of the last three years compare as follows :— Total exports.

	Quantity in 1,000,000 Tons.	Value in 1,000,000l.
January to June—		
1903	18·3	120·5
1902	15·8	111·1
1901	15·0	106·8
Increase in 1903 over 1902 ..	2·5	9·4
,, 1902 ,, 1901 ..	3·3	13·7

Compared with the corresponding figures of last year, the most noticeable increases took place in the following articles :—

Articles.	Quantity in 1,000 Tons.	Value in 1,000l.
Coal..	1,479	1,120
Earths and ores	609	1,051
Iron and iron wares	327	2,351
Chemicals and dye-stuffs	57	585
Cotton and cotton goods	7·3	1,420
Paper	9·8	600
Copper and copper wares.. ..	9·2	515
Silk and silk wares	0·2	440
Wool and woollen wares	1·8	385

The export of sugar has, for special reasons, diminished considerably :—

EXPORTS OF SUGAR.

	Quantity in 1,000 Tons.	
	January to June, 1903.	January to June, 1902.
Raw sugar ., ...	148·2	274·6
Loaf „	288·2	295·2
Other kinds	7·9	14·3

Last year the principal sugar importing countries, the United Kingdom and the United States of America, imported large quantities of German sugar in order to profit by the prevailing low prices, which were expected to advance in consequence of the Brussels Sugar Convention.

Labour market. The tendency of the labour market during the period under review has been comparatively favourable. In February the number of the unemployed showed a large decrease, applicants for every 100 vacancies numbering 175·9, as against 219·4 in February, 1902. The weather during the first months of the year permitted the resumption of work in several trades earlier than last year, for instance, in the building trade and in inland shipping. In April there were 139 applicants to every 100 vacancies. A great influx of persons seeking employment occurs every year in spring, when large numbers of young people leave school; for this reason the number of applicants in May is generally comparatively high. This year it was 141·6 against 160·6 last year. The June figure was also a low one, 141·6 against 166·1 in June, 1902. Owing to the large demand for agricultural labour the pressure on the industrial labour market was very slight, in June, the number of applicants increasing by about 2,000 only. However, the improvement is not everywhere the same. Besides the strong demand for agricultural labour, employment continued especially brisk in the building trade and the forwarding business, whereas it was slack in some branches of the iron and steel and the electrical industries. As already stated, the coal mines are reported to have engaged comparatively few fresh hands in spite of their larger output.

The clothing industry has been most prosperous ; the export trade was active and the inland business has improved considerably. The latter circumstance may be regarded as an indication of the increasing spending power of the masses of the population, which had undergone a severe diminution during 1902 and 1901.

During the general depression in 1901 and 1902, when very large numbers of workmen were thrown out of employment, the problem of coping with this calamity attracted serious attention. Suggestions were made that the workmen should be insured by the State against enforced idleness in a manner somewhat on the lines of the existing compulsory insurance against sickness, but so far these ideas have not had any practical results. Some progress has been made towards more complete and comprehensive statistics. At different times during last year a census of the unemployed was taken in various towns. The municipality of Stuttgart decided to repeat such censuses three times a year on February 1, July 1 and November 1, and a number of Würtemberg towns propose to follow this example.

The better organisation and systematic affiliation of the labour bureaus in different parts of the German Empire is energetically pushed. Quite recently it has been decided to establish a system of labour bureaus throughout Alsace-Lorraine, with head offices at Strassburg, to replace the present insufficient organisation.

At the Dresden Exhibition of German towns a great amount of information has been collected regarding the present condition of the organisation of labour bureaus in Germany. Public and private organisations of this kind are to be found principally in the south-west and north-west of Germany, and in Berlin and its environments. All the labour bureaus, public as well as private, provided during the years 1897 to 1901 work in 568,000, 629,500, 691,600, 779,600 and 1,087,000 cases respectively. The municipal labour bureaus numbered on January 1, 1903, 263 against 222 and 204 on January 1, 1902 and 1901, respectively, providing work, in each of the five years from 1898–1902, for 122,120, 160,643, 185,917, 191,847 and 221,263 individuals.

Interesting data concerning the question of the unemployed during the last year is contained in the annual report of the Union of German Printers (Deutscher Buchdruckerverband). Members of the Union were ill for 400,000 days and out of work 1,030,000 days ; this is equivalent to 12 days illness and 31 days enforced idleness per member. Notwithstanding this very unfavourable condition of the labour market and the great expenditure involved thereby, the Union disposes of funds amounting to 158,842*l*.

The last report dealing with compulsory insurance against Insurance illness refers to the year 1901. The different institutions insuring against against illness had 9,600,000 members. In 3,617,022 cases, illness. extending over 66,500,000 days, the illness involved complete incapacity for work. In the latter case the patients either receive support according to a fixed scale or are admitted into a hospital. The percentage proportion of such cases of illness is 0·38 and 6·91 days per member.

The total expenditure, amounting to 8,167,779*l*., was distributed as follows :—

	Amount.
	£
Doctors' fees	1,781,800
Medicine, &c.	1,309,749
Subventions (support)	3,649,000
Payments to hospitals, families, convalescents, &c...	1,426,579

This works out at approximately 17*s*. per member. The funds of the different institutions amounted in all to 8,550,000*l*.

Strikes and Lock-outs. Strikes or lock-outs during the period under review did not assume any great importance, labour differences bearing generally a strictly local character and affecting comparatively small numbers. Differences between employers and workmen broke out chiefly in the building trade, *i.e.*, at Cologne, Hamburg, Hanover, Bochum, Görlitz and Bunzlau. At Cologne some 4,000 hands were locked out on June 25, but a reconciliation was effected on July 14. The workmen demanded the abolition of piecework and the introduction of a minimum wage of 55 pf. (7*d*.) per hour. At Hanover the parties came to terms on August 1, the workmen resuming work meanwhile on the old conditions. An increase of wages and shorter hours already agreed upon will be introduced at a later date. At Bochum the masons struck for a minimum wage of 47 pf. (5½*d*.) per hour and a working day of not more than 10 hours. At Magdeburg 4,000 metal workers demanded the introduction of a minimum wage and a nine hours' day.

The North German Lloyd experienced in the early part of the year some difficulties with their workmen, but the firm attitude of the Board of Directors prevented the outbreak of a strike. The dock labourers desire an increase in wages, but the situation is complicated by the attitude of the company towards the Dock Labourers Union. In March the directors intimated that in future members of this Union would not be employed, and at the same time dismissed several leaders of the Union. As the company was fully prepared against the outbreak of the strike the dock labourers submitted for the time.

Serious signs of growing discontent amongst the Westphalian coal miners have found expression in the " Miners Journal " (Bergarbeiter Zeitung) and at a large meeting of miners at Essen on the July 12. The miners complain of unfairness in settling wages, unreasonable deductions therefrom, &c., and maintain that, in view of the high dividends paid by the large mining companies, they are fully entitled to higher wages. An immediate strike was recommended but abandoned on deliberation. It was resolved that the complaints should be submitted to the " Verein für bergbauliche Interessen," the mining department of the province, and to the Minister of Commerce.

New issues of State loans and shares have not been more frequent this year than last, as will be seen from the following table :—

Money market.

TABLE showing Nominal and Issue Value of State Loans and Shares.

Value in 1,000l.

	Second Half-year, 1901.		First Half-year, 1902.		Second Half-year, 1902.		First Half-year, 1903.	
	Nominal Value.	Issue Value.	Nominal Value.	Issue Value.	Nominal Value.	Issue Value.	Nominal Value.	Issue Value.
Imperial German and Federal State loans	747·5	711·5	28,250	26,141	500	500	16,800	16,563·5
Foreign State loans	2,110	888	12,500	12,187·5	4,717·5	3,486	4,435·5	4,269
Provincial and municipal loans	5,368·5	5,338	16,277·5	16,122	4,720	4,700	10,963·5	10,967·5
Mortgage bank bonds, German	4,300	4,300	11,100	11,100	7,500	7,500	12,500*	12,500*
,, ,, foreign					387·5	337·5	1,037·5	1,038·5
Other bonds	11,378·5	11,186·5	6,404·5	6,370	4,182·5	4,207	1,365	1,327·5
Bank shares	67·5		1,060	1,515·5	900	1,557·5	920	1,164
Foreign railway shares		71	100	108	977·5	1,023·5	4,281	5,641
Industrial shares	937·5	1,298·5	3,015	3,864	1,045·5	1,354	3,249	4,671·5
Total	24,959·5	23,793·5	78,707	76,903	24,880·5	24,665·5	55,551·5	58,632·5

* Estimated amounts.

NOTE.—Conversions are not included in the above table.

Of the total issue value of 58,032,500l., 46,656,000l. or 80·40 per cent. are bonds with fixed interest, 11,376,500l. or 19·60 per cent. shares. In 1902 the proportion of the shares was for the first half of the year 6·50 per cent. (4,982,500l.), for the second nearly 16 per cent. (3,935,000l.).

Large amounts of these issues, especially of the Imperial loan, have been placed on foreign markets. During the last few years France has invested rather heavily in German loans, principally Imperial and Prussian State loans.

The Imperial Government has issued a 3 per cent. loan of the nominal value of 14,500,000l. at 91·90 per cent. Besides the Imperial Government, Bavaria and Hesse have been borrowers ; Würtemberg is about to issue a loan.

Provincial and municipal loans could, with few exceptions, be placed at 3½ per cent. In several cases municipal loans have been shown in the foregoing table with 500,000l. only, although larger amounts have been registered at the Stock Exchange for future issue.

Owing to cheap money, mortgage bonds were placed in larger quantities than last year. The 3½ per cent. type is again super-seding the 4 per cent. type ; several mortgage banks have intro-duced 3¾ per cent. bonds.

The capital requirements of the German joint stock banks seem to be fully supplied at present. The amount entered in the table for fresh bank capital includes an amount of 240,000l., destined for new shares of the Banca Commerciale Italiana.

Among railway shares are included 19,500,000 dol. new Canadian Pacific shares.

A higher percentage of the industrial shares applies to new companies than during the last two years, when new capital was chiefly created for existing companies.

The average price at which industrial shares were issued was higher than last year, viz., 140·70 per cent., compared with 129·57 and 111·57 per cent. in the second and first half of 1902 respectively. The principal issues of industrial shares include :—

	Nominal Value.	Issued at—
	£	Per cent.
West Berlin Real Estate Company..	325,000	130
Chemical Works, Hönningen	120,000	140
German Car Hiring Company	150,000	150
Real Estate Company, Kurfürstendamm-Berlin ..	250,000	165
Real Estate Trading Company	250,000	160
Bergmann Electrical Works..	300,000	225
Steamship Company, Hansa (new shares) ..	250,000	106
North German Wool Carding Works (new shares)	116,000	130
Nordstern Collieries (new shares) ..	150,000	225

Investors still maintain a certain reserve with regard to dividend paying shares, and exhibit a decided preference for securities bearing a fixed rate of interest ; the demand for dividend shares is, how-ever, again increasing.

The easy state of the money market was favourable to new issues. Though slightly dearer than last year, money is still cheaper than in 1901 and 1900. The bank rate of the Imperial Bank stood at the beginning of the year at 4 per cent., was reduced to 3½ per cent. on February 11, and again raised to 4 per cent. on June 8. The average rate from January to June was 3·67 per cent., against 3·16 per cent. in 1902, 4·43 per cent. in 1901 and 5·44 per cent. in 1900.

The private discount averaged from January 1 to June 14 2·57 per cent., against 1·90 per cent. in 1902, 3·42 per cent. in 1901 and 4·61 per cent. in 1900.

An increase in the bank rate in June occurs very rarely. Owing to the cheapness of money in the first months of the year (in February the private rate of discount was temporarily 1⅞ per cent.), private banks and bankers had lent large sums to the United Kingdom and the United States, where better terms could be obtained. A large part of these loans is only repayable next autumn. When in the second half of March money became dearer in Germany and continued stiff after the Imperial loan had been issued in April, private banks were not in a position to discount all the bills offered, and had to resort largely to the Imperial Bank. From March 23 until May 31 bills increased at the Imperial Bank by 11,800,000l., and amounted on May 31 to 45,756,000l., an unusually high figure for that time of the year. The cash reserve of the Imperial Bank was at the same time comparatively low, amounting on June 8 to 45,463,500l., or 8,133,000l. less than in the corresponding period of 1902. In view of the large demands likely to be made upon the Bank at the end of the quarter the discount rate was raised to 4 per cent. In July the strain again relaxed and more normal conditions prevailed.

On June 30 the cash reserve was 44,212,900l., against 49,549,900l. in 1902 ; bills discounted 50,574,350l. (44,859,100l.), while Lombards were unusually high at 9,582,350l. (5,824,750l.). The notes in circulation amounted to 71,728,250l. (70,483,050l.).

Coal.

More favourable conditions than in 1902 prevailed in the Rhenish Westphalian district, the most important centre of the German coal production. At the end of May no stock was left at the pits except close burning coal, the demand for other qualities having kept pace with the production. The activity in the building trade and the improvement in some branches of the iron industry would seem to indicate a prospect of fair business during the ensuing months. The demand for coke was very brisk indeed during the whole six months ; a slight falling-off in July has caused the Coke Syndicate to reduce the output by 10 per cent. in August. The greater part of the blast furnace works have already concluded contracts for their coke supplies for the second half of the year. The trade in patent fuel was satisfactory.

The Westphalian Coke Syndicate, which controls the greater

part of the coke production in the Rhineland and Westphalia, sold 4,158,840 tons from January to June, *i.e.*, 36 per cent. more than 1902 and 15 per cent. more than 1901.

In Upper Silesia business has not been quite as favourable as in Westphalia, except for coke, which found a ready market at good prices. On the whole the coal market in Upper Silesia suffered from an accumulation of stock, the supply being in excess of the demand, but prices were generally satisfactory.

The output of coal in Prussia and the whole of Germany during the first half years 1903 and 1902, compares as follows :—

Quantity in 1,000,000 Tons.

	Prussia.		Germany.	
	January to June, 1903.	January to June, 1902.	January to June, 1903.	January to June, 1902.
Coal	51·74	47·61	55·47	50·99
Lignite	17·91	16·84	21·44	20·12
Coke	5·51	4·27	5·54	4·29
Patent fuel, &c.	4·25	3·71	4·85	4·20
	79·41	72·43	87·30	79·60
Imports of all kinds	..	..	7·25	6·94
Exports ,, ,,	..	..	9·89	8·41
Excess of exports	..	..	2·64	1·47
Available for home consumption	..	..	84·66	78·13

The particulars of the foreign trade of the German Empire in coal, &c., are given in the following table :—

IMPORTS.

	Quantity in 1,000 Tons.	
	January to June, 1903.	January to June, 1902.
Coal	3,087	2,826
Lignite	3,881	3,835
Coke	206	178
Patent fuel	40	36

EXPORTS.

				Quantity in 1,000 Tons.	
				January to June, 1903.	January to June, 1902.
Coal	..	..	..	8,187	7,147
Lignite	..	..	..	13	10
Coke	..	..	..	1,253	926
Patent fuel	..	..	..	490	823

The imports of coal from Belgium show an increase of 28,000 tons, those from the United Kingdom of 156,000 tons. Coal and coke were exported chiefly to the following countries :—

		Coal.		Coke.	
Country.					
		1903.	1902.	1903.	1902.
Belgium	.. ..	1,165	1,040	129	73
France ..	.. ..	548	382	441	293
Netherlands	.. ..	2,408	1,903	89	71
Austria-Hungary	..	2,613	2,489	268	265
Russia ..	.. ..	296	254	92	76
Switzerland	.. ..	542	505	62	56

Quantity in 1,000 Tons.

Nearly three-fifths of the coke imports came from Belgium, viz., 124,330 tons. Imports from the United Kingdom have decreased from 16,700 tons in January to June, 1901, to 9,916 tons in 1902 and 5,510 tons in 1903.

Belgium and France have taken much larger quantities of German coke than heretofore, whilst Mexico has likewise become a good customer for that article, the shipments to that country in the first six months of the present year amounting to no less than 77,600 tons, as compared to only 30,500 and 28,700 tons in the corresponding period of 1902 and 1901.

As to whether the Westphalian Coal Syndicate will be renewed or not is a question of paramount importance to the German coal industry. This syndicate controls about 85 per cent. of the Westphalian output, and, approximately, 45 per cent. of the entire German coal production. During the first half of 1903 the syndicated mines produced 25,500,000 tons, against over 23,000,000 tons last year, *i.e.*, 10·14 per cent. more, the total shipments of Westphalian coal having increased in the same period by about 12·5 per cent. At present the syndicate includes the great majority of the Westphalian coal mines ; during the last few years, however, it has encountered severe competition from a few very powerful collieries not belonging to the combine. To induce these collieries to join the syndicate is one of the principal objects of the negotiations now being conducted ; further important points will be to effect a satisfactory solution of the difficulties experienced with the so-called "Hüttenzechen," *i.e.*, coal mines owned by iron and steel works, and also to provide against any serious competition in the future from the opening of new mines. According to latest reports, there are good prospects of the syndicate coming to terms with the outside mine owners. Another important question, namely, whether or not the coal mined and consumed by the "Hüttenzechen" is to form part of the syndicate output, seems to have been already settled satisfactorily. It is reported that the Krupp works and the firm of Thyssen, two of the largest concerns of this class, have come to an understanding with the syndicate. If this be true, it may be expected that the other "Hüttenzechen" will more or less follow suit. Special difficulties are presented by the third question. Numerous extensive borings have been made of late years in the northern parts of the Westphalian coal district, principally by and on behalf of the International Boring Company (Internationale Bohrgesellschaft). The results have in many cases been most satisfactory, and it is expected that if the coal-fields of this region were to be developed on a large scale and in opposition to the syndicate, the latter would have to struggle hard against this competition. The syndicate, it is reported, has entered into negotiations with the interested parties, primarily the International Boring Company. The results of such negotiations have so far not been made public. Large sums would probably be necessary to acquire the rights of the International Boring Company.

The amalgamation of the Coke Syndicate and the Patent Fuel Syndicate (Brikettverkaufsverein) with the Coal Syndicate seems to be assured. Both these syndicates were already closely allied to the Coal Syndicate, but under the new arrangement they will form departments of the Coal Syndicate. The members of the Coal Syndicate and the Patent Fuel Syndicate will, on the whole, retain their present position, especially as regards their participation.

The new Coal Syndicate is to be in operation for a period of 12 years, *i.e.*, from September 15, 1903, until December 31, 1915, provided the important outsiders, specially the "Hüttenzechen" with an annual production of more than 120,000 tons, join the syndicate before the end of this year. The present mode of participation is to be modified considerably. Under the present arrangement the individual collieries participate in the total output of the syndicate according to their producing capacities, not according to the conditions of the market. Very naturally mines owning extensive and partly undeveloped property increased their share by constantly opening new shafts. Thus the sum total of the participations constantly increased at a much higher rate than was warranted by the state of the market. Reductions in the output had to be increased in turn, especially in periods of depression. Under the new scheme all claims resulting from the driving of new shafts are set aside, and the participation will be regulated according to the requirements of the market. In future an increase in the participation will only be granted if a mine has actually supplied for six consecutive months the additional quantity required by the state of the market. The quantities required by the " Hüttenzechen " for their own consumption are excluded from the participation. All internal disputes are to be submitted to a court of arbitration, whose decisions shall be considered final. The powers vested in the Board of Directors are to be extended in order to enable them to prevent, as far as possible, the increase of outside mines, and to render the working of new coal-fields by favourably situated members of the syndicate more dependent on the state of the market. The board will also have power in future to raise a contribution of 3 per cent. on the monthly invoice amount of the members for purchase of coal-fields and shares in coal mines. A 3 per cent. contribution would represent at present about 900,000*l.* per annum.

The International Boring Company, which has been frequently alluded to lately, was registered in 1895 with a share capital of 20,000*l.*, but this has been gradually raised to 50,000*l.* The financial results of the company have been very favourable indeed, it having paid dividends of 30 per cent. per annum. The boring system of this company is said to work twice as quickly as other systems. The company has carried out numerous borings for its own as well as for account of others, especially in the Lippe district (North Westphalia), on the left bank of the Rhine, in Lorraine, Belgium, the Netherlands and France, and is said to have acquired large options in all these regions.

The Prussian Government, which for years has owned extensive mines in Upper Silesia, has recently acquired considerable property in Westphalia also. The Prussian Diet appropriated the sum of 2,900,000*l.* for this purpose. The influence of the Government mines is not likely to be appreciably felt for some time, as only a small part of the fiscal property is fully developed and worked at present. Compared with the older mines the fiscal collieries suffer from the disadvantage that they are situated in the northern part of the district, where the strata of rock reach a greater distance below the surface.

Potash (kali).   Notwithstanding that the "Kalisyndicate" (Potash Syndicate) terminates only on June 30, 1905, negotiations for its renewal are already in progress. As in the case of the Coal Syndicate, it would seem to have become imperative to re-organise the syndicate in a manner calculated not only to bring the members more completely under the control of the board, but also to enable it effectively to meet competition from without. It is intended, therefore, to substitute for the existing somewhat loose combination a limited liability company, and to create a reserve fund for the purpose of acquiring mining property and shares.

Calculated on a basis of pure potash the syndicate sales increased by no less than 37,600 tons in the first five months of the year.

Portland cement.   For years the condition of the German Portland cement industry has been most unsatisfactory, owing to the prevailing disproportion between supply and demand. The inland consumption is estimated at 14,500,000 casks per annum, whereas the works can produce close on 29,000,000 casks. This enormous disproportion is due to the numerous extensions and new works erected in 1895 and the following years, partly on account of the activity in the building trade, but chiefly in the expectation that the Great Midland Canal would be built. Repeated attempts to form a German Cement Syndicate, and to regulate the prices and the production, have proved unsuccessful. The numerous local organisations compete severely against one another.

Under these circumstances very few other than the old established works, whose brands are well known, are remunerative. The South African war and the influence it exercised on the Transvaal gold mining industry has also severely affected the trade, as very large consignments of cement were formerly sent to that country. German cement is practically excluded from the principal European markets by reason of prohibitive duties, and while it is exempt from duty in Germany the import duties, including clearing expenses, per 10 tons amount to 8*l.* 10*s.* in Russia; 5*l.* 5*s.* in Austria-Hungary; 6*l.* 10*s.* in Roumania; 5*l.* in Italy; 3*l.* in Switzerland and Sweden; and 1*l.* 5*s.* in Norway. Thus only the transatlantic markets are available for the exportation of German cement. In 1902 Germany imported 51,947 tons and exported 641,520 tons. For the first six months of the last three years the imports and exports compare as follows :—

	Quantity.	
	Imports.	Exports.
	Tons.	Tons.
January to June—		
1903	25,950	374,381
1902	26,588	244,603
1901	39,719	209,153

In the principal centres of the German iron industry, Rhineland Iron. and Westphalia, iron and steel works were not quite so busy at the end of the second quarter as earlier in the year. This may be due in part to the less confident tone of the American iron markets. Nevertheless, the large orders entrusted to pig iron and steel works and to rolling mills in the first quarter, kept them well employed, especially for pig iron, rough ironware, bar iron and tyres. The prices for bars and tyres of 5*l.* 5*s.* and 6*l.* 2*s.* 6*d.* were not very satisfactory, however, and even these prices could not always be obtained. Rolled wire is weak, and the Rolled Wire Syndicate has reduced the production for the third quarter by 5 per cent. for common ingot iron and rolled wire.

It had been reported that new rolling mills were to be erected in the Saar district and in Lorraine, but according to later reports the plan has been abandoned for the present. The business in girders and fine sheet iron has been satisfactory, while that in rough sheet iron was dull, and pipes suffered from the uncertainty whether the Pipe Syndicate would be renewed. As a matter of fact the syndicate has not been renewed. The trade in machinery and boilers was unsatisfactory at unremunerative prices. The demand for scrap iron was fairly good at low prices.

The iron industry of Upper Silesia is, on the whole, flourishing. The disinclination of the rolling mills to sell at ruling prices for a time kept buyers out of the market, but the mills were fully occupied with orders in hand, and in July further large contracts were made for delivery in the third quarter. The trade in girders, pipes, rough and fine sheet iron continues fairly active. Attempts to regulate the minimum sale prices for boilers by means of a convention have so far proved abortive.

Engine builders and manufacturers of mechanical tools complain of bad trade. In a report of the society of German manufacturers of mechanical tools the unfavourable condition of the industry is attributed to the unwillingness of customers to effect new purchases in times of depression. The export trade is severely affected by the industrial crisis in Russia and high duties in Austria-Hungary. American competition made itself felt in a lesser degree, American works being fully occupied with home orders. A source of bitter complaint with the manufacturers of mechanical tools are the so-called " Gegenseitigkeitsgeschäfte " (mutual contracts), that is to say, the large iron works, when ordering mechanical tools, insist on a certain quantity of their own products, sometimes up to 50 per cent. of the value of the order, being taken in exchange. This is most onerous on mechanical tool makers, as in this industry the cost of the raw material is insignificant compared with the item of wages and general expenses.

The firm of Friedrich Krupp has been registered as a joint stock company, with a capital of 8,000,000l., the whole of the shares remaining in the possession of Miss Krupp, daughter of the late Mr. Krupp. The works include the celebrated steel works at Essen, the collieries or mines, quarries, clay pits, blast furnaces connected with the Essen steel works, also the Friedrich Krupp-Gruson Works at Magdeburg-Buckau, the steel works at Annen, and the Friedrich Krupp " Germania " shipyards at Kiel and Tegel-Berlin. The total value of the concern is estimated at 13,650,000l. Extensions are planned by the Friedrich Krupp Actien-Gessellschaft at Rheinhausen, at a cost of 1,100,000l., including three new blast furnaces, one Thomas works and several rolling mills for the supply of raw material for the Essen works as well as for sale. After the completion of the new works the corresponding departments at Essen will be closed in order to make room for the erection of additional plant for the manufacture of ordnance.

The desire of the iron and steel works to become independent in regard to the supply of raw material, especially coal, has led, during the last few years, to further large acquisitions of coal mines by such works. In 1895 seven iron and steel works owned collieries ; in 1902 their number had risen to 18, and the quantity of coal produced for their own consumption had increased from 4,000,000 tons in 1895 to 11,000,000 tons.

The formation of a German Steel Syndicate (Stahlverband) is expected to take place before the end of the year. One of the objects of this syndicate will be the regulation of the export of iron and steel, which, as a rule, was not hitherto controlled by most of the existing syndicates in this industry. It is proposed to inaugurate a system for settlements between home and foreign sales, and to determine the mode of fixing the participation quota of the individual works belonging to the combine. It is hoped that the considerable difficulties connected with these points will be overcome successfully. Primarily interested in the prospective syndicate are naturally those works which are dependent upon foreign markets for the disposal of the greater part of their production—for instance, the extensive new works in Lorraine and Luxemburg. There exists already for the export trade in the iron industry the " Abrechnungsstelle für Ausfuhrvergütungen," which grants drawbacks on the difference between home and export prices according to the quantity of raw materials used, but it is felt that another organisation is needed. The large increase in German iron and steel exports during the last two years has been obtained by selling at prices which in very many cases left no margin of profit at all or even a loss, and it is anticipated that the new syndicate will be able to conduct export operations under more favourable conditions. This view seems to be supported by the opinion of a British firm recently quoted in the German press, that there was no necessity whatever for German manufacturers of iron and steel to sell in 1901 and 1902 at such low prices as they did. The Steel Syndicate would probably increase the preponderance of the larger over the smaller works which find it already difficult to compete against their powerful neighbours ; it will presumably include the works belonging to the raw iron, rough ironware, girder and rail syndicates ; later on also the members of the sheet iron, tubes, wire and iron bar syndicates. Several of these syndicates, which terminate this year, will not be allowed to dissolve, but will be prolonged for a few months until the formation of the new Steel Syndicate.

The raw iron syndicates of Westphalia and Upper Silesia are negotiating for a price convention and a limitation of their respective business spheres, and these negotiations are expected to be successful.

Negotiations for the renewal of the Rough Sheet Iron Syndicate terminating next year were resumed in June.

The production of raw iron in the first half of 1903 compares with the corresponding period of the last three years as follows :—

Year.					Quantities in 1,000 Tons.
1903..	..	..	..	..	..	4,882
1902..	..	..	..	..	..	4,014
1901..	..	..	..	..	..	3,954
1900..	..	..	..	..	..	4,099

Thus the increase in 1903 amounts to 21·62 per cent. over 1902, 23·47 per cent. over 1901 and 19·10 per cent. over 1900.

The total production of 4,042,730 tons of raw iron in Germany from January to May, 1903, included :—

	Quantity.
	Tons.
Foundry iron and cast iron	..	..	738,274
Bessemer steel	..	..	..	..	158,216
Thomas iron	..	..	..	..	1,442,256
Specular ,, ..	..	..	..	..	315,936
Ingot iron ..	..	..	..	..	378,018

The total production for the first five months emanated from the following districts :—

	Quantity.
	Tons.
Rhenish, Prussia and Westphalia (exclusive of the Saar and Sieg)	..	..	1,621,085
Sieg, Lahn and Hesse-Nassau	..	..	302,177
Silesia	..	..	..	..	..	311,641
Pomerania ..	..	..	..	..	54,068
Hanover and Brunswick	..	..	..	149,221
Saar district	..	..	..	..	284,675
Lorraine, Luxemburg	..	..	..	1,256,444

TABLE showing the Development of the Foreign Trade in German Iron and Ironware.

IMPORTS.

Description.	Quantity in 1,000 Tons.		
	January to June, 1903.	January to June, 1902.	January to June, 1901.
Raw iron	58·3	72·1	160·0
Broken and scrap iron	26·7	15·9	20·4
Angle and T-iron	..	0·1	0·3
Railway rails	..	0·1	0·3
Malleable iron in bars..	12·0	11·2	9·9
Blooms, &c.	1·1	0·5	0·7
Plates and sheets	0·6	6·4	1·2
Tin plate	10·0	1·1	5·5
Iron wire, rough	3·1	2·8	3·8
„ coppered	0·7	5·0	0·6
Rough cast ironware ..	3·4	0·5	9·5
Railway wagon axles, &c.	0·2	0·3	0·5
Tubes	4·6	5·5	5·9
Ironware, very rough ..	4·5	4·0	6·7
„ polished	2·7	2·3	2·2
„ fine ..	0·4	0·3	0·3
Total	133·4	132·6	233·7

EXPORTS.

Description.	Quantity in 1,000 Tons.		
	January to June, 1903.	January to June, 1902.	January to June, 1901.
Raw iron	248·4	136·7	57·0
Broken and scrap iron..	62·1	92·0	47·8
Angle and T-iron	208·6	182·1	166·0
Fish plates	35·7	20·4	15·7
Railway rails	219·1	149·7	80·6
Malleable iron in bars..	182·2	173·0	136·7
Blooms, &c.	330·3	262·5	48·3
Plates and sheets	146·9	132·1	117·6
Tin plate	0·1	0·1	0·1
Iron wire, rough	81·6	77·0	71·7
„ coppered	42·8	41·8	39·7
Rough cast ironware ..	27·1	14·6	13·0
Railway wagon axles, &c.	23·9	23·0	23·4
Tubes	29·1	23·6	21·1
Ironware, very rough ..	64·7	56·6	50·5
Wire nails	26·0	29·7	26·7
Ironware, polished	41·1	34·5	27·7
„ fine ..	4·5	3·6	3·7
Total	1,831·0	1,504·0	994·0

TABLE showing the Development of the Foreign Trade in
German Iron and Ironware—continued.

TOTAL. VALUE.

		Value in 1,000l.		
		January to June, 1903.	January to June, 1902.	January to June, 1901.
Imports..	..	1,397	1,269	1,860
Exports..	..	16,618	14,155	12,006

Since 1900 the imports of pig iron from the United Kingdom
have greatly diminished, viz. :--

						Quantity.
January to June—						Tons.
1900	..	..	..	..	..	337,581
1901	..	..	..	..	..	144,004
1902	..	..	..	..	..	58,654
1903	..	..	..	..	..	49,148

The requirements of the United States market were again very
large, especially in pig iron, rails and blooms ; Belgium also bought
largely. The exports of pig iron, angle and T-iron, rails, malleable
iron and blooms to the principal countries during the first six months
of the last three years are shown in the following table :—

Country.	January to June.		Quantity in 1,000 Tons.				
			Pig Iron.	Angle and T-iron.	Rails.	Malleable Iron.	Blooms.
Belgium	1903	...	76·76	22·01	9·47	12·54	60·23
	1902	...	46·54	18·26	6·36	12·88	41·34
	1901	...	24·85	27·62	3·10	5·46	25·31
France	1903	...	14·01	0·75	...	2·78	2·44
	1902	...	17·79	0·45	...	1·83	3·52
	1901	...	14·54	1·30	...	1·63	1·80
United Kingdom	1903	...	12·91	74·23	38·47	24·02	190·36
	1902	...	12·41	62·93	21·24	31·39	157·58
	1901	...	4·08	48·08	12·97	12·63	11·67
Netherlands	1903	...	35·72	21·38	20·38	22·62	23·27
	1902	...	33·22	22·30	16·81	20·75	17·89
	1901	...	0·54	22·18	12·70	15·68	0·55
United States	1903	...	92·11	7·65	43·81	1·74	36·91
	1902	...	11·88	3·89	22·91	2·48	27·89
	1901	...	...	0·36	0·04	0·19	...

Electricity.   The electrical industry has been severely affected by the depression.
No other industry expanded so much in the years of commercial
prosperity until 1900, and ever since the tide turned and the demand
shrunk it has been difficult and often impossible to keep the large
new plant employed, and the cutting of prices has not ceased
yet. The working arrangements made by several of the

largest electrical companies at the beginning of this year ιre intended to reduce expenses, but these arrangements have been in operation too short a time to prove their utility. The combination between the firm of Siemens and Halske and the Schuckert Works at Nüremberg has resulted in the formation of the "Siemens-Schuckert-Werke Aktien-Gesellschaft," a joint stock company, with a capital of 4,500,000*l.*, of which 4,000,000*l.* are fully paid. Of this capital 2,252,500*l.* are contributed by Messrs. Siemens and Halske and 2,247,500*l.* by the Schuckert Works. The object of the undertaking is the acquisition and continuation of the business of manufacturing and selling the electrical articles and the supply of current hitherto carried on independently by both firms. A complete amalgamation has not been effected, for Messrs. Siemens and Halske retain and work independently their department for supplying electric current for telegraphs and telephones, the block and railway signalling works, incandescent lamp works and the manufacture of carbons. After a transitional period of six years profits will be divided between Siemens and Halske and Schuckert in the proportion of 55 and 45 per cent. respectively, and during the transitional period until 1908 Siemens and Halske's share in the profits will be even higher.

In the case of the association between the Allgemeine Elektricitäts-Gesellschaft and the Union Elektricitäts-Gesellschaft the arrangement provides for a pooling of the profits for a period of 30 years and their distribution among the two companies according to a fixed scale. The capital of the Allgemeine Elektricitäts-Gesellschaft is 3,000,000*l.*, that of the Union 1,200,000*l.*

The Allgemeine Elektricitäts-Gesellschaft has recently acquired an interest in the Aktiengesellschaft Gebr. Körting, of Hanover, which has a share capital of 800,000*l.*, and enjoys a high reputation as builders of gas motors. Besides the well known Körting motors they build suction and power transmitting plant and powerful double-acting cylinder gas engines. The former are intended to promote the more general use of electricity for industrial purposes and the latter to utilise the waste gases of blast furnaces, and thus create a new field for electricity in the mining industry.

The business of the Lahmeyer Electric Company, of Frankfort, was again unsatisfactory during the year ended March 31, 1903, although the loss (18,585*l.*) was much smaller than that sustained in the preceding year (124,690*l.*). This unfavourable result is attributed to the extremely low prices ruling at the end of the financial year and the lack of remunerative orders in the second half.

A " Gesellschaft für drahtlose Telegraphie m.b.H. " (Wireless Telegraph Company, Limited) has been registered by the Allgemeine Elektricitäts-Gesellschaft, and the " Gesellschaft für drahtlose Telegraphie, System Professor Braun and Siemens and Halske G.m.b.H." (Wireless Telegraph Company, System Professor Braun and Siemens and Halske, Limited). The new company has acquired the patents, inventions and methods of the Braun-Siemens and Slaby-Arco systems, also the sole utilisation of all inventions and improvements relating to wireless telegraphy which may in future be made by Siemens and Halske, the Allgemeine Elektricitäts-Gesellschaft and Professors Slaby and Braun. The electric plant will be supplied by the Allgemeine Elektricitäts-Gesellschaft and Siemens and Halske. The share capital of the company is 15,000*l*.

The Deutsch-Atlantische Telegraphen-Gesellschaft, which owns the first German transatlantic cable, pays a dividend of 5 per cent. on its capital of 1,050,000*l*. To meet the cost of a second transatlantic cable 1,000,000*l*. will be issued in 4 per cent. bonds, the interest for which is practically guaranteed by the Imperial Government, as the Empire pays a fixed sum for the use of the cable.

The Brown Boveri Company, at Mannheim, are now building a steam turbine for the Rheinisch Westfälische Elektricitätswerke, at Essen, Westphalia, for driving a three-phase alternator (5,000 volt, 5,000 kilowatt) and a continuous current dynamo (600 volt, 1,500 kilowatt) coupled directly. 10,000 horse-power, measured at the shaft of the turbine, are necessary as motive force. This is considered to be the most powerful steam dynamo extant.

Textile industry.

Since 1899 profits in the textile industry have diminished considerably. The average dividends of the textile companies quoted on the Berlin Stock Exchange fell from 8·15 per cent. in 1899 to 4·58 per cent. in 1900 and 2·91 per cent. in 1901, while for 1902 the dividends on a share capital of 5,200,000*l*. averaged 5·22 per cent. The dividends distributed by the different companies in 1902 varied between 0 and 17 per cent. The number of companies which paid no dividends fell from 24 to 14. In the first half of 1903 business in this industry has, on the whole, been satisfactory, and at the end of June continued so active in most districts that the customary dead season was hardly perceptible. Weavers and most of the spinners were working full time, dyers, printers and dressers were well provided with home and export orders, cloth manufacturers also being fairly employed, although prices were low. On the other hand, business is bad in the Crefeld silk industry, as the fashion does not favour silk this year, and the prices of raw silk were high.

The American cotton corner has affected the German cotton industry to some extent, but the influence of the corner seems to be confined to narrow limits as the mills are still well stocked with raw cotton.

Reports respecting the erection of a new jute spinning and weaving factory at Landsberg have created uneasiness in the German jute industry, which for years has been labouring under difficulties. The Association of German Jute Manufacturers estimates the number of spindles and looms in Germany at 148,764 and 7,106 respectively; of these, 134,306 spindles and 6,758 looms belong to the Association which, since July 1, 1901, stopped 22,830 spindles and 1,148 looms according to agreement, and, in addition, 4,100 spindles and 427 looms voluntarily, making in all more than

20 per cent. of the Association spindles and looms. Nevertheless, there still remains an over-production of 4·71 per cent. for the spindles and 5·62 per cent. for the looms.

Favourable results have been obtained by the introduction of electric power in the home weaving industry at Anrath, a Rhenish town, where formerly cottage hand weaving was extensively though not very profitably carried on. Since electric power was introduced the weavers, who still work in their homes, are much better off. They are employed by dealers, some of whom have also provided the new mechanical looms. These are paid for by means of small deductions from each delivery of goods until the cost is covered, when they become the absolute property of the weavers. The average price of a loom is 40*l.*, and the electric power per loom amounts to about 3*l.* per annum. In addition to a much higher productive capacity, the new system requires less exertion on the part of the operator and is a decided gain from a sanitary point of view. A single loom enables a workman to earn upwards of 1*l.* 10*s.* a week, and some weavers frequently work two looms.

On September 1, 1903, the Brussels Sugar Convention comes Sugar. into force, when all export premiums and bounties will cease in the Treaty States. In order to regulate the production and export of sugar from the Treaty States a meeting of delegates of the sugar producers of these countries was convened at Brussels on July 6, 1903, when resolutions were passed to the effect that the entire production and the quantity destined for exportation should be distributed according to a fixed plan among the respective countries. It is expected that this arrangement will be ratified by the producers.

The preserved fruit industry, which was hitherto handicapped by the high sugar prices in Germany, will, it is anticipated, derive great benefit from the Convention. The reduction of the internal consumption tax from 1*l.* to 14*s.* is apparently deemed sufficient to render the manufacture of preserves and jams profitable.

From September 1 next duty on sugar imported into Germany from countries included in the Brussels Convention and on sugar exported from and re-imported into Germany will be levied at the rate of 18 marks 80 pf. (18*s.* 7½*d.*) per 100 kilos. of refined sugar and its equivalents, and at the rate of 18 marks 40 pf. (18*s.* 4*d.*) per 100 kilos. of raw sugar.

The prospects of the beetroot harvest are good, the weather having so far been favourable to the growth and quality of the beets.

In 1901 and 1902 the sugar factory at Dingelbe, near Hildesheim, in the province of Hanover, experimenting with one of Messrs. Petry and Hecking's drum apparatus, obtained a yield of 1 cwt. dried chips from 4½ cwts. raw chips. The former was sold at 5*s.*, and as the cost of the drying process was 1*s.* 5*d.*, the cwt. of beetroots realised nearly 9½*d.* If the cwt. of dried chips is sold at 6*s.*, the cwt. of beetroot yields a little more than 1*s.* Their nutritive qualities render the dried chips an excellent substitute for maize.

LONDON :
Printed for His Majesty's Stationery Office,
By HARRISON AND SONS,
Printers-in Ordinary to His Majesty.
(1400   9 | 03—H & S   375)

No. 3087.   Annual Series.

FRANCE.

DIPLOMATIC AND CONSULAR REPORTS.

TRADE OF

MADAGASCAR

FOR THE YEAR 1902.

FOREIGN OFFICE,
September, 1903.

No. 3087 Annual Series.

DIPLOMATIC AND CONSULAR REPORTS.

FRANCE.

REPORT FOR THE YEAR 1902

ON THE

TRADE OF MADAGASCAR.

Presented to both Houses of Parliament by Command of His Majesty,
SEPTEMBER, 1903.

LONDON:
PRINTED FOR HIS MAJESTY'S STATIONERY OFFICE,
BY HARRISON AND SONS, ST. MARTIN'S LANE,
PRINTERS IN ORDINARY TO HIS MAJESTY.

And to be purchased, either directly or through any Bookseller, from
EYRE & SPOTTISWOODE, EAST HARDING STREET, FLEET STREET, E.C.,
and 32, ABINGDON STREET, WESTMINSTER, S.W.;
or OLIVER & BOYD, EDINBURGH;
or E. PONSONBY, 116, GRAFTON STREET, DUBLIN.

1903.

[Cd. 1766—21.]   *Price One Penny.*

CONTENTS.

Report on the Trade of Madagascar for the Year 1902

By MR. CONSUL SAUZIER.

(Tamatave, July 30, 1903; received at Foreign Office, August 27, 1903.)

Madagascar is the third largest island in the world and lies on the eastern side of Africa, from which it is separated by the Mozambique Canal. It has a length of upwards of 950 miles and a maximum breadth of over 320 miles.

The area with its adjacent dependencies is about 229,000 square Area. miles.

From a recent attempt at a general census the population of the Population. whole island was estimated at 2,504,000 inhabitants, exclusive of civil functionaries, military officers and soldiers. Of the first there are 760; of the second 600 and 12,511 soldiers. Out of these 2,504,000 inhabitants, 2,500,000 are Malagasies of different tribes (but from a recent journey and exploration of Mr. Guillaume Grandidier in the south it has been established that large tracts of country are densely populated, so that it would be safer to say that there are now 2,650,000 Malagasies of different tribes), 210 are Africans, 600 are Asiatics, and the remaining 3,190 are whites. Among the latter, 2,790 are French subjects and the rest are chiefly British subjects. The female population all over Madagascar seems in excess of the male.

Antananarivo, the capital, with 55,000 inhabitants, is situated in Imerina; Fianarantsoa in the Betsileo in the central provinces; Majunga on the west coast; Tamatave, Diego Suarez and Mananzary on the east coast are the principal and chief towns of Madagascar. There are two British Consuls in the island, Mr. Consul Porter residing in Antananarivo, and myself residing in Tamatave.

There are 18 principal ports which are given according to the Principal rank they occupy for the year 1902, both for imports and exports, ports. viz., Tamatave, Majunga, Diego Suarez, Mananzary, Vohemar, Nossi-Bé, Tullear, Andovoranto, Analalova, Vatomandry, Fort Dauphin, Farafangana, Sainte-Marie, Morondova, Mohanoro, Ambohibe, Maintirano, Soalala.

In May, 1895, a French Expedition under General Duchesne Government. was sent to enforce the claims of France, and on October 1, the capital having been taken, peace was concluded and the Hova Queen, Ranavalo III recognised the protectorate which France claimed over the whole island. But in January, 1896, Madagascar became a French possession by virtue of a unilateral convention by which the Queen of Madagascar alone was bound, and some months after became by law, with its dependencies, a French colony, and from that moment the Resident-General, with an Administrative Council composed of seven members, governed the whole island with numerous Residents and Vice-Residents at the chief towns of the provinces into which the island has been divided.

On September 26, 1896, slavery was abolished. This was a great boon, but slavery was never severe and harsh, at least for the last 15 or 20 years.

In February, 1897, Royalty was abolished and Queen Ranavalo deported to the neighbouring island of Réunion. The post of Resident-General was abolished and General Gallieni who occupied it was created Governor-General of Madagascar and dependencies and Commander-in-Chief.

The Residents and Vice-Residents were turned into "Administrateurs" and "Administrateurs Adjoints Coloniaux."

The administrative system of Madagascar is based upon the autonomy of the different races which people the whole island ; it gives very fair results and works very regularly. The local Governors and Chief of Districts are appointed by the Administrators after having been generally chosen by the popular vote of the inhabitants.

Forced labour abolished. The system of forced labour in the public service was in force until January 1, 1901. Under it every native between 16 and 60 years of age was required by law to work 30 days every year for Government or to pay 15 fr. (12s.). This has been replaced by an increase of the personal tax, which for the whole island had been fixed at 5 fr. (4s.). It now amounts to 1l. 4s., 16s., 12s., and 10s. according to the importance of the town or province in which the native resides.

It is fair to state that all other taxes representing forced labour have also been abolished.

Education. Education is obligatory on all children from 8 to 14 years. Numerous schools have been established all over the country by the Government, in which the teaching is absolutely unsectarian, but the natives are perfectly free to send their children to Protestant or Roman Catholic schools, of which there are also a large number.

The study of the French language is obligatory also, and it is wonderful how the young Malagasies have mastered that language.

Industrial schools in Antananarivo have been created, in which the young Hova who is clever in manual skill and dexterity will soon, under able instruction, turn out to be useful artisans, quite able to cope with their European fellow workers. Already in joinery, woodwork, masonry and brickwork the Hovas have done creditable work, and in these professional schools will soon learn to execute all sort of artistic designs.

Regular courts of law have been established in Madagascar, Judicial which deal justice to natives as well as European settlers, according system. to the laws of France. The United Kingdom abolished its jurisdiction over British subjects on April 20, 1897, so that since that date they are amenable to French law.

The "Cour d'Appel," or Appellate Court from all the minor courts of the colony, sits at Antananarivo, where there is also a Court of First Instance. There is also a "Procureur-General," who is the head of the judicial system in Madagascar, and a "Procureur de la République."

In Tamatave there is a Court of First Instance and a "Procureur de la République," while in Majunga, in Fianarantsoa, Diego Suarez and Nossi-Bé there are Justices of the Peace with extended jurisdiction.

In all the other provinces there are Administrators who are at the same time Justices of the Peace, whose competency in criminal matters is the same as that of the Court of First Instance, but in civil matters is more extended than that of a Justice of the Peace in France.

The criminal law, outside of the ordinary Correctional Courts, is administered by Special Courts established at Antananarivo, Tamatave, Diego Suarez, Nossi-Bé and Fianarantsoa.

Civil cases between natives are adjudicated upon by mixed tribunals or by the old native courts. The mixed courts are presided over in Antananarivo by the President of the Court of First Instance, and elsewhere by the Administrators or Commandants, and these are under the control of the Appellate Court.

The Customs Department has always played a considerable Customs part in this island, both during the Hova rule and since the French duties. annexation. The Hovas had some 27 posts along the east coast where duties were collected, from Ambobimarina in the north to Fort Dauphin in the south, and six posts on the west coast.

From 1886 the dues levied at certain ports were given to the Comptoir d'Escompte of Paris, as a guarantee for the loan made by that bank to the Malagasy Government. The Comptoir had the right to have a Controller in each of the ports, the receipts of which were given in guarantee.

This system lasted until the declaration of the war in 1894, when Admiral Bienaimé, who was in command of the French fleet, considered it his duty to cause a new tariff to be made, and soon afterwards the Decree of May 31, 1895, signed by General Duchesne, had force of law and was applied in Majunga, Maravoay and Tamatave. This new law allowed the 10 per cent. *ad valorem* tariff which had been fixed by the Treaty of 1865 to remain [un-changed, but made some changes in the export duties. The head of the French service was the Chief of the "Service Administratif" in Tamatave, and the other members of the staff were all French and duly sworn. The Comptoir d'Escompte had still the right to control the receipts of the dues levied which were still the guarantee of the Malagasy loan in the three above ports.

Soon after the taking of the island the whole Customs Department passed into the hands of the French authorities, and the Comptoir d'Escompte gave up its lien upon the customs receipts in the different ports in which it had an agent.

French officers were sent gradually to all the ports and places where the Hovas had established custom duties, and all the coast is now under the same fiscal system.

The law of May 31, 1895, maintained the same duty on all goods, whether French or foreign, i.e., 10 per cent. ad valorem, but soon after the annexation of Madagascar as a French colony, French goods, whether from France or from a French colony, were allowed in free of duty in those ports only where there were French custom-houses.

In July, 1897, the general customs tariff of France of January 11, 1892, was made applicable to Madagascar and dependencies, and a special tariff applicable to foreign goods imported into Madagascar was applied, by which considerable reductions were made on such articles as pepper, tea, salt fish, &c., while a higher rate upon the minimum tariff has been imposed for the remainder, such as cotton goods, drills, &c.

Subsequently, however, modifications were made in the general tariff of 1892, so that now the duties on cotton goods and drills, &c., have been so increased that foreign importation is almost prohibited.

Imports and exports.

In order to understand fully the subjoined figures of imports and exports it is well to state that at the end of 1896 and beginning of 1897, when it was mooted that the general French Customs Tariff was to be applied to Madagascar, British and foreign houses introduced large quantities of tissues of all kind, principally prints, bleached shirtings and grey calico, which fetched very good prices, and in many places cotton goods rose from 15 to 20 per cent. per bale, but as there was still a considerable importation of these goods, prices began to fall, and when the new French-made goods arrived in Madagascar the market was over-stocked, and prices fell enormously, so that the best American cotton fetched only 80 dol. (16l.) per bale and even less. The large stock of British prints and other tissues had to be sold before the Madagascar trade could be called French, which, since the application of the general tariff, it has certainly become, as almost all foreign trade has ceased with the island :—

IMPORTS.

Year.						Total Value.
						£
1896..	..	..	..	..	..	559,517
1897..	..	..	..	..	..	734,856
1898..	..	..	..	..	..	865,112
1899..	..	..	..	..	..	1,116,664
1900..	..	..	..	..	..	1,595,835
1901..	..	..	..	..	..	1,841,310
1902..	..	..	..	..	..	1,691,561

So that imports into Madagascar have more than trebled since 1896.

In 1896 cotton and linen goods from the United Kingdom and colonies amounted to 151,072*l.* ; in 1897 they increased to 169,329*l.* ; but in 1898 the value of these goods fell to 28,852*l.* ; in 1899, 25,587*l.* ; in 1900, 12,400*l.* ; in 1901, 5,564*l.* ; in 1902, 7,022*l.*

The difference in the last five years is enormous, and conclusively shows how prejudicial are the new customs tariff of 1897, and its modifications, to British trade in that branch alone.

In 1896, 1897, 1898 and 1900 the imports from the United Kingdom took second place, while in 1899 they fell to the fifth place, to rise in 1901 and 1902 to the third place.

The principal imports from the United Kingdom were coals, tissues, metal and metal goods.

EXPORTS.

Year.						Total Value.
						£
1896..	..	..	..	..	..	144,238
1897..	..	..	..	..	..	173,697
1898..	..	..	..	..	..	198,982
1899..	..	..	..	..	..	321,851
1900..	..	..	..	..	..	424,955
1901..	..	..	..	..	..	359,018
1902..	..	..	..	..	..	525,777

In 1896 the total exports to the United Kingdom and colonies were of the value of 74,890*l.* ; those to France and colonies 42,271*l.*

The exports to France and colonies increased to :—

	Year.					Value.
						£
1897 ..	..	..	..	..	..	60,797
1898 .	..	..	..	..	..	91,653
1899 ..	..	..	..	..	..	217,805
1900 ..	..	..	..	..	..	309,051
1901 ..	..	..	..	..	..	259,308
1902 ..	..	..	..	..	..	271,787

While those to the United Kingdom and colonies decreased to :—

	Year.					Value.
						£
1897 ..	..	..	..	..	..	55,619
1898 ..	..	..	..	..	..	53,431
1899 ..	..	..	..	..	..	38,059
1900 ..	..	..	..	..	..	40,153
1901 ..	..	..	..	..	..	18,421

But in 1902 rose to 130,744*l*. This was due to the great quantity of oxen exported to South Africa and Mauritius, representing 108,212*l*.

The United Kingdom by herself occupies the sixth rank with 10,044*l*. The principal exports to the United Kingdom and colonies were, rubber, rafia, wax, cattle and hides.

Now if we turn to imports and exports by the flag of the ships in which they were brought to and taken from Madagascar, we find that both in imports and exports the French flag has a great superiority over that of the United Kingdom.

The figures stand thus for imports and exports under the French flag :—

IMPORTS.

	Year.					Value.
						£
1896 ..	..	..	..	..	..	288,741
1897 ..	..	..	..	..	..	468,007
1898 ..	..	..	..	..	..	777,863
1899 ..	..	..	..	..	..	1,062,688
1900 ..	..	..	.	..	..	1,509,683
1901 ..	..	..	..	..	..	1,660,308
1902 ..	..	..	..	..	.	1,486,018

EXPORTS.

Year.					Value.
					£
1896..	..	..	..	..	..	69,396
1897..	..	..	..	..	..	94,275
1898..	..	..	..	..	..	138,565
1899..	..	..	..	..	..	259,149
1900..	..	..	..	.	..	350,920
1901..	..	..	..	..	..	285,309
1902..	..	..	..	..	..	337,944

Imports and exports under the British flag are as follows:—

IMPORTS.

Year.					Value.
					£
1896..	..	..	..	..	..	234,977
1897..	..	..	..	..	..	209,445
1898..	..	..	..	..	..	19,014
1899..	..	..	..	..	..	7,088
1900..	..	..	..	..	..	62,359
1901..	..	..	..	..	..	64,978
1902..	..	..	..	..	..	113,132

EXPORTS.

Year.					Value.
					£
1896..	..	..	..	..	..	60,198
1897..	..	..	..	..	..	33,078
1898..	..	..	..	..	..	13,961
1899..	..	..	..	..	..	20,477
1900..	..	..	..	..	..	10,092
1901..	..	..	..	..	..	15,250
1902..	..	..	..	..	..	133,524

During these seven years 7,198,258*l*. were imported under the French flag and 710,943*l*. under the British flag.

During the same seven years 1,535,558*l*. were exported under the French flag and 286,580*l*. under the British flag.

Natural products produced in Madagascar were subject to an export tariff, but this has been abolished, save for cattle, which still pay 12*s*. per head. Export duties.

The whole of the east coast is rocky in many places, and reefs also exist which render the approach to the land difficult. Harbours. At the mouths of the rivers there are bars which are dangerous to cross, and which at certain seasons of the year are almost impracticable. Those of Andovoranto, Vatomandry, Mohandro and Farafangana are so bad that in the months of June and July lighters cannot get near the ships or coasters, which are obliged to anchor out in the open roadstead, sometimes at a great distance from land.

Diego Suarez, Vohemar and Tamatave are the only harbours on the east coast where ships can anchor safely.

Tamatave.   Tamatave has 11,000 inhabitants, of whom 2,500 are whites, and about 8,500 natives and Asiatics.

The harbour, though not absolutely safe, especially for sailing vessels from December 15 to March 15, has certain advantages over the other roadsteads of the east coast. It is protected from the high sea by two lines of reefs, between which is the south pass by which vessels usually enter the roadstead, and which permit communication with the shore in almost all weather. By its geographical position it is the natural outlet of almost all the products of the coast and of the central provinces, just as it is the principal port of importation. It is in fact the emporium of almost all the trade of the island and can be justly called the commercial capital of Madagascar, for by itself, both in imports and exports, it has more than four-tenths of the trade of the whole island.

Diego Suarez.   Diego Suarez is a magnificent harbour which can hold the largest fleet. It is very secure and deep, and on that account has been chosen as the naval base in the Indian Ocean for the forces of France. The channel which leads to the roadstead is about half a mile wide and deep so that the largest vessel can enter the harbour, but its great drawback is that it is very difficult for sailing vessels to leave it during the north-east monsoon.

It is essentially a military port, and occupies the third rank with 13·32 per cent. for imports and exports. This is due to the large garrison quartered there, and to the very important military works which have been carried out and are still under construction.

On the other hand the harbours of the west coast are vast and deep, offering great security to large ships, and can moreover be always easily reached.

Majunga, with about 5,000 inhabitants, has a beautiful harbour, and is the principal port of the west coast, for, by its imports and exports in 1902 and previous years, it ranks next after Tamatave with 15·95 per cent. of the whole trade of the colony.

Shipping.   Shipping statistics show that like the trade of the United Kingdom and colonies the number of British ships has considerably diminished since 1897 :—

Year.	Number of Ships Entered and Cleared from Madagascar.	French.	British.	British Percentage.
1897	7,974	4,160	2,934	36·79
1898	12,694	7,265	4,461	35·14
1899	13,395	9,235	3,766	28·11
1900	12,823	8,738	3,717	28·99
1901	13,440	9,816	3,103	23·09
1902	12,739	9,102	2,929	22·09

By far the largest numbers of vessels entered and cleared from the following ports in 1902 :—

	Per cent.
1. Majunga	20·95
2. Analalova	14·12
3. Morondova	8·91
4. Tamatave	6·75
5. Tullear	5·63

But it should be explained that a great many dhows under French, British and red flag ply between the ports of Majunga, Analalova, Morondova and Tullear on the west coast, and the Comoro Islands, Nossi-Bé, Mayotte, Zanzibar, India and the Persian Gulf.

All vessels, whether French or foreign, pay sanitary dues of Sanitary dues. ½d. per ton on entering, but those flying the French flag, and carrying on the coasting trade along the coast of Madagascar or between Madagascar, Réunion and the Comoro Islands, are free from these dues.

Goods are landed and shipped at 4s. 10d. per ton for steamers, Lighterage. and 3s. for sailing ships, according to tonnage borne on the bill of lading.

Ballast can be had at 4s. 10d. per ton. Ballast.

The charge for water is 4s. for three casks. Water.

Three lines of steamers convey passengers and cargo regularly Steamer to Tamatave, Majunga and Diego Suarez :—1. The Messageries communi- Maritimes, from Marseilles, call twice every month homeward and cation. outward. 2. The Compagnie Havraise Peninsulaire, from Havre, once a month outward. 3. The Chargeurs Réunis, also from Havre, call monthly on the outward trip. By these three lines cargo is carried from London at through rates, and from Tamatave to London, Marseilles, Nantes and Bordeaux the rate of freight per ton (1,000 kilos.) is 1l. 12s. ; to Havre, 1l. ; to Hamburg, 1l. 16s. ; but certain articles of export, such as hides, rafia, rabannas, vegetable hair, sheep-skins, empty bags in bales, dry sundries in bags, and vanilla pay freight at the rate of 800 kilos., or 1,600 lbs. per ton.

A firm of German merchants at Tamatave have a steamer from Hamburg to Majunga, Tamatave and the east coast and back three times a year.

Lighthouses. Several lighthouses have recently been built on the coast of Madagascar ; one at Cape Amber, the extreme northern point of the island ; three at Diego Suarez harbour, three at Majunga and two in Tamatave harbour.

The one at Cape Amber is in 46° 56′ 45″ longitude and 11° 57′ 20″ latitude of Paris. It gives a white light, with regular flashes every five seconds. Its height is 115 feet from the ground and 71 yards from the sea.

The three lights at Diego Suarez facilitate the entry into and the departure from the bay during the night. (1) A white flash light every 10 seconds, placed on what is called "Le gros rocher," outside and to the soutn of the large channel, 125 feet above the sea ; (2) a white fixed light, on the "zlob des Aigrettes," height 56 feet; (3) a red fixed light on the molehead of Autsirane, situate at the entry and to the south of the harbour de la Nièvre.

Majunga.—"Katsépé" lighthouse, 100 feet high, gives a flash light every five seconds and indicates the entrance into Bombetoka Bay, and together with the Anorombato light, enables a vessel to enter by night and to come to anchor before Majunga ; (2) Anorombato light. 21 feet high ; (3) Pointe de Sable light, 23 feet.

Tamatave.—Two lighthouses, with white, red and green sectors, having each a different direction, have been constructed lately ; one called "Phare detanio" having a range of 13 miles, shows by its white lights the three entrances leading to the harbour. The other, called "Phare d'Hastie," is merely a port light, whose white light indicates the anchorage ground. By the aid of these two light-houses ships can now come to anchor by night in Tamatave harbour, which it was impossible to do previously ; there is, however, one draw-back about these lighthouses, and that is that they are not sufficiently high, and in thick or cloudy weather are not seen well enough from the high sea, and as the coast is rocky and dangerous, ships dare not come too close to search for the lights.

Lastly, a lighthouse is being built close to the entrance of Vohémor harbour. This will be a great boon to ships ; for from Cape Amber to Tamatave there is not a light, and the coast is dangerous and rocky.

Roads and inland transport. Transport from Tamatave to Antananarivo and the interior has greatly improved. A very good wagon road from Mahatsara to Antananarivo has been completed in three years at a cost of 9,000,000 fr. (360,000l.) ; it is 150 miles long, and was opened to the public on January 2, 1901.

Passengers now take the railway from Tamatave to Fooudrona, 7½ miles, then embark on small steamers through the lakes and "pangalanes" to Mahatsara, where they arrive the same night, and then take the road either in motor-cars, rickshaws, palanquin, or ox or mule carts to Antananarivo, where, by rickshaw, four days afterwards they are not only safely landed, but much cheaper than by palanquin and with less fatigue.

Goods are taken up much slower by light mule carts or ox wagon, or even by a light hand cart which two natives drag up with facility with a weight of 700 lbs. Thus, from Tamatave to Antananarivo, which is 216 miles, a passenger pays about 8*l*. first class, without food, and goods from 14*l*. to 16*l*. per ton ; while formerly a palanquin required eight men at 1*l*. 5*s*. per man, or 10*l*. without food, and a ton of merchandise cost 40*l*. The journey up to Antananarivo lasted at least eight days, while it took about a month for a ton of goods carried on men's shoulders to reach the capital.

A railway from Antananarivo to the coast is being built, the Railway, first 19 miles of which were opened by the Governor-General in October, 1902, but not to the public at large. It is a great work, well planned and well carried out by the military engineers. It has already cost 800,000*l*., another 800,000*l*. have just been voted, but the climate of the country through which the line passes is so unhealthy, the ground itself so rocky and difficult to work, that it would not be astonishing if at least another 400,000*l*. were to be required to complete the work, and put the capital within 24 hours of Tamatave, or in other words, within 24 days of Marseilles.

The want of labourers in almost all the provinces of the east coast Labour. for the last four or five years is due mainly to the fact that cost of living and taxes have almost trebled during that time ; rice has risen from 12*s*. to 1*l*. 12*s*. per ton, while taxes have also increased in the same proportion. It is not extraordinary, therefore, that the common labourer should desire his wages to be increased in proportion to the actual cost of living ; Government, moreover, has undertaken great public works, on which thousands of labourers are employed at a high rate of wages. Hence the great want of labour felt by the colonists in general.

Chinese and Indian immigration from French India has been tried in vain ; these labourers gave such trouble to their employers, chiefly the Government of the colony, that it was thought wiser to repatriate them at great cost than keep them in Madagascar, where they filled the hospitals, diminished the food supply and actually did no work.

Emigration from Madagascar is not allowed without permission Emigration. of the Governor-General ; and companies or agencies for colonies or countries not under the French flag are bound to furnish a security of at least 40,000 fr. (1,600*l*.).

All persons carrying on any trade, industry, or profession are Trading bound to pay a license, which varies from 4*s*. to 40*l*., according to licenses the importance of their transactions and the population of the town in which they are established. A special license of 1,800 fr. (72*l*.) is imposed on persons dealing in gold, banks and discount houses. Persons of Asiatic or African origin have to pay 1*l*. a year for permission to reside in Madagascar, and those who trade have to pay a license duty of from 4*l.* to 40*l.* a year according to the class of the license which they hold.

The Malagasey had no special coinage but used at first the Spanish or American silver dollar as a standard, and afterwards the French 5-franc piece, which was worth 4*s.* In order to make up the sub-divisions of the dollar of 5-franc piece the Malagasey cut up these coins into pieces varying from 2*s.* to a piece of silver of the size of a grain of rice, and weighed them in handscales with weights corresponding to the native scale of value and thus obtained change which permitted commercial transactions to be carried on. This cut money, as it was called, has been prohibited by the French Government, and in the interior transactions were in consequence difficult with the natives, but the French authorities have since bought it all up and replaced it by the silver sub-divisions of the 5-franc piece and by bullion, so that the coinage now used is the French currency, of which 46,000,000 fr. have been introduced in the colony since its conquest. The lowest copper coin is the 5-centime piece (½*d.*).

In order to facilitate trade the Government Treasury issues drafts of 100, 200, 500, 1,000, 2,000, 5,000, 10,000 and 20,000 fr. at Antananarivo, Tamatave, Majunga, Diego Suarez, Ste. Marie and Nossi-Bé at 20 days sight and at ½ per cent. premium. These drafts are good for five years from date of issue, are negotiable instruments and can be passed to the order of any one in Madagascar and France.

There are two banks in Madagascar, the Comptoir National d'Escompte de Paris, at Antananarivo, with agencies at Tamatave, Majunga, Diego Suarez and Mananzary; and the Banque Grenard, a private bank at Tamatave. These two banks issue drafts on London at 2½ per cent. premium.

Every Frenchman is entitled to a gratuitous concession of 247 acres ; and anyone can purchase lands to any extent, the price of which is about 8*d.* per acre in the north and west, and 1*s.* 8*d.* in the interior and east coast, without any other cost but that of registration within three years from the date of delivery of the title and improvement of the concession. Concessions can be given gratuitously or by way of sale by the Governor-General alone after advice from the Conseil d'Administration on the proposition of the chief of the Service des Domaines.

Madagascar was formerly celebrated for its cattle, which were so abundant that a fair sized slaughter animal was commonly sold at from 12*s.* to 1*l.* 4*s.* ; there was hardly a village where beef was not sold, and where for 1*d.* a man had not more than sufficient for himself. The large quantity of salted hides which were exported from the different ports of Madagascar also testified to the abundance of the cattle, which were generally of the horned and humped species or Madagascar zebu, which would seem to be indigenous to this island.

The Hovas very prudently forbade the exportation of cows, but allowed slaughter cattle to be taken by hundreds from different ports to supply the neighbouring islands of Mauritius and Réunion, and afterwards Natal and the east coast of Africa.

The French authorities, after the war and the wholesale slaughter of oxen, cows and heifers during the rebellion, very wisely forbade not only the export of cows and heifers, but also the killing of any, in order to allow the herds to increase and multiply.

The price of beef has since then considerably increased all over the island, and the price of a good sized bullock now in Imerina is 7*l.* or 8*l.*, while a small one fetches 4*l.* to 5*l.* In Majunga, f.o.b., the same ox is worth from 3*l.* 8*s.* to 3*l.* 15*s.*, and in Vohemar, on the east coast, from which port a considerable number are taken to Natal, Mauritius and Réunion Island, slaughter cattle are worth, f.o.b., from 2*l.* 15*s.* to 3*l.* 15*s.* each ; these slaughter cattle, alive, weigh from 600 to 700 lbs., and sometimes, but rarely, more. The export duty, which is now 12*s.* per head, is exactly the amount which the Hovas obtained formerly.

EXPORT OF CATTLE.

Year.						Value.
						£
1897..	..	..	..	..	..	21,893
1898..	..	..	..	..	..	26,144
1899..	..	..	..	..	..	33,709
1900..	..	..	..	..	..	46,233
1901..	..	..	..	..	..	32,485
1902..	..	..	..	..	..	176,050

The principal ports from which live-stock and cattle were exported from Madagascar in 1902 were :—

Name of Port.				Value.	
				Currency.	Sterling.
				Francs.	£
On the west coast—					
Analalova	..	..	..	746,500	29,860
Majunga ..	..	..	..	626,110	25,044
Tullear ..	..	..	..	586,768	23,470
On the east coast—					
Vohemar..	..	..	..	2,049,476	81,979
Tamatave	..	..	..	277,393	11,095
Diego Suarez	..	..	..	100,000	4,000
Fort Dauphin	..	..	..	30,278	1,211
Total	..	..		4,416,525	176,661

This shows what a great impetus has been given to the export of live-stock, chiefly to South Africa, for we find that during 1901 only 824,479 fr. (32,979*l*.) were exported from the whole of Madagascar, and that from the west coast the insignificant sum of 58,217 fr. (2,328*l*.) was produced by that trade ; while if the two years are compared we find in favour of 1902 for the west coast an increase of 1,901,161 fr. (76,046*l*.) and for the east coast ports an increase of 1,690,885 fr. (67,635*l*.).

Telegraphs.

Since the conquest of Madagascar in October, 1895, telegraphic communication has considerably increased ; there was formerly a telegraph line between Antananarivo and Tamatave and one from Antananarivo to Majunga, and from this last port a cable to Mozambique connected Madagascar with the rest of the world. Now on the east coast the lines from Tamatave extend to Vatomandry and Mananzary, and from Betroky in the south to Fort Dauphin. From Diego Suarez in the north east to Vohemar, Anbalaha and Maroantsetra the line goes to Ambatondrazaka and Antananarivo, so that the whole of Madagascar is now connected by telegraph lines.

The rate for inland telegrams is 10*d*. for 10 words or less, and 1*d*. (10 c.) for every additional word.

Gold.

Madagascar is rich in gold, for in almost every part of it small quantities of that valuable metal have been found, generally not deep in the ground but on the surface in the shape of nuggets, dust and a little gold sand (paillette d'or). A regular reef has not been found as yet.

The gold found since the French occupation in 1895 has increased enormously both in weight and value, for in 1896 (the first year of real statistics) the weight of gold found was 44,882 grammes, of the value of 4,488*l*. ; while in 1902 it was 1,532,000 grammes, of the value of 164,944*l*.

The following table shows the weight and value of gold found :—

Year.			Weight.	Value.	
				Currency.	Sterling.
			Grammes.	Francs.	£
1896	..	..	44,882	112,206	4,488
1897	..	..	85,444	213,612	8,544
1898	..	..	230,141	98,522	3,941
1899	..	..	423,904	729,606	29,184
1900	..	..	1,850,152	3,587,917	143,516
1901	..	..	1,188,000	3,299,676	131,987
1902	..	..	1,535,000	4,123,612	164,944

Gold cannot be carried about without a permit of origin.

Gold mining is regulated by the Decree of February 20, 1902, which grants many facilities over the old law of July, 1896.

(1400　9 | 03—H & S　380)

No. 3088. Annual Series.

SPAIN.

DIPLOMATIC AND CONSULAR REPORTS.

TRADE OF

CANARY ISLANDS

FOR THE YEAR 1902.

FOREIGN OFFICE,
September, 1903.

No. 3088 Annual Series.

DIPLOMATIC AND CONSULAR REPORTS.

SPAIN.

REPORT FOR THE YEAR 1902

ON THE

TRADE AND COMMERCE OF THE CANARY ISLANDS.

REFERENCE TO PREVIOUS REPORT, Annual Series No. 2830.

Presented to both Houses of Parliament by Command of His Majesty,
SEPTEMBER, 1903.

LONDON:
PRINTED FOR HIS MAJESTY'S STATIONERY OFFICE,
BY HARRISON AND SONS, ST. MARTIN'S LANE,
PRINTERS IN ORDINARY TO HIS MAJESTY.

And to be purchased, either directly or through any Bookseller, from
EYRE & SPOTTISWOODE, EAST HARDING STREET, FLEET STREET, E.C.,
and 32, ABINGDON STREET, WESTMINSTER, S.W.;
or OLIVER & BOYD, EDINBURGH;
or E. PONSONBY, 116, GRAFTON STREET, DUBLIN.

1903.

[Cd. 1766—22.]   *Price One Penny.*

CONTENTS.

———◆———

Reference to previous Report, Annual Series No. 2830.

Report on the Trade and Commerce of the Canary Islands for the Year 1902

By Mr. Consul Croker.

(Teneriffe, August 17, 1903 ; received at Foreign Office, August 28, 1903.)

In the hope of obtaining statistics from the customs authorities, Introductory. the report on the trade of the Canary Islands for the year 1902 has been delayed from month to month. Without such statistics it is, of course, impossible to estimate, except approximately, the volume of business done. Under any circumstances it is difficult to furnish a detailed and exact report on the import trade of these islands. The customs authorities do not require a statement of the values of the goods imported, and in view of the constantly fluctuating prices of all classes of merchandise, the statistics of weight, which alone have been accessible in previous years, are often misleading as to the value of the business. For the year under review, however, even statistics of weights have not been procurable, and the consequence is that only a general comparison can be made between the trade of 1902 and that of previous years. Pains have, however, been taken to ascertain the views of the leading men of business, and these have been verified, as far as possible, by personal investigation and inquiry.

Speaking generally, it may be said that the trade of 1902 shows a substantial increase in comparison with that of 1901, and a still more marked increase compared with that of 1900. In fact, a fair estimate of the improvement in both the export and import trade in 1902 over that of the previous year may be made by contrasting the trade of 1901 with that of 1900, the increase being proportionately the same.

Taking the islands as a whole, they may be said to have had a good year in 1902, and they are at present in a comparatively prosperous condition. The working classes have enjoyed continuous employment and their wages have been steadily on the increase. The prosperity is due, not only to the general improvement in trade, but also to the steadily increasing influx of visitors.

The trade of the islands with Spain has been gradually and consistently growing, especially as regards imports. This fact is

(382)

Exchange. undoubtedly due, to a very large extent, to the continued high rate of exchange. It was pointed out in the report on the trade of these islands for 1900 that the rise in exchange to 33 pesetas 60 c., in 1898, had had the effect of diverting from the United Kingdom to Spain a large proportion of the business in cotton and woollen textiles and manufactured iron. In 1899 the lowest point touched by exchange was 29 pesetas 18 c., but it has not since been quoted at anything like that figure. The average rate for 1901 was 34 pesetas 70 c. It is true that it was slightly lower in 1902, the average working out at 34 pesetas 7 c., an improvement of 63 c., but it must be pointed out that this reduction in the premium was largely effected by the comparatively low rates which prevailed in the early autumn. Expectations had been aroused that considerable economies in public expenditure were imminent, and the premium declined in consequence. The expectations, however, were not realised, and exchange went up to former figures. The year ended exactly as it had begun, the rate on January 1 and December 31 being 34 pesetas. The highest point reached during the year was 34 pesetas 87 c. on March 1, and the lowest 32 pesetas 86 c. on October 15.

A marked feature of the import trade was the encroachment of Italian shippers upon lines hitherto monopolised by Germany. In fact, Germany has lost considerable ground, not only to Italy, but also to Spain and the United Kingdom. Italy, on the other hand, has been making rapid advances during the last couple of years in all branches of manufactured goods, especially cottons and mercery.

Indian trade. There are eight Indian firms of importance doing business in the Canary Islands, three at Teneriffe and five at Las Palmas. These firms are entirely under Indian management, and give employment to about 70 men of their own nationality. They deal almost exclusively in silk, jute goods, wrought silver, Eastern embroidery, sandalwood, cotton goods, brass work (Eastern), porcelain and chinawares and Cashmere fabrics. The value of the goods imported by them is estimated at 25,000l. per annum. Their goods are principally transhipped at Gibraltar for these islands, and their business is done chiefly with passengers in transit.

Imports.
Cottons. The cotton business in 1902 showed a marked increase in comparison with that done in 1901. The United Kingdom maintained a commanding lead over her nearest rival, Spain, but her shipments did not increase in the same proportion as those of the latter country. German shipments fell off considerably, and the ground lost by Germany has been won by Spain and Italy. This is especially the case with the trade in cotton flannels. Even in the cheaper makes, in which Germany formerly possessed a monopoly, Italian shippers have now a considerable share of the business. France has quite lost her trade with these islands in cotton goods, and her shipments are insignificant.

Woollens. In woollen goods, however, France is doing more than hitherto.

Her shipments in 1901 were considerably in excess of those of the previous year, and in 1902 she maintained the ground she had won. Spain's share of the business increased owing to the high rates of exchange. Shipments from Germany are still falling-off, and the decrease in her trade is specially noticeable in the cheaper lines which she manufactures. The lion's share of the whole trade—considerably more than half—is still in the hands of the United Kingdom. Italy does not figure here as a competitor in woollen goods.

French goods obtained the lead in the silk market, followed by Silk. those of British, Spanish, German and Italian manufacture, in the order named. The business is small.

Spain has by far the largest share in the leather business. The Leather. shipments from Belgium, which in 1901 were more than double what she had sent the previous year, fell off considerably in 1902, and their place was taken by shipments from Italy. France and the United Kingdom obtained their usual share of the business.

The United Kingdom remained almost the sole source of the Wheat. wheat supply, 95 per cent. of the quantity imported in 1902 being shipped from that country. There was an increased demand owing to the improved condition of the labouring classes.

The shipments of maize were also larger than those of the Maize. previous year. Argentina and Morocco have no competition in this grain, but a very considerable portion of the business passes through the hands of British firms.

The same remark applies to the trade in beans, the supplies of Beans. which came from Morocco.

The United Kingdom maintained the monopoly she acquired Flour. in the flour business, and no effort has been made by the French shippers to recover the trade. Prior to 1897 the flour imported into these islands came exclusively from France.

Germany did not obtain in 1902 her usual share of colonial Colonial produce, owing probably to the high freights ruling from Hamburg produce. in comparison with those from British ports.

There are practically only two competitors for the business Rice. in rice, the United Kingdom and Spain. The former, however, does twice the business of the latter, and this position was maintained in the year under review.

The manufacture of sugar in the islands is rapidly decreasing, Sugar. owing to the smaller quantity of land now devoted to the cultivation of sugar cane. The farmers have been tempted by the prosperous condition of the banana trade to grow bananas in preference to sugar cane. There is consequently a certain prospect of an increased demand for the imported article. In 1902, however, imports were not so large as might have been anticipated, as there were large stocks of native sugar held over from the previous year. What was imported came chiefly from Hamburg, and the shipments from that port are increasing.

The coal imported into these islands during the year 1902 Coal.

amounted to about 730,000 tons. This shows a slight decrease as compared with the previous year, probably brought about by competition in the coal trade at Madeira. Speaking generally, however, the coaling business, both at Teneriffe and Las Palmas is steadily growing, and the imports in 1902 show a large increase as compared with the average for the five preceding years.

Commercial travellers. In concluding these remarks on the import trade, it may be mentioned that few commercial travellers representing British firms came to these islands. It is, however, doubtful whether material advantage would accrue from more frequent visits. Almost the entire import trade is done through local commission agents, who have a thorough knowledge of the lines they represent and also of the requirements of the customers—a knowledge it may be said which no occasional traveller could be expected to possess. The British firms which do business with these islands are well represented by both British and Spanish agents, who are kept well supplied with samples from home. These agents are most energetic, and certainly cannot be accused of wilful blindness to the needs of the market ; and, when it is remembered that it is extremely difficult for a stranger to ascertain more than approximately the credit and standing of those with whom he wishes to do business, the present system does not seem so antiquated and defective as is generally maintained.

Exports. Bananas. The most promising feature in the general trade of the islands was the extraordinary increase in the cultivation and export of bananas. When the exportation of this fruit from Jamaica to the United Kingdom began in 1900, fears were universally expressed that, in consequence of the facilities offered to the Jamaica shippers, the trade from these islands was doomed. Those anticipations, however, have completely failed of realisation. So far from the Jamaica trade having injured that from the Canary Islands, it has proved an excellent advertisement and created a demand for the fruit generally, while the superiority of the banana from here has been sufficiently observed to obtain for it, as a rule, enhanced prices. The prosperity of the trade has had the effect of hardening the price of land, and also, as has been pointed out, of reducing to a large extent the cultivation of sugar cane. The total quantity exported to the United Kingdom in 1902 from all the islands was 1,656,876 crates, valued at 284,320*l.*

Tomatoes. There was an increase in the export of tomatoes, and prices generally were well maintained. There is a growing demand, not only from the United Kingdom (which country practically monopolises the trade), but also from Spain, and if tomato cultivation were not of such a capricious nature, there would be little reason for complaint in this branch of the export trade. The exports for the year under review amounted to 432,388 boxes, valued at 111,297*l.*, the greater portion of which were shipped from Teneriffe, the quantity being estimated at 7,300 tons.

Potatoes. From Teneriffe the quantity of potatoes exported in 1902 was 110,000 cases (about 65 lbs. each case), making a total of 3,200 tons. The total quantity from all the islands was 234,966 boxes, valued at 33,600*l*.

Two sorts of onions are exported : white, which are grown Onions. chiefly in Lanzarote ; and red, which are cultivated principally at Tejina, in the north of the Island of Teneriffe. There was a fair average crop in 1902, the major portion of which was shipped, as usual, to the West Indies.

The increased and increasing demand for bananas and tomatoes Agriculture (the former especially), and consequent rise in the price of agricultural and irrigation land, are causing attention to be given to the question of irrigation. The importance of this question may be seen in the difference in the value of Terrenos de secano, or non-irrigable land, and that of Terrenos de riego, or irrigable land. The price of the former ranges from 7*l*. to 17*l*. an acre according to the height of the land, the lower lands, in this instance, being worth less than the higher lands, as they receive less natural moisture. The price of the irrigated lands situated above 1,000 feet but below 3,000 feet, is about 100*l*. an acre ; while that of good irrigable land below the 1,000 feet level is on an average 250*l*. an acre. The great difference between the value of the irrigable land below 1,000 feet and that of land above that level, is that bananas and tomatoes cannot be grown except on the former, while potatoes may be grown on land situated as high as 3,000 feet.

It is estimated that in Teneriffe there are 100,000 acres of land which are at present sterile, and which, if irrigated, could be devoted to the cultivation of bananas, tomatoes and potatoes. So far, artificial irrigation has been applied to not quite 20,000 acres, while it is the opinion of experts that if the rain supply in the central elevated portion of the island were accumulated it would suffice to irrigate some 50,000 acres.

The actual price of water for irrigation purposes is from 1*d*. to 2*d*. per cubic metre (about 300 gallons). The quantity needed for one irrigation of an acre of land is 300 cubic metres, and 25 irrigations a year are usually necessary. So that the annual cost of irrigating 1 acre is, roughly speaking, from 30*l*. to 60*l*. an acre at the above prices.

These charges may appear extremely high, but when it is considered that land on the lower levels which is not irrigated does not yield more than 1*l*. 10*s*. to 2*l*. 10*s*. net per acre, while land at the same level, but irrigated, gives a net return of up to 80*l*. an acre, it will be understood that the farmers are more than willing to pay even these prices if they can obtain the water.

At present, however, the demand far exceeds the supply, and recently two important syndicates have been formed (one in the United Kingdom and the other in Teneriffe) for undertaking the construction of large reservoirs, one in the interior of the island and the other to the north of Santa Cruz. These syndicates are in no way connected, and the farmers in the island are looking forward with great interest to the outcome of their undertakings.

According to the opinion of experts the expenditure of large capital on irrigation works would be profitable to the investors, and insure a rich and prosperous future to the islands.

Shipping.   From the annexed return of shipping it will be seen that the total number of merchant vessels entered at Santa Cruz in 1902 was 2,841, with a total tonnage of 2,894,297 tons. These figures show a decrease of 78 in the number of ships and 21,629 tons in the total tonnage as compared with the previous year.

Notwithstanding this falling-off in the total shipping at Santa Cruz, there was an increase in British shipping in 1902 of 37 vessels and 101,834 tons as compared with 1901.

On the other hand, German shipping fell off from 262 vessels with 580,026 tons in 1901, to 195 vessels with 409,332 tons in 1902, thus showing a decrease of 67 vessels and 170,694 tons in the latter year. The decrease in German shipping at the port of Santa Cruz during the past three years has been most noticeable.

Hotels.   The popularity of the Canary Islands as a resort for those in search of health or pleasure has been proved by the large increase in the number of visitors. In no previous year have there been so many, and the hotels have had a record season, having been full during the late autumn, winter and spring.

In addition to the numerous comfortable hotels at present existing in Teneriffe, a new hotel on a large scale is in course of construction on the hill overlooking the bay of Santa Cruz. Its fine position and other attractions should make it a profitable undertaking. It is being built with British capital.

RETURN of British Shipping at Santa Cruz (Teneriffe) during the Year 1902.

Nationality.	Sailing.		Steam.		Total.	
	Number of Vessels.	Tons.	Number of Vessels.	Tons.	Number of Vessels.	Tons.
British	5	2,744	738	1,458,382	743	1,461,126
Spanish	1,116	142,529	464	367,480	1,580	510,009
German	..	..	195	409,332	195	409,332
French	..	..	181	260,878	181	260,878
Italian	1	694	60	127,781	61	128,425
Belgian	..	..	33	91,463	33	91,463
Russian	..	..	13	8,713	13	8,713
Norwegian ..	2	648	11	8,114	13	8,762
Swedish	1	494	6	5,257	7	5,751
Danish	..	..	7	4,610	7	4,610
Dutch	..	..	4	3,926	4	3,926
Uruguayan ..	1	449	1	477	2	926
United States ..	..	..	1	184	1	184
Portuguese ..	1	192	..	..	1	192
Total ..	1,127	147,750	1,714	2,746,547	2,841	2,894,297
,, 1901 ..	1,157	146,927	1,762	2,768,999	2,919	2,915,926

LAS PALMAS.

Mr. Vice-Consul Swanston reports as follows :—

The changes which took place last year in the farming out of the Introductory. free port rents in the Canaries, and the entire change of the management of the Puerto Franco arrangements, have made it more difficult than ever to obtain any reliable or detailed statistics of the imports into this island for the past year.

No particulars are published or supplied as to imports or exports by the company who have rented the customs.

The year 1902 may be called an average one in the steadily increasing trade of the island.

Both imports and exports have considerably increased.

The United Kingdom still takes almost the whole of the exports, and supplies the bulk of the imports.

The principal import, coal, remains the same as last year, about Coal. 500,000 tons, nearly all from Cardiff, very little north country or other coal being brought.

The shipping returns (Annex A) show an increase of steamers Shipping. calling for coal and provisions.

The coal trade is still entirely in British hands.

In cotton goods 45 per cent. of the imports are of British origin, Cottons. 30 per cent. Spanish, the remainder is mostly from Germany and the United States.

Cotton wadding, used largely for packing bananas, came, until recently, entirely from Manchester, but now comes from the United States and Spain.

The woollen goods are mostly British, but the import is only Woollens. about one-third of the quantity of cotton goods imported.

In textiles generally, the United Kingdom holds the bulk of the Textiles. trade. Germany and Spain (Barcelona) being the most serious competitors. Cheap merinos and cotton suitings, also fancy flannelettes, are coming in increasing quantities at very low prices from Germany.

In all textiles here a low to medium quality at a cheap price sells most readily.

Chemical manure is an increasing import into the island, almost Chemical entirely from the United Kingdom. manures.

Sulphates of ammonia, superphosphates and nitrates of soda, potash and dried bloods are largely imported for artificial manures, the ingredients being mixed here in many different proportions to suit the fancy of the fruit growers, who have of late years been trying many experiments on their fruit plantations.

The competition that has arisen in the United Kingdom between Bananas. the Jamacia and Canary bananas, has induced the grower here to make every effort to strengthen and improve the fruit.

For the better qualities of hardware, and for ironware, tin plates Hardware. and tinware the United Kingdom holds its place in the trade and supplies the bulk, but in cheap cutlery, bolts, locks, nails and wire Germany and Belgium are getting an increasing share. A large number of cheap iron bedsteads have recently been brought from Seville, but the British make is preferred for strength and durability.

Furniture.

The business in furniture is small, and as the Canary carpenters are most skilful, and turn out very strong work, most is made here, but in the past year considerable quantities of cheap showy furniture, mostly veneered work, have been brought from Barcelona, and sells readily.

Provisions.

In provisions, flour, rice and biscuits come almost entirely from London and Liverpool, maize from the Argentine Republic and Morocco.

Cost of living.

The cost of living here has more than doubled in the past 10 years, this applies to most of the ordinary necessities of life, and is to be accounted for by the large number of steamers calling here for coal and provisions, and the large number of visitors to the island.

Potatoes and eggs.

A large and increasing trade is done in shipping potatoes and eggs to the South African ports.

Candles and soap.

Soap and candles (except those used in the churches) come entirely from the United Kingdom.

Starch.

Starch is now supplied cheaper from Germany than elsewhere.

Beer and alcohol.

Light beers, and also gin, now come almost wholly from Germany, as also the bulk of the alchohol used in wine making in the island.

Sugar.

The supply of sugar grown and made in the island not being sufficient for its consumption, considerable quantities have been imported from Hamburg.

Timber.

The bulk of the timber used for building purposes comes from Canada and the United States, but nearly all the cut wood used for crates and cases for the enormous quantities of bananas, tomatoes, and potatoes exported, comes from Norway, ready sawn in shooks, the bundles tied with wire. It is to be regretted that this trade is not in Canadian hands. There seems no reason why this cut wood should not come from Canada, if the lumber firms there would give the matter their attention, and use care and exactness in executing the orders and shipments. The value of the crates and boxes in which the fruit is shipped from the island must total up to some 80,000l. per annum, probably more. The import navigation duty on wood from Canada is 3 pesetas 50 c., or 2s. 0½d. per 1,000 kilos., while from Norway the duty is only 2 pesetas 50 c., or 1s. 5½d. per 1,000 kilos. However, considerable orders have now been sent to Canada, and there is little doubt but that (from the samples I have seen and the prices quoted) Canada can well supply all that is wanted in wood by the fruit shippers. More land where water is available is planted with bananas every year, and it will be seen from the return of exports (Annex B) that the shipments of fruit show an increase in value of 209,721l. since 1901.

Annex A.—RETURN of all Shipping at the Port of Las Palmas Grand Canary, during the Year 1902.

Nationality.	Sailing.		Steam.		Total.	
	Number of Vessels.	Tons.	Number of Vessels.	Tons.	Number of Vessels.	Tons.
British	6	2,328	1,338	3,542,500	1,344	3,544,828
American ..	5	3,689	..	..	5	3,689
Austro-Hungarian	1	561	13	21,482	14	22,043
Argentine ..	..	..	1	2,520	1	2,520
Belgian	..	..	4	5,472	4	5,472
Dutch	..	..	21	37,884	21	37,884
Danish	2	935	18	26,461	20	27,396
French	..	..	98	286,775	98	286,775
German	..	..	227	473,324	227	473,324
Italian	2	956	70	145,864	72	146,820
Russian	1	478	13	20,419	14	20,897
Spanish	819	263,589	1,271	581,377	2,090	844,966
Swedish and Nor- wegian ..	6	2,184	27	58,319	33	60,503
Uruguayan ..	1	504	..	..	1	504
Total ..	843	275,224	3,101	5,202,397	3,944	5,477,621

Annex B.—TABLE showing Exports of Fruit and Vegetables from Las Palmas to London and Liverpool during each Month of the Year 1902.

To LONDON.

Month.	Number of Packages.				
	Bananas.	Tomatoes.	Potatoes.	Oranges.	Sundries.
January	36,187	3,395	305	12	109
February	46,494	4,419	307	..	15
March	42,895	8,557	2,198	..	162
April	50,133	21,438	21,969	..	11
May..	46,976	23,787	39,705	..	60
June	79,434	4,226	171	..	2,959
July..	41,066	..	..	48	15
August	58,041	..	..	..	27
September	65,842	..	..	..	384
October	67,147	2,015	..	65	576
November	43,006	10,954	..	343	1,469
December	48,567	12,395	206	742	458
Total ..	625,788	91,186	64,861	1,210	6,245

To Liverpool.

Month.	Number of Packages.				
	Bananas.	Tomatoes.	Potatoes.	Oranges.	Sundries.
January	26,368	2,183	40	31	158
February	44,284	5,697	134	..	32
March	41,714	11,148	223	..	101
April	70,580	27,346	11,965	..	72
May.,	69,998	24,241	27,427	..	21
June	67,486	6,768	1,055	..	74
July..	80,434	..	..	..	5,819
August	75,757	..	..	..	28
September	90,605	..	..	....	45
October.	83,943	1,038	..	205	105
November	85,490	6,924	..	370	664
December	21,380	9,689	..	52	514
Total	708,039	95,034	40,844	658	7,633

The approximate values, packed and ready to ship, are as follows :—

	Value.
	£
Bananas	363,771
Tomatoes	74,488
Potatoes	31,712
Oranges	396
Total	470,367
„ 1901	260,646
Increase	209,721

LONDON :
Printed for His Majesty's Stationery Office,
By HARRISON AND SONS,
Printers in Ordinary to His Majesty.
(1400   9 | 03—H & S   382)

No. 3089.   Annual Series.

FRANCE.

DIPLOMATIC AND CONSULAR REPORTS.

TRADE OF

SENEGAL AND DEPENDENCIES

FOR THE YEAR 1902.

FOREIGN OFFICE,
September, 1903.

No. 3089 Annual Series.

DIPLOMATIC AND CONSULAR REPORTS.

FRANCE.

REPORT FOR THE YEAR 1902

ON THE

TRADE OF SENEGAL AND DEPENDENCIES.

REFERENCE TO PREVIOUS REPORT, Annual Series No. 2866.

Presented to both Houses of Parliament by Command of His Majesty,
SEPTEMBER, 1903.

LONDON:
PRINTED FOR HIS MAJESTY'S STATIONERY OFFICE,
BY HARRISON AND SONS, ST. MARTIN'S LANE,
PRINTERS IN ORDINARY TO HIS MAJESTY.

And to be purchased, either directly or through any Bookseller, from
EYRE & SPOTTISWOODE, East Harding Street, Fleet Street, E,C.,
and 32, Abingdon Street, Westminster, S.W.;
or OLIVER & BOYD, Edinburgh;
or E. PONSONBY, 116, Grafton Street, Dublin,

1903.

[Cd. 1766—23.]   *Price Twopence.*

CONTENTS.

———

*Report on the Trade of Senegal and Dependencies for the Year
1902 by Mr. H. G. Mackie, Acting British Consul at Dakar.*

(Dakar, July 29, 1903; received at Foreign Office, August 31, 1903.)

The difficulty experienced in obtaining material for the compila-
tion of this report has retarded its publication.

Several important changes have been introduced into the
administrative organisation of French West Africa by a decree
dated October 1, 1902. *Re-organisa-
tion of govern-
ment.*

For closer political union the general superintendence of these
vast possessions, which comprise the colonies of Senegal, French
Guinea, Ivory Coast and Dahomey, is vested in a Governor-
General resident in Senegal, who alone corresponds with the home
Government. Each of these dependencies, however, possesses
a government and fiscal policy of its own and is administered by a
Governor. For this reason the trade of each colony is reviewed in
separate reports. The principal local administrative reforms
occur in the colony of Senegal, with which this report more particularly deals.

For administrative purposes Senegal, until the recent enactment,
was sub-divided into numerous scattered districts in which no less
than four distinct forms of government existed. These have now
been reduced to two, viz. (1) the communes of Dakar, St. Louis,
Rufisque and Goree, which possess Municipal Councils elected
every four years by the natives, who exercise the franchise on an
equality with French citizens; as such they are eligible for election
and possess judicial rights both in penal and civil procedure, except
as regards succession, marriage and probate; and (2) hamlets
and villages situated in territories ceded by ancient treaties, acquired
by conquest, or placed under French rule by local authorities, not
entrusted with municipal privileges or represented in the Council
but directly administered by the State. France has now abolished
(3) native administration in territories where headmen chosen by
the Government served as channels of communication between the
State and people, and over which France only exercised indirect
control; and (4) political protectorates, which enjoyed complete

autonomy. Henceforth these territories will be directly administrated by the State.

The administration of the French Sudan, which forms a hinterland for all the colonies on the west coast, has merged into that of Senegambia–Niger, with the exception of Dinguiray, Siguiri, Kurussa, Kankan, Kissidouyou and Beyla, which have been absorbed by French Guinea ; Odjeune, Kong and Bouna, now included in the colony of the Ivory Coast, and the canton of Kuala and the Say territories, transferred to the colony of Dahomey.

Area and population. Senegal has an area of about 806,000 square miles and a population approximating 4,523,000, including some 3,000 Europeans and 4,000 half-castes.

Revenue. The principal sources of revenue arise from direct or personal contribution, customs, posts and telegraphs, and registration taxes. The estimated receipts for the current year are 5,257,684 fr. (210,300*l*.), and expenditure 5,204,949 fr. (208,200*l*.).

Import and export trades. The value of the import and export trades of Senegal is as follows :—

Year.	Value.		
	Imports.	Exports.	Total.
	£	£	£
1900	1,872,205	1,317,285	3,189,490
1901*	2,168,366	1,061,400	3,229,766
1902*	1,434,800	989,100	2,423,900
1902 (specie).. ..	277,000	257,000	534,000

* Exclusive of specie.

Cotton goods. Cotton materials being worn by the natives for clothing, the demand is considerable.

The sale of bleached, dyed and printed cottons is practically confined to the towns, while the unbleached and blue baft goods are disposed of in the villages along the coast and in the interior.

As regards British goods, the white grades, and especially the cotton cambrics invoiced at 30 to 35 c. per metre, are the most popular. These sell at 50 to 60 c. per metre. Dyed goods, known in this market as " Roum," also command a ready sale, especially the grades 32 inches wide, invoiced at 30 to 45 c., which fetch 50 to 75 c. These goods are supplied almost exclusively by the United Kingdom. Other grades, however, come from France and Germany.

Cotton prints are less satisfactory. Their colours fade and run in washing, and they are gradually falling into disrepute. Even the higher grades do not sell for more than 50 c., and are being rapidly displaced by goods from Rouen and Alsace, which are retailed at 75 c., while the wholesale price is only 5 c. in favour of the British article. The same applies to the coarser grades, which are becoming unsaleable, and are being supplanted by goods of Swiss and Dutch manufacture. A grade of French origin, known as "toile de Vichy," finds favour with the natives, and successfully competes with British homespuns. It is retailed at 1 fr.

British muslins and twilled cottons retain their popularity, but if the manufacturers could be induced to alter the width to 32 inches, a larger demand might possibly be created. There is also room for improvement in the quality of the twilled goods.

Active work is being carried on in this country by French Education. missionaries, in whose hands the labour of education largely rests. Grants in aid of education to the extent of 353,000 fr. (14,120*l.*) are made annually, the principal contributors being the towns of Dakar, St. Louis, Rufisque and Goree, but the number of scholars in these towns does not appear to exceed 2,000. The education question is now being carefully considered by the authorities, who are about to introduce reforms which will necessitate an increase of the town grants to 406,075 fr. (16,243*l.*) in 1904. A school for the sons of native chiefs is in course of erection at St. Louis.

The town of St. Louis, founded in 1626, is the present capital of St. Louis. French West Africa. It is built on a sand spit near the mouth of the Senegal River, and is the residence of merchants and agents. Being the terminus of the caravans engaged in the transit trade with the Sudan, its port serves as an outlet for the merchandise brought by camels from the interior. A large proportion of its commerce is also derived from the river traffic.

The bar of silting sand which obstructs the estuary of the river St. Louis fairseriously hampered the trade of the port during 1902. At certain factory conseasons of the year the water rises to a level sufficient to admit dition of. of the passage of large vessels, while at others there is barely enough water for the river craft. Last year, however, the condition of the bar was so unsatisfactory that many British vessels wisely cancelled their charters and went elsewhere in search of homeward cargoes ; only two reached St. Louis. Several Danish and Norwegian vessels, attracted by the remunerative freights offered by the St. Louis merchants, attempted to force a passage over the bar and were badly damaged in doing so. In some instances clauses were rashly inserted in the charter parties imposing liability for the delivery of cargoes at St. Louis "at the ship's expense." These vessels were forced to remain in idleness for many weeks awaiting a rise in the water. Government grants have been made in aid of dredging operations, which will, it is believed, render the river navigable as far as Salde, a distance of 280 miles. In the meantime British shipowners would do well to take note of the unsatisfactory condition of the channel.

To avoid a passage over the bar, anchorage is being provided at Guet N'Dar, situated on the coast near St. Louis, where an iron wharf is being erected.

The railway about to be built between Thies and Kayes will, it is expected, divert much of the transit trade of St. Louis to Dakar.

(378)

Dakar, increasing prosperity of.

Dakar, which a few years ago was a mere assemblage of rude native huts, with a bungalow here and there for the accommodation of the officials, now ranks as first in importance among the towns of this colony. It is also the chief French sea port on this coast, and bids fair to become, in view of its close proximity to some of the great ocean routes, a port of call and coaling station of considerable importance.

Dakar commands a formidable strategical position, has an extensive system of defensive works, and is admirably adapted as a naval base and port of refuge. The promontory on which it is built is a remarkable tongue of land on the extreme west of the hinterland, with which it is connected by a neck of level ground. The town itself consists for the most part of broad and regular thoroughfares, the appearance of which is being rapidly improved by the addition of large buildings, some of which will be imposing structures.

Transfer of seat of government.

The west coast being singularly destitute of harbours, the value of Dakar as a commercial centre is materially enhanced. It is in fact the only port of Senegal capable of affording safe anchorage for the largest ships, and it is owing to its natural advantages that the French Government have decided to make it the capital of these vast possessions. It is expected that some impetus will be given to the trade of this port by the transfer next autumn of the seat of government from St. Louis, the present capital, to this town. The enthusiastic energy which the Governor-General has imparted to the advancement of civilisation and commerce augurs well for the future of Dakar, the improvement of which will be carried out under his immediate supervision.

Considerable additions to shipping accommodation have been authorised and are under construction. The harbour is being dredged to a uniform depth of 28 feet over a surface of 500,000 square yards, and will be provided with jetties and commodious wharves, alongside of which vessels of large tonnage will be able to load and discharge instead of by lighters. The shipping of this port derives considerable shelter from the Island of Goree, conveniently situated close to the Cape Verde peninsula.

Three conspicuous lighthouses, which are being re-fitted with lamps of modern pattern, and several beacons afford additional security to shipping. The construction of a dry dock has also been decided upon.

Goree.

The small fortified island and free port of Goree was at one time a prosperous commercial centre and the official residence of French lieutenant-governors, but it has lapsed into a state of decadence, its trade and population having been absorbed by Dakar. It is, however, destined to become the temporary residence of the Governor-General pending the erection of the Government House, public offices and buildings, which are being provided for the accommodation of that official and his staff at Dakar. The organisation of a steamboat communication with Dakar will, for a time at least, help to stimulate the commercial activity of Goree.

Rufisque, situated south of the bay formed by the Cape Verde Rufisque. peninsula, is the chief outlet for the export of groundnuts, the annual shipments of which have attained the substantial figure of some 50,000 tons. It possesses extensive depôts for the storage of this product, and is connected by rail with Dakar and St. Louis. In view of its increasing prosperity it has been decided to build a breakwater to protect shipping from the troublesome south-easterly winds to which they are at present exposed. It has three metallic piers, but cargoes are worked by means of lighters.

The trade and prosperity of Senegal, so abruptly checked by Insanitary the yellow fever epidemic of 1899–1900, is happily showing signs condition of of gradual recuperation. Although this colony is at present free towns, detri-mental effect from epidemic diseases, public health continues to be menaced by of on trade. the unrestrained pollution of the towns by the natives. The present unsatisfactory sanitary conditions, which have prevailed for so long, are formidable obstacles to commercial expansion, and their detrimental effects are reflected in the trade of the colony, which is entirely in the hands of a few wealthy and long-established firms.

The difficult problem of water supply has at last been success- Reforms. fully solved, and the town of Dakar is now provided with water. The opening of the waterworks this year, to be followed by the sewage of the town shortly to be taken in hand, indicate that the long neglected problem of sanitation is at last receiving attention. These and many other well considered schemes have been retarded by the absence of official means of carrying them into effect, but it is confidently hoped that when M. Roume, the Governor-General, who has already displayed so much adminis-trative skill, returns from leave to take up his residence at Dakar, methods of bureaucracy will no longer be allowed to hamper the spread of civilisation. By a series of beneficent measures, fostered at great cost to the mother-country, the Government are endeavour-ing to build up and consolidate their power in their West African possessions. The construction of railways, subsidising of coasting steamers for the establishment of steamship services between French West African settlements, opening up of river communica-tion, increasing of land and cable telegraph lines, harbour works, and the advancement of education and agriculture, are among the many schemes for the spread of civilisation engaging the atten-tion of the Government. The recent grant to the colony of a loan of 65,000,000 fr. (2,600,000l.) by the home Government sufficiently indicates that these problems are being seriously grappled with.

The Messageries Maritimes Company has been a large contributor Dakar as a to the prosperity of Dakar, which it has placed within five days' coaling reach of Europe. The company's fine fleet of fast ocean-going station. steamers engaged in the South American trade make use of Dakar as a coaling station and provisioning entrepôt, for which it possesses all the necessary resources.

The company's coal depôt is, however, inadequately equipped, the most conspicuous deficiency being the absence of steam hauling power. Owing to this deficiency the rate of loading does not exceed 110 tons a day and the discharging of colliers 200 tons. Under contract with the Government the company also provides coal for the naval department, for which it has to maintain a permanent stock of 5,000 tons.

Besides its own sheds, which accommodate 11,000 tons, and an open space for the storage of some 8,000 tons, it receives the use of a Government shed with a storing capacity of 11,000 tons. Sixteen 40-ton lighters, a steam tug, a slipway and a small engineering shop complete its equipment.

British trading interests at this port are more extensively represented by coal than any other branch of industry. An interesting feature in this connection is the establishment at Dakar of the "Compagnie Française des Charbonnages." This company has secured certain trading privileges enjoyed by a firm that has recently closed its business connections with this colony.

The company owns 14 lighters, representing an aggregate tonnage of 1,800 tons, 3 water tank barges, 3 steam tugs, a launch and a hulk capable of storing 1,100 tons. It has a 20 years' lease of a depôt on shore for the storage of 3,000 tons, and a wharf adjoining the depôt on which steam cranes have been erected. The building of another wharf, with steam hauling appliances and coal sheds capable of holding 10,000 tons, will be commenced as soon as the formalities for the grant of the necessary concession are complete. Unhampered by competition and favoured with the advantages of a geographical position that places the depôt within easy reach of some of the large ocean lines, there is every hope of an expansion of trade in the near future.

Coal does not appear in the import lists, but it is estimated that the quantity of Welsh coal consumed in 1902 amounted to 40,000 tons. 2,700 tons of patent fuel (briquettes) were imported last year.

British shipowners should take note of the fact that the privileges of immunity from port and anchorage dues enjoyed by this company are strictly limited to coal cargoes, and that, should any other merchandise be discharged, these dues will be imposed.

Shipping.   Communication with Europe is maintained by the fast steamers of the Messageries Maritimes Company, who receive a subsidy from the Government for running a regular fortnightly mail service. The usual length of the voyage is eight days from Bordeaux and five days from Lisbon. The steamers of the Chargeurs Reunis and Fraissinet lines likewise touch at Dakar; the former once a fortnight and the latter once a month.

Messrs. Elder, Dempster and Co. have secured the bulk of the carrying trade between this colony and the United Kingdom, as well as the passenger and goods traffic between Dakar, Bathurst, Sierra Leone and other West African ports.

A coasting steamship company is being formed for the establish- Coasting ment of regular services between Dakar, St. Louis, Goree, Rufisque, steamship services. Carabane and Ziguinchor. The mail service now being organised between this port and Casamance has been steadily agitated for during the past two years. The Government has responded by the grant of a subvention to the new coasting company, which will undoubtedly supply a much felt want. On each voyage to and from Casamance the steamers will touch at Bathurst, where they will enjoy exemption from port dues in return for the maintenance of a regular fortnightly postal service.

The subsidising of this company is regarded as a precursor to the gradual development of an extensive bounty-fed coastal service, which the Government may eventually extend to the Ivory Coast and Dahomey.

Much prominence has been given of late to colonial cable con- Telegraph struction schemes, plans having been prepared for the laying of cables. cables between Dakar–Brest, Tamatave–Reunion, Reunion–Mauritius and Saigon–Pontianak. A recent telegram from France announces the grant by the Government of the necessary funds for connecting Dakar with Brest by a cable to be opened in about 11 months. This cable will complete an important telegraph system by which all the French colonies on the west coast, with the single exception of the French Congo, will be placed in direct tele-graphic communication with the mother-country entirely by means of French cables and overland lines.

Agriculture in Senegal has long been neglected, but the organisa- Agriculture. tion and encouragement of this important enterprise is now re-ceiving the attention of the Government. The soil, on which but little labour is bestowed, is nevertheless found to yield a remunerative return.

The advancement of agriculture is sure, sooner or later, to find Need of agri-expression in increased purchases of agricultural implements. cultural implements. Business in this branch of industry would seem to admit of develop-ment, as the natives, when provided with a few implements by the authorities, readily appreciated the benefits derived from their use.

The steady decrease from year to year in the rainfall of this colony is regarded as a disquieting sign.

The reports from most of the districts, notably Cayer, Baol, Crops. Thies, Sine, Combo, Ziguincher and Lower Casamance, are eminently satisfactory. In fact, in some of these districts the crops of ground-nuts have doubled the previous year's yield, while millet and maize have given abundant returns. On the other hand, from some of the districts, happily in the minority, the reports are unsatisfactory owing to failure of the rains.

Groundnut growing has become an important industry which Groundnuts. admits of much development. With the adoption of more advanced methods of tillage, the productive powers of the areas under cultiva-tion could, it is believed, be doubled, while even under the existing primitive methods of working, wide new areas could be brought under tillage and the yield materially increased. The chaff provides an abundance of fodder for local consumption at a period when it is specially valuable.

Groundnuts figure conspicuously in the export lists of the colony, from which the following has been abstracted :—

Year.				Quantity.	Value.
				Tons.	£
1899	..	..	..	..	84,279	484,763
1900	..	..	..	..	138,840	969,612
1901	..	..	..	..	121,657	844,690
1902	..	..	..	..	108,600	820,990

The decrease in the exports of the last two years is attributed to the competition of India and Egypt in the markets of Europe.

Maize is extensively cultivated, especially in the Fouta district. An official publication last year calls attention to the fact that this colony is capable of producing crops almost sufficient to meet the demands of the French home market.

Much care is bestowed on the cultivation of rice by the natives of Casamance ; it is also produced in the districts of Oualo and Saloum, where it is much prized for its superior quality, but cannot be obtained in large quantities. The alluvial lands in the districts watered by the Senegal River have been found to be admirably adapted to rice cultivation, which will doubtless be extended to those territories before long.

Senegal is a cattle rearing country. Its live-stocks are plentiful, especially in the breeding districts of Oualo, Cayor and Baol. There should be a ready demand in some of the West African colonies less favoured in this respect, where the dearth of animal produce is often severely felt by European settlers.

Some of the more influential merchants in St. Louis are contemplating the organisation of a monthly steamship service between that port and Sierra Leone for the export of cattle and sheep, taking return cargoes of kolas and possibly calling at intermediate ports for trading purposes.

South African farmers with surplus stocks would do well to turn their attention to the West African markets, especially to those of Sierra Leone and other British colonies.

With the establishment this year of a regular steamship service between this port and Casamance, which is a well wooded district, trade in timber may be developed. Some of the hard woods are, from their remarkable durability, peculiarly adapted for use as piles for bridges and wharves, while others are suitable for the manufacture of household furniture.

The pacification of the Sudan has had an important bearing on the gum trade. While the Egyptian Sudan was closed to trade the prices attained nearly 5 fr. per kilo., but since these territories have been opened up to commerce the prices have fallen to 50 c.

Senegal is also specially adapted to the cultivation of rubber, Rubber. for which there is a growing and remunerative demand, a reddish quality called "Akou" fetching as much as 6 fr. 50 c. per kilo. locally (2s. 4d. per lb.). A medium quality called "Mandiago" is sold for about 4 fr. per kilo., while an inferior quality can be obtained for 2 fr. per kilo. (9d. per lb.).

Among the numerous rubber plants cultivated here the *Landolphia Fomentosa* and *Vogelii* may be mentioned as giving good results.

A few years ago much attention was given to the cultivation of rubber by the Government, with the result that it soon became an industry of some importance. In view of the steadily declining output, the necessity of further State aid and encouragement is badly felt and is being urged upon the authorities by the local merchants.

The principal European markets are Liverpool and Hamburg.

A duty of 5 per cent. *ad valorem* is imposed on rubber exported from Senegal, except at Casamance, where 7 per cent. *ad valorem* is charged on all exports.

Sir Alfred Jones' schemes for the encouragement and develop- Cotton. ment of cotton growing in our West African possessions have been paid the tribute of imitation in this colony. M. Chevalier, Doctor of Natural Sciences, during his recent visit to Senegal and the Sudan, expressed his opinion that cotton could be grown with success in both these territories. As regards Senegal, the Cayer and N'Diander districts he considered best suited to its cultivation in view of their proximity to the coast and railway. The Government, it is reported, have now taken the matter in hand and are securing the services of an eminent French naturalist for the purpose of studying cotton growing in Egypt, with a view to its ultimate extension to this colony. This industry will doubtless be aided by bounties.

Kola nuts are extensively consumed by the natives throughout Kola nuts. this colony, by whom they are much prized for certain stimulating properties attributed to them. The kola nut is almost exclusively imported from Sierra Leone, and is also the staple trade of the Sierra Leone merchants resident in this colony. The octroi duty on this commodity was recently increased to 30 per cent. *ad valorem*, but the authorities have now reduced the tax to its former level.

The trade of French West Africa, which was no more than Progress con- 31,000,000 fr. (1,240,000*l*.) in 1891, rose to 40,000,000 fr. (1,600,000*l*.) fined to sea in 1895, and attained to 65,000,000 fr. (2,600,000*l*.) in 1899; it reached border. 79,000,000 fr. (3,160,000*l*.) in 1900 and exceeded 100,000,000 fr. (4,000,000*l*.) in 1901. As these figures indicate, the trade of this Consular district has trebled since 1891, but while the material progress has been great, it has been confined to the sea border; the vast inland territories, for lack of railway communication, remaining in their initial stage. A recent report to the French Chamber of Deputies on the economic conditions of the vast regions known as the French Sudan describes them as rich in natural resources but still in the tribal stage of development. It urges railway penetration as a measure imperatively called for in the interests of this uncivilised colony, which embraces an area of some 300,000 square miles and contains an estimated population of upwards of 4,000,000, over which France has only recently secured a footing of political ascendency. The railway systems of the British colonies on the West African coast are described at some length, and stress is laid on the fact that our settlements already possess, in proportion to superficial area, a mileage 2·7 times greater than that of this dependency. It then gives an illustration of the stimulating influence of a railway on the trade of an undeveloped country by comparing the exports of the district traversed by the Dakar–St. Louis Railway—the only complete line in this colony— with those of previous years. The exports of groundnuts, now the staple produce of the district, rose from 4,800 tons before the existence of the railway to 32,000 tons in 1889, and have now attained 95,000 tons per annum.

Public works.   In 1899 the government of this colony authorised the raising of a loan of 14,000,000 fr. (560,000*l.*) for public works, which had not kept pace with the spread of the settlement. This sum was to have been devoted almost exclusively to harbour works and water supplies. The loan, however, was not realised, and on the outbreak of yellow fever in that year all public works were suspended.

After the lapse of several years spent in comparative inactivity, renewed impetus has been given to public works, which now include railways and other communications, by the grant this year of a loan of 65,000,000 fr. (2,600,000*l.*) by the home Government.

This sum is to be distributed as follows :—

	Amount.	
	Currency.	Sterling.
	Francs.	£
French Guinea	29,000,000	1,160,000
Senegambia–Niger	26,000,000	1,040,000
Ivory Coast	10,000,000	400,000

Public works in Senegambia include :—

	Amount.	
	Currency.	Sterling.
	Francs.	£
Thies–Kayes projected railway ..	500,000	20,000
Harbour works	12,000,000	480,000
Improvement of navigation of Senegal and Niger rivers ..	5,000,000	200,000
Sanitation	5,450,000	218,000

It is noteworthy that Article 5 of the Decree authorising the colonial loan has undergone an important modification. It provided that the plant required for the railway extensions in West Africa should, as far as possible, be of French origin, and that for transport purposes preference should be given to vessels under the French flag. The words " as far as possible " have been eliminated by the French Senate, thus setting up a monopoly in this important branch of industry. *Railway plant.*

The disadvantageous physical configuration of the French West African possessions has proved a formidable obstacle to railway penetration schemes. This colony being singularly destitute of navigable rivers, the vast inland territories to be opened up by the French Sudan Railway are so far removed from the influences of the sea that the work of construction has occupied nearly a quarter of a century and has cost upwards of 3,360,000*l.* The progress of this undertaking has been impeded by the difficulties in transporting railway plant, which has to come across a bar of silting sand at the estuary of the Senegal River. Higher up the river, navigation, even by river craft, is only possible for short periods and at uncertain seasons. During the yellow fever epidemic of 1899–1900 traffic on this river was suspended, and much valuable material perished from long exposure to rain and heat, while last year, owing to insufficiency of water, very little progress was possible. *Sudan Railway.*

The object of the railway is to afford the means of facilitating the military occupation of the French Sudan, to open up vast territories to the trade of Senegal, and to link the River Senegal with the Niger. Starting at Kayes on the Senegal, it passes in a south-easterly direction through Bafoulabe, Kita and Bammaku, finally reaching Koulikoro on the Niger.

The construction of the railway was undertaken by the French Government in 1880. In 1880–81 9,852,751 fr. (394,110*l.*) were voted by the Government; in 1882 7,548,785 fr. (301,950*l.*) were spent, while the distance covered was only 16 kiloms. (10 miles); in 1883 4,671,000 fr. (186,840*l.*), and in 1884 3,209,000 fr. (128,360*l.*) when the 53rd kilometre (33rd mile) was reached at a cost of 112,400 fr. per kilom. (7,252*l.* per mile). Notwithstanding the heavy outlay the line, which was constructed by native labour, had to be condemned as hopelessly defective. When in 1888 the line had been extended to within a mile of Bafoulabe, the progress of the work was checked by the withholding of further grants for a period of four years.

The surveys were only commenced in 1891, when experts were sent out from France for the purpose, and these operations extended over a period of six years. In 1898 a convention was concluded between France and Senegal and the Sudan, by which the colonies undertook to contribute 1,000,000 fr. (40,000*l.*) collectively per annum towards the railway, loans were raised and Treasury grants made. As a result of these and other vigorous measures the work is now actively progressing. In 1902 the constructive works extended to the 416th kilometre (258th mile) ; in 1903 they will cover a distance of 500 kiloms. (311 miles) and reach the terminus at Koulikoro in 1904. Hopes are confidently entertained that the entire line (350 miles) will be open to traffic in 1905.

The total expenditure is officially stated to have amounted to 83,976,628 fr. (3,359,065*l.*), and includes the following figures :—

	Amount.
	Francs.
1880–84 (period of construction by State)	25,287,536
1885–90 („ suspension of regular work)	1,243,532
1891–98 („ survey)	3,962,545
1899–1903 (period of construction by State and colony) ..	36,915,111
Loans and Treasury advances	16,369,904

Kayes–Thies Railway. The success of the French Sudan Railway is so dependent upon the Senegal River, which is often impracticable for traffic purposes for several months in the year, that the French Government have recognised the importance of connecting this railway with the Dakar–St. Louis line, which it will join at Thies, a station on that line. The projected line will cross the Baol, a well populated and fertile country.

An annual subvention of 100,000 fr. (4,000*l.*) has been offered by this colony, while the funds necessary for carrying out the surveys of the line have been granted by the French Government. On the completion of this line Dakar will be in direct railway communication with the Niger River.

Dakar–St. Louis Railway. Owing to the advantageous terms of the concession the Dakar–St. Louis Railway was completed within three years.

According to the original terms of the concession the Government undertook to defray the loss of working the railway, and guaranteed a net income to the company of 3,400 fr. per kilom. (219*l.* per mile) of railway, or 5 per cent. on the invested capital, which was fixed at 68,000 fr. per kilom., but in 1882 the amount guaranteed was reduced to 1,154 fr. per kilom. (74*l.* 9*s.* per mile), in consideration of the payment of 12,680,000 fr. (507,200*l.*). The constructive works were pushed forward by leaps and bounds regardless of cost. The Government, growing alarmed at the outlay, finally introduced a measure by which the working expenditure was regulated by contract. As an encouragement to reduce the working expenses the company received 2 per cent. in 1890, increased to 10 per cent. in 1895, of the difference between the contract price and the actual working expenditure, if the latter did not exceed the former. This measure had the desired effect. The company, eager to secure the bonus offered, effected such rigorous economy that the receipts of the railway exceeded the working expenses in 1898. The railway (164 miles) has cost the French Government 35,391,115 fr. (1,415,600*l.*), which includes a contribution towards the cost of construction of 507,200*l.*, the remainder representing annual payments in respect of guarantees of interest covering a period of 19 years (1883–1902).

The earnings of the railway were originally estimated at 1,200 fr. per kilom., and were not expected to exceed 1,500 fr. ; these have now attained to upwards of 12,000 fr. per kilom. (770*l.* per mile).

The rolling-stock of this railway is as follows:—14 large locomotives, 15 small locomotives, 16 brake vans, 60 carriages, 310 wagons.

The wooden sleepers are being replaced by iron sleepers. The weight of each rail per metre (3·28 feet) is 44 lbs., and the dimensions of the wooden sleepers 5 feet 3 inches by 8 inches by 4 inches. The iron sleepers weigh 70 lbs. The gauge is 3·28 feet.

The Konakry–Koroussa line, destined to connect the coast with the Niger, is the only railway built by this dependency on its own initiative and without State aid. The total distance to be traversed by this railway, which is being built in sections, is 550 kiloms. (342 miles). At present two sections appear to be under construction, one from Konakry to Friguiabe, 93 miles, and another from Friguiabe to Timbe, a distance of 137 miles. The funds for the undertaking have been obtained from loans advanced by the Caisse des Depôts et Consignations, which, up to the present, amount to 12,000,000 fr. (480,000*l.*). Konakry-
Koroussa
Railway.

The constructive works were undertaken by a firm of contractors in 1900, but in 1902 the government of French Guinea took over the works. The progress of the railway has been enormously assisted by the employment of native sub-contractors, who provide labourers on their own terms and act as responsible mediums between the military engineers entrusted with the work and the natives. The Governor-General, who inspected the railway in May last, refers in flattering terms to the success the colony has achieved in this enterprise, which he largely attributes to the excellent results the system of native labour has given.

Great activity has marked the progress of this railway, which reached the 149th kilometre (93rd mile) in May last. Constructional difficulties have, however, occurred between the 27th and 44th kilometre and the 90th and 107th kilometre, but it is expected that these will be overcome by the end of this year, when the first 150 kiloms. will be opened to traffic. The first railway bridge, 98 feet long, is now complete and two others of 197 and 262 feet are in an advanced stage of construction. The first locomotive was expected in June last ; a large quantity of railway plant, including rolling stock-sufficient for the maintenance of traffic over the first 93 miles of railway, will arrive in October next.

The cost of the first section of this railway has amounted to 480,000*l*., which, contrary to expectation, has not exceeded the original estimates.

Kotonou–Tchaourou Railway.

The Kotonou–Tchaourou Railway is the third under construction, which will have its terminus on the Niger. The total length of the line, including a branch to Whydah, is stated to be 435 miles, of which 56 miles are open to traffic. The building of the railway was entrusted to Messrs. Borelli and Co., of Marseilles, to whom in 1900 the colony gave a concession, subsequently transferred to the " Compagnie Française des Chemins de Fer au Dahomey," of which the principal clauses are as follows : (1) The colony ceded 295,000 hectares (728,900 acres) of land, including mining rights, to the company ; (2) the colony undertook the substructure, *i.e.*, earthworks, culverts, &c., in sections of 31 miles per annum ; (2) the colony undertook to pay the company a subvention at the rate of 2,000 fr. per kilom. (129*l*. per mile) of railway opened to traffic for a period of eight years.

The company, with a capital of 5,000,000 fr. (320,000*l*.), undertook : (1) the superstructure, *i.e.*, ballasting, rails, stations, rolling stock, &c. ; (2) to cede to the colony a share in the earnings of the line as soon as the gross receipts exceed 6,000 fr. per kilom. (387*l*. per mile) ; (3) the concession to the company is for 75 years, on the expiration of which the line becomes the property of the colony.

Elements of difficulty and complexity have been introduced into the concession by Clause 1, by which extensive land grants were made to the company. It seems that the ceding of the land constitutes a serious infraction of native rights and that claims for indemnity are likely to arise.

The 205 kiloms. of substructure will cost 2,600,000 fr. (104,000*l*.) and superstructure 11,000,000 fr. (440,000*l*.). The kilometric cost of the railway works out at about 66,000 fr. (4,225*l*. per mile), or 20,000 fr. less than the kilometric cost of railway construction in France. Considering that railway construction in an uncivilised country must necessarily be beset with numerous difficulties, the initial cost of this line has, so far, been kept down in a very creditable manner.

The work progressed at the rate of 32 miles per annum until the line reached the Lama lagoon, over which the railway embankment had been built. The swampy nature of the ground necessitates the reconstruction of the earth works, which is likely to prove a work of some difficulty, and delay the completion of the line for a year at least.

As this line will enter into direct rivalry with the railway under construction in the neighbouring British colony of Lagos, competition, it would seem, is likely to become an important factor in African railway policy at no distant date.

Out of the colonial loan the sum of 10,000,000 fr. has been assigned to the Ivory Coast for railway construction purposes and harbour works.

Ivory Coast Railway.

RETURN of Shipping at the Ports of Dakar, St. Louis and Rufisque during the Year 1902.

Nationality.	Dakar.				St. Louis.				Rufisque.				Total.			
	Entered.		Cleared.		Entered.		Cleared.		Entered.		Cleared.		Entered.		Cleared.	
	Number of Vessels.	Tons.	Number of Vessels.	Tons.	Number of Vessels.	Tons.	Number of Vessels.	Tons.	Number of Vessels.	Tons.	Number of Vessels.	Tons.	Number of Vessels.	Tons.	Number of Vessels.	Tons.
French	158	291,900	156	288,900	68	45,559	64	44,272	45	33,280	42	34,737	271	370,739	262	367,909
British	49	61,743	49	61,743	2*	1,605	2	1,605	25	27,007	26	29,867	76	90,355	77	93,215
German	15	12,660	15	12,660	3	1,723	3	1,723	18	18,093	9	10,176	36	32,476	27	24,559
Norwegian	7	4,907	7	4,907	3	1,893	3	1,893	8	7,310	7	9,488	18	14,110	17	16,288
Danish	7	2,615	7	2,615	4	1,320	4	1,320	5	2,954	6	4,472	16	6,889	17	8,407
Dutch	3	2,341	3	2,341	3	2,846	3	2,846	4	3,769	3	2,182	10	8,956	9	7,369
Swedish	2	2,033	2	2,033	...	...	...	...	3	2,984	5	4,727	5	5,017	7	6,760
Italian	2	2,084	2	2,084	...	...	...	...	3	4,389	4	5,251	5	6,473	6	7,335
Other nationalities	3	1,427	3	1,427	1	63	1	63	3	1,818	3	256	7	3,308	7	1,746
Total	246	381,710	244	378,710	84	55,009	80	53,722	114	101,604	105†	101,156	444	538,323	429	533,588
„ 1901	...	...	...	...	...	...	...	...	...	...	...	...	377	544,406	373	537,681
Total British shipping, 1901	...	...	...	...	...	...	...	...	...	...	...	...	76	119,602	73	114,153

* 14 vessels of 11,991 tons in 1901.

RETURN of Principal Articles of Import during the Years 1901–02.

Articles.	Value.	
	1901.	1902.
	£	£
Live-stock	1,062	1,548
Preserved meats, milk, cheese, &c.	23,495	24,502
„ fish	1,547	1,970
Farinaceous foods..	293,546	108,690
Fruits and seeds	144,461	140,686
Groceries and tobacco	197,087	123,747
Oil	66,487	52,622
Timber	22,473	24,372
Wines, spirits and mineral waters	153,654	85,347
Fuel and building materials ..	76,084	58,924
Metals	12,159	11,745
Chemicals	6,391	5,763
Colours	8,384	5,285
Pottery	3,055	2,253
Glassware	28,045	11,627
Cottons and tissues	798,411	421,443
Stationery	6,854	6,899
Leather goods	17,538	12,314
Ironwork and machinery	186,553	234,716
Arms and ammunition	17,620	18,850
Furniture	4,635	5,472
Woodwork	6,929	6,716
Instruments	717	804
Straw and basket work ..	2,339	587
Various and fancy articles ..	80,929	24,437
Total*	2,168,866	1,434,800

* Exclusive of specie.

VALUE of Cotton Fabrics, with Principal Countries of Origin, Imported during the Year 1902.

Articles.	Total of Imports.	Principal Countries of Origin, included in the Total of Imports.			
		United Kingdom.	France.	Foreign Origin.*	Germany.
	£	£	£	£	£
Unbleached ..	1,690	1,230	130	160	..
Bleached	35,180	21,250	8,756	4,830	216
Dyed	146,358	93,960	25,995	24,700	1,675
Printed	13,390	7,800	3,382	1,040	816
Blue baft	131,020	2,330	97,404	..	..
Other goods ..	8,094	3,100	2,906	1,390	553
Total	335,722	129,670	138,573	32,120	3,260
„ 1901 ..	672,212	200,522	318,956	63,055	4,613

* Including British, imported from France.

Table E.—Export of Groundnuts, Gum and Rubber, during the Years 1901–02.

Articles.	Countries Exported to.	1901.		1902.	
		Quantity.	Value.	Quantity.	Value.
		Tons.	£	Tons.	£
Groundnuts	France	89,262	614,132	82,414	626,080
	United Kingdom	134	542	76	559
	Germany	8,240	60,221	10,712	84,843
	Belgium	3,336	24,376	..	..
	Netherlands	16,809	119,598	13,183	89,737
	Other countries	3,975	25,819	2,215	19,771
Gum	France	3,149	116,438	3,037	65,880
Rubber	France	318	38,748	465	75,876
	United Kingdom	..	8	43	6,918
	Germany	38	5,509	34	5,542
	Other countries	..	50	..	..
	Total	..	1,005,441	112,179	974,706

IVORY COAST.

Mr. Vice-Consul Armstrong reports as follows :—

Commerce.

The trade of the Ivory Coast is most important, as will be shown by the table of statistics attached. There are six large commercial firms in the colony, each with branch houses at all the important ports on the coast, and trading posts at the chief towns in the interior. The year 1900 was one of the most favourable no doubt, exceeding that of the following years owing to the fact that the sale of powder was prohibited on account of a slight insurrection in the interior, and this of course in turn diminished exports.

The chief articles of export from the Ivory Coast are : rubber, palm oil, mahogany, palm kernels, coffee, ivory and gold dust. It will be seen by Table C that the largest of these exports is rubber, of which the United Kingdom receives nearly all. Palm oil is shipped chiefly to France, and the other exports are mostly taken to the United Kingdom.

The mahogany trade.

The mahogany trade has always been one of the most remunerative of the Ivory Coast, and furnishes the means of livelihood to many natives. Although last year's prices were by no means good in Liverpool (for that is by far the best market), they are much better now and the natives are only awaiting the rainy season, when the logs will be floated down the lagoons and rivers.

The chief imports are : cotton goods, coming chiefly from the United Kingdom (see Table B), gin, salt, powder, rice, tobacco, building materials, wines, spirits, provisions, beads, arms, machinery (mining and engineering), miscellaneous articles and live-stock.

Statistics show that the United Kingdom does by far the largest trade with the Ivory Coast, France follows next, and then Germany and other countries.

A great advance has been made by the construction of telegraph Public works. lines, which extend to all the principal ports, business towns, civil and military posts, &c., in the colony, and it is now in direct overland communication with the Gold Coast and Senegal.

Brick yards have been started and large quantities both of bricks and tiles are being made. In connection with this enterprise, the Government foundry shop, with lathes, circular saws, &c., has no doubt done a great deal for the rapid construction of buildings, &c., and also for the manufacture of such pieces of machinery as generally it was necessary to send to Europe to replace, thus causing much delay.

The Printing Department has shown wonderful improvement in the last year.

The old Government House at Bassam has lately been turned into a hospital, and as it is well situated it will no doubt prove of great value to the colony.

Telephonic communication now exists with Bassam and Bingerville, and one can also speak with several other parts of the colony.

A French company has now taken over the cable line for French West Africa, which was until February last the property of the West African Telegraph Company.

The principal place of interest is the Government seat at Bingerville, which is situated on the Lagoon at a distance of 19 miles from Bassam, and has shown itself of great importance and a safeguard for the health of the Government employés.

But a large sum of money has been expended in Bassam by the commercial houses in buildings, &c. That Bassam does the largest business of any port in the colony cannot be denied, partly owing to the fact that it is the centre of native trade, but chiefly owing to the fact that there is a wharf which insures the safe landing and despatch of people and goods, the value of which is well known to all who are acquainted with the huge surfs prevalent on the Ivory Coast.

A great deal has been done in the past year towards effecting satisfactory conditions at Bassam, but there is still a great deal of room for improvement, and there is no doubt that it will remain the chief port till such time as the Lagoon will be cut, thus affording a good harbour. This work is at the present time being seriously considered, and, coupled with the fact that a railroad is to be built with the view of assisting in the formation of a harbour, it will be a very serious rival for Grand Bassam, but owing to the extensive and deep water lagoons it will be in touch by water with this port. Should this harbour be successfully created, the Ivory Coast will prove to be a most important factor to the French colonies, as it will afford an excellent coaling station; and it will also insure the rapid and safe loading and unloading of goods.

The importance of Grand Bassam as a commercial centre is due Lagoons.

to the extensive lagoons with which it is connected, and as these are navigable for steam launches for a distance of 56 miles in a westerly direction parallel with the coast, and also for great distances in a northerly direction, it will be readily seen what a great advantage they become for trading purposes.

The most prolific palm tree areas are situated on the borders of these extensive lagoons, and it is from these trees that the palm nut is taken for making palm oil, which is one of the largest of the Ivory Coast exports.

Grand Bassam is also situated at a point where two of the largest rivers flow into the sea, viz., the Rivers Comoe and May, the former being navigable for steam launches for a distance of 32 miles, to a small town which is the terminus of the caravan route from the Soudan, where the rubber is carried to be sold.

On the borders of these lagoons the mahogany tree is also found, the transport of which to the coast is made very easy and cheap by means of floating. The mouth of the Comoe River running into the sea, is navigable only at certain times of the year, and even then it is very dangerous and only used for landing new launches imported from Europe, when they are too large to permit of their being safely landed by the wharf company.

Extensive lagoons also exist on the frontier adjoining the British Gold Coast, and a survey is now being made to cut a canal and thus join the two large lagoons. This will prove of great value to the commercial interests of the colony.

Mail service. The Ivory Coast is well supplied with steamer services : The Chargeur Réunis Line from Bordeaux ; the Frassinet Line from Marseilles ; the Compagnie Belge Maritime du Congo from Antwerp and Southampton ; the British and African Steamship Company from Liverpool and Hamburg ; the Woerman Line from Hamburg and Southampton ; the African Steamship Company from Liverpool ; the Compagnie Fabre from Marseilles. The lines from Marseilles and Bordeaux keep the colony regularly supplied with mails from France, but the British Mail Service is uncertain ; now, however, that Elder, Dempster and Co. are making their boats calling at Southampton touch at Grand Bassam regularly for mails and passengers only, these unsatisfactory conditions will cease to exist.

Health. The health of Grand Bassam, as compared to other places on the coast, is not good. This is due in all probability to the extensive swamps which exist in several parts of the town. Yellow fever is the most destructive and it is closely followed by blackwater fever. Great efforts are being made to fill up these swamps with sand, and no doubt in the course of another year they will all be finished.

Bingerville is very healthy, due to the fact that it is on a hill and above the mist which arises from the Lagoon. On account of the serious epidemic of yellow fever, a lazaretto is to be constructed on the east side of the River Comoe, in order to prevent the spread of this disease.

Grand Bassam has been in quarantine for yellow fever during July, August and September of 1902, and for three months in 1903. This will prove most disastrous to the colony. The mahogany trade, which has promised so much, will be seriously diminished. Logs exposed to the hot sun awaiting the arrival of a steamer are being cracked and spoilt, and serious losses to shippers are inevitable.

Trade with the interior has ceased, and every day of the prolonged quarantine means loss to the merchants, and thus to the Treasury.

Jackville and Assinie, the two ports on either side of Bassam, the former being in lagoon communication by steam launch, have also been quarantined, which prevented the landing of goods consigned to Bassam at these ports. Although no cases of the epidemic occurred at these two last mentioned ports, it was deemed necessary to quarantine them, owing to their close connection with Grand Bassam, consequently goods consigned to these three ports have been taken back to Europe, thus entailing great expense.

All towns other than Bassam on the Ivory Coast are healthy as compared to the general health of West Africa. This is due in all probability to the fact that there are more Europeans in Bassam than any other town. The population for 1902 was about 80, out of which 16 deaths occurred from yellow fever and about the same number from other causes. The population for 1903 was about 65, and out of this total 13 deaths from yellow fever occurred from January 1 to May 13.

Bingerville, which comes next to Bassam in European population, is fairly healthy. The same may be applied to Grand Lahou, Jackville and Assinie.

The mining industry has within the last year shown itself of the greatest importance in the colony, and has been the cause of the great influx of British subjects, both engineers and prospectors, into this colony. The country is undoubtedly a rich one, and of course it will take some time to prove the value of the concessions. Should these concessions prove as rich as some suppose them to be, the Ivory Coast will take its place as one of the leading gold-bearing colonies of West Africa. *Mining.*

Everything has been done by the Government to prevent litigation, and the great feature of the success of this enterprise is that the natives are not the concessionaires but the Government, who grants all concessions in its name to those who wish to invest. This step cannot be too highly praised, as one who knows the Coast will at once confirm the statement that the natives are not above selling concessions twice, provided that they are paid twice, and this has always proved the bone of contention in other colonies.

At present the companies floated for the exploration of this colony are limited, but money, and in most instances British capital, is being expended in large quantities to prove the wealth of the colony.

One of the greatest grievances, however, to the leaders of this enterprise is the labour question, and it can be said without hesitation that 200 native labourers from this eastern and most thickly populated district are not forthcoming. This is no doubt owing to the fact that they find commerce a source of greater remuneration to them than the present wage, namely 1*s.* per diem salary and 3*d.* per diem as subsistence. Skilled labour, such as masons, engineers and carpenters, is plentiful and the average rate of pay for this class of workmen is 3*s.* per diem.

The natives of the eastern portion of the colony are by no means what one would term industrious, but this is largely due to the fact that they can be absolutely independent of the goods that European trade offers, if they so wish. They can live entirely on the products : (1) Of their gardens, which consist chiefly of plaintain and cassava, Indian corn, pepper, palm nuts, fruits, such as bananas, pine-apples, oranges, limes, guavas, &c. ; (2) fish ; (3) flesh, such as deer, cattle, goats, sheep, &c. Added to this each village has its own treasury so to speak, that is to say, that there is usually in the hands of the chiefs more or less valuable hoards of gold dust, and they all have their small placer mines, which is ample to keep them well supplied in clothing, which consists of cotton prints manufactured in the United Kingdom. Of course, with their primitive method of mining, that is, washing the ground in calabashes, it is not very remunerative, but ample to keep them in European goods which they require, although the immigration of whites into their territories has had a tendency to stop their mining, as, being so secretive, they are afraid that the " white man " will find their rich mines.

That there is gold can be proved from the fact that all natives have gold ornaments, such as rings, earrings, &c., and also nuggets of the most highly coloured gold are by no means rare ; the gold in each instance being that taken from this colony. Ancient workings prove that this country was worked hundreds of years before it was known to Europeans.

TABLE A.

Year.				Value.		
				Imports.	Exports.
				£ s. d.	£ s. d.
1897 ..	..	..	..	183,164 9 7	358,720 14 5
1898 ..	..	..	..	221,094 1 7	422,159 14 5
1899 ..	..	..	..	255,195 8 10	489,725 12 10
1900 ..	..	..	..	363,234 17 8	686,218 9 7
1901 ..	..	..	..	291,439 14 5	553,147 16 10

Table B.—IMPORTS of Cotton Goods during the Year 1901-02.

Country.	Value.
	£ s. d.
France..	12,729 14 5
United Kingdom and colonies	155,785 17 8
Germany	6,897 15 2
Other countries	1,141 8 0

Table C.—EXPORTS during the Years 1900-01.

Articles.	Value.	
	1900.	1901.
	£ s. d.	£ s. d.
Mahogany	48,322 9 7	38,510 11 2
Palm kernels..	21,133 8 0	20,259 16 10
,, oil	59,024 0 10	52,990 16 10
Coffee	2,472 4 0	7,196 9 7
Rubber	189,320 11 2	112,772 0 0
Ivory	479 19 2	1,115 18 5
Gold dust	1,001 13 7	2,569 4 0

Table D.—EXPORTS by Countries during the Year 1901.

Articles.	Value.		
	United Kingdom.	France.	Germany.
	£ s. d.	£ s. d.	£ s. d.
Mahogany	27,207 5 8	5,723 16 9	5,579 8 9
Palm kernels	10,944 0 10	8,494 4 0	821 12 0
,, oil..	18,603 14 5	34,387 2 5	..
Coffee	906 0 0	6,290 9 7	..
Rubber	103,734 17 8	3,641 2 4	5,396 0 0
Ivory	685 7 3	430 11 2	..
Gold dust	1,004 17 7	1,564 6 5	..

LONDON :
Printed for His Majesty's Stationery Office,
By HARRISON AND SONS,
Printers in Ordinary to His Majesty.
(1400   9 : 03—H & S   378)

No. 3090. Annual Series.

ITALY.

DIPLOMATIC AND CONSULAR REPORTS.

TRADE OF

LOMBARDY

FOR THE YEAR 1902.

FOREIGN OFFICE,
September, 1903.

No. 3090 Annual Series.

DIPLOMATIC AND CONSULAR REPORTS.

ITALY.

REPORT FOR THE YEAR 1902

ON THE

TRADE AND AGRICULTURE OF LOMBARDY.

REFERENCE TO PREVIOUS REPORT, Annual Series No. 2773.

Presented to both Houses of Parliament by Command of His Majesty,
SEPTEMBER, 1903.

LONDON:
PRINTED FOR HIS MAJESTY'S STATIONERY OFFICE,
BY HARRISON AND SONS, ST. MARTIN'S LANE,
PRINTERS IN ORDINARY TO HIS MAJESTY.

And to be purchased, either directly or through any Bookseller, from
EYRE & SPOTTISWOODE, East Harding Street, Fleet Street, E.C.,
and 32, Abingdon Street, Westminster, S.W.;
or OLIVER & BOYD, Edinburgh;
or E. PONSONBY, 116, Grafton Street, Dublin.

1903.

[Cd. 1766—24.]   *Price Twopence Halfpenny.*

CONTENTS.

Report on the Trade and Agriculture of Lombardy for the Year 1902

By Mr. Consul Towsey.

(Milan, August 17, 1903; received at Foreign Office, August 19, 1903.)

Trade in this district during the year 1902 was very satisfactory.

Imports of raw material and manufactured goods reach Milan Imports. by different routes. Some arrive direct and appear in the customs returns of Milan, others are landed at Genoa, Venice and other ports, are entered at the customs there and afterwards forwarded by rail inland to this and other places. Others again come overland from the neighbouring and other countries, pass through the frontier stations at Chiasso, Luino, Ala, &c., but in the statistics they are not distinguished from the goods destined to other parts of Italy. The same occurs with regard to exports; considerable quantities proceed from Lombardy to Genoa and Venice, whence they are exported, whilst other quantities go out of Italy through the frontier stations mentioned above. These naturally figure in the export returns of those places with exports from other parts of Italy. Under these circumstances it is practically impossible for complete statistics to be compiled exclusively for Lombardy or even for Milan alone.

Thanks to the courtesy of the customs authorities I am enabled to give tables of imports and exports for Milan and tables of the imports and exports that have passed through Chiasso and Luino, compiled from data supplied by them.

The tables for Milan—although incomplete for the reasons given—and the brief analysis which follows them, may serve to convey some idea of what goods have been imported and exported, but the quantities stated should be considered as below the actual quantities that entered and left Milan.

RETURN of Imports Entered at the Custom-House of Milan
during the Year 1902.

Customs Category.	Articles.	Countries from which Imported.		Quantity.
1	Wine	Austria-Hungary..	Gallons	122
		France	,,	11,211
		Germany	,,	949
		United Kingdom..	,,	27
		Other countries ..	,,	3,707
		Total ..	,,	16,016
	,, in bottles.. ..	Austria-Hungary..	Number	299
		France	,,	64,319
		Germany	,,	7,830
		United Kingdom..	,,	237
		Other countries ..	,,	3,031
		Total ..	,,	75,716
1	Beer	Austria-Hungary..	Gallons	7,093
		Germany ..	,,	2,150
		Switzerland ..	,,	755
		Total ..	,,	9,998
	,, in bottles	Austria-Hungary..	Number	50
		France	,,	288
		Germany	,,	6,160
		United Kingdom..	,,	36
		Other countries ..	,,	50
		Total ..	,,	6,584
1	Spirits	Austria-Hungary..	Gallons	31,846
		France	,,	4,781
		Germany	,,	336,859
		United Kingdom..	,,	257
		Switzerland ..	,,	1,142
		Other countries ..	,,	40
		Total ..	,,	374,925
1	,, in bottles ..	Austria-Hungary..	Number	605
		France	,,	7,174
		Germany	,,	1,053
		United Kingdom..	,,	441
		Switzerland ..	,,	200
		Other countries ..	,,	213
		Total ..	,,	9,686
1	Oils, fixed, mineral an volatile, also petroleum	Austria-Hungary..	Tons ..	1,124
		France	,, ..	14
		Germany	,, ..	305
		United Kingdom..	,, ..	3
		Switzerland ..	,, ..	22
		Other countries ..	,, ..	3
		Total ..	,, ..	1,471

RETURN of Imports Entered at the Custom-House of Milan
during the Year 1902—continued.

Customs Category.	Articles.	Countries from which Imported.			Quantity.
2	Coffee, sugar and colonial articles	Austria-Hungary..	Tons	..	4
		France	,,	..	174
		Germany	,,	..	75
		United Kingdom..	,,	..	169
		Switzerland ..	,,	..	35
		Other countries ..	,,	..	166
		Total ..	,,	..	623
:3	Chemical products (acids, oxides, chlorides)	Austria-Hungary..	,,	..	66
		France	,,	..	190
		Germany	,,	..	1,162
		United Kingdom..	,,	..	32
		Switzerland ..	,,	..	85
		Other countries ..	,,	..	6
		Total ..	,,	..	1,541
.3	Soap and perfumery ..	Austria-Hungary..	,,	..	2
		France	,,	..	54
		Germany	,,	..	109
		United Kingdom..	,,	..	21
		Switzerland ..	,,	..	4
		Other countries ..	,,	..	2
		Total ..	,,	..	192
4	Colours, dyes, varnishes	Austria-Hungary..	,,	..	108
		France	,,	..	162
		Germany	,,	..	2,338
		United Kingdom..	,,	..	34
		Switzerland ..	,,	..	94
		Other countries ..	,,	..	6
		Total ..	,,	..	2,737
.5	Hemp, flax, jute ..	Austria-Hungary..	,,	..	314
		France	,,	..	11
		Germany	,,	..	369
		United Kingdom..	,,	..	72
		Switzerland ..	,,	..	7
		Other countries ..	,,	..	5
		Total ..	,,	..	778
·6	Cotton	Austria-Hungary..	,,	..	35
		France	,,	..	46
		Germany	,,	..	485
		United Kingdom..	,,	..	475
		Switzerland ..	,,	..	117
		Other countries ..	,,	..	9
		Total ..	,,	..	1,167
7	Wool	Austria-Hungary..	,,	..	80
		France	,,	..	99
		Germany	,,	..	602
		United Kingdom..	,,	..	579
		Switzerland ..	,,	..	76
		Other countries ..	,,	..	20
		Total ..	,,	..	1,456

(377)

RETURN of Imports Entered at the Custom-House of Milan
during the Year 1902—continued.

Customs Category.	Articles.	Countries from which Imported.			Quantity.
8	Silk	Austria-Hungary..	Lbs.	..	475,589
		France	,,	..	583,421
		Germany	,,	..	397,386
		United Kingdom..	,,	..	21,203
		Switzerland ..	,,	..	291,221
		Other countries ..	,,	..	55,167
		Total ..	,,	..	1,773,987
9	Wood and straw ..	Austria-Hungary..	Tons	..	70
		France ..	,,	..	146
		Germany	,,	..	187
		United Kingdom..	,,	..	63
		Switzerland ..	,,	..	21
		Other countries ..	,,	..	4
		Total ..	,,	..	491
10	Paper and books ..	Austria-Hungary..	,,	..	299
		France	,,	..	109
		Germany	,,	..	658
		United Kingdom..	,,	..	49
		Switzerland ..	,,	..	39
		Other countries ..	,,	..	22
		Total ..	,,	..	1,176
11	Hides and skins.. ..	Austria-Hungary..	,,	..	37
		France	,,	..	74
		Germany	,,	..	387
		United Kingdom..	,,	..	224
		Switzerland ..	,,	..	16
		Other countries ..	,,	..	60
		Total ..	,,	..	798
12	Iron, scrap, and filings..	Austria-Hungary..	,,	..	32
		France	,,	..	558
		Germany	,,	..	6,120
		United Kingdom..	,,	..	741
		Switzerland ..	,,	..	2,581
		Other countries ..	,,	..	105
		Total ..	,,	..	10,137
12	,, in pigs	Austria-Hungary..	,,	..	57
		France ..	,,	..	151
		Germany	,,	..	906
		United Kingdom..	,,	..	205
		Switzerland ..	,,	..	16
		Other countries ..	,,	..	48
		Total ..	,,	..	1,383
12	,, and steel	Austria-Hungary..	,,	..	939
		France	,,	..	572
		Germany	,,	..	10,522
		United Kingdom..	,,	..	106
		Switzerland ..	,,	..	142
		Other countries ..	,,	..	349
		Total ..	,,	..	12,630

RETURN of Imports Entered at the Custom-House of Milan during the Year 1902—continued.

Customs Category.	Articles.	Countries from which Imported.			Quantity.
12	Iron in plates	United Kingdom	Tons	..	177
		Germany	,,	..	36
		Other countries	,,	..	6
		Total	,,	..	219
12	Ironware and tools	Austria-Hungary	,,	..	27
		France	,,	..	56
		Germany	,,	..	253
		United Kingdom	,,	..	22
		Switzerland	,,	..	13
		Other countries	,,	..	9
		Total	,,	..	380
12	Copper, brass, bronze, nickel, lead, tin	Austria-Hungary	,,	..	133
		France	,,	..	443
		Germany	,,	..	700
		United Kingdom	,,	..	24
		Switzerland	,,	..	40
		Other countries	,,	..	46
		Total	,,	..	1,386
12	Machinery	Austria-Hungary	,,	..	122
		France	,,	..	143
		Germany	,,	..	1,326
		United Kingdom	,,	..	589
		Switzerland	,,	..	201
		Other countries	,,	..	51
		Total	,,	..	2,432
12	Scientific instruments	Austria-Hungary	,,	..	7
		France	,,	..	36
		Germany	,,	..	126
		United Kingdom	,,	..	7
		Switzerland	,,	..	15
		Other countries	,,	..	16
		Total	,,	..	207
12	Railway carriages	Austria-Hungary	,,	..	226
		Germany	,,	..	29
		Total	,,	..	255
13	Mineral ores	Austria-Hungary	,,	..	11
		France	,,	..	10
		Germany	,,	..	6
		Other countries	,,	..	1
		Total	,,	..	28
13	Stones, bricks	Austria-Hungary	,,	..	55
		France	,,	..	966
		Germany	,,	..	166
		United Kingdom	,,	..	4
		Switzerland	,,	..	3
		Other countries	,,	..	2
		Total	,,	..	1,216

RETURN of Imports Entered at the Custom-House of Milan
during the Year 1902—continued.

Customs Category.	Articles.	Countries from which Imported.			Quantity.
13	Earthenware	Austria-Hungary..	Tons	..	163
		France	,,	..	278
		Germany ..	,,	..	777
		United Kingdom..	,,	..	34
		Switzerland	,,	..	13
		Other countries ..	,,	..	17
		Total	,,	..	1,282
13	Glassware	Austria-Hungary..	,,	..	605
		France	,,	..	251
		Germany ..	,,	..	695
		United Kingdom..	,,	..	16
		Switzerland	,,	..	29
		Other countries ..	,,	..	152
		Total	,,	..	1,748
14	Cereals	Austria-Hungary..	,,	..	53
		France	,,	..	26
		Germany ..	,,	..	179
		United Kingdom..	,,	..	34
		Other countries ..	,,	..	233
		Total	,,	..	525
14	Fruits, dried and green	Austria-Hungary..	,,	..	14
		France	,,	..	8
		Germany ..	,,	..	16
		Other countries ..	,,	..	35
		Total	,,	..	73
15	Animal produce..	Germany ..	,,	..	161
		France	,,	..	138
		Austria-Hungary..	,,	..	62
		Switzerland	,,	..	43
		United Kingdom..	,,	..	8
		Other countries ..	,,	..	197
		Total	,,	..	609
16	Miscellaneous	Germany ..	,,	..	442
		France	,,	..	122
		United Kingdom..	,,	..	88
		Austria-Hungary..	,,	..	52
		Switzerland	,,	..	51
		Other countries ..	,,	..	3
		Total	,,	..	758

A brief analysis of the data at the custom-house from which
the above table is compiled furnishes the following details :—

Wine. Wine in the wood and in bottles was principally from France.

Beer. Beer comes mostly from Austria-Hungary and Germany. There
is a considerable consumption thereof here.

Spirit. Germany supplies the greatest quantity of spirit which is mostly of the class entered at the customs as "pure." Cognacs, cherry brandy, absinthe, also appear in fairly good quantities from France.

Oils comprise fixed oils from Germany, olive oil from France, Oils. linseed oil from Austria-Hungary, France and Germany, and other kinds from the United Kingdom.

Mineral oils, including petroleum, from Austria-Hungary and to a lesser extent from Germany.

Essential oils in small quantities from the United Kingdom, France and Germany.

Coffee from Brazil (139 tons out of the 142 tons entered) Coffee. and chicory from Germany.

Sugar is represented by 313 tons, in about equal proportions Sugar. from the United Kingdom and France. The other colonial products consist of cocoa, chocolate, cinnamon, cloves, spices, tea and biscuits.

Chemical products are largely imported, the greater part being Chemical from Germany and consist of acids, oxides, chlorides, nitrates, products. sulphates, salts, &c., but as regards medicines the United Kingdom, France and other countries enjoy a fair share of this trade.

Soap of the ordinary and scented qualities come more from Soap and Germany than from other countries, and it is the same in the case perfumery. of perfumery.

Colours, dyes and varnishes include colours of various descrip- Colours, dyes tions, mainly from Germany. Indigo from India. Varnishes and varnishes. of French make and also of British and German. Black lead pencils, ink and shoe blacking form part of this category and to a not inconsiderable extent, but here again Germany takes the lead.

The quantity given of hemp, linen and jute is made up principally Hemp, linen, of yarns and tissues from Germany and Austria-Hungary, and of jute. linen, in which the United Kingdom ranks first.

Cotton is a comprehensive item and includes yarns, tissues, Cotton. prints, brocades, muslins, velvets, cotton singlets, braids, trimmings, lace, &c. In yarns and tissues the United Kingdom holds the first place followed by Germany, but in velvets their places are reversed, while in singlets Germany represents the greater share, as she does also in galloons though not in tulles. The other countries exporting to a lesser amount are Austria-Hungary and France.

1,456 metric tons of wool appear in the return and consisted Wool. of 162 tons of carded and combed wool, waste and worsted; 60 tons of horsehair; 383 tons of yarns, threads and heavy carded tissues; 672 tons of felt, combed tissues, &c.; 150 tons of heavy felt goods, carpets, &c.; and 27 tons of trimmings and sewn goods. The two countries that contributed most were Germany and the United Kingdom, the latter being first in carded and combed tissues, rugs and carpets.

Wood and straw includes sawn timber from France and Austria- Wood and Hungary, cabinet wood from France, furniture and wooden utensils straw. from Germany, Austria-Hungary, the United Kingdom and France, carriages from all these countries, wickerwork and strawplaiting for hats, &c.

Paper and books. More than half the quantity of paper and books stated consisted of white and coloured writing paper, about 350 tons were in prints, lithographs and cardboard, while of books there were about 194 tons. Of the total quantity only 49 tons appear to have come from the United Kingdom.

Iron and steel. Iron and steel, other metals and machinery all come under the twelfth category. It is a large one, and the details thereof would occupy too much space, suffice it to say that "iron and steel" include hammered and rolled iron, rods, bars, tubes. It will be seen that of the 12,630 tons given in the table, 10,522 tons came from Germany.

Iron plates. Iron plates were mostly of the galvanised and oxidised qualities, and more from the United Kingdom than from Germany.

Copper, brass and bronze. Copper, brass and bronze in ingots, sheets, pipes, rods, dies and ornamental work. "German silver" appears in the customs returns under other metals.

Boilers and machinery. Boilers and machinery consist of multitubular boilers, tools, steam engines, with and without boilers, mostly from the United Kingdom; hydraulic engines and motors, agricultural machinery, weaving, spinning and carding machinery, electrical dynamos from Germany, Austria-Hungary and the United States, and some from the United Kingdom; sewing machines, with and without stands, are also included, as well as parts of machinery and apparatus of copper, &c., for heating, distilling, &c.

Earthenware. Earthenware includes terra-cotta, porcelain, ordinary stoneware, majolica, chinaware both plain and coloured.

Glassware. Glassware includes window panes, mirrors, glasses, bottles and broken glass.

Cereals. Besides small quantities of rye and oats, cereals include pearl barley, rice for making starch, flour of different kinds, and starch from the United Kingdom, France, Austria-Hungary, but principally from Germany.

Animal produce. Animal produce is an important item. It consists of potted meats, extracts of meats, game, tinned fish, caviare, condensed milk, canned goods generally, cheeses, candles, wax, glue, feathers, sponges, mother-of-pearl, buttons, amber, manures, &c.

Miscellaneous articles. Miscellaneous articles are small wares, toys, fans, musical instruments, rubber, elastic bands, electric wire, insulators, &c., watches, clocks, caps, hats, artificial flowers, umbrellas, rifles, pistols, cartridges and sundry other things.

The above remarks apply only to such imports as are entered at the Milan customs, and not to those that reach Milan from the sea ports or from the frontier stations, where they have already been entered.

TABLE of Exports from Milan during the Year 1902 as shown by the Customs Returns.

Customs Category.	Articles.	Countries to which Exported.		Quantity.
1	Wines and spirits ..	Germany	Gallons	1,380
		France	,,	115
		Total ..	,,	1,495
	,, in bottles ..	Germany	Number	7,977
		France ..	,,	135
		Austria-Hungary..	,,	432
		Other countries ..	,,	8,932
		Total ..	,,	17,476
2	Sugar, milk	United Kingdom..	Tons ..	540
		France	,, ..	8
		Germany	,, ..	3
		United States ..	,, ..	1
		South America ..	,, ..	3
		Other countries ..	,, ..	14
		Total ..	,, ..	569
3	Chemical products and medicines	France	,, ..	31
		Turkey	,, ..	11
		United States ..	,, ..	27
		Other countries ..	,, ..	46
		Total ..	,, ..	115
6	Cotton	South America ..	,, ..	178
		Turkey	,, ..	65
		United States ..	,, ..	28
		United Kingdom..	,, ..	22
		Other countries ..	,, ..	102
		Total ..	,, ..	395
7	Wool	France	,, ..	10
		Germany	,, ..	13
		Total ..	,, ..	23
8	Silk	France	Lbs. ..	252,447
		Germany	,, ..	147,648
		United Kingdom..	,, ..	66,000
		Austria-Hungary..	,, ..	19,718
		United States ..	,, ..	15,514
		Other countries ..	,, ..	151,696
		Total ..	,, ..	653,023
9	Wood and straw ..	Germany	Tons ..	45
		France	,, ..	22
		Other countries ..	,, ..	9
		Total ..	,, ..	76
10	Paper and books ..	France	,, ..	5
		Germany	,, ..	3
		Other countries ..	,, ..	3
		Total ..	,, ..	11

TABLE of Exports from Milan during the Year 1902 as shown by the Customs Returns—continued.

Customs Category.	Articles.	Countries to which Exported.		Quantity.
12	Iron, steel, metals ..	United Kingdom..	Tons ..	75
		France	,, ..	8
		Germany	,, ..	5
		United States ..	,, ..	8
		South America ..	,, ..	38
		Other countries ..	,, ..	13
		Total ..	,, ..	147
12	Machinery	France	,, ..	23
		Germany	,, ..	14
		Total ..	,, ..	37
12	Optical instruments ..	France	,, ..	12
		Germany	,, ..	11
		Total ..	,, ..	23
13	Marble,alabaster,earthen- ware and glassware ..	France	,, ..	18
		Germany	,, ..	7
		Total ..	,, ..	25
15	Animal produce.. ..	South America ..	,, ..	198
		France	,, ..	30
		United States ..	,, ..	21
		Germany	,, ..	12
		United Kingdom..	,, ..	3
		Other countries ..	,, ..	37
		Total ..	,, ..	301
16	Miscellaneous	Germany	,, ..	90
		France	,, ..	78
		Other countries ..	,, ..	22
		Total ..	,, ..	190

Exports.

The principal articles of export that appear in the customs returns of Milan are dairy produce, chemicals and medicines, cotton tissues and silk, but, as in the case of imports, the figures given in the foregoing table are not to be taken as complete.

On reference to the returns for Chiasso and Luino, which are appended to this report, it will be seen that some of these articles

Dairy produce.

figure for larger amounts. This is especially the case with regard to milk, butter, cheese, poultry and eggs, which are chiefly the produce of Lombardy and Upper Italy. The traffic in this produce, particularly with the United Kingdom, is considerable and on the increase.

Silk.

As is well known, an extensive trade is carried on in silk in this district, and the exportation thereof is very considerable. What the actual quantity is it is not easy to ascertain. According to the official returns sent herewith the quantity exported from Milan in 1902 was 653,023 lbs.; from Como, 1,306,690 lbs.; and the quantities that passed outwards at Chiasso and Luino were 12,135,160 and 2,879,956 lbs. respectively, making a total of 16,974,829 lbs. There is every reason to believe that, although this may all be from Lombardy, it does not represent the total quantity exported therefrom, as no mention is made, for instance, of the large and increasing quantities that are exported to the United States viâ Genoa, the value of which, I am told, was about 2,600,000*l*. during the year ended June, 1902. The total quantity exported from Italy in 1902 was 32,523,396 lbs., of which, I am informed, the greater part was from Lombardy.

The exports of silk manufactured goods for the year 1902, as compared with the three preceding years, were :— Silk manufactured goods exported.

Year.						Quantity.
						Lbs.
1902 ..	..	..	..	..	..	2,489,315
1901 ..	..	..	..	..	..	2,582,743
1900 ..	..	..	..	..	..	2,225,447
1899 ..	..	..	..	..	..	1,791,359

Owing to the excessive dryness which prevailed in 1902, the crops of cereals were generally below the average, especially in the case of maize, wheat was less so. Rice, though again below the average, was of good quality. Agriculture. Crops.

The production of olive oil in Lombardy is of a limited character, the total average yield of the whole region being about 132,000 gallons.

Oranges and lemons are grown in the province of Brescia, where it is estimated there are 22,000 trees yielding 3,600,000 fruit.

The subjoined table gives the crops in hectolitres for the last three years, the area under cultivation and the average yield of each article.

While on the subject of agriculture I may mention that I hear that the estimated importation of agricultural machinery and implements may be reckoned as follows :— Agricultural machinery.

For—	From—	Quantity.	Total.
		Tons.	Tons.
Lombardy	United Kingdom	730	
	France	30	
	United States	940	
	Germany and Austria-Hungary	770	
			2,470
Venetian provinces ..	United Kingdom	50	
	United States	400	
	Germany and Austria-Hungary	600	
			1,050
	Total for Upper Italy ..	..	3,520

From France come corn sifting machines and sprays for treating vines ; from the United States, mowers, reapers, hay forks, binders, ploughs, chilled ploughs, potato diggers, hay and straw pressers ; from the United Kingdom, threshing machines, hand pumps, horse gears and a few mowers and reapers ; from Germany, ploughs and small drills.

A great number of ploughs are used in Italy, where there seems to be a preference for the American type. Swedish cream separators are in use. The German goods are said to be cheap.

RETURN of the Production of Maize, Wheat, Rice, Wine and Olive Oil in Lombardy during the Years 1902-1906.

Quantity in Hectolitres.

Articles.	Area under Cultivation in Hectares.	Average Yield per Hectare.	Average Annual Yield.	Provinces of Lombardy, 1902.								Total.		
				Pavia.	Milan.	Como.	Sondrio.	Bergamo.	Brescia.	Cremona.	Mantova.	1902.	1901.	1900.
Maize ...	304,000	25·98	7,897,000	750,000	1,800,000	400,000	60,000	740,000	1,800,000	1,300,000	1,000,000	7,860,000	8,000,000	7,135,000
Wheat ...	290,000	15·96	4,600,000	624,000	900,000	273,000	3,500	374,300	510,000	540,000	755,000	4,010,000	4,380,000	4,800,000
Rice ...	82,800	56·23	4,656,000	2,325,000	940,000	...	...	6,000	8,000	115,000	473,000	3,869,000	3,888,000	4,856,000
Wine ...	223,000	9·42	2,100,000	680,000	40,000	89,000	165,000	75,000	240,000	156,000	438,000	1,578,000	2,250,000	2,420,000
Olive oil ...	3,000	2·07	6,200	...	...	640	...	100	3,560	...	...	4,300	3,800	5,340

NOTE.—1 hectare = 2·471 acres; 1 hectolitre = 22 gallons, liquid measure, or 2·75 bushels for corn, &c.

Silk cocoon
crop, 1902.

The total crop of cocoons in 1902, according to calculations made by the Silk Association, amounted to 41,935 tons, in 1901 to 40,330 tons, and in 1900 to 42,716 tons. The average for 10 years from 1892 to 1901 was 40,930 tons.

There was an increase in production in Piedmont, Lower Lombardy, Emilia and the Marches, little change in Venetia, and a falling-off in the Uplands of Lombardy and in Tuscany.

The following table gives the returns for 1900–02 for the whole Kingdom of Italy divided into regions :—

Regions.	Quantity.		
	1900.	1901.	1902.
	Tons.	Tons.	Tons.
Piedmont	7,357	6,842	7,167
Lombardy	16,710	15,539	16,423
Venetia ..	8,572	8,315	8,523
Liguria ..	210	200	215
Emilia ..	3,005	2,825	3,022
Marche and Umbria ..	2,478	2,429	2,646
Tuscany	1,871	1,778	1,601
Latium ..	115	110	120
South Adriatic ..	140	150	155
South Mediterranean ..	1,951	1,840	1,750
Sicily ..	305	300	310
Sardinia..	2	2	3
Total ..	42,716	40,330	41,935

TABLE showing Total Quantities of Cocoons Sold on the Principal Italian Markets and Centres, and Average Prices of the Yellow Pure, or Superior Quality, during the Year 1902 compared with the Years 1900–01.

Markets.	1900.		1901.		1902.	
	Quantity.	Average Price.	Quantity.	Average Price.	Quantity.	Average Price.
	Kilos.	Lire.	Kilos.	Lire.	Kilos.	Lire.
Acqui	130,690	3·221	105,910	3·443	110,950	3·511
Alba	391,370	3·326	340,330	3·589	356,632	3·630
Alessandria	225,981	3·255	187,724	2·994	231,475	3·201
Ancona	671,364	3·525	670,492	3·075	697,693	3·247
Arezzo	521,353	3·506	530,310	3·280	451,110	3·470
Arsiè	20,350	3·390	10,330	3·122	17,740	2·980
Arzignano	225,000	3·650	225,000	3·450	196,000	3·350
Asti	649,180	3·246	522,430	3·420	685,360	3·496
Belluno	3,800	3·750	2,000	3·450	2,300	3·300
Bergamo	1,800,000	3·775	1,700,000	2·843	1,750,000	2·947
Bologna	572,050	3·146	464,751	3·420	569,840	3·490
Borgo Bugginno	247,730	3·600	187,485	3·366	164,471	3·220
Bra	165,000	3·248	176,600	3·731	192,800	3·426
Brescia (province)	3,402,518	...	2,609,946	...	3,173,774	...
Brescia (market)	39,693	3·314	22,010	2·671	70,532	2·890
Busca	106,400	3·250	41,500	3·422	38,500	3·500·
Canelli	155,800	3·500	121,100	...	188,600	3·450
Carmagnola	137,900	2·970	86,680	3·393	84,450	3·535·
Carrù	58,100	3·400	43,300	3·625	64,100	3·664
Casale Monferrato	108,220	3·304	100,550	3·320	113,832	3·500
Castelfranco Veneto	190,000	3·600	185,000	3·220	250,000	3·050·
Castelnuovo d'Asti	58,750	2·957	32,580	3·175	39,070	3·870
Cavour	142,100	2·972	160,120	3·430	147,111	3·426
Ceva	94,950	3·233	104,400	3·217	117,750	3·347
Cesena	168,874	3·106	140,487	3·100	142,087	3·370
Chivasso	26,150	2·985	20,000	3·177	22,250	3·259
Cittadella	199,800	3·490	175,000	3·060	105,000	2·890
Città di Castello	15,216	3·850	18,600	3·290	17,400	3·400
Civitella di Romagna	5,134	3·480	7,384	3·480	3,320	3·340
Cologna Veneta	489,203	...	416,366	...	519,220	...
Como	...	...	...	...	89,380	3·723
Correggio	22,035	3·123	16,778	2·830	15,498	3·040
Cortemilia	85,960	3·288	71,100	3·488	77,600	3·397
Cortona	16,000	3·630	15,600	3·400	19,510	3·333
Cosenza	235,160	3·254	332,160	2·852	272,980	3·600
Crema	238,459	3·143	184,366	2·948	238,306	2·802·
Cremona (province)	3,500,000	...	3,200,000	...	3,700,000	...
Cremona (market)	148,065	3·187	104,128	2·772	158,829	2·732·
Cuneo	931,580	3·549	1,023,440	3·464	673,700	3·458
Dicomano	1,850	3·083	2,000	3·050	800	3·050
Dogliani	68,480	3·250	71,700	3·415	73,700	3·420
Empoli	26,900	3·306	13,250	3·049	15,600	3·403
Faenza	43,901	2·970	55,448	3·101	55,554	3·269
Fano	46,507	3·120	49,885	2·783	45,069	3·205
Feltre	36,490	3·530	29,170	3·400	32,790	3·300
Figline Valdarno	108,200	3·187	121,000	3·275	132,500	3·737
Fiorenzuola d'Arda	53,710	3·134	47,650	2·857	60,151	3·034
Firenze	380,000	...	350,000	...	320,000	...
Forlì	333,350	3·080	334,735	3·339	311,469	3·416
Fossano	171,680	3·475	212,123	3·685	218,100	3·736
Fossombrone	168,510	3·491	162,879	3·204	231,388	3·397
Gallarate	104,843	3·413	100,972	2·992	91,452	3·319
Guastalla	44,780	3·120	27,084	2·800	87,172	2·820
Imola	101,430	2·971	97,931	2·967	88,440	3·210·
Ivrea	145,400	2·988	95,650	3·447	104,432	3·400
Jesi	351,705	3·332	386,025	3·084	379,590	3·399
Legnago	80,480	3·100	85,390	2·760	98,730	2·840
Lodi	258,640	3·165	218,017	2·887	281,760	2·788
Lonigo	597,950	3·463	521,800	2·990	638,800	3·065
Lucca	138,850	3·520	119,300	3·130	108,320	3·334
Lugo	202,008	2·750	217,410	2·962	196,400	3·120
Macerata	66,466	3·244	72,768	3·047	110,772	3·414
Mantova (province)	1,629,685	...	1,527,100	...	1,700,000	...
Mantova (market)	310,427	3·115	270,152	2·569	293,749	2·607
Marradi	16,831	3·700	21,240	3·600	14,910	3·250
Meldola	110,471	3·276	104,962	3·450	140,761	3·700·
Milano	3,430,000	...	3,260,000	...	3,400,000	...
Mirandola	21,508	3·070	22,513	2·400	21,790	2·989
Modena	97,146	3·306	91,355	3·047	110,960	2·966
Mondovi	194,000	3·380	217,100	3·560	183,200	3·388
Montevarchi	99,000	3·473	77,000	3·170	83,000	3·500
Morciano di Rom.	29,041	3·257	27,142	3·084	28,883	3·134
Motta di Livenza	113,800	3·600	327,400	3·190	149,000	3·170
Nizza Monferrato	57,040	3·279	44,250	3·320	65,600	3·490

TABLE showing Total Quantities of Cocoons Sold on the Principal Italian Markets and Centres, and Average Prices of the Yellow Pure, or Superior Quality, during the Year 1902 compared with the Years 1900–01—continued.

Markets.	1900.		1901.		1902.	
	Quantity.	Average Price.	Quantity.	Average Price.	Quantity.	Average Price.
	Kilos.	Lire.	Kilos.	Lire.	Kilos.	Lire.
Novara	400.175	3·175	347,506	3·064	397,231	3·070
Novi Ligure	10,825	3·019	6,274	2·913	5,340	3·365
Osimo	292,828	3·304	251,437	3·069	279,197	3·242
Parma	193,811	3·272	129,399	2·873	172,127	3·020
Pavia	11.780	3·452	8,890	2·937	8,490	2·798
Pergola	15,228	3·646	11,865	3·200	15,206	3·207
Perugia	76,894	3·432	72,900	3·306	79,374	3·364
Pesaro (province)	374,568	3·338	353,547	3·063	427,571	3·290
Pesaro (market)	128,537	3·144	112,853	2·951	104,156	3·157
Pescia	199,500	3·300	142,150	3·250	138,600	3·450
Piacenza (province)	265,390	3·141	228,830	2·857	240,290	2·898
Pinerolo	269,880	3·254	327,710	3·579	340,650	3·625
Pisa	36,400	3·511	31,915	3·075	21,000	3·244
Pistoia	175,800	3·416	135,500	3·000	122,000	3·550
Ponte dell 'Olio	13,950	3·170	19,700	2·810	26,410	2·980
Pontedera	17,400	3·429	9,300	3·112	12,550	3·347
Racconigi	496,800	3·260	372,100	3·601	491,750	3·595
Ravenna	8,897	2·610	6,044	2·424	4,834	2·621
Recanati	15,808	3·316	21,805	2·988	18,089	3·330
Reggio Emilia	108,290	3·190	78,421	2·880	69,606	3·060
Rieti	17,259	3·301	8,140	3·192	10,650	3·371
Rimini (province)	158,511	3·175	133,004	3·086	134,605	3·272
Rimini (market)	70,513	3·127	55,541	3·082	51,120	3·261
Rivarolo Canavese	7,100	3·025	9,000	3·250	6,800	3·245
Rocca S. Casciano	83,180	3·460	93,554	3·613	72,560	2·900
Roma	23,046	3·200	20,000	2·900	15,240	3·072
Rovigo	10,198	3·200	7,687	2·900	7,930	3·186
S. Arcangelo	27,598	3·197	36,667	3·182	39,302	3·423
Santa Sofia	37,660	3·266	38,051	3·469	27,961	3·320
Saluzzo	369,400	3·174	233,900	3·489	301,600	3·626
Sassuolo	19,790	3·350	21,800	3·190	16,280	3·250
Savigliano	171,000	3·500	163,500	3·650	102,600	3·400
Savignano	23,569	2·910	24,958	3·300	10,560	3·370
Sinigaglia	25,761	2·938	33,039	2·728	38,905	3·248
Spoleto	7,774	3·083	1,750	2·847	1,610	3·232
Stradella	174,628	3·142	172,406	2·974	190,452	3·059
Teramo (province)	98,425	4·465	115,381	4·405	111,473	4·029
Torino	666,000	2·963	538,000	3·416	578,500	3·467
Treviso (province)	1,400,000	3·505	1,300,000	...	1,350,000	...
Udine	1,315,000	3·393	1,255,000	3·175	1,300,000	2·975
Udine (market)	25,303	3·230	28,786	3·039	39,302	2·661
Urbino	12,830	3·432	9,380	3·120	12,366	3·264
Venezia	500,000	...	480,000	...	475,000	...
Verona (market)	46,760	3·337	30,965	2·703	38,296	2·829
Verona (province)	3,250,000	3·184	3,050,000	2·853	3,200,000	2·876
Vicenza	1,600,000	3·476	1,680,000	3·220	1,700,000	3·040
Vigevano	75,812	3·084	65,584	2·675	78,379	2·903
Vignola	23,011	3·336	19,704	2·857	21,090	2·832
Villafranca Piemonte ...	61,430	3·215	55,950	3·420	103,840	3·613
Voghera	341,409	3·407	255,379	3·144	344,599	3·002
Average	...	3·292	...	3·148	...	3·348

NOTE.—The averages for 1899 and 1898 were 3·929 and 2·938 lire respectively.

TABLE showing Quantities of Silk which have passed through the Silk Condition Houses in Milan during the Year 1902 as compared with the Year 1901.

		Quantity.	
		1902.	1901.
		Lbs.	Lbs.
Silk—			
Organzine		3,382,940	3,872,374
Tram		3,491,081	3,196,083
Raw..		14,335,519	11,659,373
Other		460,130	406,648
Total		21,669,670	19,134,478

TABLE showing Imports and Exports of Cotton during the Year 1902 as compared with the Year 1901.

IMPORTS.

Articles.	Country.	Quantity.		Increase or Decrease in 1902.
		1901.	1902.	
		Tons.	Tons.	Tons.
Raw cotton ..	North America ..	95,646	105,711	+ 10,065
	India..	26,919	26,480	— 438
	Egypt	8,094	8,244	+ 149
	Other countries ..	4,461	6,921	+ 2,460
	Total	135,121	147,357	+ 12,236
Cotton yarn ..	France	56	21	— 35
	Germany	263	307	+ 44
	United Kingdom ..	341	342	+ 1
	Switzerland	136	148	+ 11
	Other countries ..	14	8	— 5
	Total	811	827	+ 16
„ cloth ..	France	114	140	+ 25
	Germany	418	514	+ 96
	United Kingdom ..	555	579	+ 24
	Switzerland	172	161	— 11
	Other countries ..	92	107	+ 14
	Total	1,353	1,503	+ 150

EXPORTS.

Articles.	Country.	Quantity.		Increase or Decrease in 1892.
		1901.	1902.	
		Tons.	Tons.	Tons.
Cotton yarn ..	Austria-Hungary ..	673	144	— 529
	Roumania	307	797	+ 489
	Turkey	4,987	4,492	— 495
	Africa	467	422	— 45
	America, Central and South	1,885	2,480	+ 595
	Other countries ..	1,253 ·	472	— 781
	Total	9,575	8,808	— 767
„ cloth ..	Austria-Hungary ..	864	228	— 636
	France	327	250	— · 76
	Germany	199	111	— 87
	Roumania	229	1,175	+ 946
	Switzerland	290	204	— 85
	Turkey	4,335	3,691	— 644
	Africa	1,486	1,265	— 220
	America, Central and South	6,619	6,758	+ 138
	Other countries ..	1,947	1,477	— 470
	Total	16,299	15,163	— 1,136

Spindles.

☞ The increase of spindles in 1902 and the first six months of 1903, including those being put up, may be estimated at about 250,000.

Looms.

The number of looms has also increased, but in lesser proportion, perhaps about 5 per cent. of the total.

Trade in first part of season, 1903.

In the first part of this season (1903) business was brisk, and spinners, weavers and printers had orders to keep them going for some months. Owing to high prices in cotton, however, business in new orders was very inanimate and the latter part of the season not encouraging.

Piercing of Simplon tunnel.

The piercing of the Simplon tunnel on August 1, 1903, had reached a distance of 7,400 yards on the south side (Iselle) and a total, together with that on the north side (Brigue), of 18,138 yards, which is detailed as follows :—

	Length.		
	South Side (Iselle).	North Side (Brigue).	Total.
	Yards.	Yards.	Yards.
Length on July 1, 1903 ..	7,400	10,308	17,708
Progress per month	193	237	430
Total, August 1, 1903 ..	7,593	10,545	18,138

The average progress of mechanical boring on the south side was 18 feet 7 inches per working day. The flow of water from the tunnel was 253 gallons per second, whereas on the north side the average progress of mechanical boring was 24 feet 8 inches per working day. The flow of water from the tunnel was 9½ gallons per second.

An exhibition will be held in Milan in 1905 during the months of April to October to celebrate the opening of this tunnel; the result of which will give another impetus to the ever-increasing importance of Milan as an industrial and commercial centre. International sections are :—(1) Means of transport by land and aërial navigation ; (2) means of transport by sea ; (3) prévoyance (i.e., legislation on behalf of workmen, employés, &c., workmen's friendly and provident societies, &c.) ; (4) decorative art ; (5) labour pavilion for industrial art. The Fine Arts section is for national exhibits only. The exhibition is under the patronage of His Majesty the King of Italy. *Milan Exhibition, 1905.*

A National Exhibition of Agriculture and Industry will be held at Brescia in May, 1904. It will comprise sections for exhibits connected with co-operative systems, hygiene, sport and sacred art. Two of the groups of the agricultural section will be international and open to foreign firms who are already represented by agencies in Italy. This exhibition also is under the patronage of His Majesty the King of Italy. *Brescia Exhibition, 1904.*

The population of Milan, according to the census taken on December 31, 1881, was 321,839. On February 8, 1901, when the census was again taken, the population had risen to 491,460. At the end of December, 1902, it was estimated to be 506,510, which, during the first six months in 1903, had increased to about 510,000 :— *Population.*

Year.	Births.		Deaths.		Marriages.		Illegitimate Births.	Births, deaths and marriages.
	Number.	Per 1,000.	Number.	Per 1,000.	Number.	Per 1,000.		
							Per cent.	
1902	13,271	27·09	10,594	21·27	3,753	7·54	7·8	
1901	13,116	27·25	10,915	22·31	3,536	7·23	7·10	
1900	12,371	25·53	10,878	22·10	3,740	7·60	...	
1899	12,222	25·84	10,507	21·82	3,393	7·05	...	
1898	12,674	27·38	10,211	21·70	3,174	6·74	...	

The net profits of the municipality on the city tramways were less than in 1901 owing to strikes, but the total number of tickets issued was 75,406,025, as compared with 67,606,611 in 1901. The tramways are constantly extending. *Share of profits of municipality in city tramways.*

TABLE showing Average Cost of Provisions in 1902 as compared
with the Years 1901 and 1900.

Articles.			Average Cost.		
			1902.	1901.	1900.
			£ s. d.	£ s. d.	£ s. d.
Wheat	.. ..	Per 220 lbs.	1 0 7	1 1 4¾	1 0 5
Maize	.. ..	,,	0 13 7¼	0 14 1¼	0 13 1¾
Rye	.. ..	,,	0 15 0½	0 15 8½	0 14 11¼
Rice	.. ..	,,	1 11 8¼	1 10 4¼	1 10 7½
Potatoes	.. ..	,,	0 7 2	0 8 0	0 6 4¾
Wheat-bread	..	Per lb. ..	0 0 1·74	0 0 1·83	0 0 1·75
Butter	.. ..	,, ..	0 0 10·35	0 1 0	0 0 10·80
Beef	.. ..	,, ..	0 0 7·76	0 0 6·55	0 0 6·55
Veal	.. ..	,, ..	0 0 9·03	0 0 9·82	0 0 8·73
Pork	.. ..	,, ..	0 0 8·30	0 0 7·64	0 0 7·85

The year 1902 was again a satisfactory one for the Albergo
Popolare or "Rowton House." The average number of cubicles
occupied per day was 344, as compared with 221 in 1901 ; the
daily average of visitors was 19 ; the daily average of baths was 10.
It may be added that in the first six months of the present year
the daily average of cubicles occupied has risen to 383, which is a
still further increase of 39 per day. The Albergo continues to
gain popularity and favour. As was stated in last year's report,
the class of people who took advantage of this institution was

distinctly superior to what was expected. The Committee has now
purchased a plot of ground consisting of 3,000 square metres upon
which to erect a dormitory where the poorest classes will be
provided with clean sleeping accommodation at 20 c. (less than 2d.)
per night. It will contain 320 beds.

The Milan "Museo Commerciale," an institution whose chief
object is the expansion of commerce, sent out 17,253 letters during
the year 1902 and received during the same period 15,702 letters.
These figures are exclusive of circulars, printed matter, &c., and
other work. Inquiries from abroad numbered 2,854.

A considerable sum of money is now disposable for large and
extensive improvements of the railway station at Milan, to be
carried out as rapidly as time and circumstances will permit.

RETURN of Imports into Italy during the Year 1902 viâ Chiasso (Lombardy).

Customs Category.	Articles.	Countries from which Imported.		Quantity.
1	Mineral waters	Germany	Tons ..	41
		Austria-Hungary..	,, ..	21
		Total ..	,, ..	62
1	Wines	France	Gallons	317
		Spain	,,	485
		Other countries ..	,,	1,635
		Total ..	,,	2,437
1	,, in bottles.. ..	France	Number	1,332
		Germany	,,	7,400
		Other countries ..	,,	3,288
		Total ..	,,	12,020
1	Beer	Belgium	Gallons	1,354
		Germany	,,	8,735
		Switzerland ..	,,	50,292
		Total ..	,,	60,381
1	,, in bottles	Other countries ..	Number	5,150
1	Spirits, Cognac	United Kingdom ⎫ Germany .. France .. ⎬ Switzerland ⎭	Gallons	2,090
		Other countries ..	,,	2
		Total ..	,,	2,092
1	Oils	Austria-Hungary..	Tons ..	158
		Germany	,, ..	79
		Other countries ..	,, ..	60
		Total ..	,, ..	297
2	Coffee, chicory, chocolate, sugar	Belgium .. ⎫ Germany .. ⎬ United Kingdom ⎪ Switzerland ⎭	,, ..	2,572
3	Chemical products (acids, caustic soda whereof 1,226 tons from France, oxides, acetates, carbonates, sulphates, glycerine, gums, resins, &c.)	Belgium .. ⎫ France .. ⎬ Germany .. ⎪ Switzerland ⎭	,, ..	9,887
		Other countries ..	,, ..	46
		Total ..	,, ..	9,933
4	Colours, varnishes ..	United Kingdom..	,, ..	2
		France	,, ..	11
		Germany .. ⎫ Switzerland ⎬	,, ..	1,207
		Other countries ..	,, ..	22
		Total ..	,, ..	1,242

LOMBARDY.

RETURN of Imports into Italy during the Year 1902 viâ Chiasso (Lombardy)—continued.

Customs Category.	Articles.	Countries from which Imported.		Quantity.
5	Hemp, flax, jute ..	Belgium	Tons ..	3,047
		Germany	„ ..	19
		Other countries ..	„ ..	145
		Total ..	„ ..	3,211
6	Cotton	United Kingdom ⎫ Germany ⎬ Switzerland ⎭	„ ..	825
		Other countries ..	„ ..	218
		Total ..	„ ..	543
7	Wool	United Kingdom..	„ ..	425
		France	„ ..	354
		Austria-Hungary..	„ ..	5
		Belgium .. ⎫ Germany .. ⎬ Switzerland ⎭	„ ..	1,855
		Total ..	„ ..	2,639
8	Silk	United Kingdom..	Lbs. ..	138
		Germany .. ⎫ Switzerland ⎬ China .. ⎭	„ ..	231,721
		Japan .. ⎭	„ ..	4,301
		Other countries ..	„ ..	37,032
		Total ..	„ ..	273,192
9	Wood and straw ..	United Kingdom..	Tons ..	16
		France	„ ..	28
		Germany	„ ..	59
		Austria-Hungary..	„ ..	2,500
		Switzerland ..	„ ..	7,907
		Belgium .. ⎫ Germany .. ⎬ Switzerland ⎭	„ ..	29
		Other countries ..	„ ..	339
		Total ..	„ ..	10,878
10	Paper and books ..	Germany .. ⎫ France .. ⎮ Switzerland ⎮ Belgium .. ⎬ United Kingdom ⎮ Other countries ⎭	„ ..	1,819
11	Hides	Belgium .. ⎫ Germany .. ⎮ United Kingdom ⎬ France .. ⎮ Switzerland ⎮ Other countries ⎭	„ ..	205
12	Mineral ores	France	„ ..	10
		Germany	„ ..	42
		Other countries ..	„ ..	30
		Total ..	„ ..	82

RETURN of Imports into Italy during the Year 1902 viâ Chiasso (Lombardy)—continued.

Customs Category.	Articles.	Countries from which Imported.			Quantity.
12	Metals	France ..	Tons ..		49
		Germany	,, ..		1,173
		Belgium	,, ..		104
		Germany .. ⎫	,, ..		97
		Switzerland ⎬			
		Other countries ..	,, ..		205
		Total ..	,, ..		1,623
12	Scrap iron and filings ..	Germany	,, ..		3,850
		Austria-Hungary..	,, ..		11
		Switzerland ..	,, ..		1,513
		Total ..	,, ..		5,374
12	Pig iron	United Kingdom..	,, ..		50
		France	,, ..		5,407
		Germany	,, ..		1,086
		Switzerland ..	,, ..		41
		Belgium	,, ..		22
		Total ..	,, ..		6,606
12	Iron and steel	United Kingdom..	,, ..		9
		France	,, ..		23
		Germany	,, ..		33,922
		Austria-Hungary..	,, ..		4
		Switzerland ..	,, ..		237
		Belgium	,, ..		1,236
	Burnished ironware, and needles, pins, &c.	Belgium .. ⎫ Germany .. ⎬ United Kingdom ⎪ Switzerland ⎭	,, ..		70
		Other countries ..	,, ..		126
		Total ..	,, ..		35,627
12	Boilers and machinery..	United Kingdom..	,, ..		3,071
		Germany	,, ..		5,299
		Switzerland ..	,, ..		2,668
		Other countries ..	,, ..		9
		Belgium	,, ..		356
		Total ..	,, ..		11,403
12	Scientific instruments ..	Germany	,, ..		81
		Belgium	,, ..		5
		Other countries ..	,, ..		18
		Total ..	,, ..		104
12	Railway carriages ..	Germany	,, ..		1,202
		Belgium	,, ..		274
		Other countries ..	,, ..		414
		Total ..	,, ..		1,890
13	Stones, bricks	Germany	,, ..		2,700
		France	,, ..		375
		Switzerland ..	,, ..		405
		Belgium	,, ..		225

RETURN of Imports into Italy during the Year 1902 viâ Chiasso (Lombardy)—continued.

Customs Category.	Articles.	Countries from which Imported.		Quantity.
13	Stones, bricks—contd.— Marble, alabaster, building stones, mineral earths	Belgium .. France . Germany .. Switzerland } Tons ..		1,384
		Other countries ..	,, ..	62
		Total ..	,, ..	5,151
13	Coal	Germany	,, ..	29,557
13	Earthenware	Germany .. ., United Kingdom.. Other countries ..	,, .. ,, .. ,, ..	208 7 9
		Total ..	,, ..	224
13	Glassware	Germany .. Austria-Hungary.. Belgium .. Other countries ..	,, .. ,, .. ,, .. ,, ..	99 18 533 18
		Total ..	,, ..	673
14	Cereals	Germany .. Netherlands Switzerland .. Other countries ..	,, .. ,, .. ,, .. ,, ..	615 9 3 49
		Total ..	,, ..	676
14	Fruit and vegetables ..	Germany .. Switzerland }	,, ..	72
		Other countries ..	,, ..	44
		Total ..	,, ..	116
15	Horses and cattle ..	Switzerland ..	Number	5,146
15	Meat, poultry, game, fish	Belgium .. Germany .. Switzerland } Tons ..		77
15	Butter, cheese, lard, milk	Germany .. Switzerland }	,, ..	15
		Other countries ..	,, ..	437
		Total ..	,, ..	452
15	Other animal produce ..	France .. Germany .. Switzerland } Other countries ..	,, .. ,, .. ,, ..	30 2,136 67
		Total ..	,, ..	2,233
3	Soap and perfumery ..	Germany .. Switzerland ..	,, .. ,, ..	30 35
		Total ..	,, ..	65

RETURN of Imports into Italy during the Year 1902 viâ Chiasso (Lombardy)—continued.

Customs Category.	Articles.	Countries from which Imported.		Quantity.
16	Miscellaneous	Germany .. Switzerland Belgium .. Other countries ..	} Tons .. ,, ..	439 10
		Total ..	,, ..	449

RETURN of Exports from Italy during the Year 1902 viâ Chiass (Lombardy).

Customs Category.	Articles.	Countries to which Exported.		Quantity.
1	Wines in casks	Germany .. .. Switzerland ..	Gallons ,,	935,264 1,818,586
		Total ..	,,	2,753,850
1	,, in bottles ..	Germany .. .. Switzerland ..	Number ,,	737 15,984
		Total ..	,,	16,721
1	Spirits	France .. .. Switzerland .. Other countries ..	Gallons ,, ,,	286 1,078 462
		Total ..	,,	1,826
1	Oils: olive oil and lin- seed oil, &c.	Germany .. .. Switzerland .. Other countries ..	Tons .. ,, .. ,, ..	235 503 22
		Total ..	,, ..	760
2	Sugar, spices, colonial articles	United Kingdom.. Germany .. .. Switzerland .. Other countries ..	,, .. ,, .. ,, .. ,, ..	18 20 32 21
		Total ..	,, ..	91
3	Chemical products ..	Germany .. .. Switzerland .. Other countries ..	,, .. ,, .. ,, ..	295 643 318
		Total ..	,, ..	1,256
3	Medicines, drugs, &c. ..	Germany .. .. Switzerland .. Other countries ..	,, .. ,, .. ,, ..	3 43 3
		Total ..	,, ..	49

RETURN of Exports from Italy during the Year 1902 viâ Chiasso (Lombardy)—continued.

Customs Category.	Articles.	Countries to which Exported.			Quantity.
3	Soap and perfumery ..	Germany	Tons	..	10
		Switzerland ..	,,	..	38
		Total ..	,,	..	48
4	Colours, dyes	Germany	,,	..	92
		Switzerland ..	,,	..	385
		Total ..	,,	..	477
5	Hemp, flax, jute ..	Germany	,,	..	2,257
		Switzerland ..	,,	..	530
		Belgium	,,	..	899
		Other countries ..	,,	..	21
		Total ..	,,	..	3,707
6	Cotton	Germany	,,	..	464
		Switzerland ..	,,	..	419
		Other countries ..	,,	..	18
		Total ..	,,	..	901
7	Wool	France ..	,,	..	34
		Germany	,,	..	200
		Switzerland ..	,,	..	218
		Belgium	,,	..	9
		Netherlands ..	,,	..	26
		Total ..	,,	..	487
8	Silk	United Kingdom..	Lbs.	..	170,775
		France	,,	..	2,662
		Germany	,,	..	5,297,175
		Switzerland ..	,,	..	6,577,632
		Belgium	,,	..	4,056
		Netherlands ..	,,	..	3,388
		Other countries ..	,,	..	79,472
		Total ..	,,	..	12,135,160
9	Timber and furniture ..	United Kingdom..	Tons	..	87
		Germany	,,	..	266
		Switzerland ..	,,	..	3,751
		Other countries ..	,,	..	467
		Total ..	,,	..	4,571
9	Straw and wicker work (including 2,298,307 straw hats)	United Kingdom..	,,	..	2,113
		Germany	,,	..	160
		Switzerland ..	,,	..	501
		Belgium	,,	..	21
		Other countries ..	,,	..	613
		Total ..	,,	..	3,408
10	Paper and books ..	Germany	,,	..	43
		Switzerland ..	,,	..	294
		Other countries ..	,,	..	133
		Total ..	,,	..	470

RETURN of Exports from Italy during the Year 1902 viâ Chiasso (Lombardy)—continued.

Customs Category.	Articles.	Countries to which Exported.			Quantity.
11	Hides and skins.. ..	United Kingdom..	Tons	..	· 19
		Germany	,,	..	431
		Switzerland ..	,,	..	409
		Other countries ..	,,	..	22
		Total ..	,,	..	881
12	Iron, scrap and filings ..	Germany	,,	..	80
		Switzerland ..	,,	..	142
		Total ..	,,	..	222
12	,, in pigs	Germany	,,	..	20
		Switzerland ..	,,	..	53
		Total ..	,,	..	73
12	,, and steel	Germany	,,	..	26
		Switzerland ..	,,	..	179
		Total ..	,,	..	205
12	Brass, copper, bronze, spelter, silver	Germany .. Switzerland }	,,	..	57
		Other countries ..	,,	..	14
		Total ..	,,	..	71
12	Machinery	Germany	,,	..	233
		Switzerland ..	,,	..	355
		Total ..	,,	..	588
12	Scientific instruments ..	Switzerland ..	,,	..	18
		Other countries ..	,,	..	9
		Total ..	,,	..	27
13	Stones, bricks, chalk, cement	Germany	,,	..	1,169
		Switzerland ..	,,	..	4,592
		Belgium	,,	..	12
		Other countries ..	,,	..	216
		Total ..	,,	..	5,989
13	Sulphur	Germany	,,	..	553
		Switzerland ..	,,	..	333
		Total ..	,,	..	886
13	Coal	Switzerland ..	,,	..	7,335
13	Earthenware	Germany	,,	..	89
		Switzerland ..	,,	..	373
		Other countries ..	,,	..	11
		Total	,,	..	473

RETURN of Exports from Italy during the Year 1902 viâ Chiasso
(Lombardy)—continued.

Customs Category.	Articles.	Countries to which Exported.			Quantity.
13	Glassware	United Kingdom	Tons	..	8
		Germany	,,	..	64
		Switzerland	,,	..	246
		Total	,,	..	318
14	Cereals (rye, flour, rice, bran, chestnuts, &c.)	Germany	,,	..	386
		Switzerland	,,	..	3,891
		Holland	,,	..	12
		Other countries	,,	..	1,719
		Total	,,	..	6,008
14	Fruit, vegetables, flowers	United Kingdom	,,	..	31
		Germany	,,	..	7,742
		Switzerland	,,	..	16,405
		Belgium	,,	..	298
		Other countries	,,	..	28
		Total	,,	..	24,504
15	Horses, mules, cattle	Switzerland	Number		60,548
15	Fresh and salted meat, &c.	Germany	Tons	..	85
		Switzerland	,,	..	219
		Other countries	,,	..	82
		Total	,,	..	386
15	Fish, fresh and dried	Germany	,,	..	16
		Switzerland	,,	..	49
		Other countries	,,	..	87
		Total	,,	..	152
15	Butter	United Kingdom	,,	..	2,911
		Germany	,,	..	394
		Switzerland	,,	..	1,005
		Other countries	,,	..	115
		Total	,,	..	4,425
15	Cheese	United Kingdom	,,	..	2,107
		Germany	,,	..	764
		Switzerland	,,	..	645
		Total	,,	..	3,516
15	Eggs	United Kingdom	,,	..	4,894
		Germany	,,	..	4,095
		Switzerland	,,	..	4,695
		Belgium	,,	..	2,696
		Netherlands	,,	..	312
		Total	,,	..	16,692
15	Other animal produce	Germany	,,	..	26
		Switzerland	,,	..	304
		Total	,,	..	330

RETURN of Exports from Italy during the Year 1902 viâ Chiasso (Lombardy)—continued.

Customs Category.	Articles.	Countries to which Exported.		Quantity.
16	Miscellaneous	United Kingdom..	Tons ..	1,078
		France	,, ..	30
		Germany	,, ..	272
		Switzerland ..	,, ..	209
		Belgium	,, ..	11
		Other countries ..	,, ..	101
		Total ..	,, ..	1,701

RETURN of Imports into Italy during the Year 1902 viâ Luino (Lombardy).

Customs Category.	Articles.	Countries from which Imported.		Quantity.
1	Wines	France	Gallons	298
		Germany ..	,,	1,024
		Spain	,,	128
		Switzerland ..	,,	204
		Total ..	,,	1,654
1	,, in bottles ..	France	Number	299
		Germany	,,	4,363
		Switzerland ..	,,	940
		Spain	,,	459
		Total ..	,,	6,061
1	Beer	Switzerland ..	Gallons	26,131
1	Spirits	Unspecified ..	,,	1,379
	,, in bottles ..	,, ..	Number	1,044
1	Oils	Germany	Tons ..	28
		Other countries ..	,, ..	12
		Total ..	,, ..	40
2	Coffee, sugar, chicory ..	Belgium	,, ..	421
		Switzerland ..	,, ..	48
		Other countries ..	,, ..	18
		Total ..	,, ..	487
3	Chemical products ..	United Kingdom..	,, ..	664
		Germany	,, ..	2,574
		Switzerland ..	,, ..	1,369
		Total ..	,, ..	4,607
4	Colours, varnishes ..	Germany	,, ..	823
		Switzerland ..	,, ..	153
		Total ..	,, ..	976

RETURN of Imports into Italy during the Year 1902 viâ Luino (Lombardy)—continued.

Customs Category.	Articles.	Countries from which Imported.			Quantity.
5	Hemp, flax, jute ..	Belgium	Tons	..	587
		Germany	,,	..	47
		Switzerland ..	,,	..	22
		Other countries ..	,,	..	8
		Total ..	,,	..	665
6	Cotton	Germany	,,	..	201
		Switzerland ..	,,	..	133
		France	,,	..	69
		Total ..	,,	..	403
7	Wool	Germany	,,	..	384
		Belgium	,,	..	233
		France	,,	..	120
		Switzerland ..	,,	..	107
		Other countries ..	,,	..	14
		Total ..	,,	..	858
8	Silk	France	Lbs.	..	1,834
		Germany	,,	..	118,236
		Switzerland ..	,,	..	260,389
		Total ..	,,	..	380,459
9	Wood and straw ..	Switzerland ..	Tons	..	10,880
		France	,,	..	2,562
		Germany	,,	..	30
		Austria-Hungary..	,,	..	11
		Other countries ..	,,	..	218
		Total ..	,,	..	13,701
10	Paper and books ..	Germany	,,	..	3,700
		Switzerland ..	,,	..	1,252
		Other countries ..	,,	..	2
		Total ..	,,	..	4,954
11	Hides and skins.. ..	Germany	,,	..	225
		Switzerland ..	,,	..	152
		Belgium	,,	..	18
		Other countries ..	,,	..	2
		Total ..	,,	..	397
12	Iron slag and filings ..	Switzerland ..	,,	..	872
		Germany	,,	..	292
		France	,,	..	10
		Total ..	,,	..	1,174
12	,, in pigs	France	,,	..	1,040
		Germany	,,	..	740
		United Kingdom..	,,	..	72
		Switzerland ..	,,	..	57
		Total ..	,,	..	1,909

RETURN of Imports into Italy during the Year 1902 viâ Luino (Lombardy)—continued.

Customs Category.	Articles.	Countries from which Imported.			Quantity.
12	Iron and steel	Germany	Tons	..	20,033
		Switzerland ..	,,	..	288
		Belgium	,,	..	25
		Total ..	,,	..	20,346
12	Metals	Germany	.,	..	779
		Belgium	,,	..	146
		Netherlands ..	,,	..	19
		Other countries ..	,,	..	18
		Total ..	,,	..	962
12	Machinery	Germany	,,	..	4,024
		Switzerland ..	,,	..	1,996
		United Kingdom..	,,	..	1,346
		France	,,	..	27
		Other countries ..	,,	..	214
		Total ..	,,	..	7,607
12	Heating apparatus ..	Germany	,,	..	142
12	Scientific instruments ..	Germany	,,	..	90
		Switzerland ..	,,	..	24
		Other countries ..	,,	..	2
		Total ..	,,	..	116
12	Railway carriages ..	France	,,	..	467
		Switzerland ..	,,	..	60
		Belgium	,,	..	28
		Total ..	,,	..	555
13	Coal	Germany	,,	..	18,338
13	Stones, bricks, &c. ..	Germany	,,	..	1,517
		Switzerland ..	,,	..	942
		Belgium	,,	..	268
		France	,,	..	266
		Other countries ..	,,	..	4
		Total ..	,,	..	2,997
13	Earthenware	Germany	,,	..	290
		Other countries ..	,,	..	3
		Total ..	,,	..	293
13	Glassware	Germany	,,	..	106
		Belgium	,,	..	47
		Other countries ..	,,	..	8
		Total ..	,,	..	161
14	Cereals	Germany	,,	..	379
		Switzerland ..	,,	..	131
		Total ..	,,	..	510

RETURN of Imports into Italy during the Year 1902 viâ Luino
(Lombardy)—continued.

Customs Category.	Articles.	Countries from which Imported.			Quantity.
14	Fruit and vegetables ..	Germany	Tons ..		31
		Switzerland ..	,, ..		54
		Belgium	,, ..		11
		Other countries ..	,, ..		3
		Total ..	,, ..		99
15	Cattle	Switzerland ..	Number		4,094
15	Meat and poultry ..	Switzerland ..	Tons ..		19
		Other countries ..	,, ..		3
		Total ..	,, ..		22
15	Other animal produce ..	Germany	,, ..		2,165
		Switzerland ..	,, ..		1,156
		Belgium	,, ..		25
		France	,, ..		15
		Total ..	,, ..		3,361
16	Miscellaneous	Germany	,, ..		363
		Switzerland ..	,, ..		41
		Total ..	,, ..		404

RETURN of Exports from Italy during the Year 1902 viâ Luino
(Lombardy).

Customs Category.	Articles.	Countries to which Exported.			Quantity.
1	Wines	Germany	Gallons		730,697
		Switzerland ..	,,		1,190,135
		Total ..	,,		1,920,832
1	,, in bottles ..	Germany	Number		5,365
		Switzerland ..	,,		8,564
		Total ..	,,		13,929
1	Spirits	Switzerland ..	Gallons		704
	,, in bottles.. ..	Switzerland ..	Number		160
		Germany	,,		146
		Total ..	,,		306
1	Oils	Germany	Tons ..		761
		Switzerland ..	,, ..		1,253
		Total ..	,, ..		2,014
2	Sweets, spices and colonials	Austria-Hungary..	,, ..		71
		Germany	,, ..		21
		Switzerland ..	,, ..		4
		Total ..	,, ..		96

RETURN of Exports from Italy during the Year 1902 viâ Luino (Lombardy)—continued.

Customs Category.	Articles.	Countries to which Exported.			Quantity.
3	Chemical products ..	Switzerland ..	Tons	..	891
		Germany	,,	..	2
		Other countries ..	,,	..	13
		Total ..	,,	..	906
3	Herbs, roots, medicines, perfumery, &c.	Switzerland ..	,,	..	131
		Germany	,,	..	38
		Total ..	,,	..	169
4	Colours and dyes ..	Germany	,,	..	221
		Switzerland ..	,,	..	105
		Total ..	,,	..	326
5	Hemp, flax, jute ..	Germany	,,	..	1,759
		Switzerland ..	,,	..	1,588
		Total ..	,,	..	3,347
6	Cotton	Switzerland ..	,,	..	258
		Germany	,,	..	124
		Total ..	,,	..	382
7	Wool	Switzerland ..	,,	..	434
		Germany	,,	..	227
		United Kingdom..	,,	..	43
		Other countries ..	,,	..	462
		Total ..	,,	..	1,166
8	Silk	Germany	Lbs.	..	986,427
		Switzerland ..	,,	..	1,303,313
		North America ..	,,	..	590,216
		Total ..	,,	..	2,879,956
9	Wood and straw ..	Switzerland ..	Tons	..	2,176
		Germany	,,	..	53
		Other countries ..	,,	..	140
		Total ..	,,	..	2,369
10	Paper and books ..	Switzerland ..	,,	..	93
		Germany	,,	..	9
		Total ..	,,	..	102
11	Hides and skins.. ..	Switzerland ..	,,	..	281
		North America ..	,,	..	23
		Germany ..	,,	..	22
		Belgium	,,	..	17
		Total ..	,,	..	343
12	Iron and steel	Switzerland ..	,,	..	270
		Germany	,,	..	11
		Total ..	,,	..	281

RETURN of Exports from Italy during the Year 1902 viâ Luino
(Lombardy)—continued.

Customs Category.	Articles.	Countries to which Exported.		Quantity.
12	Metals	Switzerland ..	Tons ..	229
12	Machinery	Switzerland ..	,, ..	286
		Germany	,, ..	26
		Total ..	,, ..	312
13	Stones, bricks, cement ..	Switzerland ..	,, ..	8,740
		Germany	,, ..	5,243
		Total ..	,, ..	13,983
13	Sulphur	Switzerland ..	,, ..	1,827
		Germany	,, ..	1,405
		Total ..	,, ..	3,232
13	Earthenware	Switzerland ..	,, ..	98
13	Glassware	Switzerland ..	,, ..	29
13	Graphite..	Germany	,, ..	1,623
		Switzerland ..	,, ..	822
		Total ..	,, ..	2,445
13	Coal	Switzerland ..	,, ..	1,491
14	Cereals	Germany	,, ..	4,823
		Switzerland ..	,, ..	· 5,725
		Belgium	,, ..	1,700
		Total ..	,, ..	12,248
14	Fruits	Switzerland ..	,, ..	13,662
		Germany	,, ..	9,614
		Belgium	,, ..	210
		Netherlands ..	,, ..	143
		Total ..	,, ..	23,629
15	Horses, mules, cattle ..	Switzerland ..	Number	32,842
		Germany	,,	14,612
		Total ..	,,	47,454
15	Animal produce.. ..	Germany	Tons ..	300
		Switzerland ..	,, ..	945
		Belgium	,, ..	119
		Netherlands ..	,, ..	45
		Total ..	,, ..	1,409
16	Miscellaneous	United Kingdom ..	,, ..	15
		Germany	,, ..	196
		Switzerland ..	,, ..	203
		Other countries ..	,, ..	103
		Total ..	,, ..	517

Lightning Source UK Ltd.
Milton Keynes UK
UKHW021834010421
381406UK00003B/196